TIME TO GROW

STUDY GUIDE FOR THE TELECOURSE

INTELECOM

AUTHOR

David Thornbrugh

EDITORS

Kathryn Opsahl and Evelyn Brzezinski

A television-based course in Child Development, Infancy through Adolescence, developed and produced by Coast Community College District and INTELECOM in association with the Instructional Telecommunications Consortium.

McGRAW-HILL, INC.

New York   St. Louis   San Francisco   Auckland   Bogotá   Caracas
Lisbon   London   Madrid   Mexico   Milan   Montreal
New Delhi   Paris   San Juan   Singapore   Sydney   Tokyo   Toronto

This book is printed on recycled paper containing a minimum of 50% total recycled fiber with 10% postconsumer de-inked fiber.

TIME TO GROW
STUDY GUIDE FOR THE TELECOURSE

3 4 5 6 7 8 9 0 MAL MAL 9 0 9 8 7 6 5 4 3

Cover: *Baby at Play*, Thomas Eakins;
National Gallery of Art, Washington, D.C.
John Hay Whitney Collection.

The editors were Jane Vaicunas and Nomi Sofer;
the production supervisor was Richard A. Ausburn.
Malloy Lithographing, Inc.,was printer and binder.

CONTENTS

FOREWORD

BEFORE YOU BEGIN THIS COURSE . . .

All of the 26 lessons in this course will follow the same pattern. Each lesson consists of three parts: readings from your textbook – Child Development: Its Nature and Course, Second Edition, by L. Alan Sroufe, Robert G. Cooper, and Ganie B. DeHart; a video program; and this telecourse guide. While you've read many textbooks and seen many television programs, you may never have worked with a document such as the telecourse guide. So before you start any of the reading, we'll give you a little information about how the guide is organized and how it can help you throughout your study of child development. Each lesson will consist of the following parts:

LESSON ASSIGNMENT – This section presents a concise listing of the assignments and steps that you should follow to master the lesson objectives and achieve the lesson's goal. The term "steps" is used to reinforce the idea that learning is a process.

INTRODUCING THE LESSON – This section is a "friendly" advance organizer – a motivator – for what the lesson covers. Such organizers help make learning more meaningful, ensure better retention, and, we hope, pique your interest.

GOAL –This single sentence tells you the overall purpose of the lesson. It helps you keep in mind the overriding principle guiding the lesson.

LESSON OBJECTIVES – These objectives form the framework for the content of each lesson. Learning these objectives will enable you to reach the lesson's goal.

VIEWING GUIDE – The Viewing Guide presents points to be considered before, during, and after watching the video portion of the lesson. This section is designed to guide your viewing, to help you see the important parts of the video. To do a thorough job of understanding these points, you may needs to watch the video more than once.

UNDERSTANDING THE LESSON – This section summarizes the important points of the lesson by integrating the key terms, concepts, and principles within the particular assigned readings and offering you some focusing questions. The section is designed to help you apply the material from the text as you prepare to watch the video. Reading this section before viewing will help the video be even more meaningful. Reading it again after viewing will reinforce learning.

<u>SELF-TEST</u> – Several multiple choice and short essay questions are presented to help you review material and prepare examinations.

<u>ANSWER KEY</u> – Answers to the SELF-TEST items are provided at the end of the telecourse guide.

IN CONCLUSION . . .

Keeping in mind the purpose of each section of the telecourse guide will support your learning as you proceed through the 26 lessons. And along with the videos and your text readings, using this telecourse guide effectively will reinforce your learning. We hope you enjoy this course.

ACKNOWLEDGEMENTS

Creating a telecourse guide such as this one takes the cooperation of many individuals, each working in his or her special area of expertise. We owe thanks to a team of academic professionals whose sound advice, based on their years of teaching experience, directed the academic integrity of this telecourse guide. Their work involved helping to craft the guiding objectives for the course and reviewing all the lessons for the telecourse guide and the exam bank.

Our thanks for assistance on this telecourse guide goes to Dr. David Lane, who served as the instructional designer for the course and the author of the exam banks. In addition, we acknowledge the hard work of the members of the academic advisory committee for *Time to Grow*, as follows: Elizabeth H. Brady, Cal State Northridge (retired), Northridge, CA; Dr. Michael Catchpole, North Island College, Port Alberni, British Columbia; Dr. Betty Hutchison, Foster G. McGaw Graduate School, National-Louis University, Evanston, IL; Dr. Lilian Katz, ERIC Clearinghouse, Urbana, IL; Dr. Tom Luster, Michigan State University, East Lansing, MI; and Dr. Mary Knox Weir, Long Beach City College (retired), Long Beach, CA.

David Thornbrugh
Kathryn Opsahl
Evelyn Brzezinski

Interwest Applied Research
Beaverton, Oregon

MODULE I:

BEGINNINGS

1

The Nature and Theories of Development

LESSON ASSIGNMENT

Completing the following steps will help you master the lesson objectives and achieve the goal for this lesson:

STEP 1: Read the INTRODUCING THE LESSON section to provide a context for what you will learn in this lesson.

STEP 2: Read the lesson's GOAL and LESSON OBJECTIVES so that you will know what you are expected to learn.

STEP 3: Read the text assignment, Chapter 1, pages 4 to 33. Pay particular attention to the key terms and concepts in the Chapter Summary on page 33; they will help you when you watch the video.

STEP 4: Review the VIEWING GUIDE in the telecourse guide. It lists several points to consider as you watch the video.

STEP 5: Watch the video.

STEP 6: Read the UNDERSTANDING THE LESSON section in the telecourse guide. Make sure you understand the key terms and can answer the focusing questions included there.

STEP 7: Complete the SELF-TEST.

STEP 8: Go back to the LESSON OBJECTIVES and make sure you can respond to each of them.

INTRODUCING THE LESSON

I t is probably safe to make a few general assumptions about anyone who is reading this introduction. You are probably an adult who is able to read and understand these written words. You most likely are able to perform certain complicated actions, such as driving a car, operating a bank's cash machine, programming a video cassette recorder to record a favorite show – maybe. You sustain numerous relationships with other people, in varying degrees of intimacy, from a nodding acquaintance with the clerk at your local grocery to deep and lifelong ties to your parents – you may even be a parent yourself.

In short, you are an independent, fully grown human being with a certain amount of experience who is capable of making most of your own decisions.

But this hasn't always been you, has it? Not so very long ago, you were sweating and fumbling through the anxieties of adolescence, unsure of your changing body, tormented – and tantalized – by burgeoning sexual desires, plagued by doubts about yourself, your friends, the world around you.

Going back, before adolescence, you were another creature entirely, not so tall, lighter in weight, less sophisticated in thought, but able to form general notions of the shape and nature of the world, already adept at certain skills and sports.

With one more leap into the past you were just beginning school, approaching that first day of classes with a mixture of dread and enthusiasm. You'd already mastered the basic skills that you'd need for a lifetime of pleasures and toil – speech, walking, basic social interactions – but you'd just begun to prepare for reading, adding up a few simple numbers, and perhaps assuming your first responsibilities – feeding your goldfish daily, for example.

Finally, you go all the way back, beyond your first memories, to where only snapshots or embarrassing videotape footage can take you. In these you see your first steps, your first word, even your first bath.

It's a long way from that earlier incarnation in infancy to the person who sits at a desk today, absorbing these words and translating them into concepts. Some of the steps along the way were dramatic ones and probably stand out in your memory: your first bicycle ride, the first night you spent away from home, your first kiss. Other abilities which you now take for granted came gradually, often indiscernibly: the ease with which you make a long-distance telephone call, for example, or swim several laps, or make the decision to pay bills instead of watching that rerun of the Wizard of Oz.

Looking at pictures of yourself as a teenager, a child, an infant, it is hard not to feel a sense of amazement at the great distance you've come and the amount that you've changed. And it isn't just that you have grown taller, developed muscles and coordination, and honed skills as you've grown. Your grasp of the world, your way of thinking, have grown and deepened as you've matured. Over the years since your birth, you've developed into the person you are today.

The idea of *development*, of an organism growing through progressive, cumulative phases into new, more complicated stages, is the subject of this telecourse. Through the text material and the video lessons you will begin to see how each human being follows a similar course of growth throughout her or his life, but at her or his own pace and with certain individual differences. Within the context of development, you will see how each human being, beginning as an infant, follows similar but unique paths to adulthood.

Lesson 1 presents the basic framework of the concepts of developmental psychology and explains how this course will apply its principles to the study of child development. The developmental perspective explains the ways in which a child of six months differs from the same child at age four, six, and ten. In Lesson 1, you will begin to appreciate how each stage of childhood emerges from the accomplishments of earlier stages. Like the brightly colored Russian folk dolls that nestle one within another, the person you are today emerged, in an orderly, systematic, and guided fashion, out of a sequence of earlier selves.

GOAL

The purpose of this lesson is to introduce you to the fundamental themes of developmental psychology, which is a coherent framework for explaining and understanding the various changes – of both a qualitative and quantitative nature – that an individual goes through as he or she grows.

LESSON OBJECTIVES

After reading the text assignment, completing the exercises in this telecourse guide, and viewing the lesson's video portion, you will be able to:

1. Summarize what is meant by a developmental perspective in reference to the study of children.

2. Name and describe the key features of development change.

3. Distinguish between the normative and dynamic aspects of development.

4. Describe the factors on which development depends.

5. Explain what a theory is and how it is useful.

6. Recognize the basic concepts and developmental states of Erikson's psychosocial theory and Piaget's theories of cognitive development.

7. Recognize the basic concepts of social learning (cognitive) theory; of information-processing approaches to cognitive development.

8. Distinguish among laboratory experiments, naturalistic observation, and natural experiments.

VIEWING GUIDE

Lesson 1 presents a comprehensive outline of the major components of the developmental perspective of child development, a collection of concepts which will become increasingly familiar to you as you progress through this course. After reading the text material and learning the important terms included there, you are ready to view the lesson's video portion. First, review the questions in the Self-Test at the end of this telecourse guide lesson to give you an idea of important points to watch for in the video. Then read the following Points to Consider to give you an idea of what the video will cover. Keep these points in mind while watching.

Points to Consider

☐ *The developmental point of view*: The principles of development as an explanation of how children change from age to age form the background of this telecourse. As you watch the video and read the text material, be aware of how children change both *qualitatively* and *formatively*. Note also these three main aspects of development: children differ from one age to another; a child's capacities emerge from earlier capacities; and development is coherent over time.

☐ *Making sense of development*: The way we are born and grow has fascinated philosophers and scientists since ancient times, but the modern science of childhood development owes a special debt to several pioneers. Pay attention to the importance of the theories of Charles Darwin in current theories of childhood development. Notice the continuity between more recent explanations of development and earlier ones, such as those of John Locke.

☐ *Theories*: There are several theories that help us understand how individuals develop. As you learn about the several stages of childhood development, keep in mind how they would be explained by the different theories of Jean Piaget, Sigmund Freud, John Bowlby, and others. Notice also how the various theories differ in some degree because of the different focus which each theorist took.

☐ *Tools for study*: Our understanding of how individuals grow and develop depends upon a solid body of carefully gathered data and many insightful observations – both formal and informal. As you view the video, take note of how a child's behavior in a controlled laboratory experiment might differ from its behavior in an uncontrolled natural setting. Be aware of the strengths and weaknesses of the various methods for studying development, and try to identify when a particular approach is most appropriate.

UNDERSTANDING THE LESSON

In the Greek legend of the tragedy of Oedipus, Oedipus is the only person who can answer the riddle of the Sphinx: "What creature is it that walks on four legs in the morning, two at noon, and three in evening?" Oedipus's correct answer was a human being, who crawls as an infant, walks in adulthood, and in old age leans upon a cane.

Since ancient times, the question of how individual humans are created, born, and grow from helpless infancy through the stages of childhood into the self-reliance of adulthood has fascinated philosophers and natural scientists – not to mention mothers and fathers. From the cryptic wisdom contained in the riddle of the Sphinx to modern theories based upon laboratory observations, the questions of child development have been answered in a number of original and provocative ways.

Basic Principles of Development

As the examples from both your textbook and the video make plain, a child's reactions and behavior change with time. A 5-month-old baby stares solemnly as her big sister bobs up and down in front of the baby's crib, trying in vain to play peekaboo. Yet in two or three months, the same baby shrieks gleefully every time her sister's head reappears at the edge of the crib. What has taken place in the intervening months to make the infant enjoy the game?

By understanding the idea of *developmental perspective* as explained in this lesson, you will begin to appreciate the coherence and elegance of how we develop from almost helpless infants into self-sufficient adults. In the concept of development, each of us proceeds through a series of stages that mark *qualitative* changes in how we handle the world. Older children are able to master more and progressively harder challenges because their capabilities are being transformed into new levels of skill.

The other component of development is *behavioral reorganization*, which means that a child gains more advanced ways of organizing or putting information together as he or she grows older. Compare, for example, how a toddler places one block atop another with how a 4 year old uses Lego units to construct a rocket. Broadly speaking, most 4 year olds will have much greater abilities to coordinate their block-building movements, formulate strategies of building, and imagine new building plans.

When we look at the changes in body and behavior that are typical at each age – just as the block-building movements described above – we are looking at development *normatively*. But just because something is typical at a certain age doesn't mean that all children experience it then. When we look at within-individual progress, we are looking at behavior *individually*.

Keep in mind that each change in behavior and understanding grows naturally out of the abilities that were there before, in conjunction with interactions with environmental influences. A basic theme of development is that the changes we experience from infancy through adolescence are orderly, cumulative, and directional. That is, our development follows a genetically planned sequence of events that build upon one another in stages of increasing complexity.

Key Terms

Development
Normative development
Individual development
Qualitative change
Quantitative change

Focusing Questions

1. A 2 year old shrieks with glee as she makes short hops; 12 years later, she wins the broad jump in junior high. Is her improved performance over the years an example of qualitative change?

2. What are some examples of the ways in which children reorganize their thoughts and actions to form more complex patterns of behavior as they grow older?

A Framework for Understanding Development

The eighteenth-century musician Wolfgang Amadeus Mozart composed his first minuet at the age of five and performed before the Viennese court at the age of six. While brilliance such as Mozart's is so far out of the ordinary as to be astounding, young Mozart still had to develop his musical abilities in the same orderly manner as you or I would to learn to play the guitar. As you learn in this lesson, Mozart's musical skills developed out of the interaction of (1) his inherited genetic abilities, (2) his progressive stages of achievement, and (3) the influences of his environment.

Developmental theorists base their understanding of this three-part process partly on the evolutionary theory of Charles Darwin. Evolutionary theory holds that an interaction of inherited traits and environmental influences determines the success of individual species, and serves as our model of child development. For example, in the case of Mozart, genetic factors contributed to his early musical genius, but it was the environmental influence – largely in the shape of education and early performing – that shaped his extraordinary career.

Darwin is just one of the many scientists and philosophers who have debated the causes and courses of human development. One view, put forth by the English philosopher John Locke, held that children are at birth totally neutral, and that all their subsequent values and beliefs are imposed upon them by their parents, teachers, and society in general. Taking an alternative tack was the French philosopher Jean Jacques Rousseau, who believed that children are born in a state of innocence and then corrupted by the teachings of society. (From Rousseau comes the idea of the "Noble Savage," the concept of primitive peoples as morally superior to so-called civilized peoples.)

To a certain degree, various camps of child development still debate the relative importance of heredity and environment on each individual – a controversy known as "nature versus nurture." The position taken in this telecourse, however, is that it is pointless to try assigning more weight to either genetic or environmental factors. In keeping with most contemporary developmentalists, in this course you will study the many ways in which heredity and environment interact to shape the various stages of an individual's life.

Focusing Questions

1. How does the principle of natural selection as set forth in Charles Darwin's theory of evolution apply to current models of human development?

Explaining Development

As you will have learned from the video and the text material, child development experts don't always agree. Scientists who study childhood growth and behavior often differ in their views because they follow different theories of development. A theory is a unified set of principles explaining a set of phenomena, a field of behavior, or nature. A fully-developed theory is similar to the instructions a friend gives you to approach her house for the first time: take the North Shore exit, turn left at the Dairy Queen, then drive three miles and go right at the laundromat. Another researcher might approach the same destination from the opposite direction, and so would look for different landmarks. But both would arrive at the same place – in this case, the specific instance of child behavior.

In the field of child development, there are numerous theories. But five prominent theories that guide researchers in their travels are featured in this course. Of these, three emphasize qualitative change, including those based on *psychoanalytic* approaches. The principles of psychoanalysis were laid down by Sigmund Freud, who analyzed human behavior in light of the emotional conflicts individuals face at different stages of their lives. In early psychoanalytic theories of development, the qualitative changes of an individual's growth are explained by the concepts of the id, the ego, and the superego. All these psychoanalytic concepts begin with the emotional structures of individual human personality.

Another major theory of qualitative change was developed by Jean Piaget, who built his theory of development around how the thinking of children at different ages changes. To Piaget, the difference between the ways that 2 year olds behave as compared to 4 year olds is a matter of their changing cognitive abilities – that is, how they think about the world and themselves. To Piaget, we become less self-centered – or egocentric – as we grow older because we are better able to understand how the feelings and needs of other people might differ from our own. Piaget's construct of decentering and reversibility is central to his theory and relates to ways of seeing the world as much as to human relationships.

The third theory to take a qualitative approach to child development was proposed by John Bowlby, whose *adaptational theory* draws heavily from both Darwin's theory of evolution and Freud's ideas about individual development. Adaptational theory (which is sometimes also called *attachment theory*) combines the idea that babies are born with certain genetic behaviors with the psychoanalytic notion that the value or efficiency of these behaviors will be greatly affected by the individual's environment. In other words, while an infant may be born with an ingrained urge to seek intimacy with its parent, how that parent responds – or doesn't respond – to the child may affect the infant's reactions to others for the rest of its life.

Of the two theories that focus on the gradual nature of developmental changes, *information-processing theory* holds that children become better at solving problems as their powers of attention, memory, and thinking improve gradually over time. Information theorists concentrate on how children think when solving problems, including those that involve social situations.

Social learning theory, on the other hand, tends to explain changes in individual behavior largely by how children are affected by such factors as punishment, reward, and imitation. Based on the principles of behaviorism, social learning theory holds that development is gradual and cumulative, and that children learn through watching how others behave, a process called modeling. Social learning theorists tend to be more interested in how children of the same age approach a problem in different ways as opposed to how children of different ages react differently to a similar situation.

When considering these several theories, it is important to remember that they reach different conclusions about the various facets of development because they each begin from different points of reference. The theories often present different views of similar circumstances because they are looking at them through different theoretical lenses, so to speak. All, though, have important insights to offer.

Key Terms

> Psychoanalytic approaches
> Developmental approaches
> Adaptational approaches
> Social learning theory
> Information-processing theory

Focusing Questions

1. Why hasn't any one theory of child development arisen that all researchers can accept?

2. A 3-year-old girl and her parents are taking a walk in the park when the mother notices that the child's shoelaces are untied. But as the mother bends down to tie the laces, the little girl pushes her aside and says "No, I want Daddy to do it." How might a child developmentalist who was influenced by Freudian psychology interpret the child's actions? How might a Piagetian developmentalist interpret them?

Methods for Studying Development

Although child developmentalists approach their field under the guidance of several differing theories, all researchers use the same basic methods to test their hypotheses. In the video, you will have seen examples of the main methods of studying child behavior, of which the *experiment* is one. In laboratory settings, researchers can isolate particular child behaviors or stages of development and set up tests or measurements that are very precise and controlled. Throughout this telecourse, you will see examples of experiments in child development that are designed to study such things as the acuity of infant vision or the ability of toddlers to perceive depth, among others.

But because the results of laboratory experiments do not always relate to the actual world, as well as because there are some types of human behavior that cannot ethically be manipulated, researchers have looked to the biological sciences for *observational methods*. Using techniques of observation and recording similar to those of scientists observing animals in the wild, researchers go into schools, homes, and playgrounds to carefully note how children behave, both alone and with others. Some researchers even construct special laboratories that look like a day care playroom or even a private home and use this setting to observe how children behave in a natural setting. Educators are now beginning to use observational methods in their work.

In a *natural experiment*, researchers select subjects to study for certain traits or behaviors from among the ages or family groups that are naturally available. Say, for example, a researcher is interested in the effect that being raised by only one parent might have on the average age of learning to walk. Because it would be impossible, both ethically and practically, to split a child's parents apart deliberately just for the sake of an experiment, the researcher seeks out single-parent households to study. He or she would then compare these against selected groups of two-parent households and use the differences to support any conclusions.

Another important tool of child developmentalists is the study of change over time. By selecting a group of children of similar age and, as much as possible, background, and following their development in a particular category for a number of weeks, months, or years, researchers can gain valuable information. In a *longitudinal study*, the researchers select one group of children all the same age and follow their development in a certain selected area over a number of months or years. In a *cross-sectional study*, on the other hand, the researchers compare children of different ages at one point in time. The important thing to keep in mind about the two methods is that they are ways of studying change over time – a vital concern of child developmentalists.

Key Terms

Longitudinal study
Experiment
Natural experiment
Observation

Focusing Questions

1. Suppose you are interested in studying gender differences in how 4 year olds react to long periods of separation from their parents. What are some of the advantages to setting up a laboratory experiment? Some of the disadvantages? What are some of the reasons you might prefer to rely on observation for your data? Some of the reasons against relying on observation?

2. Why is the study of animal behavior in nature, known as ethology, important to the study of child development?

Questions for Understanding

As you read these questions, often raised by parents, educators, and other childcare providers, first try to answer the questions yourself. Then read the answer following each question and compare your response to it.

1. *My 3-year-old son has made amazing advances in his abilities to understand concepts, get along with others, and more and more, to do things on his own. According to developmental theory, how have all these incredible changes taken place since he was born?*

People who are concerned with how children grow and change, such as doctors, educators, and childcare professionals, apply a number of theories to explain how we grow from infancy to adulthood. But though any two theories may disagree on how or why a specific change occurs in an individual's development, they generally agree on the principles of developmental psychology.

A main principle of developmental psychology is that children differ in several important ways from one phase of growth to the next. A 3 year old is not only taller and heavier than a 1 year old – a quantitative change – he or she is also more emotionally complex and capable of making different types of response than is the younger child – examples of qualitative change.

Another main tenet of a developmental perspective is that each stage of a child's growth is a natural outcome of the child's previous level of development. In other words, one level of development sets the stage for the next.

The third main principle of a developmental approach is that an individual's development is coherent over time. That is, although you as an adult are more capable, in most ways, than you were as a child, your current capabilities can probably be traced back to inclinations or skills you began exhibiting at a very early age. Although you have experienced many changes in your capabilities and point of view during your life, they have taken place within a framework of personal inclinations, preferences, and abilities that have remained fairly stable since childhood.

A fourth factor is the influence of the environment. There may be special circumstances in the child's life – a high quality preschool, for example – that affect the child's development. The complex interaction of heredity and environment must never be underestimated.

2. *I've heard that babies usually begin to show a fear of strangers when they're about 7 months old. Yet my daughter, who is now nearly 15 months old, has never been the least bit afraid of strangers. Should we be concerned that she isn't developing normally?*

Not at all. While the emotional event that you mention does develop in many children in the beginning of their second half year, it isn't an inevitable step in a set sequence that a child must go through to be "normal." The fear of strangers is a common stage of emotional development that children go through and, as such, is an example of normative development. Normative development refers to the changes that most children share, and includes such other milestones as beginning to walk and to talk.

Keep in mind, however, that development also includes an individual component, which accounts for how each child develops in unique ways. For one thing, this means that, even for a particular stage of development, the various individuals among any group of children the same age will move through the stage at different rates. For example, babies born at roughly the same time will begin walking at varying times. Individual development also refers to the fact that each of us has a distinctly different personality which guides and colors our individual reactions to the significant milestones of development. In the case of your daughter, it sounds as though her specific, individual personality may have had the greatest influence on how she reacted to strangers.

3. *What does Charles Darwin's theory of evolution have to do with childhood development?*

Modern child developmentalists have drawn upon the theories of Charles Darwin to explain a number of characteristics with which human beings all seem to be born. According to Charles Darwin, over time an animal species will evolve a set of characteristics which best allow that species to survive in its environment. The mechanism which allows the species to select and pass on these traits is called natural selection. Biologically, traits which favor an individual's survival are transferred from generation to generation in the individual's genes.

By applying these concepts to human behaviors, developmentalists were able to account for such general human traits as sociability, language skills, curiosity, and our amazing capacity for learning. Darwin's ideas have had a major role in shaping how current developmental theory explains the relation between heredity and environment in individual development.

It is important to realize, however, that differences between humans cannot be fully explained by the heredity which is passed along in our genes. Environment, in its broadest sense, from physical to political, is a critical factor in development.

4. *How do Piaget's beliefs about the way young children think about themselves differ from Freud's concept of the ego?*

Piaget structured much of his theory of childhood development around the idea that children first interpret all aspects of the world through their own ego. By this, he meant that young children are incapable of understanding that other people have completely different points of view, as well as feelings all their own. In this sense, Piaget didn't mean that children are self-centered in the selfish, "me-first" way which an adult might be. Rather, he meant that babies seem at first to view themselves as the center of the universe and only gradually develop a sense of other people as separate individuals.

In Freud's original formulation of individual development, on the other hand, the ego is conceived as just one component of an individual's forming self. According to Freudian theory, a newborn baby possesses only an id, which is conceived of as the sum total of all an individual's primitive drives and instincts – the sexual urge, for example, can be generalized as one component of the id. Gradually, over the first few years of life, the individual's ego develops and begins to assume control of the impulses flowing from the id. Over time, each individual develops a superego, which can be roughly generalized as a conscience, to help guide individual behavior.

5. *I've heard of something called information-processing theory. Is this a type of computer program?*

Although information processing is a term used in the field of computers, in the context of this course, it actually refers to a theory of child development that is mainly concerned with how children develop cognitively. By this we mean how children develop mentally, and especially how they develop problem-solving skills. Information-processing theorists explain the changing capabilities of children at different stages by the amount of experience the child has accumulated, among other things. In addition, biological and maturational change also influence cognitive processes. In general, information processing theory holds that a child's attention, memory, and thinking ability improve as he or she grows older, enabling him or her to better interpret new situations and apply a greater number of solution strategies. In terms of developmental theories, information-processing theorists take the view that change develops gradually, though they share with Piagetians an emphasis on the importance of cognitive development.

6. *There are many developmental theories. Which one is right?*

When considering any scientific question that is explained by several theories, it is inaccurate to question which one is the "right" explanation. Especially in a category as open to interpretation as human behavior, a variety of explanations are bound to crop up.

The important thing to remember when studying a number of different, perhaps even contradictory, theories is that each one represents a particular point of view from which all other conclusions flow. For example, the developmental theories put forward by Sigmund Freud, Jean Piaget, and John Bowlby all begin with the assumption that developmental changes are qualitative; that is, children of different ages have changed fundamentally in how they think, feel, and react to situations. These three theories offer different interpretations of similar events, mainly because each approaches the selected instance from a different perspective. While Freud was most interested in how individual emotional development affected overall growth and Piaget focused on the role played by cognitive factors, Bowlby built his theory around a combination of these two aspects, adding in a social component.

Keep in mind that all three of these theories – as well as the two others described in the lesson and several others that aren't even covered in this course – are widely accepted, comprehensive sets of principles that have all made important contributions to our understanding of child development. But it's important to realize that earlier theories are "true" only in their own time. As we learn more with each new study, what seemed a sensible theory at one time may be proven incorrect by later data.

SELF-TEST

The following multiple choice and short answer test questions should help you assess your understanding of the points covered in the text and the video. After answering all the questions, check your answers against the key and use the accuracy of your answers to gauge how well you have met the lesson objectives.

Multiple Choice Questions

1. An attempt to summarize current observations in light of past observations and to predict future ones is one possible definition for

    a. theory.
    b. experiment.
    c. correlation.
    d. hypothesis.

2. At 6 months old, Angela just blinks and stares when her family's cat slinks by; three years later, after the cat dies, Angela goes around the house explaining that "Kitty went to heaven." Seen through a developmental perspective, Angela's changed conceptualization of a cat during the intervening three years represents a(n)

    a. quantitative change.
    b. qualitative change.
    c. organizational change.
    d. example of continuity.

3. According to popular legend, Albert Einstein didn't learn to talk until he was well out of the usual range for beginning to speak. This story is an example of the application of

    a. individual development.
    b. formative development.
    c. behavioral reorganization.
    d. information processing.

4. Marvin is a dedicated baseball fan who can't wait until his infant son becomes old enough to enjoy watching big-league games with his dad. When Sam is 6 months old, Marvin props the baby up against a sofa on the living room floor and practices rolling a softball to his son. To practice playing catch with Sam, however, Marvin is going to have to wait until Sam has grown enough to be able to focus on the ball, coordinate this visual information with his motor abilities, and then grasp the ball. For Sam to be able to do this depends upon

    a. all of the following.
    b. the physical capabilities he has already mastered to that point.
    c. his genetic makeup.
    d. the degree of encouragement his father gives him to play.

5. By and large, current developmentalists deal with the question of the relative importance of genetic versus environmental influences on individual development by asserting that

   a. inherited characteristics usually dominate.
   b. environmental influences usually dominate.
   c. a combination of inherited and environmental factors work together to shape development.
   d. the link between the two factors is so controversial as to be meaningless.

6. A mother carefully holds her infant up in a plastic bathtub set in a sink, supporting his neck as she splashes warm water on the child's belly. According to the theories of Erik Erikson, at least partially as a result of the mother's treatment of the baby during its baths, the child

   a. may form life-long sexual associations with water.
   b. learns that care givers are dependable and can be trusted.
   c. begins to form a budding sense of self autonomy.
   d. begins to form an early sense of separateness from its mother.

7. According to Jean Piaget's theory, it wouldn't make much sense to try to teach an 8-month-old baby the concept of numbers because

   a. the child is still too egocentric to handle abstract concepts.
   b. an 8-month-old has not yet developed the necessary cognitive capabilities.
   c. the child is still fixated in the oral stage at this age.
   d. an 8-month-old's id will resist learning at this age.

8. Suppose you are interested in gathering information on children's preference for a specific style of toy. You might choose to conduct your study through a laboratory experiment because

   a. laboratory experiments offer greater control and precision.
   b. the results from laboratory experiments aren't open to interpretation.
   c. laboratory experiments solve the problems of ecological validity.
   d. the methods of naturalistic observation are poorly developed.

9. While browsing through the classified ads in the newspaper, you come across this ad: "Wanted, for scientific research project, two-parent families with three children, preferably of both sexes, with all children in elementary school. Families with working father making between $25,000 and $30,000 preferred." This ad is LEAST LIKELY to be looking for subjects for a

   a. laboratory experiment.
   b. cross-sectional study.
   c. longitudinal study.
   d. natural experiment.

10. Social learning theorists liken an individual's memory to a tape recorder that is always set to record; if a current situation requires new behavior, the individual will "tape over" old messages and learn new

behavior. According to this view, the most important aspect of learning is

a. age.
b. maturation.
c. experience.
d. genetics.

Short Answer Questions

The following questions should be answered in a paragraph or two. You should identify several key points for each answer and use these to form the framework for your response.

1. What are the key features of the developmental perspective?

2. What are the five main theories of child development discussed in this lesson and what are their main points?

3. Suppose you are interested in finding out the age at which children first begin showing an awareness of gender differences. What are the types of research methods available to you; what are some of their strengths or weaknesses?

2

Children in Context

LESSON ASSIGNMENT

Completing the following steps will help you master the lesson objectives and achieve the goal for this lesson:

STEP 1: Read the INTRODUCING THE LESSON section to provide a context for what you will learn in this lesson.

STEP 2: Read the lesson's GOAL and LESSON OBJECTIVES so that you will know what you are expected to learn.

STEP 3: Read the text assignment, Chapter 2, pages 43-76. Pay particular attention to the key terms and concepts in the Chapter Summary on pages 75-76; they will help you when you watch the video.

STEP 4: Review the VIEWING GUIDE in the telecourse guide. It lists several points to consider as you watch the video.

STEP 5: Watch the video.

STEP 6: Read the UNDERSTANDING THE LESSON section in the telecourse guide. Make sure you understand the key terms and can answer the focusing questions included there.

STEP 7: Complete the SELF-TEST.

STEP 8: Go back to the LESSON OBJECTIVES and make sure you can respond to each of them.

INTRODUCING THE LESSON

The type of carp known in Japan as koi have a remarkable characteristic: their growth depends upon the size of the pool they are contained in. When koi are hatched and raised in small containers or pools, they will stop growing once they reach a certain size, perhaps two or three inches long. But if the breeder moves these mature fish to a much larger pool, the fish begin growing again and will continue until they reach a length of well over a foot – depending upon how much room they now have to swim in.

By and large, human beings don't react to changes in their environment quite so dramatically as koi do. But just like fish – or any other living organism – the development of an individual human being depends greatly upon a number of surrounding influences. These influences, in the form of biology, family, social and economic background, and culture, as well as individual development, represent the particular pond into which every human infant lands at birth.

Development, in other words, depends a great deal upon *context*. No matter how well equipped genetically an infant might be to flourish, if the child's environment is a harsh one from the moment of birth, that child's potential may never be fully realized. Say, for example, a girl is born with a set of genes that gives her the potential to some day be an Olympic swimmer. But if that baby is born to a mother who is impoverished, perhaps even homeless, the child may not be properly nourished, destroying any chances she may have had to compete for gold medals. The same might be true if the girl's parents belong to a cultural group that believes girls should be submissive and "feminine," norms that forbid her from competing athletically.

An especially unfortunate example of how children develop within specific contexts unfolded during late 1989 and 1990 in Romania. In that formerly closed Communist country, the government of Nicolae Ceausescu enforced laws aimed at making people have more children. But many parents, because they couldn't afford to feed their unwished-for babies, gave them up to state orphanages, where they were often raised under extremely unfavorable conditions. Visitors to the understaffed institutions have brought back reports of thousands of children with severe developmental problems, including apathy, lethargy, and inability to speak or walk.

The importance of context to healthy child development extends beyond such dramatic examples, however. In this lesson you will learn how each infant is shaped – from birth – by an embracing network of family ties, social expectations, cultural standards, and economic boundaries. In addition to the genetic code that guides our physical development, each of us is channeled through life along paths laid down in part by parents, siblings, friends, teachers, and numerous others. This lesson will also introduce you to how some very important contexts of development, including the family, are changing and discuss what effects scientists think these changes will have on children.

GOAL

The purpose of this lesson is to show you how children develop within a range of contexts – biological, environmental, social and economic, and cultural – and to demonstrate how even development itself forms a context for the growing child.

LESSON OBJECTIVES

After reading the text assignment, completing the exercises in this telecourse guide, and viewing the lesson's video portion, you will be able to:

1. Name and discuss the four major contexts within which development occurs.

2. Recognize the influence of the historical context in which children develop.

3. Discuss the role of the family in the development of the child and how the changing nature of the family and family life today is affecting children.

4. Discuss the concept of "non-shared environments" and their effects on children from the same family.

5. Explain the influence of such social settings as day care, peer groups, and schools to human development.

6. Explain the relationship among cultures and parenting and child development.

7. Indicate how development itself provides a context for future development.

8. Recognize how the different contexts in which development occurs interact.

VIEWING GUIDE

In this lesson, you begin seeing how child development unfolds within a variety of circumstances. After reading the text material and learning the terms, you are now ready to view the lesson's video portion. First, review the self-test questions at the end of this telecourse guide lesson to give you an idea of important points to watch for in the video. Then, read the following Points to Consider and keep them in mind while watching.

Points to Consider

☐ *Inborn biology*: How do a child's inherited characteristics contribute to its development? Can inborn tendencies be shaped by environmental factors, or are we born frozen into certain specific behaviors?

☐ *Family affairs*: Like the cables that pull a rising tent into shape, family ties are an important influence on infants. How do the behavior and expectations of the family create a context for development? And how does the arrival of a new son or daughter – or brother or sister – alter the relationships within the family?

☐ *Money and status*: What are some of the ways in which low-income parents act to ensure a healthy and secure upbringing for their children? What are some of the special difficulties facing teenage, unwed mothers?

☐ *Children in context*: The values which a child learns are largely a product of its particular culture – which in this lesson refers to the rules, customs, values, and expectations of a particular society. As you watch the video, see what you can learn about how the three children of differing cultural backgrounds vary in their views on gender roles; on competition; on the importance of schooling.

UNDERSTANDING THE LESSON

Have you ever bought a novel because of the glowing reviews on its cover, only to discover that the story was no good? "An all-embracing sense of the absurd," was the opinion of the reviewer for the Dallas Herald – or so you thought. If you'd seen the rest of that quoted sentence – in its original context – you would have gotten a different impression entirely: "In 'Flickering Neon,' the author fails miserably to create a coherent story, a believable motive, or any sense of suspense or intrigue. In fact, the only readers who will enjoy this book are ones with an all-embracing sense of the absurd."

In some cases, context isn't just important; it's everything. In other circumstances, trying to understand why people behave as they do can be as misleading as judging books by the advertising on their jackets. If we wish to understand how children develop, we must first comprehend how each stage of development occurs within specific, discernible contexts.

The Biological Context

Many models of baby strollers or mobile walkers have a row of movable, brightly colored beads strung across their restraining bars. While choosing a stroller, mom or dad probably won't insist on placing their child in the seat to see if he or she will fiddle with the beads; they can safely assume that the toys will attract their offspring's attention – at least for awhile.

This curiosity that humans are born with, our urge to reach out and tinker with objects, is part of our genetic makeup as it has evolved through thousands of years. It, and similar urges and drives as described in the text and on the video, make up the *biological context* of human development. We are born possessing certain tendencies or behaviors that unfold according to a generally similar schedule of development for all infants and children – such as the urge to babble at a certain age, for example, or the tendency that toddlers have to tag along behind an older sibling.

As you have already seen in the video and read in the text material, numerous layers of context surround all of us as we develop. At the center of development, and influencing all influences that follow, however, is the context of the body and its hereditary inclinations.

Key Terms

> Canalization

Focusing Questions

1. If you wish for your son or daughter to be bilingual, when might you want them to begin taking lessons in Spanish, Japanese, or whatever language you choose?

2. Suppose you are babysitting your 18-month-old niece, and you have just pulled her away from the doors of a china cabinet – for the third time in two minutes. While your first impulse may be to scold her, what can you remind yourself about the reasons for her behavior that may lessen your frustration?

The Child's Immediate Environment

While lying on her back, 4-month-old Sheila gazes intently at the bright-colored plastic birds in a mobile that twists slowly above her head. Occasionally she stretches out her hand and tries to capture one of the fascinating objects. In her concentration on the slowly turning toys, Sheila is responding to the influence of objects in her immediate environment – and as soon as she's able to haul herself up onto the bars of her crib, she'll be interacting directly with her environment by grabbing one of the birds.

As you've seen in the video, objects and people form the immediate environment of the child. And for most children, "people" first means family: mother, father, brothers, sisters, aunts, uncles – though not always in that order or even restricted to relatives. Generally, an infant's family are the ones who give her or him those first nurturing hugs and those first examples of speech, those first dizzying tosses into the air.

Today's child developmentalists view the family as a system of interconnecting relationships in which each member is directly and indirectly affected by all the other members. Not only is the child affected by the quality and amount of attention it gets from its parents and siblings, but they in turn are affected by the child. For example, young parents may find that they have to stop going out for movies when a baby daughter arrives; older children may suddenly discover that Mommy doesn't have as much time for them as she did before baby brother arrived. Developmentalists also call this *reciprocal determinism*. As you advance through this course, you will encounter further examples of the family as an *open system*, which means that it is dynamic and constantly changing, both affecting and affected by new family members.

The role of fathers and siblings in child development is now recognized as very important, whereas researchers used to concentrate primarily on the role of the mother. For example, studies indicate that mothers who had parenting problems improved in their child caring when they found a supportive spouse. This indicates, not surprisingly, that children benefit from marital harmony. The presence of brothers and sisters also contributes to the child's development. Older siblings provide direct stimulation for infants, as well as serving as role models. The point here, however, is that all the relationships in a family are important to a child's development and affect all the members in a complex web of reciprocal influences.

Traditionally, researchers presumed that children in the same family would experience their family circumstances in much the same way. However, studies of siblings growing up in the same family suggest that this is not the case. Siblings in the same family can have quite different experiences, and these different experiences, called *non-shared environmental influences*, may help explain why children from the same family are so often very different in terms of personality.

Take the example of siblings who differ in age by ten years – a 4 year old and a 14 year old – and imagine that their parents are having marital difficulties and eventually divorce. The siblings may experience the discord and the divorce very differently. The teenager may cognitively process the events quite differently from the preschooler. Moreover, when things get tense, the teenager may be freer to go to a friend's house for hours at a time, while the preschooler must endure another argument between his parents. If one of the children is temporarily difficult, he or she may become a scapegoat for frustrated parents, while the other child escapes criticism.

When the parents divorce, the preschooler may live in poverty throughout his school years, while the teenager will have spent most of his school years living above the poverty line. Thus, children in the same family may have quite different experiences that have developmental significance.

Key Terms

> Sensitive care
> Transactional model
> Birth order effects

Focusing Questions

1. What are some of the possible effects on children of watching TV for many of hours each week? How might playing video games affect the developing child?

2. Will babies who are born prematurely always develop more slowly than normal-term babies? Can "preemies" be expected to always have developmental problems later? What factors in the infants' context may affect their later development?

The Social and Economic Contexts

To a newborn infant, the economic and social status of its family are among the most powerful and immediate of the indirect contexts shaping its development. In recent years, rising costs and changing societal norms have made it more likely that a given child will be raised in a household with a working mother. Single-parent families have also become much more common. Children of single parents may be indirectly affected by the lack of the social support that a two-parent family may be more likely to offer. While the effects on children of being raised by just one parent tend to vary, studies show that poverty is almost invariably a cause of problems for child development. As for divorce, research indicates that negative effects on children are reduced when the conflict between the parents is lessened or resolved, even though the result to the child is the loss of one parent.

Many children are now raised by a working mother, whether she is alone or with a partner. Among the several complex relations that determine how maternal employment affects offspring, researchers seem to agree that mothers who are satisfied with their employment status, whatever it is, seem to have fewer child-rearing problems. This finding is reflected in the case story of Mikey Gordon and his parents, Frank and Christine, as presented in your textbook.

Outside of the family, one of the first contexts for children is, increasingly, day-care centers. Besides providing children with adult influences outside the family, day care also gives many children their first chance at being around other children their own age – their peers. We first begin learning how to deal with others as equals in such peer group settings, in equal-status or *symmetrical* relationships. Through symmetrical relationships, we begin learning about fairness, reciprocity, and cooperation. Children who do not attend day care will enter into similar relationships when they begin attending school.

Key Terms

Family day care

Focusing Questions

1. What are the important factors that determine whether or not a prematurely born child gets "sensitive care" from its parents?

The Cultural Context

On a Tokyo street, a Japanese mother meets a former teacher. As the woman bows deeply and respectfully, she reaches up and behind to the infant she carries on her back and pushes the child's head down with hers.

On a Philippine island, a foreign visitor stops to talk with a 7-year-old girl who is carrying an infant. "Is that your little brother?" asks the foreigner. "No, she is my cousin," says the girl.

On a steep trail leading to a village in Nepal, a woman trudges slowly upward carrying a load of bundled cut grass on her back. As she walks, she speaks encouragingly to her 6-year-old daughter who paces her footsteps, likewise bent under a smaller, but still towering, bundle of animal fodder.

The different expectations of various cultures are the last of the major contexts of development as explained in this lesson. The culture we are raised in will have a great effect on our gender roles, our values, our attitudes toward work, the expectations placed on us by our families and future mates – even upon our senses of self. Children begin absorbing cultural values from family members and will face further examples of cultural norms when they begin playing with peers of similar backgrounds and then begin attending school.

As you have observed in the video and read in the text, cultures have different values – often radically so – because such values are *adaptive*. In other words, a Japanese child is taught very early that he or she has a clearly established status in society, whereas an American child learns that her place in society depends largely on what she does to earn it.

Key Terms

Subcultures

Focusing Questions

1. What kind of cultural values might an American school child be learning during a game of hide-and-seek?

2. In Japan, in 1991, kindergartners act out the adventures of the cartoon character Doraemon, a blue robot cat; in American schoolyards, in 1991, games often center around the exploits of the Teenage Mutant Ninja Turtles. Are these examples of children behaving in ways that indicate different cultural values?

Questions for Understanding

As you read these questions often raised by parents, educators, and other childcare providers, first try to answer the questions yourself. Then read the answer following each question and compare your response to it.

1. *Will the children who are being adopted out of Romanian orphanages by U.S. parents have developmental problems?*

   As you read in your text, it is difficult to say for certain what effects neglect or abuse during the early years of life will have on a child's future development. Children who are separated from their parents before age 4 and reared in an institution are liable to suffer long-term negative consequences. Older children may have more problems but probably because they have experienced deprivation for a longer time. Children almost invariably respond to improvements in their environments. They may suffer long term negative effects, relative to other children, but they will also show improvement if they experience nurturant relationships.

2. *Should parents worry if their child is unable to ride a bicycle by age 6 or 7?*

   Certain human behaviors are contained in each individual's genetic makeup and appear at roughly similar times for all children. Examples of such "canalized" behaviors would be the urge of babies to begin babbling at a certain age, or to begin walking. A skill such as riding a bicycle, on the other hand, depends mainly upon the developing motor skills of the child – eye-hand coordination, balancing abilities, muscular development, and so on. In other words, learning to ride a bicycle is not a specific stage along the continuum of child development. When a child begins riding a bicycle depends as much on his or her attitudes of self-confidence and feelings of apprehension about learning a new skill – as well as both peer and parent pressure – as it does on individual development. Thus, the stage at which any particular child rides a bicycle depends upon several contexts. No, parents should not worry.

3. *With all the different self-help books on the market for parents and the variety of theories about how children develop, how can parents know what is good advice?*

While conscientious new parents will want to seek out good information on caring for their newborn, they should also feel confident in relying on their own instincts and common sense. The biological context shaping a newborn's responses to its environment also encloses its parents in a network of hereditary impulses and responses. It would be a rare mother who needed training in how infants cry to recognize the difference between a restless baby and an injured one.

On the other hand, human beings are not computers; putting in the same information often brings radically different results in different children. Theories of child development are useful because they offer frameworks for understanding how an infant might develop given a specific set of circumstances. For example, the transactional model of Arnold Sameroff offers one guide to understanding how the two-way influence between parents and child, in concert with the family's social and economic circumstances, shapes the child's development over the long term.

4. *Which of several children born in a family will probably be the most well balanced?*

While the several siblings of one family will probably show differences in behavior and outlook as they develop – what scientists call "birth order effects" – it would be a mistake to look upon these differences as better or worse. Rather, the ways in which first-born children develop differently from their second-, third-, or fourth-born siblings are better considered as variations in how individual human personality unfolds. For example, though scientists agree that first-born children are likely to be more achievement-oriented than younger siblings, who in turn are apt to be more gregarious, they do not assign a judgmental value to these tendencies. The important point to remember is that each individual is part of a dynamic family system, in which each member influences and is affected by all others.

5. *Do children suffer from being raised in non-nuclear families?*

As recently as 15 or 20 years ago, a "normal" American family was generally thought of as being like the ones depicted on popular TV situation comedies of the day such as "Father Knows Best," "I Love Lucy," "The Ozzie and Harriet Show" – even "The Flintstones." Nowadays, however, children are being raised by single, working mothers, by lesbian and gay couples, by divorced fathers who work at home. The "average" American family has mutated so quickly that researchers have not had time to do the long-term research necessary to determine what effects a variety of child-rearing environments have on child development.

Over the short term, however, most researchers agree that the newly emerging family styles do not of themselves threaten to cause later developmental problems for children. For example, homosexual parents report no more trouble with their children than do heterosexual parents, nor do their children seem to have any special problems in gender identity. The process is more important than family structure. How people relate to the child is probably more important than who is doing the relating and within what structure.

6. *New immigrants to America often have difficulties adjusting because their values conflict with those of their new country. In this case, how can we call cultural values "adaptive," as the lesson does?*

The idea that cultural values often arise for the purpose of producing people who are well adapted to a particular society is in line with the main theme of this lesson; that is, cultural values are adaptive, but specifically within the context of a particular culture. In the example of the young Japanese girl depicted in the video, Miyumi's parents exert pressure on her to achieve high grades. This is in keeping with Japanese society, where future jobs and status depend very much on what university one attends. Children are expected to get very high grades. Thus in Japanese society, the expectations of Miyumi's parents that she get high grades are adaptive.

If, on the other hand, Miyumi does get good grades and her American friends resent her for it, her cultural values may cause her problems – because they are being applied out of their normal context.

SELF-TEST

The following multiple choice and short answer test questions should help you assess your understanding of the points covered in the text and the video. After answering all the questions, check your answers against the key and use the accuracy of your answers to gauge how well you have met the lesson objectives.

Multiple Choice Questions

1. Carrie is 17 and her brother Glen is 6. Their parents' income is much higher now than it was when Carrie was 6, and a grandparent with significant health problems has recently moved in with the family. These differences in Carrie's and Glen's experiences as they grow up are called

   a. non-shared environmental influences.
   b. genetic context.
   c. non-traditional families.
   d. cultural influences.

2. Six-year-old Arnold gets exasperated when he tries to play with a group of friends and his 4-year-old brother Andrew insists on tagging along with them. Part of the reason for his younger brother's urge to join Arnold's group is

   a. the result of Andrew's failure to relate to his mother.
   b. a genetic inclination among humans to socialize.
   c. a given condition of his immediate environment.
   d. the result of their family's economic condition.

3. In the early 1800s, 8-year-old children commonly worked 10 hours a day, 6 days a week in British cotton mills. A modern example of how historical context shapes child development would be the

   a. increasing numbers of babies born to crack-addicted mothers.
   b. laws requiring that American children must receive an education.
   c. high proportion of the children of Asian immigrants who are admitted to Harvard and Yale.
   d. increase in the number of children being raised by single mothers.

4. The old cliche, "You can't teach an old dog new tricks," indicates how difficult it is for most people to change their behavior once they've matured. Biologically, the term for this is

   a. canalization.
   b. readiness.
   c. context.
   d. development.

5. The most dominant part of a child's immediate environment is his or her

   a. genetic makeup.
   b. cultural background.
   c. family.
   d. health.

6. Arnold Sameroff's transactional model describes how children and parents affect each other in what developmentalists call a bidirectional effect. This transactional model is an example of

   a. the closed nature of the family system.
   b. the importance of the mother-child relationship.
   c. a developmental context.
   d. a developmental theory.

7. Development itself becomes a context for further development because it

   a. can reverse the effects of genetic predisposition.
   b. is governed by the culture in which a child lives.
   c. affects how a person handles the challenges of each new stage of development.
   d. affects a child's system of values.

8. In New York's Bedford-Stuyvesant neighborhood, 10-year-old Karen Kim works after school in the grocery store owned by her Korean parents. Her Hispanic neighbor, 10-year-old Connie Rodriquez, attends catechism class at St. Mary's Parish Church after school. The way these girls spend their time after school is dictated mainly by their different

   a. rates of biological development.
   b. cultural contexts.
   c. social and economic contexts.
   d. historical contexts.

9. When single parent Jennifer Smith dropped her 3-year-old son Aaron off at day care for the first time, he cried. When she returned to pick him up, however, he cried at having to leave. Aaron told his mother he liked playing with kids his own age because none of them could be his boss. By this, Aaron means that his day-care relationships are

   a. social.
   b. biological.
   c. symmetrical.
   d. reciprocal.

10. If a child from a single-parent, low-income home where the parent is an alcoholic does poorly in school, the main reason is likely to be

   a. an inability to relate to peers.
   b. the difficulties of the child's particular economic context.
   c. a combination of several contexts affecting the child.
   d. poor biological development because of poor nutrition.

Short Answer Questions

The following questions should be answered in a paragraph or two. You should identify several key points for each answer and use these to form the framework for your response.

1. Discuss the importance of the father's role in a child's development.

2. Describe some reasons children from U.S. subcultures might have difficulty adapting to a traditional North American classroom.

3. Your text states that one in five U.S. children lives in poverty. What are some consequences of this environment for the developing child?

3
Conception and Prenatal Development

LESSON ASSIGNMENT

Completing the following steps will help you master the lesson objectives and achieve the goal for this lesson:

STEP 1: Read the INTRODUCING THE LESSON section to provide a context for what you will learn in this lesson.

STEP 2: Read the lesson's GOAL and LESSON OBJECTIVES so that you will know what you are expected to learn.

STEP 3: Read the text assignment, Chapter 3, pages 80-112. Pay particular attention to the key terms and concepts in the Chapter Summary on pages 112-113; they will help you when you watch the video.

STEP 4: Review the VIEWING GUIDE in the telecourse guide. It lists several points to consider as you watch the video.

STEP 5: Watch the video.

STEP 6: Read the UNDERSTANDING THE LESSON section in the telecourse guide. Make sure you understand the key terms and can answer the focusing questions included there.

STEP 7: Complete the SELF-TEST.

STEP 8: Go back to the LESSON OBJECTIVES and make sure you can respond to each of them.

INTRODUCING THE LESSON

From efforts as simple and small as a birdhouse to projects as grandiose as a space shuttle, we create things according to specific plans. A 10-year-old boy or girl assembles a plastic model of an F-15 fighter jet by following the numbered steps of the instruction sheets that come in the box. In a symphony, the violinists, french horn players, and kettle drummers combine all their separate efforts into the glory of "The 1812 Overture" according to the score written by Tschaikovsky and under the direction of a conductor. Before Stephen Spielberg exposed one foot of film to make *E.T.*, he and his screenwriter put in long hours writing the movie's script.

In many ways, a human being also grows and develops according to a very specific set of instructions – though if the "blueprints" for a single human being could somehow be printed, the resulting stack of paper would probably rise higher than a 10-story building.

Each one of us begins life as a single cell. And all the incredible complexity of organs, bones, blood, tissues, and electrochemical exchanges that will eventually become "us" is contained within the confines of that single cell, in the form of genes. For each one of us, genes play the role of blueprints, instruction sheet, musical score.

But describing an individual's genes as his or her "blueprint" for existence is misleading. As you learned in Lesson 2, human development depends greatly upon a number of contexts. The genetic plan for an individual that is created when a sperm unites with an egg does not dictate the final form of that person in the same way as does, say, the foundation of a building or the keel of a ship. Just as a sprouting geranium seed, for example, will be shaped by its soil, sunlight, and nutrients, so will a variety of factors – the immediate environment, the mother's age, economics – likewise shape the growing human life, both before and after it enters the womb.

In this lesson, you continue your exploration of the multitude of influences that come together in the development of a single human being. The video portion and text material sketch in the outline of what genes are and how they dictate the splitting of cells and the multiplication of forms and functions that unfold with the growth of a fertilized egg. You will see how development proceeds from conception into pregnancy and how the prenatal period foreshadows the orderly and cumulative stages of infant and child development.

And finally, you will learn how the genetic material in a single cell – through a combination of differentiation, reorganization, and qualitative changes – emerges from the womb as a unique human infant.

GOAL

The purpose of this lesson is to unravel for you some of the mysteries of the genetic code and explain how prenatal development proceeds, from conception through a series of orderly, cumulative stages, to birth.

LESSON OBJECTIVES

After reading the text assignment, completing the exercises in this tele-course guide, and viewing the lesson's video portion, you will be able to:

1. Relate the key aspects of development to the prenatal period.

2. Explain what genes and chromosomes are and how they influence development.

3. Recognize how a child's gender is determined and the process of pre-natal genetic development.

4. Indicate how genes interact with one another and the environment.

5. Name the three major periods of prenatal development and describe the major characteristics of each in terms of both the developing child and its mother.

6. Explain what a teratogen is and why teratogens generally do more harm to embryos than to fetuses.

7. Identify different procedures that are used to detect fetal problems.

8. Explain how the environmental context influences prenatal development.

VIEWING GUIDE

In the previous lessons, you have studied how a host of conditions and circumstances shape the development of a human being. Now, in this lesson, you will begin following the path of human life from the moment of conception. After reading the text material and learning the terms, you are ready to view the lesson's video portion. First, review the self-test questions at the end of this telecourse guide lesson to give you an idea of important points to watch for in the video. Then read the following Points to Consider to give you an idea of what the video will cover. Keep these points in mind while watching.

Points to Consider

☐ *First drafts*: What are the processes that reproductive cells undergo before they are united in a fertilized egg? How do these processes differ from subsequent cellular actions that allow a single cell to begin repli-cating, differentiating, and reorganizing itself into the tissues, bones, and fluids of the developing human body?

☐ *Beginnings*: What are some of the conditions that must be right before a woman can conceive? Do environmental factors have any effect on fertility, or is the ability to conceive determined genetically?

☐ *On the count of three*: How do the rapidly multiplying cells of an embryo change during the three stages of prenatal development? What are the differences between qualitative and quantitative changes, and when do they occur?

☐ *Outside effects*: Are there stages during prenatal development when a fetus is more vulnerable to influences from outside the mother's womb than at other stages? How effectively does the child's "support system" – placenta, amniotic sac, and umbilical cord – protect it from foreign substances?

UNDERSTANDING THE LESSON

Most of us, at one time or another, daydream about inheriting a large sum of money from some distant relative. An unexpected inheritance, we think, would give us the freedom to do things we've always dreamed of but couldn't afford: take a vacation in the Bahamas, buy a Ferrari, fly to London on the Concorde for an afternoon of shopping.

But in one sense, we're all born rich. Thanks to the complex mechanics of human heredity, each of us is granted a legacy of inestimable worth – the unique combination of genes that we receive from our parents. Locked up in the single cell of a fertilized human egg is all the potential experience of a lifetime, poised at the start of a process of development that nine months later has become a separate individual – you, for example.

Genes and Heredity

By now, you will have discovered in the video and textbook some of the intricacy of the process of conception. You have also likely begun to appreciate the complex process by which two people – a woman and a man – create another human being.

Individual human development has its roots in heredity, which is the combined set of characteristics, traits, and potentialities that each person gets from his or her parents. Every cell in the human body except egg and sperm contains 46 *chromosomes*: threadlike parts of the nucleus that are composed of DNA (deoxyribonucleic acid), each containing thousands of genes imprinted with specific individual physical traits. Chromosomes are linked in pairs of 23, like the bannisters of a spiral staircase – one rail from the mother, one rail from the father. These duplicates, which are similar in size, shape, and genetic information, are called *homologues*.

The process that allows a single cell to evolve into the millions of differentiated cells of a human infant begins with *mitosis*. In mitosis, a form of cell division that continues throughout the individual's life, the chromosomes duplicate themselves and then split into two daughter cells, each containing 46 chromosomes. A different type of cell division, called *meiosis*, takes place in the reproductive cells. This process reduces the number of chromosomes in egg and sperm cells to 23 each so that the fertilized egg or *zygote* has the required 46 chromosomes. Meiosis occurs in three stages. In the first stage the homologous chromosomes arrange themselves into maternal and paternal pairs. They connect at certain points, and corresponding segments may *cross over* from one side of the pair to the other. During the second stage, the pairs separate, moving to opposite ends of the cell. The cell divides, producing new cells made up of randomly assorted genes from the mother and the father. In the final stage, the chromosomes of the new cells duplicate through mitosis and again move to opposite sides of the cell and divide. This results in four *gametes* – egg or sperm cells – each with half of the chromosomes of the original cell and a new combination of genetic instructions.

When the 23 chromosomes of the egg combine with the 23 chromosomes of the sperm, they unite in the 46 chromosomes required to produce a new human being. Just how that particular individual develops, however, isn't simply the result of the genetic instructions coded on those 46 chromosomes. The crucial role that context plays in the developmental history of every individual begins at conception and continues throughout the prenatal period. The determination of gender, for example, begins at the time of conception, but requires further steps through the prenatal period and later in life to complete the process. Two X chromosomes in the 23rd chromosome pair of a fertilized egg start the development of a female. A Y chromosome in the 23rd pair begins the process that will produce a male. Through the first six weeks of development the sex gland tissues look exactly the same in males and females. In the 7th week the Y chromosome finishes its work by triggering part of this tissue to differentiate into testes. In the absence of the Y chromosome the tissues differentiate into ovaries. From this point on sex development is shaped by hormones – glandular secretions that are part of the internal makeup of the embryo. The hormones direct the prenatal formation of reproductive organs and at puberty stimulate the development of the secondary sexual characteristics.

Key Terms

> Alleles
> Genotype
> Phenotype
> Modifier genes

Focusing Questions

1. The DNA that makes up each chromosome has the ability to "unzip" and copy itself. What role does this ability play in the reproductive process? How does it contribute to individual heredity?

2. What is the significance of the "crossing over" of genetic material from the cell's male and female contributors during meiosis?

Conception

The moment of birth exerts a strong appeal to human consciousness. We say that ideas are born – as are nations, art movements, revolutions, and even the universe itself. We give poignancy to failure by saying an effort was misconceived or stillborn. But, like the rest of development, birth is just one of the stages along a continuum of events, and not even the first. Life begins at conception.

And like every other aspect of human development, conception occurs within specific contexts and along orderly sequences. For humans, successful conception begins with the production within the female's ovaries of an egg cell, or ovum, every 28 days. The ovum is released into the fallopian tubes and travels down them into the uterus. If the ovum isn't fertilized within 24 hours, it disintegrates and is lost from the body during the woman's next menstrual period.

If, however, a single sperm cell meets with the egg and penetrates it, fertilization occurs, producing a zygote. In the fallopian tube, the zygote continues to develop into a blastocyst which will embed itself on the uterine wall, beginning the first of the prenatal stages. If two eggs are released by the ovum and fertilized simultaneously, the result is fraternal, or dizygotic, twins. If, however, the egg duplicates itself after being fertilized and the two cells move apart, the result is identical, or monozygotic, twins.

As you learned in the text and video portion, however, events do not always proceed like this. A certain number of couples who wish to reproduce are unable to; they are infertile. The causes of infertility include a variety of factors such as a failure to ovulate, blocked fallopian tubes, and a low sperm count. You saw in the video several couples who were attempting to overcome infertility through various methods, which include corrective surgery, artificial insemination, and in vitro fertilization – the so-called "test tube baby" method.

Focusing Questions

1. Does a surrogate mother contribute any genetic material to the child she carries? How do you think the surrogate mother's body might affect the fetus's development?

2. What are some of the reasons for higher rates of miscarrying, infertility, and other such problems in women who become pregnant after the age of 40?

Earliest Stages: Prenatal Development

The common units for measuring a woman's pregnancy – first, second, and third trimesters – gauge prenatal development from the point of view of the mother. Many women will feel drowsy and tired during the first trimester and experience the type of nausea called morning sickness. Though all pregnant women stop menstruating, the phenomenon of "spotting" – vaginal bleeding that may resemble menstruation – may lead some women to believe they aren't pregnant and to continue habits that may be bad for the developing fetus, such as smoking or drinking. In the second trimester, the mother will begin feeling the fetus's movements and gaining weight. In the third trimester, many women find the extra weight of the growing fetus to be very tiring and may be kept awake at night by the kicking of the fetus.

There are distinct characteristics to each stage of pregnancy. The first period is from conception to week two, or the *germinal period*. During this time, the single fertilized cell that is the zygote divides and forms the structure called a blastocyst. The blastocyst embeds itself in the wall of the uterus and its cells begin differentiating into specialized forms and functions. The part of the blastocyst known as the trophoblast extends tendrils into the blood-enriched uterine walls and begins drawing in nutrients and oxygen from the mother's blood vessels.

By the second stage of prenatal development, the *embryonic period* (week two through eight), the blastocyst has become firmly implanted and is now known as an embryo. The placenta – a mass of tissue that supplies oxygen and nutrients to the embryo – forms, as does the umbilical cord. The amniotic sac forms around the embryo, cushioning it. The embryo itself begins a period of rapid differentiation called organogenesis, in which all the body's vital organs begin to form, along with other major body parts. By the end of the embryonic period, the baby's eyes, heart, limbs, and bones will have begun to take shape. During the embryonic period, the developing fetus is highly vulnerable to any substances which are not filtered out by the placenta, such as alcohol, various drugs, and diseases.

The *fetal period*, from week nine to birth around week 38, is a time of growth and refinement for the forming organism – now called the fetus. By the fifth month, the fetal heart is beating regularly and the fetus has adopted a regular sleep-wake cycle. The fetus begins to exhibit responsiveness to any stimulation – in an overall, "global" way at first, then more locally. For instance, touching a 10-week-old fetus on the foot makes it arch its entire trunk; a similar touch at 18 weeks causes the fetus to pull back just its foot – another example of phased, qualitative change. By the end of the fetal period, the original single fertilized egg is nearly at the end of its course of development into an infant, ready to be born.

Key Terms

Embryonic induction

Focusing Questions

1. Does a pregnant woman's blood flow directly from her into her developing child?

2. Scientists speak of how certain genes in the developing fetus can be "turned on" or "turned off." What does this mean? Can any embryonic cell, under the right circumstances, develop into any possible organ or structure?

Environmental Influences

In March 1991, a woman in Seattle, Washington, who was nine months pregnant got an unexpected – and unappreciated – lesson in the possible effects of environmental factors on prenatal development. The woman was in a restaurant and ordered a strawberry daiquiri. Two restaurant employees, however, refused to serve her, citing the possible dangers of exposing her fetus to alcohol. One waiter steamed the label off a bottle of liquor and gave it to the woman, pointing out its warning of the possible effects – including fetal alcohol syndrome – of alcohol on the unborn.

In the subsequent publicity, doctors were found who supported both sides of the strawberry daiquiri controversy: some said that the woman shouldn't consume any alcohol at all while pregnant, no matter how far along she was in gestation; other doctors held that the alcohol in a single drink wouldn't hurt a fetus in its ninth month of development. All the doctors cited did agree, however, that what a woman ingests during her pregnancy does have an effect on her developing child, though of varying degrees at different stages of development. As you know from your reading and viewing, any environmental agents that can cause abnormalities in a fetus are called *teratogens*.

The list of teratogens is long and includes the obvious ones such as heroin and "crack," HIV and rubella, and birth-control hormones. Also, the unborn child may be affected if the mother suffers from great stress or poor nutrition during her pregnancy. Developing fetuses are most vulnerable to damage from teratogens during the embryonic period when the major body parts are forming and cell differentiation is rapid and widespread. Changes at this time are permanent and irreversible. Obviously, it is highly important for a pregnant woman to take great care during the early stages of her pregnancy. Unfortunately, however, it may be difficult for some women to know that they are pregnant during these early, crucial stages.

A number of techniques exist for detecting some birth abnormalities. Ultrasound, for example, produces a computer image of the fetus by bouncing sound waves off it and is increasingly used because it is non-invasive. To detect other defects, however, the process called *amniocentesis* is still the best method. This method involves inserting a needle into the mother's abdomen and drawing off a sample of amniotic fluid. *Chorionic villus sampling*, which provides the same information as amniocentesis but can be done earlier, is a type of genetic testing in which cells are suctioned from the developing placenta through the uterus and vagina. While the advent of these and other techniques have given prospective parents greater chances for detecting any abnormalities in their developing child, they have also increased the possible responsibility involved in deciding how to handle an imperfect fetus.

Focusing Questions

1. What kinds of fetal abnormalities can tests such as ultrasound, amniocentesis, and chorionic villus sampling detect? What are some of the moral dilemmas which a pregnant woman and her partner might find themselves in as a result of such testing?

2. Why would a pregnant woman want to avoid any contact with anyone who has rubella?

Questions for Understanding

As you read these questions, often raised by parents, educators, and other childcare providers, first try to answer the questions yourself. Then read the answer following each question and compare your response to it.

1. *How much chance do parents have of predicting what their children will look like?*

Prospective parents are naturally curious about how their children will look. But while parents can make certain guesses about their offspring that are more likely to be accurate than others – two tall people can reasonably anticipate offspring of similar height, for example – they'll never be able to foresee exactly what shapes their children are actually going to take.

The reason for this lies in the way genes interact with one another. A person's observable physical characteristics – known as their pheno-type – are determined by his or her genes – known as their genotype –

which aren't observable. In other words, trying to guess what genes two people will contribute to their children is like trying to tell if a person can speak more than one language just by looking at her or him.

The genes that determine characteristics are received as matched pairs from parents and are called alleles. If the genes for a particular trait are the same, they are homozygous; if different, they are heterozygous. In heterozygous genes, the alleles are either dominant, recessive, or co-dominant. In addition, many traits are influenced by dozens of genes – polygenic effects – creating enormous diversity among people, even people within the same family. Thus, for the most part, trying to foresee what your children will look like is a hit-or-miss effort.

2. *What are "fertility drugs"? How do they work?*

Because the most common cause of infertility in women is a failure to ovulate or release egg cells from the ovaries, special drugs are available that induce increased egg production. These drugs have proven successful in helping some previously infertile women become pregnant – sometime spectacularly so, since the way these drugs work occasionally results in multiple conceptions.

3. *When should a pregnant woman be most careful about what she eats or ingests in terms of how it affects her baby?*

A developing fetus is probably most vulnerable to outside influence during the embryonic period. During this stage, the blastocyst undergoes radical qualitative change, forming into an oval that then becomes indented. Cells begin migrating inward and forming three different types of tissue: endoderm, which become internal organs; mesoderm, which become muscles, skeleton, and blood; and ectoderm, which form the central nervous system, sensory organs, and skin. Then, after these tissues have migrated to various parts of the embryo, they begin adapting into specific organs and structures depending upon the type of tissue they are in contact with. This process is known as embryonic induction.

During this period of rapid change, from about the second to the eighth week of pregnancy, the developing organism is highly susceptible to the influence of various chemicals or substances. And though the placenta, umbilical cord, and amniotic sac offer barriers against foreign materials, they do not filter out everything. Viruses, alcohol, and a range of other drugs, for example, can slip through and damage the growing embryo.

4. *When is a woman too old to consider having a child?*

In recent years, it has become fairly common for women who have passed the age of 40 to conceive and deliver healthy babies. Because of advances in medical technology and increased awareness among older women of the importance of proper prenatal care, many women over 35 safely conceive and bring healthy babies to term. Also, women over 40 who have had one or two previous children are more likely to have a trouble-free pregnancy than women having a first child past the age of 40.

On the other hand, statistical evidence shows that both teenagers and women over 35 have higher rates of miscarriage, stillbirths, and infant deaths than women in between those ages. Probable reasons, for teenagers, include immature reproductive organs and a greater chance of being unable to provide good nutrition and prenatal care. Among the problems confronting an older pregnant woman are the thinning of uterine walls after age 30 and possible damage to her supply of ova over the years. This age group runs a high risk of chromosomal disorders such as Down syndrome. Nonetheless, the rate of Down syndrome is still only one in sixty-five for women conceiving after age 45.

5. *My wife and I have heard that stress can possibly damage an unborn child. Should we try to avoid all arguments during her pregnancy?*

While it is very hard to measure something as subjective as stress, some studies have been developed that measure negative life events such as divorce or job loss. According to some of these tests, the children of woman who experienced high levels of stress during pregnancy were more likely to be irritable as newborns, and some developed later behavioral problems.

Stress, however, seems only to be a problem for a developing fetus when the problem is intense and long term. A probable negative result of such stress might be an alteration in available oxygen to the fetus due to adrenaline in the mother's bloodstream. Having an occasional disagreement and flare of emotions is highly unlikely to have any ill effect on the unborn child. Many people, in fact, may find repressing emotions more stressful than releasing them.

6. *Why is it usually only males who are born with colorblindness?*

It is true that certain genetic problems are much more likely to afflict men than women: for example, colorblindness, hemophilia, and dyslexia. And the reason is that, genetically speaking, women are the basic pattern of the species. Women have two X chromosomes; one can override if the other X is defective. For males, the one Y chromosome cannot override a defective X.

When a normal embryo inherits 23 chromosomes from its mother and 23 chromosomes from its father, the child's sex is determined by the 23rd pair. From the mother, it can only receive an X chromosome; but from the father, it can receive either an X or a Y chromosome. If it receives a Y, the embryo will be a boy. But the father's shorter Y chromosome carries little genetic material beyond the "message" of maleness.

In other words, in a "female" zygote, if one set of 23rd chromosomes contains a genetic flaw, they have a chance of being cancelled out by dominant normal genes on the matching 23rd chromosome – both are X, remember. In a "male" zygote, however, any genetic anomalies on the 23rd X chromosome will not be covered up by matching material on the 23rd Y chromosome, and so the abnormality will be expressed – as colorblindness is, for example.

SELF-TEST

The following multiple choice test questions should help you assess your understanding of the points covered in the text and the video. After answering all the questions, check your answers against the key and use the accuracy of your answers to gauge how well you have met the lesson objectives.

Multiple Choice Questions

1. The gender of a fertilized egg is determined by

    a. hormones.
    b. the 23rd chromosome pair.
    c. the mother.
    d. the sex glands.

2. An example of the importance of environmental factors on development during the prenatal period would be

    a. crossing over of genes during meiosis.
    b. how developing tissues change according to their locations in the fetus.
    c. the possible effect teratogens may have on the embryo.
    d. the role played by the short Y chromosome in determining male gender.

3. When Joanne was born, she was diagnosed as having the genetic disorder known as PKU; her body lacked the enzyme needed to use the common chemical phenylalanine found in foods. Joanne inherited this condition from her parents because the determining genes she received from them were on

    a. homozygous alleles.
    b. dominant alleles.
    c. co-dominant alleles.
    d. heterozygous alleles.

4. One example of how the actions of some genes are triggered or "turned on" by other genes at certain stages of development is

    a. the combination of alleles that produce blue eyes.
    b. how two X chromosomes produce a female.
    c. the production of 4 gametes during meiosis.
    d. the secretion of estrogen during puberty.

5. A blastocyst becomes an embryo when

    a. it has developed a placenta.
    b. it is embedded in the uterus wall.
    c. organogenesis is complete.
    d. placenta prevaria occurs.

6. Anyone shopping for a used car usually kicks its tires; a pediatrician examining a new baby for the first time checks its ears. The pediatrician does this because

   a. an infant's hearing is a good indicator of neural development.
   b. abnormalities in ear development may indicate life-threatening problems in the kidneys.
   c. kidneys and ears form at the same time in prenatal development thus defects in one often predict defects in the other.
   d. it's simply a part of the routine examination.

7. One week after James was born, he would scream in apparent agony even at very light noise or when his mother changed him. At two years, James hadn't begun walking, and clearly avoided stimulation as much as possible. Before he was born, James's mother was most likely

   a. addicted to heroin.
   b. a 3-pack-a-day smoker.
   c. an alcoholic.
   d. exposed to rubella.

8. Compared with a 15-year-old girl, a 40-year-old woman will

   a. probably have a less stressful pregnancy.
   b. have a better chance to have a trouble-free pregnancy.
   c. have about the same chances of getting pregnant.
   d. have a smaller supply of ova.

9. In the 1943 film comedy, *The Miracle of Morgan Creek*, a young woman becomes a national celebrity after giving birth to six babies. Today, such an event is very much a real-life possibility because of the advent of

   a. fertility drugs.
   b. laparoscopy.
   c. amniocentesis.
   d. lower infant mortality rates.

10. Cells from a developing placenta are suctioned through the vagina and cervix of a pregnant woman via a small tube. This process is called

    a. amniocentesis.
    b. ultrasound.
    c. fetal monitoring.
    d. chorionic villus sampling.

Short Answer Questions

The following questions should be answered in a paragraph or two. You should identify several key points for each answer and use these to form the framework for your response.

1. A couple hoping to have children have been trying to conceive, without success, for several years. What options might a physician discuss with the couple to help them overcome their apparent infertility and possibly conceive a baby?

2. Although the placenta can protect a developing embryo or fetus from some environmental dangers, viruses can pass through the placenta and cause birth defects or death. Discuss some of these viruses, their effects, and measures, if any, that may prevent severe consequences.

3. The average full-term baby weighs about 7½ pounds at birth. Babies weighing 5½ pounds or less at birth may be at risk for a variety of problems. What are some reasons for low birth weight? Discuss some of the difficulties low birth weight infants may experience.

4

Birth and the Neonate

LESSON ASSIGNMENT

Completing the following steps will help you master the lesson objectives and achieve the goal for this lesson:

STEP 1: Read the INTRODUCING THE LESSON section to provide a context for what you will learn in this lesson.

STEP 2: Read the lesson's GOAL and LESSON OBJECTIVES so that you will know what you are expected to learn.

STEP 3: Read the text assignment, Chapter 3, pages 89-97, and 107-113; and Chapter 4, pages 126-141, and 146-147. Pay particular attention to the key terms and concepts in the Chapter Summary on pages 112-113, and 154-155; they will help you when you watch the video.

STEP 4: Review the VIEWING GUIDE in the telecourse guide. It lists several points to consider as you watch the video.

STEP 5: Watch the video.

STEP 6: Read the UNDERSTANDING THE LESSON section in the telecourse guide. Make sure you understand the key terms and can answer the focusing questions included there.

STEP 7: Complete the SELF-TEST.

STEP 8: Go back to the LESSON OBJECTIVES and make sure you can respond to each of them.

INTRODUCING THE LESSON

Throughout our lives, most of us experience moments of extreme surprise, maybe even shock. At the end of a particularly trying day at work, you step through your apartment front door – and twenty gleeful friends bound from behind the furniture, shouting "Happy Birthday!" While cruising at 35,000 feet, the 727 you're flying in hits a low-pressure air pocket and plummets several thousand feet. Being surprised is always . . . a surprise.

But sudden shocks are nothing new to individual human beings. After all, conscious life begins with a big surprise – birth. After nine months of gradual, cumulative development within the cushioned shelter of the womb, a human infant is turned upside down, squeezed through the birth canal, and then coaxed forth into the world.

As the last drops of amniotic fluid drain out of its lungs, the newborn reflexively breathes in a first lungful of air and experiences its first smells. Sounds, previously muffled by its mother's body, fill the infant's ears. Hands caress it, and light beats against its tightly clenched eyes. For the first time, air and temperatures different from that of its mother's body touch its skin, still glistening with the fluids of birth. At least from the point of view of the participating adults, life comes as a rude awakening to a newborn.

Certainly the moment of birth marks a major transition in the development of the human infant. But as adults, we should probably be cautious about projecting our developed capacity to register surprise onto the newborn. Obviously, at birth our abilities to experience emotions – if possible at all – are greatly different from what they will become. For another thing, a newborn's senses are to a large extent still undeveloped, and so the sudden onslaught of sounds, sights, and sensations are not nearly as unsettling as we might think. While being born certainly does represent a major change for the infant, the baby is well prepared for the attendant shocks.

In this lesson, you will examine the moment of birth as one of the most significant milestones in a child's development – certainly, in the eyes of parents, the most dramatic. In keeping with the theme of this course, you will see how the experience of birth is shaped by a variety of developmental contexts, which include prenatal influences that occur both within and outside the fetal environment and the effect that the child's family has upon it. In turn, you will see how the approaching birth and arrival of a new infant affect the lives of its parents, plus those of any siblings.

You will also learn about recent changes in how babies are being born in hospitals and special birth centers in the United States and other countries and how these new means of delivery can benefit both infants and parents. Increasingly, parents prepare for the birth of a child by attending special training sessions in birth, and the text material and video portion will introduce several of these approaches. This lesson will help you appreciate how important a developmental event birth truly is for the infant – as well as how well prepared for the event the baby is.

GOAL

The purpose of this lesson is to describe the biological sequences that culminate in the birth of a child, as well as to describe a sense of what the experience of birth is like – from the viewpoints of both the mother and the neonate.

LESSON OBJECTIVES

After reading the text assignment, completing the exercises in this telecourse guide, and viewing the lesson's video portion, you will be able to:

1. Recognize that birth is a radical transition for the fetus.

2. Outline the sequence and procedures involved in the birth process.

3. Describe, in general, the appearance of the newborn child.

4. Indicate the psychological and social effects on all family members as they adjust to living with an infant.

5. Suggest ways in which new birthing techniques and procedures provide psychological as well as physical benefits for parents and infants.

VIEWING GUIDE

In this lesson, you will study the dramatic and emotional moment when a new child first enters the spotlight. But as clearly as birth represents a starting place, you will further learn how birth is just one more of the important but sequential steps of a child's development. After reading the text material and learning the terms, you are now ready to view the lesson's video portion. First, review the Self-Test questions at the end of this telecourse guide lesson to give you an idea of important points to watch for in the video. Then read the following Points to Consider to give you an idea of what the video will cover. Keep these points in mind while watching.

Points to Consider

☐ *The big day*: Birth proceeds in a series of definite stages which, taken together, make up the length of time a woman will be in labor. Notice, also, what changes the fetus undergoes just prior to birth.

☐ *The varieties of birth*: In the video, you will see mothers and their partners learning one of several methods of "natural birth." Consider why these types of training have become popular and just what they offer to mothers and neonates. Also, notice how the status of the father in delivery rooms has changed over the past generation or two.

☐ *What to expect of a newborn*: A baby may not be born with 20-20 vision or the hearing of a guard dog, but a healthy baby will have some sensory development. Try to imagine just what the world looks, sounds, feels, and smells like to a newborn. In the video, watch for the immediate steps that delivery room personnel will take to determine the baby's health and well being.

☐ *First acts*: You will be viewing scenes of newborns reacting – often quite loudly – to birth. Notice how the experience seems to be affecting the baby, and just how alert or interested the baby seems. Pay attention to the range of behaviors, if any, which infants are capable of at birth.

☐ *Early influences*: Although the physical act of birth is generally the same for all mothers and infants, the expectations about the arrival of a new baby vary from family to family and culture to culture. While watching the video, be aware of how different social, economic, and familial contexts can have an influence on the experience of birth for everyone involved.

UNDERSTANDING THE LESSON

As this course repeatedly emphasizes, the stages of child development are gradual and cumulative, with few moments of high drama. The moment of conception is by nature unseen and unremarked; even the astounding growth and differentiation of the zygote through the three stages of pregnancy can only be inferred from signs that are filtered through the mother's slowly changing body. And later, such heralded events as speech, walking, and the dawning of self awareness occur in small increments, slowly, over time. By and large, the significant milestones of a child's development are passed without obvious cymbal-crashing or blowing of trumpets.

Except, that is, for the moment of birth. Cultures the world over celebrate few events as uniformly as they do the birth of a new member of the community. A birth is one of the most dramatic and emotionally moving events of human experience. After nine months of growth, after the early moments of morning nausea for some mothers, after her abdomen first begins to swell, after the first stirrings and kickings, the baby emerges. For the first time, this new person has a face and must be named. The moment of birth marks a clear and significant moment of transition for everyone involved – baby, mother, father, and other family members.

Being Born

As you learned in the previous lesson, human development begins with conception, and the general outline of an individual's development is contained in the 46 sets of chromosomes which it inherits from its parents. During the three trimesters of pregnancy, the growing infant becomes an increasingly real presence to the mother. By the end of the fourth month, she has felt the quickening of fetal movements and soon others can feel the moving fetus by touching her abdomen.

As for the fetus itself, the last month or two before birth is a period of weight gain and refinement in the growth of body parts. Since the twelfth week, the fetus has been inhaling and exhaling amniotic fluid. The fetus has also adopted a regular sleep-wake cycle. Even while within the womb, the infant is showing an increasing tendency to react to its surroundings and to be influenced by context. As you will learn in Lesson 5, these behaviors are early signs of the baby's preadaption to the changes it will soon face.

As the moment of birth approaches, the fetus moves into a head-down position. This is the safest position for birth, as it usually prevents the child's being strangled by its own umbilical cord, a more possible danger during a breech, or bottom first, birth. In the first stage of labor, the mother's body experiences contractions that move the baby into the birth canal. As contractions become stronger and more frequent, the cervix dilates to its full limit – a process which takes from an hour to as much as a day.

The second phase of a normal labor begins with the *crowning* of the baby's head through the cervix into the vagina. With contractions now occurring at about a minute apart and lasting 45 seconds, the baby's head and shoulders slip out, the head turns to the side, and the rest of the body quickly follows. In the final stage of labor, the continuing contractions in the uterus expel the placenta and other "afterbirth" membranes.

Focusing Questions

1. In Lesson 3, you learned about some of the effects that outside agents, called teratogens, can have on the developing embryo. What are some of the signs of these effects that might appear in a newborn? How might some of these developmental effects complicate the process of birth?

Methods of Birth

Since the end of World War II, most babies in the United States have been delivered in hospitals. Doctors approached a birth as a medical problem and in most cases excluded fathers from the delivery room. In movies of the time, waiting rooms filled with anxious husbands pacing the floor and smoking cigarettes are common cliches. Delivery rooms, like operating theaters, were brightly lit and designed for maximum efficiency. Anesthetics were administered to women in labor in up to 95 percent of births.

In recent years, though, the atmosphere in delivery rooms has been changing. A general desire among pregnant women and their partners all over the world for more "natural" methods of childbirth has had a large effect on how children are born. It is now common practice in hospitals for the baby's father to be present during birth, and many delivery rooms are now specifically designed to be less "hospital-like," with bright colors evident and comfortable furniture on hand. Some hospitals have added "birthing rooms" that, at first glance, often resemble hotel rooms.

Today pregnant women are very often active participants in the preparations for their child's birth, through a number of programs that train them in the methods of natural childbirth. One of the most popular of these is the *Lamaze method*, in which prospective parents attend pre-birth classes in breathing techniques and other exercises to ensure a safe, natural birth. One of the main aims of approaches such as Lamaze is to enable a woman to experience birth without the use of any anesthetics or other drugs. Though western doctors have traditionally used anesthetics during labor to ease the mother's pain, anesthetics lower the mother's blood pressure and thereby reduce the supply of oxygen available to the child.

Another important trend in Western methods of birth has been the increasing practice of midwifery. A midwife – who can be either a male or female practitioner – is a health professional who is generally involved with the expectant mother for a much longer time than are mainstream medical specialists. Midwives usually are present during the entire length of a woman's labor, and many provide long-term counseling and advice on family planning and contraception following the birth. In one Seattle, Washington, hospital in 1990, one out of four babies was "birthed" by a midwife.

In most cases, however, midwives coordinate their activities with an obstetrician, in the event of any possible *birth complications*. Such complications might include indications by fetal heart-rate monitors that the fetus is suffering distress, or the possibility that the mother's pelvis is too small to allow passage of the baby's head. Such cases may require a *Caesarean section*, a surgical procedure in which the infant is delivered through an incision in the mother's abdomen and uterus. Some controversy attends the wide practice of Caesarean sections by doctors in this country; from 1965 to the mid-1980s, the incidence of this operation increased from 5 to 23 percent.

Key Terms

> Birth complications
> Caesarean section
> Lamaze method

Focusing Questions

> 1. Why do the Lamaze and other methods of natural birth emphasize the importance of proper breathing techniques during labor?
>
> 2. What are some of the possible negative effects on the infant of anesthetics and analgesics given to its mother during labor?

Characteristics of Newborns

There is always high emotion in a delivery room at the moment of birth. Not surprisingly, even doctors and midwives who have assisted in the deliveries of dozens of infants report feeling a regular sense of thrill, as well as awe. Nine months following the unremarked and unnoticed moment of conception, another human being has arrived upon the scene.

In the video portion of this lesson, you saw the wet, tiny figure of the newborn being held above its tired but exhilarated mother. Like nearly any other healthy, well-developed baby, its eyes were clenched tight against the light, and its skin radiated a healthy glow. Within a few moments of birth, you saw a nurse administering an Apgar scale, checking and rating the infant's heart rate, respiratory efforts, reflex irritability, muscle tone and skin color. You also heard the doubts expressed by a child developmentalist as to the overall validity of the test, unless it is rigorously applied.

As a rule, babies adjust to birth remarkably quickly. Within a short time, the newborn will be nestled in its parents' arms, its eyes open, awake and apparently alert. While a newborn's vision is certainly limited, it is able to distinguish differences in lightness and darkness, is sensitive to movement, and can see objects which are within a few inches of its eyes. Furthermore, researchers have demonstrated that newborns have an inborn tendency to concentrate on faces, generally by focusing on outlines.

As you will learn in more detail in the next lesson, fetuses have demonstrated their ability to hear by moving in the womb in response to loud noises. After birth, the baby will hear sounds when they are 10 to 20 decibels above the level at which an adult first hears them. If the wind blows through some trees outside the hospital window, for example, the baby may well hear the leaves rustling. Infants use distinct facial expressions and body movements to indicate a sensitivity to various odors – for one thing, they don't like the smell of rotten eggs. And babies arrive with a full complement of taste buds and are able to distinguish the flavor of a weak sugar solution from the taste of plain water – probably in preparation for the sweetness of mother's milk.

Key Terms

Apgar scale

Focusing Questions

1. A young father picks up his newborn daughter for the first time. What action will the man almost instinctively take to ensure that his new baby can more or less "see" him?

2. Which of the newborn's senses – sight, hearing, taste, smell, or touch – is probably the first one to enable the infant to "recognize" its mother?

A Newborn's States and Reflexes

New parents are often unprepared for the rhythms of their newborn infant. A baby, after all, is not yet focused upon any priorities beyond sleeping, eating, and being comforted. Babies will generally sleep about 16 hours per day, divided about equally between day and night.

Developmentalists categorize a baby's level of alertness into six *states*, including quiet sleep, active sleep, awake and quiet, awake and active, fussing and crying. And though some parents may find it hard to believe, babies actually spend less than 10 percent of their time crying. Infants cry for a number of reasons, including hunger, and they need to be soothed by care givers. Newborns are also biologically preconditioned to soothe themselves, through such things as thumb-sucking, a reflexive action that they may begin while in the womb.

Even at birth a newborn will demonstrate certain definite behaviors, though almost strictly of the reflexive variety. For instance, if you touch an infant on the cheek, he or she will turn his or her head in that direction while opening his or her mouth – an automatic reaction known as the *rooting reflex*. If the infant then captures your finger in his or her mouth, the baby will begin vigorously sucking, another innate reflex. And, of course, shutting the eyes at the first light of birth, as well as breathing, are both reflexes. These and other reflexes make up part of a child's capabilities at birth which doctors use as a gauge of the baby's health; these reflexes will be studied further in the next lesson.

Another important ability that even infants possess is some control of their eye movements. Newborns show a tendency to gaze around, as though actively looking for something to look at. And though their eye movements are neither accurate nor smooth, newborns tend to try following with their eyes an object that is moved across their field of vision. Probably in intuitive recognition of this, care givers tend to move their heads slowly and from side to side when talking with infants.

Focusing Questions

1. Which of the three types of crying do you think an infant is making when it cries at birth?

2. Suppose you are carrying a 1- or 2-day-old baby around. Would you expect the infant to be completely passive, without any apparent interest in its surroundings, or would you expect the child to gaze around, and perhaps even move its head as you walked?

The Importance of Context in Prenatal Development and at Birth

Like every other stage of an individual's life, birth takes place within a context. The circumstances of each birth are shaped by the newborn's particular genetic makeup, prenatal experience, and parents' economic circumstances, among other things. The arrival of a new baby also has a great impact on its parents and any other family members. The scenes from the video portion showing expectant parents and their older children emphasize the fact that the baby is being born into an environment that will begin shaping the child's development almost immediately.

Also, as you learned in the previous lesson, the newborn has already been shaped and influenced by a variety of prenatal factors, including the combination of its genes, the sequence of developmental stages during pregnancy, and the gain in weight of the fetus just before birth. The fetus has also been influenced by factors that originate outside its mother's body, whether in the form of possibly damaging teratogens or a poor diet for its mother.

Like every other stage of development, an infant's birth takes place within the context of the individual's own body, the family, and the world at large. If, for example, a pregnant mother lacks adequate medical care as a result of poverty, she may not receive proper testing or preparation before the birth. In the case of a woman who is using drugs and doesn't know that she is pregnant within the crucial first trimester, her fetus can suffer numerous serious defects. As for the various new trends toward more natural birth discussed in the lesson, pregnant women from poor backgrounds are less likely to be offered some of these options. Thus, not all babies are "born equal," and the circumstances of birth are but the beginning of a lifelong set of influences that shape an individual's life.

Focusing Questions

1. How might the birth experience of a baby born to an unmarried 17-year-old mother differ from that of a baby born to a 28-year-old married mother of one other child?

Questions for Understanding

As you read these questions, often raised by parents, educators, and other child care providers, first try to answer the questions yourself. Then read the answer following each question and compare your response to it.

1. *I've heard that it's now possible to learn the gender of our baby before it's born.*

   That is quite true. Ultrasound, a technique that bounces sound waves off a fetus and then uses the information to compile a computer image of the fetus, will also tell you the baby's sex. The technique is used for a variety of purposes such as diagnosing heart defects and rhythm disturbances, as well as to guide instruments during other sample-taking techniques. Interestingly, it is not uncommon for some parents to request that their physician not tell them if their unborn child is male or female, even if the physician has ordered the test for another reason. But to know or not to know is, in this case, one of the more pleasant decisions facing parents before their child is born.

2. *What are some of the difficulties that may arise during birth?*

   While birth is a natural process for the majority of women, complications can arise. If, for example, the fetus hasn't turned itself around in proper head-down direction, it may emerge feet or bottom first. This can cause problems because a baby takes longer to be born in this position; in addition, there is a danger of the umbilical cord becoming tangled or pinched. If this happens, the child could be seriously deprived of oxygen, a condition known as *anoxia*.

   Babies who are delivered past their projected date of birth may grow too large to be delivered safely. Another danger of *postterm* babies is that, by overstaying their welcome, they deplete the placenta of oxygen. In such cases, doctors may induce labor by administering a contraction-stimulating drug, *oxytocin*. Doctors also sometimes perform a Caesarean section to solve the problems of certain difficult deliveries.

3. *What does it mean if my baby is born prematurely? Is it a problem?*

   While the term "premature" simply means that a baby is born early. Prematurity itself is not necessarily a problem. The determining factor in how well any infant can survive outside the womb is its size and the degree of its development. The average birthweight of a full-term baby is 7½ pounds; only 6 percent of babies born in the United States fall below 5½ pounds. These babies suffer a mortality rate twice that of heavier babies.

   While neonatal intensive care wards have developed an amazing ability to sustain the life of "preemies," thanks largely to advanced technology, there are limits below which infants cannot survive outside the womb. It is unusual for any infant with a birthweight under two pounds to survive.

   Keep in mind, also, that low birthweight can be caused by factors other than premature delivery, such as retarded growth and development in the uterus. Babies born prematurely, but after seven months of gestation, may survive with no ill effects. On the other hand, babies who are born with a comparatively low birthweight do run higher risks for later difficulties than higher birthweight babies of the same gestational age.

4. *Sometimes, when our week-old daughter cries, my wife will say things like, "Oh, she needs changing." Then, other times, she'll say, "Okay, now she's hungry." I can't hear any difference in her crying, but apparently my wife can.*

It is true that babies have different patterns of crying for different needs. When a baby is hungry, it tends to start slowly, signaling its state by whimpering, then gradually escalate to louder and longer cries. If your daughter becomes upset at something, such as a loud noise in her room, she'll let you know by beginning to cry in an immediate, loud outburst. Should she hurt herself, perhaps by being pricked by an open safety pin, she'll let loose with a high-pitched, high-intensity wail, followed quickly by loud crying.

Research shows that mothers respond most quickly to cries of pain as compared to the other two types of crying. Studies have also shown that nurses in hospital nurseries develop the ability to discriminate among the three types of crying – so you should be able to also, given enough time.

5. *Recently, I heard about individuals who aren't midwives, but assist at deliveries by being present and offering support to the woman in labor.*

It sounds like you're referring to a new category of trained woman who has given birth herself, called a "doula." Doula is a Greek word that refers to a woman who guides a new mother. Unlike midwives, who are often trained as nurses, doulas offer emotional support to a woman in labor, in the form of hugging, hand-holding, and words of encouragement or explanation.

Although not enough research has been done yet on the efficacy of the presence of doulas at deliveries, the stated intent of a doula is to lessen a woman's anxiety in hopes that their bodies will perform as they should. In one of the few studies which has been done, as reported in a recent *Newsweek* article, only 8 percent of the women assisted by doulas had Caesarean sections, as compared with 18 percent in a control group.

6. *Is being born painful for a baby?*

According to conjecture based on the latest scientific data, researchers have concluded that being born is probably not painful to the child. From the fetus's point of view, the main discomfort of birth comes from being squeezed during passage through the birth canal. But an infant's sense of pain is much less developed than an adult's.

Probably the biggest shock to the newborn comes from the sudden flood of light striking its eyes. In recognition of this, many hospitals now keep the lighting turned down low in their delivery rooms. In fact, recent trends in the U.S. and Europe toward "homey" birth centers reflect an increasing awareness of the importance of the feelings of both the mother and the newborn during birth.

SELF-TEST

The following multiple choice and short answer test questions should help you assess your understanding of the points covered in the text and the video. After answering all the questions, check your answers against the key and use the accuracy of your answers to gauge how well you have met the lesson objectives.

Multiple Choice Questions

1. Usually, the last stage in the fetus's preparation for birth is to

    a. begin "breathing" amniotic fluid into its lungs.
    b. shift around so its head is pointed toward the birth canal.
    c. develop a sleep and wake cycle that is in general synchrony with the mother's.
    d. begin moving in response to sounds from outside the womb.

2. The drug which doctors use to induce labor is called

    a. anoxia.
    b. orthanogenesis.
    c. teratogen.
    d. oxcytocin.

3. Which of the following is NOT part of an Apgar test?

    a. Waving a hand before the baby's eyes to see if it blinks
    b. Tweaking the baby's nose to make it sneeze
    c. Pushing against the baby's arms and legs to check its muscle tone
    d. Taking the baby's pulse

4. In William Shakespeare's tragedy *Macbeth*, the main character is told by witches that he should not fear being killed by his many enemies, "for none of woman born shall harm Macbeth." At the climax of the play, however, when Macbeth tells this to his rival Macduff, Macduff answers by saying, he "was from his mother's womb untimely ripped" – in other words, Macduff had been delivered by Caesarean section.

    This plot twist was especially effective in Shakespeare's day because the procedure was rare, and it nearly always killed the mother. Now, Caesareans are performed in this country

    a. only when the mother's life is in danger.
    b. in about one out of every four births.
    c. in about one out of every three births.
    d. in about one out of every two births.

5. One of the main advantages to natural forms of childbirth is that babies born by them are

    a. unaffected by the mother's anxiety.
    b. not born in a traditional delivery room.
    c. not exposed to the possible ill effects of anesthetics or analgesics.
    d. less likely to be born prematurely.

6. Parents in North America tend to try to arrange sleeping patterns for infants to

   a. allow the infant to be fed as often as possible.
   b. match the sleep time of the rest of the family.
   c. keep the crying state to a minimum.
   d. allow waking time when the family can enjoy the company of the infant.

7. A crying baby is capable of soothing itself, by relying on behaviors that derive from the

   a. rooting reflex.
   b. breathing reflex.
   c. grasping reflex.
   d. sucking reflex.

8. You visit a friend who proudly shows you her 2-day-old baby. You are lucky to have arrived when the baby is awake and alert. You lean forward until you are about six inches away from the baby's face and mutter a few soft, nonsensical goo-goos and gah-gahs at her, moving your head slowly from side to side. What the baby is probably seeing is

   a. a clear image of your face.
   b. a slightly blurred, general outline of your face.
   c. a dark, unfocused blur.
   d. almost nothing.

9. Besides determining gender, ultrasound can be used to determine if a baby has

   a. Down's syndrome.
   b. Tay-Sach's Disease.
   c. an open spinal column.
   d. a cleft lip.

10. From the neonate's point of view, probably the most memorable sensation upon leaving the womb is caused by

    a. being exposed to light for the first time.
    b. having to breathe air for the first time.
    c. being exposed to sounds directly for the first time.
    d. the squeezing caused by the contractions of the mother's uterus.

Short Answer Questions

The following questions should be answered in a paragraph or two. You should identify several key points for each answer and use these to form the framework for your response.

1. Sheila has been in labor for 18 hours; her husband Phillip is concerned about how fatigued his wife is. Unfortunately, Sheila's contractions seem to have stabilized at about 15 minutes apart, and her cervix is not yet fully dilated. Now their doctor tells them that she believes the baby is in the feet-first, or breech, position. What are some of the points which the doctor is now likely to present to the couple?

2. Describe some of the changes that have taken place in practices of childbirth in this and other countries over the past couple of decades.

3. Describe what the newborn's behavior will be like within 24 hours of its birth in terms of infant states.

5

First Adaptations

LESSON ASSIGNMENT

Completing the following steps will help you master the lesson objectives and achieve the goal for this lesson:

STEP 1: Read the INTRODUCING THE LESSON section to provide a context for what you will learn in this lesson.

STEP 2: Read the lesson's GOAL and LESSON OBJECTIVES so that you will know what you are expected to learn.

STEP 3: Read the text assignment, Chapter 5, pages 124-155. Pay particular attention to the key terms and concepts in the Chapter Summary on pages 154-155; they will help you as you watch the video.

STEP 4: Review the VIEWING GUIDE in the telecourse guide. It lists several points to consider as you watch the video.

STEP 5: Watch the video.

STEP 6: Read the UNDERSTANDING THE LESSON section in the telecourse guide. Make sure you understand the key terms and can answer the focusing questions included there.

STEP 7: Complete the SELF-TEST.

STEP 8: Go back to the LESSON OBJECTIVES and make sure you can respond to each of them.

INTRODUCING THE LESSON

We all enter the spotlight of life in much the same condition: vernix-covered, wrinkled, shocked, and howling. After nine months' gestation, each of us faces our first challenge of survival – to draw breath into the lungs and begin existence outside of the womb. With that initial, dramatic intake of air, we're thrust suddenly upon the stage and commanded to perform. It's hardly any wonder that the second reaction of many newborns to birth is a loud, healthy cry.

Not surprisingly, parents throughout time have tended to hear that first vocalization as a cry of alarm, of helplessness. A newborn infant is a vulnerable, incomplete thing, unequipped to care for itself in even the smallest of ways. We're born totally dependent upon others for everything we need.

This view, at any rate, has been both the popular and the scientific perception of human infancy for thousands of years. At one time, a newborn was seen as "a white paper unscribbled with observations of the world." This concept – known as *tabula rasa* (blank slate) – stipulated that an infant was an unmarked surface upon which only experience would draw in the features of a personality and a mind.

But recent advances in the study of infant behavior indicate that perhaps we're not as helpless as we seem to be at birth. Instead of entering the world completely unprepared, we arrive with a set of reflexes, "pre-wired" behaviors and innate capabilities that greatly aid us in our first appearance on the stage of life.

Still, newborn humans remain fairly uncommunicative. Beyond those initial squalls and coos, babies are able to tell us very little, at least in ways we can easily understand. How do we know what an infant sees, hears, tastes and feels? What is a newborn capable of, and how much can he or she perceive? When do we begin to learn, to interact with the environment and with others? To what degree do we even recognize that there is a world beyond the tips of our fingers, beyond the sensors of our skin? Do we come into the world with any skills for handling it and, if so, what are they?

In this lesson you will begin to appreciate the astonishing degree to which humans are prepared for life – by becoming familiar with an array of *built-in capacities* that improve our chances for survival. You will learn to recognize the behavior traits that allow the infant to begin interacting with its world, and even begin manipulating and comprehending it. You will study how scientists have developed experiments that allow them to measure the perceptual processes of even newborn infants, or neonates. And, finally, you will understand how the first phase of independent human existence contains within it the seeds of much of the behavior that each of us needs to meet the challenges of life.

GOAL

The purpose of this lesson is to show you the full range of capabilities that human beings are born with, as well as introduce you to the ways each of us begins learning – from day one.

LESSON OBJECTIVES

After reading the text assignment, completing the exercises in this tele-course guide, and viewing the lesson's video portion, you will be able to:

1. Recognize and appreciate the capabilities of the very young infant.

2. Define the term *reflex* and give examples of reflexes that are survival mechanisms, reflexes that will later be incorporated into more complex voluntary behaviors, and reflexes that disappear as a result of central nervous system development.

3. Describe the sensory capabilities of infants.

4. Discuss the concept of *perception* as it applies to development and relate it to the emergence of an infant's visual perceptual abilities.

5. Describe key principles and patterns in motor development during the first year of a child's life.

6. Compare the various ways in which an infant can learn.

VIEWING GUIDE

The theme of Lesson 5 is that, far from being born helpless and unprepared, babies in fact arrive in the world impressively well-equipped to survive and begin living. After reading the text material and learning the important terms included there, you are ready to view the lesson's video portion. First, review the questions in the Self-Test at the end of this tele-course guide lesson to give you an idea of important points to watch for in the video. Then, read the following Points to Consider to give you an idea of what the video will cover. Keep these points in mind while watching.

Points to Consider

☐ *Adaptations at birth*: Newborns have several important reflexes to help them survive. Look for some of these reflexes and the purposes they serve.

☐ *Taking measure*: Newborn infants are unable to talk, and have limited abilities to indicate their responses to stimuli. Pay attention to how developmental scientists study and measure the capabilities and limitations of infants. Consider how understanding infant capabilities helps us.

☐ *Infant perception*: The video looks at how infants process information received from the world around them. Look for information about when babies can recognize a parent and other familiar people by the sound of their voices. Think about whether a baby could detect the smell of a bouquet of roses placed near the crib.

☐ *First learning*: The concept of infant "learning" has been debated for many years. Think about the differences between the learning of a one- or two-day-old baby and yourself. If infants *are* capable of learning, look for the forms that it takes. Look at the examples given in the video and consider, for instance, if a baby cries because her diapers are wet, whether that is a case of contingency learning or simply a natural occurrence. Watch for definitions of the different types of *conditioning*, and how they shape the way infants learn.

UNDERSTANDING THE LESSON

To the early psychologist William James, it was plain that the experience of birth to the baby was "one great blooming buzzing confusion." An infant, after all, has no prior exposure to the air, to light, to sound – no contact with anything beyond the liquid embrace of the womb. In earlier times, people "knew" that babies were born both blind and deaf and acquired these senses only as their brains matured. It was natural to assume that the neonate was unprepared for its sudden expulsion and needed constant care and attention simply to survive.

We certainly look incompetent enough when we're born. It takes most of us until we are over a year old before we utter our first one-syllable word, let alone begin walking. But we're hardly the pitiful lumps of helplessness at birth that we were once thought to be.

Infant States

Infant developmentalists divide an infant's states into quiet sleep, active sleep, awake and quiet, awake and active, fussing and crying. The first few weeks of an infant's active life represent a time of transition from the womb. Newborns sleep an average of 16 hours a day – much to the relief of their exhausted mothers and fathers. However, they seldom sleep more than four hours at a stretch, so parents quickly learn to enjoy their baby at 2 a.m. (if that's possible). During these early weeks, many of the infant's waking hours are spent in feeding.

While all babies will exhibit behavior that falls within this pattern, it is important to recognize the range of differences among them. We begin to manifest our personalities from a very early age. This is attested to by the comments of numerous parents with more than one child: "Janey was such a restless baby, she even fussed when she nursed. Bill, on the other hand, was always a quiet baby."

Key Terms

> Infant states
> REM sleep

Focusing Questions

1. How do infants communicate their various states, such as discomfort, hunger, or contentment?

2. Why is it important to study infant states?

Infant Reflexes

A reflex is any behavior that can be triggered automatically by a specific stimulus. One example of a reflex is when a doctor taps your knee during a medical examination to elicit a kick. Infants are born equipped with certain reflexes that are essential for survival – taking a breath, for example. Others, such as the tendency of a newborn to be startled, then throw its arms up and grasp – known as the *moro reflex* – might be left over from evolution.

Other responses that appear to be "wired in" from birth are the *rooting reflex*, which causes an infant to turn its head toward the direction of a touch to its mouth or cheek, and the *sucking reflex*, which is triggered by putting a nipple in the mouth. Obviously, being born with these two "hunt and nurse" reflexes already in place gives us a tremendous advantage over hunger. Both reflexes will fade after about four months as infants' brains develop, their reflexes come under cognitive control, and they begin to gain voluntary control over eating and swallowing.

Reflexes also appear to give us practice in actions that we'll need later in our development. The *grasping reflex*, which causes newborns to cling tightly to any object placed in the palm of their hand, is one example.

Another is the *stepping reflex*, an early involuntary reaction that later gives way to voluntary control. Some researchers have postulated that it represents at least a precursor to walking, though the reflex disappears between the ages of one and four months. One recent theory about the source of the stepping reflex, however, is that it is actually a pre-natal reflex, the result of a response that allows the fetus to turn around in the womb. According to this idea, the purpose of the stepping movement is to prevent adhesion to the walls of the womb.

Key Terms

Survival reflexes

Focusing Questions

1. If you shine a light in a baby's eyes and the baby squeezes its eyes shut, is that an example of a reflex?

The Sensory World of the Newborn

Infants are far from blind. For instance, to say that a two-week-old infant's ability to see detail is 20/300, as your text does, sounds extreme. Put another way, however, the newborn doesn't seem quite so bad off. An infant can see a human finger within nine feet, the iris of a parent's eye at about four feet, and a medium-sized freckle at eleven inches. This ability to distinguish fine details is called *acuity*.

On the other hand, infants are much less sensitive to differences in brightness than are adults. Faraway objects are unclear to infants not only because they are blurry, but because they tend to blend in with their surroundings in the infant's perception. When parents bend down until they're nose-to-nose with the baby, they not only bring themselves into clearer focus for the child, but they're also making their image larger to the infant, better illuminated and putting it into sharper contrast.

Infant vision is also blurred because the newborn's lenses do not yet focus fully in response to the distance of an object, a process called *accommodation*. But these limitations are temporary and acuity changes as the infant develops.

Key Terms

Saccade

Focusing Questions

1. Measured in decibels, how much louder must a sound be for an infant to hear as compared with an adult's ability to hear it?

2. Can infants taste and smell as soon as they're born?

Early Visual Perception

Anyone who saw the third Indy Jones movie will appreciate the principle involved in the visual cliff study of depth perception as described in the text. In "Indiana Jones and the Last Crusade," the hero must cross a chasm that, at first glance, appears unbridged. Indy perceives that there is indeed a chasm and his first impulse is not to cross. However, he steps out into the chasm on the basis of trust and quickly realizes that the apparent gap is an illusion, and that a camouflaged bridge does extend across the depths.

In real life, camouflaged bridges do not usually appear. But the ability to detect depth changes – such as in stairs or on a cliff – remains very important. And as the experiment designed by Gibson and Walk indicated, human beings are born with an ability to detect drop-offs. Research by others showed that even children as young as two months old begin to show interest in discrepancies between the heights and depths of adjoining areas. As you saw in the video, even though they can feel the hard surface of the glass supporting them, the babies on the see-through platform could detect the apparent drop under them. And since, unlike the adult Indiana Jones, they hadn't yet learned to overcome their apparent perceptions, the babies demonstrated a clear preference for the opaque side.

Apparently, even at such a young age, we are able to "read" *binocular depth cues*. One such cue, *convergence*, occurs when your eyes rotate inward as an object comes closer to your nose. Another binocular cue is *retinal disparity*, which is information about depth that we gain because our eyes are set apart from one another, giving us two angles of viewing comparison. Obviously, accurate visual perception is crucial for many of the important learning tasks children and adults face every day. And as this lesson shows, the refinement of this perceptual process begins at birth.

Key Terms

Perception
Monocular depth cues
Linear perspective
Interposition

Focusing Questions

1. Can a person with only one eye make any judgments about depth?

2. Given the results of the visual cliff experiment as shown in the video, would you let a crawling infant play on the edge of the Grand Canyon?

Motor Skills

Developmentalists generally feel that motor skills develop along general, predictable patterns. Your text discusses the development of some specific motor skills involving the eye, hands and arms, and legs and feet. One of the first motor skills to develop occurs in the eye, with saccadic eye movements. These fast, jerky eye movements that allow us to catch up with moving targets may begin developing within one month of birth. *Pursuit eye movements* work to keep a moving target in the center of vision, and generally begin emerging a month or so after saccadic movement develops. Adults show an intuitive awareness of a baby's slower capacities for tracking when they move an object slowly in front of a baby's face, much in the same manner that a grocery store clerk moves a bar code on an item slowly across a laser scanner.

Use of the hands and arms develops in its own way. An infant's voluntary control over reaching and grasping follows the pattern of first having reflexive responses disappear as the infant acquires the ability to stop the reflexive behavior. Then, at about six months, voluntary reaching and grasping takes over.

Finally, regarding leg and feet movement, a child reaches the stage of walking only after going through the stages of development as described in your text: from leg-kicking through crawling to exploratory "cruising" to those initial tottering first steps alone. Then our first steps are taken hesitantly and with the full sole, feet spread widely apart. Like reaching and grasping, infants need to "lose" their reflexive leg movements in order to gain voluntary control over their legs and feet and thus learn to walk.

Key Terms

Cephalocaudal development
Proximodistal development

Focusing Questions

1. What happens next after a child's early reflex systems are inhibited as its motor skills develop?

Infant Learning

In the text, you were introduced to various forms of learning in infants, of which one of the earliest is *habituation*. With habituation, after repeated exposure to a new sensation or event, the infant decreases its attention to the event.

In another kind of learning, *associative learning*, the baby connects the occurrence of one event with another. This can be demonstrated in situations which involve *classical conditioning* in which a baby is taught to connect two things which usually are not associated. For instance, usually an unconditioned stimulus such as a nipple in the mouth will elicit the unconditioned response of sucking. In classical conditioning, however, even young babies can learn to give a conditioned response to a conditioned stimulus. This would happen if the infant started sucking every time the baby saw mother prepare for nursing – such as being held in a certain position – even though it wasn't time to nurse. In this case, the sucking response was "conditioned" to the conditioned stimulus of the mother preparing to nurse. When a conditioned response is no longer associated with its stimulus – when the child realizes that just being held doesn't mean nursing is imminent – the response usually fades away through a process called *extinction*.

Another type of learning is instrumental or *operant conditioning*. Operant learning is when children change their behavior as a result of the feedback or consequences they receive. Positive and negative reinforcement lead to increased behavior; punishment leads to decreased behavior. The process by which a child's behavior is reinforced to encourage a specific result – such as learning to speak – is known as *shaping*.

Imitation is a learning skill that scientists believe develops in infants through four steps. Up to about six months, infants are able to mimic a few simple actions which they can already do, such as sticking out the tongue. At about six months, as cognitive control increases, they begin trying to duplicate behaviors or sounds that are completely new to them, which come out as babbling. In the third stage, at about 12 months, they become much more adept at repeating the actual sound of words they hear. And in the final stage, at about 18 months, they become skilled mimics, able to duplicate actions and sounds with only a little monitoring.

Key Terms

   Operant conditioning
   Negative reinforcement
   Shaping
   Extinction

Focusing Questions

   1. How do classical and operant conditioning differ?

   2. What is the difference between negative reinforcement and punishment?

Born Prepared

The text stresses the simple nature of the behaviors on which most studies of infant learning are based. The reason for this is simple – infants are more likely to demonstrate learning when doing things they already are capable of, which are usually behaviors that are reflexive and have survival value. This tendency to perform behaviors we already have is called *preparedness*. Simply put, this means that infants are prepared to learn how to eat, crawl, gain control of their hand clasping and other necessary motor skills, as opposed to more difficult behavior – twiddling their thumbs, say, or catching a ball. Other animal species, such as horses or deer, are born with other types of preparedness, such as an ability to run soon after birth – a clear survival benefit. Human infants are likewise born prepared to pay attention to certain kinds of things. The way infants study the outline of a face, as described in your text, and their demonstrable interest in human voices are examples of this preparedness.

Key Terms

> Preparedness
> Preadaptations

Focusing Questions

> 1. If a baby closely studies your face when you bend down close, is this an example of preadaptation?

Questions for Understanding

As you read these questions, often raised by parents, educators, and other childcare providers, first try to answer the questions yourself. Then read the answer following each question and compare your response to it.

> 1. *As the parent of a week-old baby, I'm wondering when we can expect our child to sleep through the night?*
>
> At least to some degree, what constitutes a "good night's sleep" depends on how old we are. As noted in the text section on infant states, newborns spend as much 16 hours a day sleeping. The only problem – from the point of view of parents – is that these sleep times are divided fairly equally around the clock. By around the eighth week, however, most babies are beginning to sleep more at night than during the day. But it may be months before Mom and Dad can plan on sleeping throughout the night undisturbed by a cry from their offspring's crib.
>
> 2. *How much of dad's and mom's face can baby make out?*
>
> An infant's ability to see detail clearly – the trait called acuity – is quite limited. One reason for this is that a newborn has trouble adjusting the lenses of its eyes to objects as they approach, an action known as accommodation, which is essential for good focusing. An infant's ability to perform the tracking movement known as a saccade is also only about one-fifth that of an adult's. Further, the cranial nerves involved in optic and olfactory functions are the only ones other than those in the cortex which are not yet myelinized at birth.
>
> 3. *What are size constancy and shape constancy and when do infants develop them?*
>
> When a friend approaches you from a block away, she grows in your eyes from an apparent few inches tall to her true height. Even though her image on the retina of your eye is growing, you perceive her size as remaining the same all along, a process known as size constancy. Similarly, should your friend approach you on a flight of stairs, you will still perceive her shape as remaining the same, even though it appears to change as her position shifts in relation to yours. This is called shape constancy.
>
> Most researchers believe that infants first develop shape constancy around two or three months. Size constancy, on the other hand,

doesn't seem to emerge until around six months of age. This order of development makes sense, as it ensures that babies first recognize the objects around them as always the same, or stable. This is an important stage in the infant's developing awareness of just who its care givers are, and how they differ from a mobile dangling over its bed or a stuffed animal.

4. *I've heard that it's to an infant's advantage to learn to walk early. Should parents try to accelerate their child's efforts to walk? Will this give the child a head start in any other areas of development?*

For most psychologists and developmental experts, the answer to this question is "no." While the onset of walking varies, most children are walking by the age of 15 months. This follows a developmental path that is generally the same for all children: an initial stepping reflex is replaced by voluntary control; sitting up; crawling; standing with help; standing with self-support; standing alone; and walking alone. According to one study described in your text, it is possible to help a child walk sooner by exercising its stepping reflex, which seems to be adapted into early walking behavior. However, this method produced walkers only slightly sooner than babies who weren't given extra encouragement. More importantly, there appears to be no evidence that children who walk unusually early fare any better than others in a variety of performance categories once they get older.

5. *How well do infants hear?*

While infant hearing isn't as acute as adult hearing, it is well developed at birth. In fact, the main hearing organ of the inner ear – the cochlea – is operating four months before birth; the basic neurological wiring that enables the infant to discriminate between different tones and intensities is probably available two months before birth; and the infant is prepared to direct attention toward sounds approximately one month before birth. But this is an observation that any new parent will have made within a few days or weeks of cooing at their newborn.

6. *Do babies dream? They spend so much time sleeping, I wonder if it serves more purpose to them than just providing rest?*

Infants spend about 50 percent of their sleep time in REM sleep, which in adults is an indicator of dreaming. It's hard to imagine what neonate dreams would be like, since adult dreams consist of remembered and rearranged events and people. What experience could an infant have to base dreaming upon? On the other hand, adults tend to become irritable if deprived of REM sleep, and so do infants.

Some researchers have theorized that infant REM sleep represents random neurological firing in the brain, similar to the "idling" of a car's engine. If infants do dream, they probably are perceiving "light shows" of color and other sensual impressions. Most new parents, however, will hardly need to be encouraged to let their child sleep as long as he or she may need to in order to get sufficient REM sleep. Interestingly, other types of sleep – for instance, that indicated by delta waves – may be even more important than REM sleep.

SELF-TEST

The following multiple choice and short answer test questions should help you assess your understanding of the points covered in the text and the video. After answering all the questions, check your answers against the key and use the accuracy of your answers to gauge how well you have met the lesson objectives.

Multiple Choice Questions

1. Which type of reflex is in some way a rehearsal for an important behavior you probably use every day?

   a. Rooting reflex
   b. Moro reflex
   c. Stepping reflex
   d. Sucking reflex

2. Miranda, five months old, reaches up and grabs a handful of her mother's hair, making her mother yelp exaggeratedly. Miranda grins; she has just demonstrated her understanding of the type of learning known as

   a. contingency.
   b. shaping.
   c. conditioning.
   d. imitation.

3. Which of the following infant reflexes disappears LAST?

   a. Babinski
   b. Moro
   c. Stepping
   d. Tonic Neck

4. Researchers are able to make reasonable claims about the acuity of infants because babies

   a. have fully developed eyes at birth.
   b. have fully developed cranial connections at birth.
   c. are able to focus on projected slides.
   d. clearly demonstrate a preference for looking at stripes of varying width.

5. Visual accommodation is the ability of the eyes to

   a. track a moving object.
   b. adjust their focus as an object approaches.
   c. adjust to the size of an object as it approaches.
   d. adjust to the shape of an object as it approaches.

6. Karina is playing in the science museum on a floor which goes from being carpeted to having glass-covered parts over a beautiful garden in the courtyard below. She does not want to crawl on to the glass-

covered areas although this part is meant to be walked on. This reluctance to crawl across the glass area covering an apparent drop is LEAST likely to be guided by which of the following factors?

    a. Her memories of falling
    b. Binocular depth cues
    c. Linear perspective
    d. Retinal disparity

7. At about seven months old, babies begin relying on interposition to give them information about an object's

    a. shape.
    b. relative size.
    c. distance away.
    d. proportions.

8. Cephalocaudal development means that motor skills in infants develop

    a. from head to toe.
    b. from the extremities inward.
    c. from the center outward.
    d. evenly throughout the body.

9. Baby Tyler is crying in the play area at the day care center. His father comes in and all of a sudden Tyler stops and pays attention to his voice. This is called

    a. habituation.
    b. instrumental conditioning.
    c. proximodistal development.
    d. an orienting response.

10. If you encourage a child to repeat a specific sound by increasing your praise with each improvement in her pronunciation of the word, you are practicing

    a. habituation.
    b. shaping.
    c. classical conditioning.
    d. imitative learning.

Short Answer Questions

The following questions should be answered in a paragraph or two. You should identify several key points for each answer and use these to form the framework for your response.

1. In what ways is infant learning different from adult learning?

2. How does the process of perception change in the infant from birth to about one year?

3. Give two examples of learning – one that would best be explained by classical conditioning and one that would best be explained by operant conditioning.

6

Infant Cognitive Development

LESSON ASSIGNMENT

Completing the following steps will help you master the lesson objectives and achieve the goal for this lesson:

<u>STEP 1</u>: Read the INTRODUCING THE LESSON section to provide a context for what you will learn in this lesson.

<u>STEP 2</u>: Read the lesson's GOAL and LESSON OBJECTIVES so that you will know what you are expected to learn.

<u>STEP 3</u>: Read the text assignment, Chapter 5, pages 158-186. Pay particular attention to the key terms and concepts in the Chapter Summary on pages 186-187; they will help you when you watch the video.

<u>STEP 4</u>: Review the VIEWING GUIDE section in the telecourse guide. It lists several points to consider as you watch the video.

<u>STEP 5</u>: Watch the video.

<u>STEP 6</u>: Read the UNDERSTANDING THE LESSON section in the telecourse guide. Make sure you understand the key terms and can answer the focusing questions included there.

<u>STEP 7</u>: Complete the SELF-TEST.

<u>STEP 8</u>: Go back to the LESSON OBJECTIVES and make sure you can respond to each of them.

INTRODUCING THE LESSON

Suppose that you are trying to assemble a 1000-piece jigsaw puzzle – a picture of Mt. Everest, for example. You begin with a pile of cardboard pieces, of roughly the same size, in different shapes and colors, all jumbled together. How do you go about fitting all the pieces together to form a whole? How do you create order out of chaos?

Probably, you start by sorting the pieces according to similarities. Pieces with straight edges – frame pieces – go into one pile. Sky-colored pieces go into a separate pile, as do pieces that seem to be parts of the mountain. You base your decisions on what you know about mountains, colors, shapes, and other clues to reality. In other words, you organize the information before you according to various categories that you recognize.

But what if you have no "clues" as to how things go together? Suppose, further, that you are unable to use words to describe the pieces that you're moving around. In fact, you can't even "decide" to move your hand to pick up that blue-colored piece of cardboard and put it beside that straight-edged piece – because you have no "idea" of "beside." Try to imagine what it is like to have very limited thoughts, ideas, and concepts. How could you get anything done without the ability to think?

Very crudely, this state seems to be what we're born into. A newborn baby is faced with a task as seemingly impossible as our imaginary effort to assemble a jigsaw puzzle with no controllable mental abilities. To an adult observer, the infant must create its world from scratch, and apparently without many of the tools for understanding that he or she will have acquired within a few years. How do infants put the puzzle together?

The question of how we begin to think is a fascinating one. In this lesson, you will learn how infants begin to make sense of their surroundings, how they begin to understand the world by giving order and shape to its events. You will see how these mental skills, called *cognitive abilities*, develop in the infant through an orderly series of stages, and how cognitive skills build upon previously developed skills.

Perhaps most surprisingly, you will observe just how actively a baby engages its world. Although our first responses to our environment are reflexive ones, we very quickly begin *adapting* these reflexes to adjust to the multitude of new sensations that are bombarding us. Almost from birth, babies actively participate in the world.

Through the textbook material and the examples depicted in the video portion, you will see how an infant's cognitive abilities develop in an orderly fashion. In the first few years of life, a baby begins to understand the connection between *cause* and *effect*. He or she begins to grasp the difference between *means* and *ends* and to develop a sense of *object permanence*. And, finally, infants begin to develop a sense of *memory*, an essential final link between understanding and learning.

In this lesson, you will study modern theories of how infant cognition develops, based largely on the groundbreaking observations of Jean Piaget. Piaget's six stages of *sensorimotor* development are especially important to the study of child development. In this lesson, you will gain an appreciation of the incredible accomplishment that a baby achieves by the time he or she first pauses to think through an action before taking it.

GOAL

The purpose of this lesson is to demonstrate how an infant begins developing an array of thinking skills – cognitive abilities – that enable him or her to understand and participate in the world.

LESSON OBJECTIVES

After reading the text assignment, completing the exercises in this telecourse guide, and viewing the lesson's video portion, you will be able to:

1. Describe Piaget's sensorimotor period of cognitive development and its six stages.

2. Define object permanence and discuss its gradual development during the sensorimotor period.

3. Indicate the course of memory development in the first 12 months of life.

4. Compare Piaget's theory of cognitive development to alternatives suggested by Fischer, Case, and Bruner.

5. Describe the constraints on cognitive functioning that are characteristic of infancy.

6. Identify the three general themes of cognitive development in the first 2 years of life.

VIEWING GUIDE

In this lesson, you will learn how an infant begins to develop the ability to think. From birth to about 2 years old, an infant's cognitive development follows an orderly series of expanding capabilities that lead from reflexive actions to symbolic or representational thought. After reading the text material and learning the terms, you are now ready to view the lesson's video portion. First, review the self-test questions at the end of this telecourse guide chapter to give you an idea of important points to watch for in the video. Then, read the following Points to Consider to give you an idea of what the video will cover. Keep these in mind while watching.

Points to Consider

☐ *Something to think about*: If babies are born unable to think, how can they perform any actions at all? According to Piaget's theory of cognitive development, what role does accident play in how infants begin adapting to the stimulation they receive?

☐ *Thinking about objects*: Why is it so important for humans to develop an awareness that objects exist outside of an individual's perception? What evidence led Piaget to conclude that newborns are incapable of understanding that objects have permanence? How does a baby's behavior toward objects change throughout the course of the sensorimotor period?

☐ *First memories*: Do newborns have any memory at all? Very few people are able to remember their infancy; does this mean that babies have no long-term memory? Why does memory have to develop before a baby can learn to talk?

☐ *Expert opinion*: What are some of the limits to cognitive development which Piaget believed a child faces in the first two years of life? In Piaget's theory of cognitive development, what are the roles played by adaptation and equilibration? What are the theories of the neo-Piagetians and how are they different from the theories of developmentalists such as Jerome Bruner?

UNDERSTANDING THE LESSON

The urge to explore is deeply human. Tens of thousands of years ago, when a land bridge connected Alaska with Siberia, curious people drifted across from Asia into North America – compelled perhaps by need, perhaps by curiosity. During the European age of exploration, crews of sailors in tiny wooden ships circumnavigated the globe in spite of extreme hardships. Our need to comprehend has also led the human mind inward, splitting the atom and decoding the double helix of DNA. In imagination, the urge to discover has launched Sinbad the Sailor on his seven voyages and propelled the crew of the Starship Enterprise across new frontiers.

Anyone who has ever watched the miraculous unfolding of an infant's mind in the first two years of existence knows this human tendency to seek out brave new worlds. Each individual, after all, begins exploring his or her surroundings almost at birth. And from those first discoveries, each of us builds a coherent universe.

Infant Cognitive Development: A Framework

At birth, the newborn is faced with an enormous amount of information to absorb. Every sensation is new – breathing for the first time, eating, feeling the air. The question of just how infants are affected by the sudden change in their environment and how they begin mentally organizing the world is one that has been a central concern of child developmentalists.

As you have seen in the video portion, researchers in child development have devoted a great deal of attention to the question of just how infants begin acquiring the mental skills – cognitive abilities – which they need to interact successfully with their environment. It is important to remember that a child's cognitive development is tied to gaining greater control over his body; this control allows him to be able to explore his world.

In Lesson 1, you briefly studied the theories of pioneering child developmentalist Jean Piaget. Piaget described infants as moving actively toward an understanding of the world along six developmental steps that cover the first two years of life. Because newborn dealings with the world are limited to what they can feel through their sensory systems and affect through their motor activities, Piaget called this time the *sensorimotor period*.

In stage 1 of the sensorimotor period, from birth to about 1 month, an infant's responses to the world are limited by his or her reflexes. And although, as you learned in Lesson 5, reflexes are automatic, they form the basis of the first efforts that the baby makes to master his or her own body. Within the first month, for example, the baby begins to modify the sucking impulse by sucking more or less vigorously perhaps depending on how hungry or sleepy he or she is; in other words, the baby is learning to make adjustments based on changing information.

In stage 2, from about month 1 to month 4, the baby increasingly practices simple, repetitive movements of the body, which Piaget called *primary circular reactions*. For example, a baby playing with a rattle will shake it over and over again, seemingly just for the pleasure of practicing this early skill. According to Piaget, the repeated action that the baby engages in is automatic and unconscious at this stage, but nonetheless marks the emergence of new behaviors from strictly reflexive ones.

During stage 3, from about 4 to 8 months, the baby moves to actively investigate the consequences of its own actions – what Piaget called *secondary circular reactions*. At this stage, the baby is forming a rudimentary understanding of the connections between itself and the world. Banging a spoon on the highchair tray is a good example of a secondary circular motion.

In stage 3, the infant for the first time directs its awareness outside what it can sense with just its own body. In addition, there is a marked improvement in eye-hand coordination and the ability to grasp objects. Still, though, the baby's awareness is limited to the sensory results that it gets from certain motor actions – for example, to the recognition that "If I kick like this, that interesting rattling noise happens."

By stage 4, from about 8 to 12 months, infants begin combining two or more simple actions, or *schemes*, to reach a goal. By a scheme, Piaget meant a simple, organized pattern of behavior. At this stage, the infant begins putting together previously mastered motor skills to accomplish a goal different from the action's original one. For example, opening a cupboard and pulling out all the pots and pans is something a baby might experiment with at this stage. Piaget called this new behavior *coordination of secondary schemes*. Now the infant is able to anticipate the consequences of future actions.

Piaget called stage 5, from about 12 to 18 months, the time of *tertiary circular reactions*. As the phrase circular movements implies, the child is still repeating simple actions, but now it varies them to discover new consequences. During this stage, when a child accidentally encounters a new sensation, it actively explores how he or she can alter the sensation by acting on it in different ways.

A baby dropping food from a high chair might, for example, experiment with dropping from the left and from the right, dropping high and low, or throwing cereal on the floor. At this stage, the child is beginning to grasp the relationship between cause and effect. It is a time of very active behavior – as any harried parent of a 1 year old can testify.

Stage 6, from about 18 to 24 months, is called the time of *the beginning of representational thought*, and marks the end of the sensorimotor period. Now the child is beginning to form *symbolic* thoughts about actions; for the first time, in other words, the child is starting to think before acting.

A young baby playing with a shape toy will try to put the square peg in various holes and eventually – through trial and error – find the right hole. An older baby who is capable of representational thought will do the trial and error part in his mind, imagining what will happen if he tries the square peg in the round hole and deciding against it.

This growing ability to act things out mentally is shown in the increased "pretending" that children practice during this stage. Stage 6, the end of Piaget's sensorimotor stages, marks a significant leap in the child's cognitive development. In Piaget's view, however, the stage 6 child is still not "thinking" in words yet. Keep in mind, also, that his or her thoughts are still limited to actions that he or she can perform.

Key Terms

> Goal-directed chains
> Representational thought

Focusing Questions

1. At which of Piaget's sensorimotor stages does an infant appear to begin actively anticipating the results of its behavior? When do a baby's actions become intentional?

2. At what stage do babies begin to mimic the behavior of their care giver or care givers? Why is the ability to imitate someone else's actions an important step forward in an infant's capabilities?

Developing the Concept of Objects

Imagine for a moment that you are getting ready to leave your home. You've thrown on a jacket, taken your checkbook, and reached for your car keys in their usual place on the bedroom dresser – but they aren't there. "Now, where did I put them?" you immediately wonder, and begin trying to remember the last place you saw them. Without ever considering it, you begin your search for the keys on the assumption that you *have* keys – you "know," in other words, that they exist.

This apparently simple realization of the existence of objects outside yourself is one of the most important concepts you learned as a baby. Acquiring a sense of object permanence is one of the first and biggest steps that a baby takes toward representational thought.

According to Piaget, infants are born with no capability to conceive of an object existing once it has gone out of their immediate sight. To a newborn, the appearance of her mother's face is just another image that materializes over the crib. If Mommy's face is there, she'll look at it; if not, she doesn't actively search for it. By the end of her second year, however, the child knows who Mommy is, that she has a life outside of the child's own, and that Mommy will come and go depending on conditions that the child has little control over.

In Piaget's view, an infant actively constructs a sense of object permanence by the end of his or her second year, and along a course of development roughly parallel with the six sensorimotor stages. In stage 1, for example, the infant responds to those items or people that are directly in front of his or her eyes; if the baby's mother steps away, the baby looks at other things. In stage 2, the infant develops "passive expectation," and will continue to gaze at the spot where a person or thing has just left. But the baby hasn't yet begun actively searching for the missing person or object, and continues to act according to the rule, "out of sight, out of mind."

By stage 3, as you saw in the video, infants are beginning to reach for partially covered objects, but seem unable to visualize an object that has been covered up. At this stage, babies still need perceptual cues to trigger their interest in an object. By stage 4, however, the baby has begun to realize that things exist even when he or she can't see them. For the first time, infants now begin actively searching for objects that have been taken out of their sight. But at this stage, the infant still has an imperfect understanding of the "rules" of object behavior, as you saw demonstrated in the various experiments involving toys hidden from babies under blankets.

In stage 5, a baby grasps that an object is likely to be where he or she saw it last, and so begins looking there. Even now, though, the baby is not quite able to comprehend the possibility of an object being moved from the position where he or she last saw it. This next jump in cognitive ability, to a mature sense of object permanence, takes place in stage 6, when the baby is finally able to imagine that an object can move, even when the baby can't see it. When it happens the infant has achieved a sense of object permanence.

It is important to be aware of how some recent researchers have questioned or modified Piaget's original descriptions of how infants develop object permanence. For example, T.G.R. Bower used a series of experiments based on infants' rate of sucking to study their reaction to how objects disappear suddenly from their sight. Though inconclusive, Bower's results indicate that even infants as young as 2 months old may have a higher awareness of objects than Piaget believed. And in the clever experiment of the turning screen described in your text, Rene Baillargeon gathered evidence suggesting that infants of 5 to 7 months old have some awareness that objects exist out of their sight.

In general, recent researchers have concluded that infants develop object permanence at somewhat earlier stages than Piaget thought. This difference probably reflects the "fine-tuning" of experiments that developmentalists after Piaget have brought to bear on the stages of cognitive development, and not a fundamental disagreement with his general theory.

Focusing Questions

1. At stage 4, an infant looks for a hidden object in the place where he or she previously saw it, even if the child watched it being moved and hidden since the first time. Piaget thought that the child believed that searching in the first hiding place was what brought the object back, which is a form of "mistaken" logic. Why do most modern developmentalists disagree with Piaget's conclusions about why the child makes the "stage 4 mistake"?

2. Why is the concept of object permanence such an important step in a child's cognitive development?

The Infant's Developing Memory

Let's imagine again that you're still looking for your car keys. Your first – and unconscious – assumption was that your car keys were *somewhere*, even though they weren't where you expected them to be. Your first thought – at least, your first repeatable thought – was, "Now, where did I put them?" You immediately began ransacking your memory for the vital information you needed to find your car keys.

Memory is one of the most important cognitive skills that a human being possesses. Without memory, it is difficult to imagine how we could learn any skills more advanced than the simple motor skills that we develop through the repetition based on our first reflexes. Language, social interactions, tool-use, associative thought – all are incomprehensible without the ability to consciously call up remembered events, lessons, examples, categories. Memory forms a major link that allows us to construct a meaningful whole of our sensations and impressions.

Developmentalists have performed numerous experiments aimed at determining just how an infant's memory develops over the first six months of life. As you learned in Lesson 5, infants are born with a certain degree of memory ability, based largely on the principle of preparedness. However, developmentalists have been unable to show that newborns are capable of remembering beyond a 24-hour period. By 2 to 4 months old, though, infants have clearly gained the ability to remember simple tasks for up to about one week. And although these memories begin fading after a second week, other research indicates that the infants will remember for a longer time if they are shown some reminder of the object they're intended to remember. In other words, young infants remember something longer if they're "cued" to it somehow.

By the second half-year, infants give several signs of their developing long-term memory. Learning their first words around the end of the first year, for example, is a clear demonstration of the ability to store words and the objects they represent in memory. By this time babies are clearly remembering the features of the important people in their lives. And at some point in their second half year, infants cross a crucial hurdle of cognitive development when they begin to categorize items. In one study, for example, infants 10 months old demonstrated an ability to categorize different animals by the animals' types of feet.

Another perceptual ability that begins developing about halfway through an infant's first year is the ability to distinguish groups of things by how many are present; this ability is called *numerosity*. Using very simple tests involving drawings of two or three dots, researchers Prentice Starkey and Robert Cooper were able to demonstrate numerosity in infants 6 to 8 months old.

In general, the memory of all normal infants will gradually become more robust, complex and long lasting during their first year. Keep in mind, however, that during the sensorimotor period, the child's memory is limited to things it can see, touch, taste, hear, or otherwise interact with physically.

Focusing Questions

1. Why are recognition tests widely used by researchers who are interested in how infant memory develops?

2. If an infant's brain is predisposed to remember certain kinds of information over others, what sort of information might it remember?

Explanations of Cognitive Development

When it comes to theories of how infant cognition develops, Jean Piaget occupies much the same position in childhood development as the painter Pablo Picasso does in modern art – he can't be ignored. Not all current experts agree with Piaget's conclusions, but they all have built at least partially upon his original work. Piaget based his theory of cognitive development in children on the belief that children actively construct their views of the world, rather than passively absorbing the information that flows into them from the environment.

Piaget believed that a child begins forming its knowledge of the world through the interplay of its perceptions with its motor skills – the process whereby the brain interprets information from the senses, giving it order and meaning. This is the basis of Piaget's framework of cognitive development during the sensorimotor period; an infant learns and progresses in understanding through what it can reach, grasp, ingest, or otherwise interact with and perceive physically. In this context, Piaget referred to grasping and eating as examples of schemes, which arise out of reflexes. Infancy is a time of acting without "thinking," though thinking will arise out of the cumulative stages of cognition as described in the sensorimotor period.

As a child moves through the stages of cognition, according to Piaget, he or she continually adjusts to the changing conditions brought on by growth through adaptation. In the context of cognitive development, adaptation means the tendency of each individual to change his or her behavior to meet a new situation.

Contained within Piaget's concept of adaptation are the two subprocesses of *assimilation* and *accommodation*. Say, for example, that a baby who has the three schemes of grasping, biting, and shaking is confronted with a new object – a doll, for instance. First, the baby tries to assimilate the new object by applying old behaviors to it – that is, by grasping it, biting it, and shaking it. But suppose these already-learned approaches aren't very satisfying when applied to the soft cotton terrycloth of the doll. This new material, the baby may discover, is more pleasant to stroke; by stroking the doll, the infant accommodates to it, and adds a new scheme of behavior to her repertoire.

In Piagetian developmental theory, adaptation is always accompanied by assimilation and accommodation. These tendencies move the child forward along its course of development toward mental structures that allow the child to coordinate its rapidly growing amounts of sensory and motor information. As for the reason that the infant is urged to move toward more sophisticated skills and greater understanding, Piaget called this *equilibration*. Very simply, the principle of equilibration as it applies to cognitive development means that when a child's strategy – or scheme – for dealing with a situation doesn't fit, he or she will try to match its action to the situation – it will try to achieve equilibration. Another way of explaining the tendency toward equilibration is to say that infants strive to get their actions in synchronization with their circumstances.

But as important as Piaget's theories remain to child development specialists, not all experts agree with them. In creating his set of six sensorimotor stages, for example, Piaget stipulated that a child achieving a certain level of object permanence would also be at a similar stage of development for another task, such as being able to understand cause and effect. Later researchers such as Fischer, however, have found that individual development does not occur evenly in all areas. Though Piaget recognized this problem, which he dubbed *decalage*, he was never able to adequately account for it.

Cognitive psychologist Jerome Bruner agrees with Piaget that motor activity plays a central role in infant cognitive development, but unlike Piaget, he feels that even newborns have some representative ability, or a rudimentary way of representing their environment. Bruner also attributes intentionality to newborns, which they apply to the set of innate action patterns that they are born with, such as looking and sucking to master a specific goal.

Key Term

Executive processing space

Focusing Questions

1. Can babies apply the principle of adaptation to acquire *any* behaviors or skills which might be useful to them? What kind of limitations are there to the skills that an infant can assimilate and accommodate?

2. Do Piaget's theories of infant cognitive development cover all the possible cases as seen by current developmentalists? What are some of the ideas which have been developed by the neo-Piagetians?

Questions for Understanding

As you read these questions, often raised by parents, educators, and other childcare providers, first try to answer the questions yourself. Then read the answer following each question and compare your response to it.

1. *Our 7-month-old son Josh has a new game: While seated in his high chair, he scoops up a spoonful of mashed potatoes and plops it in his hair. Then he looks at his 6-year-old brother to see if he is laughing. Is Josh being a monster on purpose?*

    While it sounds like Josh is acting purposefully, he certainly isn't intentionally acting badly. At Josh's age, which is probably Piaget's sensorimotor period 4, he is beginning to combine actions together in *goal-oriented chains* – in this case, using a spoon to put food onto his head, then looking at his older brother for the laugh he expects. Rather than misbehaving, Josh is actively expanding his cognitive abilities – though in a rather messy fashion.

2. *In a weird movie I saw once, the main character was supposed to be able to remember being born; in fact, he was conscious even of being in the womb. I know this is far-fetched, but do we really know when a child develops awareness?*

The concept of individual awareness is a slippery one. Even as an adult, your level of awareness varies according to your circumstances. While driving, for example, how conscious are you of your various actions of steering the car, applying the brake, looking in the rearview mirror? And since children do not begin acquiring language until well into their second year, it is very difficult to judge just how much they comprehend of the world.

Generally, however, child developmentalists agree that by the end of their first year, children have begun to anticipate the near-term effect of their actions, and to combine two or more behaviors together. By the end of the second year, a child has begun to think symbolically, which for the first time allows him or her to think of an action before acting on it. And while 2 year olds are beginning to use simple words, they are still using them in unstable, idiosyncratic ways. Two year olds are also rapidly developing a long-term memory, though their behavior is still tied to the concrete and the immediate.

So, in brief, while a child at 2 years old will have largely mastered the distinction between objects and him- or herself and be able to understand who you are in relation to other adults, he or she is still a long way from an adult's awareness of the world.

3. *Why do child development researchers seem so interested in how babies react to recognition tests?*

Recognition tests are an important means of studying infants because they give a way of assessing just how long infants of different ages can remember simple pictures of forms. Because children even as young as 4 months can be trained to remember angled lines, researchers can measure their short- and long-term memories. The reactions that infants have in recognition tests enable researchers to hypothesize about how well babies recognize and remember more complicated figures, such as their parents' faces.

4. *To what extent is my newborn baby's mind an empty vessel, just waiting for knowledge to come pouring in?*

Starting with the developmental theories of Jean Piaget, child developmentalists have come to see the newborn child as an active participant in its cognitive development. The child participates in its discoveries about its new existence, shaping the forces acting upon it through the processes of assimilation and accommodation.

Within the first two years of his or her life, your child will have learned that objects exist, that they differ from one another, and that they have permanence. He or she will also have grasped that an action here has an effect over there – the principle of cause and effect. He or she will have begun understanding basic concepts, including those of space and time, and will be able to organize objects and occurrences by categories. And the process the child uses to master these cognitive skills is a directed, dynamic one.

5. *I've read about babies whose parents tried to turn them into math prodigies by hanging numbers over their cribs. Is it possible to help my baby learn faster?*

While you can and should do all you can to encourage your child to learn to the best of his or her ability, it is also important to recognize the limits on what babies can learn. Especially during infancy, your child's knowledge of the world will come strictly through action. That is, he or she gathers information through chewing, sucking, kicking, and moving. In the ordinary course of cognitive development, your child can't absorb any ideas – such as digits that represent numbers – until he or she begins thinking representationally, at about 2 years old. Even at that age, the ideas must still be based in the concrete.

6. *How long does it take for my baby to remember who I am?*

At one week of age, babies will orient to the sound of their mother's voice rather than the voice of another woman. At around 4-8 weeks of age a child will show a "smile of recognition" at the sight of a familiar care giver. And as you learned in Lesson 5, a 3-month-old can pick out a picture of its mother from among other faces.

Research has shown that even babies as young as 2 months old do have a form of long-term memory, but can only remember people or events when they are shown cues to trigger the memory. If this is a characteristic of long-term memory in very young infants, then it seems reasonable to assume that a mother or father's face is an often-seen "cue" that is likely to help the child remember who you are.

SELF-TEST

The following multiple choice and short answer test questions should help you measure your understanding of the points covered in the text and the video. After answering all the questions, check your answers against the key and use the accuracy of your answers to gauge how well you have met the lesson objectives.

Multiple Choice Questions

1. By the term "sensorimotor," Jean Piaget meant that infants

    a. rely more on their senses of seeing, hearing, tasting, and so on than at any other period of their development.
    b. solve problems using their sensory systems and motor activities.
    c. make sense out of the world through motor activities.
    d. begin using symbolic mental processes as their motor abilities develop.

2. An example of a secondary circular reaction would be a baby

    a. repeating new words after its mother.
    b. learning to eat with a spoon.
    c. throwing a toy against different targets to compare the results.
    d. shaking a rattle repeatedly because the effect was interesting.

3. If a 4-month-old is waving a rattle and drops it, she won't look around for it. According to Jean Piaget's theories, she doesn't react because

   a. her short-term memory remains undeveloped.
   b. she has no concept of "rattle" to remember.
   c. she doesn't understand object permanence.
   d. her motor skills are insufficiently developed.

4. While playing with your 15-month-old cousin, you hide a marble under one of three boxes. Then, as she watches, you hold the marble in your fist and move it to a different box. But when the little girl looks for the marble, she looks under its first hiding place. Your cousin's sense of object permanence comes after stage

   a. 3.
   b. 4.
   c. 5.
   d. 6.

5. Through habituation, infants demonstrate an ability to remember

   a. at birth.
   b. in their first week.
   c. in their second week.
   d. in their first month.

6. What is the most important reason that recognition tests are used to test the memory of babies under the age of 6 months?

   a. The tests' images correspond to the child's early ability to conceptualize.
   b. Simple visual stimuli are all that babies of that age can perceive.
   c. Babies' span of attention is too short for any other kind of test.
   d. The infants cannot yet use language.

7. Most current researchers in child development accept Piaget's belief that

   a. both infants and older children are active learners.
   b. general logical structures limit understanding at each stage of development.
   c. infants remain at the same sensorimotor level for several different skills.
   d. the problem of decalage is a minor one.

8. Executive processing space is the name of the theory of working memory developed by

   a. Fischer.
   b. Bruner.
   c. Case.
   d. Piaget.

9. At 2 months of age, Malcolm Williams is limited to practicing what he learns

    a. through contact with his environment.
    b. by his underdeveloped neural system.
    c. through accidental events involving his own body.
    d. through accidental events involving his family.

10. A month-old infant sucks on a bottle's nipple until he is full, then stops; an 8-month-old girl drops a spoon from her high chair every time her mother replaces it; a 14-month-old boy experiments with dropping different-sized toys into the toilet. Even at their different stages of development, each child is learning through

    a. action.
    b. analogy.
    c. representation.
    d. reflection.

Short Answer Questions

The following questions should be answered in a paragraph or two. You should identify several key points for each answer and use these to form the framework for your response.

1. A 6-month-old baby in his high chair accidentally knocks a toy to the floor. An older sibling picks it up and replaces it, and the baby once again pushes the toy so it falls to the floor. After several such interactions, the older child eventually becomes frustrated with the repetition and thinks the baby is being annoying on purpose. What is actually happening at this stage of the baby's development to make him act this way?

2. Discuss the behaviors children in the second six months of life display that show they have developed a long-term memory.

3. Your text uses the term working memory to describe the information-processing capacity of a child in the first year of life. What role does this working memory play in a baby's ability to perform more and more complex tasks?

7

Infant Social and Emotional Development

LESSON ASSIGNMENT

Completing the following steps will help you master the lesson objectives and achieve the goal for this lesson:

STEP 1: Read the INTRODUCING THE LESSON section to provide a context for what you will learn in this lesson.

STEP 2: Read the lesson's GOAL and LESSON OBJECTIVES so that you will know what you are expected to learn.

STEP 3: Read the text assignment, Chapter 6, pages 190-225. Pay particular attention to the key terms and concepts in the Chapter Summary on pages 224-225; they will help you when you watch the video.

STEP 4: Review the VIEWING GUIDE section in the telecourse guide. It lists several points to consider as you watch the video.

STEP 5: Watch the video.

STEP 6: Read the UNDERSTANDING THE LESSON section in the telecourse guide. Make sure you understand the key terms and can answer the focusing questions included there.

STEP 7: Complete the SELF-TEST.

STEP 8: Go back to the LESSON OBJECTIVES and make sure you can respond to each of them.

INTRODUCING THE LESSON

One evening, when you stop at your local video rental shop, you ask about the friendly young man who usually works there; you haven't seen him for a few days. "Oh, his father is sick, and he had to go back home," you're told. You express regrets at the news, and feel sad. You'll miss the clerk's casual friendship. Your brief chats as you rented movies were one of the numerous links in the network of social contacts that constitute your personal neighborhood.

Social interactions of this sort, in degrees of intimacy from the greeting you give your mail carrier to the leap of emotion you feel when you hear your mother's voice on the phone, make up the framework of much of our lives. A human life is a social life. Responding to other members of our species comes as naturally and easily to most of us as breathing.

And, like breathing, most of your skills in human relations began with programmed responses that you were born with; we begin life with certain preadaptations that give us an important headstart on the developmental tasks ahead of us. Because the human infant is unable to care for itself for many years, its survival depends almost completely on others. But that dependency isn't totally a matter of the whims of care givers. Infants are born with the ability to elicit comfort, nurturing, and attention from others. Biologically speaking, babies are cute for a reason.

During the first year of life, a baby undergoes a series of social and emotional developmental stages that, under the proper circumstances, allow it to form deep and significant *attachments* with the important people in its life. At first, the child displays reflexive behaviors – such as involuntary smiles – that tend to attract attention and stimulation from care givers, including parents and siblings. Gradually, the child's motor abilities improve; reflexive jerks and twitches evolve into deliberate clutchings of hands and turnings of the head. The child's vision improves, and it is able to distinguish among Mom, Dad, Sister, and Brother. By the end of the child's first year, the arrival – and sometimes the departure – of a recognized care giver elicits immediate emotional responses, whether of squealing laughter or piteous wails. The child is an active participant in a network of relationships, reacting with clear signs of emotional attachment to the important people in its life.

In this lesson, you will explore just how quickly and thoroughly a child develops emotionally and socially. You will learn how the tendency for human infants to form attachments to care givers is apparently an innate one, and you will learn the ways infants are predisposed to form these attachments. Through the framework of developmental theory, you will learn how infants are guided and encouraged by the attention of their care givers, and soon begin demonstrating the reciprocal behavior that social relationships depend upon. You will observe how an infant progresses from early reflex responses such as crying and sleeping, to the full range of emotional responses, including anger, joy, frustration, and surprise.

GOAL

The purpose of this lesson is to give you an understanding of how human infants are born predisposed to begin forming social relationships, beginning with attachment to care givers – the first of a lifetime's emotional and social involvements.

LESSON OBJECTIVES

After reading the text assignment, completing the exercises in this telecourse guide, and viewing the lesson's video portion, you will be able to:

1. Indicate the ways in which newborns are preadapted to become social.

2. Characterize what constitutes sensitive parental care, and recognize the influence contextual factors have on the quality of child care.

3. Describe the development of complex emotions that begin to emerge in the second half year of life.

4. Describe the formation of the attachment relationship between infant and care giver.

5. Give examples of several different patterns of attachment and discuss how the characteristics of care givers and the temperament of infants contribute to the quality of attachment.

6. Summarize the possible consequences of poor infant care and suggest types of intervention that can be effective.

7. Relate changing patterns of family and of work to the need for child care.

8. Recognize the controversy that exists regarding the relation between infant day care and the quality of infant-mother attachment.

VIEWING GUIDE

In this lesson, you will follow the course of an infant through its first year of life as it forms its first attachments to other human beings, in the form of the profound attachment to its parents – a relationship that, you will discover, is two-way from a surprisingly early age. By the end of the first year, a child has woven a strand for itself in the network of social connections and begun to feel the range of human emotions. After reading the text material and learning the terms, you are now ready to view the lesson's video portion. First, review the questions in the Self-Test at the end of this telecourse guide lesson to give you an idea of important points to watch for in the video. Then read the following Points to Consider and keep them in mind while watching.

Points to Consider

☐ *First ties*: According to developmentalists, infants are born *predisposed* to form *attachments* with care givers. Notice the evidence that developmentalists cite for this conclusion. In the video portion, you will see instances of parents speaking in simplified language to their newborn; be aware of reasons why this might be the best way to talk to babies.

☐ *Beginning to cope*: Children begin developing a wariness or even fear of strangers at about 7 months old. As you learn about the concept of *separation anxiety*, consider how this concept might relate to the traditional idea of "spoiling" a baby.

☐ *The varieties of attachment*: As you read about and see filmed examples of the attachments that babies form with care givers, be aware of the types of attachment that are possible. As you study the material, try to imagine the process of emotional development undergone by a child who is raised in extreme solitude.

☐ *Matters of temperament*: Developmentalists refer to a baby's activities, moods, and the way a baby responds emotionally as *temperament*. Think about the relation between an infant's temperament and its possible later personality. Be aware of the role, if any, researchers believe an infant's apparent temperament provides as a guide to the child's later outlook, moods, behaviors, or even values.

☐ *Quality counts*: You will see several instances in the video of the kind of "tuned in" quality childcare known as *sensitive care*. Remain aware of how a baby stimulates interactions that typify a sensitive care giver's attentions. As you study the research that has been done on how neglectful and abusive care damages children, think about the long-term consequences of poor-quality care and whether or not the ill effects can be canceled out in later years.

UNDERSTANDING THE LESSON

Most of us, if we search our memories, can recall at least one occasion in our childhood when we were separated from our mother or father in a crowd. You're in a department store, surrounded by a forest of adult legs soaring up into dresses or pants, and you reach over to grab Mom or Dad's leg for reassurance. But the face peering benignly down at you is a strange one; you've lost your parent.

No matter how long ago such an event occurred, you probably can tap at least a glimmer of your long-ago feeling of panic. Your sudden realization that you were alone among strangers was a terrifying one because you depended so greatly upon your parents; you were attached to them by a myriad of emotional bonds.

The child's first moments of pleasure are shared with his or her primary care givers, and in moments of stress, it is mother or father that the child turns to first. The ties that a child forms with his or her care givers mark a crucial step in the process of the child's developing emotions. The sense of security, confidence, and stability that a child finds in a positive attachment with its care givers forms the basis of a lifetime of social and emotional interactions.

Development in the First Half Year

As adults, we have little trouble identifying just how we go about forming relationships. We approach people, talk to them, listen, and respond, taking note of their facial expressions, their tone of voice, their body posture – as well as whether they return our phone calls. An infant, however, lacks the developed motor and cognitive skills that we employ so effectively. And yet, within months of being born, a baby is gurgling happily at the gentle sing-song of its mother's voice, or kicking its feet ecstatically at the prodding of its father's finger. How does a baby begin forming its first relationships with others?

To begin, infants are preadapted to interact socially, just as you learned in Lesson 5 that they are preadapted with physical reflexes to develop later motor skills. A baby's reflexive, involuntary cries in response to changes in arousal levels are its first means of signaling to others. If – and only if – the child's cries are met with appropriate response from care givers, the child will eventually begin initiating such interactions in a deliberate and reciprocal manner.

Infants are also predisposed to respond to stimuli such as the light and dark contrasts found in human faces, as well as to the human voice. Human infants turn their heads automatically in the direction of a person's voice. Furthermore, studies have shown that infants adjust to the rhythm of their care givers and demonstrate differences in behavior when their style of care is changed. Some researchers interpret this sensitivity of infants to an early ability to learn. At the very least, it demonstrates an innate tendency to adjust to social influences.

However, these early interactions are not so much *between* baby and others as they are *from* others to baby. Before true social exchanges can take place, the baby must begin to develop *reciprocity* with its care givers. Over the first four or five months of its life, as the baby gains greater control over his or her motor skills and begins staying alert for longer periods, care givers can begin to guide the infant's attention. As the infant is increasingly able to voluntarily respond to or turn away from stimuli, an attentive care giver is able to frame or direct the baby's responses to an ever greater extent. Like the teleprompter that TV newscasters read from, care givers are able to "cue" infants to respond in ways that lead toward true reciprocity.

But, as you learned from your text, the way that care givers interact with infants is crucial to the infants' development. The way in which a care giver paces, modifies, and elicits an infant's attention is called *attunement*, and can be done either poorly or well. Properly done, attunement is included within the types of behavior known as *sensitive care*. Through sensitive care, a baby begins to be initiated into the kinds of stimuli and reactions to its behaviors that, eventually, it will voluntarily participate in. In newborns, however, this interaction remains strictly under the direction of the care giver. True reciprocity develops gradually over the first year of a child's life.

Within about ten weeks of birth, the baby begins to respond with pleasure to stimuli from her or his care givers. By about age 4 or 5 months, the infant has begun to differentiate one or two special care givers' faces from all others, and has begun to stop smiling at strangers. And at 6 months, the baby is both reacting to, and deriving from, the care giver's attentions – the foundation of a lifetime of social behavior.

Key Terms

Sensitive care

Focusing Questions

1. Should a mother who is attuned to her baby be able to control his or her patterns of sucking when the child is breast-feeding?

2. Does a newborn have any voluntary abilities, such as being able to turn his or her head in the direction of someone's voice?

Development in the Second Half Year

Ten-month-old Seth approaches the fuzzy round doll sitting on the floor in front of him. Though Seth doesn't recognize its goggle eyes and yellow and black stripes as those of a bumble bee, he does know something new and interesting has been placed on his floor, and he quickly crawls forward. Stretching out a hand, he pushes the squat bug on its head – and suddenly jerks his hand back as the battery-operated doll squawks loudly and scuttles away from him. Seth's jaw drops, his eyes widen – and his face puckers up in the beginning of a long, loud yowl. Seth has been surprised, and he's letting the world know that he doesn't like it.

By his obvious surprise, Seth is demonstrating the great strides in emotional development that infants make during their second half year of life. Distinct emotional responses and clear attachment to principal care givers are both indications of the dramatic, qualitative developmental changes that infants experience at this time.

Infants in their second half year also continue to develop the ability to distinguish among the different people in their environment. A significant sign of the child's increasingly mature emotions is the appearance around month 7 of *stranger distress*, which is simply an apparent fear of strangers. Where a few months earlier, the sight of any person's face was likely to make an infant smile, now the sight of a new face will cause the child to stare, turn away, and often begin to cry.

The degree of wariness that babies exhibit toward strangers also depends upon the context of the situation. A baby may be less afraid of an approaching stranger if his or her mother or father is nearby, or if the new person shows some sensitivity to the baby's comfort. According to some researchers, this tendency to react to a stranger depending upon the context of the meeting shows an ability of the child to "evaluate" the situation. In this view, the degree of unease depends on how secure the baby feels in regards to the presence of a trusted care giver and, perhaps, whether the child perceives that he or she can crawl or turn away from the stranger. But more importantly, it depends on the child's current status regarding cognitive development.

Another significant emotion that infants begin showing around this time is *separation anxiety*. Anyone who has ever babysat and had the experience of holding a squirming, shrieking baby while the parents hurry out the door will recognize this emotion. Developmentalists relate separation anxiety to the child's cognitive advances because, to miss a care giver, the child must be able to recognize that he or she exists while out of the child's presence. The child is also now giving signs of its developing will, in that it chooses to cry only when its mother or father leaves against its wishes. These developments are also further indications of the child's growing sense of self.

Also in the second half year, the child is increasingly able to cope with emotionally arousing situations. Previously, the child was able to cope with excessive stimulus or even trauma only by withdrawing, through such mechanisms as deep sleep, turning away, or beginning to cry. Now, however, the child's coping responses become more subtle and flexible. For example, when distressed or over-stimulated, the child begins to purposefully signal the care giver by calling, gesturing, or giving other signals.

Key terms

> Stranger distress
> Separation anxiety

Focusing Questions

> 1. If an 8-month-old boy is in a room with his mother when a stranger enters, what will the boy's reaction probably be if he sees his mother frowning? If he sees her smiling?
>
> 2. Why might infants younger than 7 months old be easier to care for during a hospital stay than slightly older infants?

First Attachments

When young Seth, as described earlier, became upset after being surprised by his new motorized toy, his response was swift: he cried and looked in his mother's direction, raising his arms to be picked up. In addition to demonstrating his growing emotional complexity, Seth also exhibited another important developmental milestone of an infant's first year, that of attachment to his care givers.

As you have studied already in the text material and video portion, developmentalists refer to attachment as the interaction between infants and their primary care givers. Attachment grows between infants and care givers as a result of repeated episodes of interaction which allow the involved parties to coordinate their behavior. When a hurt or upset infant seeks out a specific person for comfort, or crows gleefully and demands to be picked up when that person enters the room, he or she is giving signs of attachment. Similarly, in the musical *My Fair Lady*, when Professor Henry Higgins sings about Eliza Doolittle that he's "grown accustomed to her face," he's singing about attachment.

Keep in mind that attachment is different from "bonding." The term bonding refers to the emotional ties parents feel for their infant almost as soon as it is born. Attachments take much longer to form. And though attachment is usually observed between infants and mothers and fathers, infants will become attached to whomever cares for them on a regular basis. Attachment appears to be a vital need in an infant's regular emotional development, as is shown in the example of orphaned baby monkeys who cling to a terry cloth doll in times of distress.

As for why humans seem to be biologically predisposed to form emotional attachments, the developmentalist John Bowlby theorizes that early human infants who stuck closer to their care givers had a higher survival rate than those who didn't. Through the mechanism of natural selection, human infants developed a predisposition to focus their attention on care givers. But though all children will normally form attachments to their care givers, the degree and quality of the attachment varies widely among children. In Bowlby's attachment theory, such differences are accounted for by the differences in the quality of care which care givers provide; other researchers, however, emphasize the role of an infant's inborn temperament. Probably, the answer to different forms of attachment draws from both theories.

Bowlby describes high quality care as a "secure attachment relationship," meaning that the baby behaves toward its care givers in an organized and smooth manner, and has confidence in how it will be treated. Secure attachment develops when the baby experiences consistent attention and appropriate responses to its signaled needs. Over time, the infant develops confidence that its signals will be heeded, and begins to form a capacity for reciprocal communication.

In the video portion of the lesson, you saw examples of securely attached infants interacting with their care givers. These children are able to confidently leave their care givers to explore new surroundings, yet clearly prefer being in the care giver's proximity. Such babies smile often at their care givers, seeking them out to share discoveries, and do not exhibit unprovoked anger.

On the other hand, children who are *anxiously attached* show insecurity in their relations with care givers – typically through two patterns. Children who develop *anxious resistant* attachments consistently seek out care givers, but in a contradictory way. Such children may insist on being picked up by the care giver, then immediately squirm to be put down. A main characteristic of resistant attachments seems to be a feeling of ambivalence toward care givers. Children who attach in an *anxious avoidant* pattern, on the other hand, seem to consciously keep away from care givers. Recently, researchers have introduced a third category of anxious attachment, referred to as "disorganized/disoriented," to describe infants who react in a dazed or confused manner around the care giver.

Key Terms

> Attachment
> Secure attachment
> Anxious attachment
> Anxious resistant
> Anxious avoidant

Focusing Questions

1. Some care givers tend to over-stimulate their children by insisting on interacting with the child even after it has turned away, or by being overcontrolling. How is the child likely to react to such overly persistent attention from a care giver, and what kind of interaction between parents and child is likely to be the result?

2. What are some of the probable causes of anxious attachments?

Temperament

Generally, we describe friends and acquaintances according to their outlook or behavior. We say one person is gloomy, another sunny and easy-
going, a third shy and retiring. What we're trying to categorize by these
terms is a person's *temperament*, a variety of behaviors that a person char-
acteristically displays in interactions with his or her environment. Researchers studying children's temperament tend to assume that an individual's
temperament is genetically or biologically rooted, with the environment
after birth then modifying these tendencies.

Child developmentalists are interested in just how stable a child's temperament will prove to be over time. Much research has been devoted to
the question of whether an infant's temperament can be used to predict the
individual's adult behavior or personality. As a whole, current research
indicates that a certain range of an infant's behavior – negative emotional-
ity, reactivity, positive affect – are quite stable by the end of the first year,
but do not serve as a good guide for predicting future behavior.

Key Words

Temperament

Focusing Questions

1. Why would a researcher studying the genetic roots of temperament be interested in the developmental patterns of twins? Why
   might you expect greater similarities in temperament between
   identical than between dizygotic twins?

2. Suppose a newborn is generally restless and irritable, with a tendency to cry for long periods. According to current developmental research, should their parents worry about their baby's future
   temperament? Could an increase in sensitive care improve the
   situation?

The Importance of Quality Care

As you know from previous lessons, the course of individual development is
inextricably entwined with context. This is no less true for emotional development than for motor skills or cognitive development. The quality of care
that an infant receives from its care givers has a great effect on how its
emotions, behaviors, and thinking powers will be shaped.

Under the best of circumstances, an infant will receive the type of
attentive, attuned attention known as "sensitive care." Sensitive care givers
engage their babies in an intuitive ballet of response and counter-response
based on a careful awareness of the baby's needs. Sensitive care givers
spend many hours learning the moods and signals of their baby and are
willing to modify their own behaviors to suit the baby's. With sensitive care,
a baby soon learns that the smile that follows some enjoyable sensation,
such as a parent blowing against her child's belly, elicits more of the good
feeling, in a positive feedback loop. Sensitive care builds secure attachment and instills feelings of confidence in its recipients.

Unfortunately, not all infants receive sensitive or even adequate care. Infants who are severely deprived of stimulation during early infancy display abnormal development, including possible abnormalities in the nervous system. Studies have shown that children who were reared from infancy in institutions had later difficulties in establishing close contacts with peers, and developed problems later in life as parents. Interestingly, studies have also shown that, even in institutional settings, infants who receive a certain amount of social interaction respond positively, as measured in how often they smiled at and vocalized with adults.

An extreme example of poor development is *nonorganic failure to thrive*, a syndrome characterized by very low growth, delayed motor development, and withdrawn or apathetic affect. Research indicates that failure to thrive results from poor quality care which ranges from inconsistent feeding to indifferent or neglectful behavior from care givers. The abusive or neglectful behavior that appears to contribute to failure to thrive stems from a variety of contexts, including a negative life history for the mother, her current levels of stress and depression, plus the degree of social support that she receives.

Focusing Questions

1. How permanent is the damage done to a child who suffers from failure to thrive syndrome? Can children whose social and emotional development gets off to an abnormally slow rate "catch up" with children who receive sensitive care? Are the duration of the neglect and the child's age when it occurred factors?

Questions for Understanding

As you read these questions, often raised by parents, educators, and other child care providers, first try to answer the questions yourself. Then read the answer following each question and compare your response to it.

1. *I'll have to return to work at least part-time within three months after having my baby. Will she form attachments with her day care worker instead of me?*

   The question of what effect day care has on the emotional and social development of children under one year old is an important one. Unfortunately, the studies done so far in this area have been inconclusive. Some researchers, however, believe that infants less than a year old who are placed in day care are at higher risk for anxious attachment than children who are raised at home.

   There is general agreement, however, that the quality of the day care a child receives is very important in how it affects the child's developing relationships. Babies who receive sensitive care, both during any time spent in a day care center and at home, appear to suffer few if any long-term negative effects from being placed in substitute care during the week.

   Perhaps the important point about early day care for your child, after the obvious one of making sure that you select a high quality day care provider, is to make sure that you concentrate on providing your own sensitive care to the child during your times together in the evenings and on the weekends.

2. *People always talk about the "innocence" of babies. Yet, in the three months since our son was born, I keep noticing how clever he can be at anticipating our actions. It almost seems like he's the one training us to jump at his command, not the other way around.*

While infants are of course dependent upon their care givers for all their needs, even very young children have a remarkable ability to perceive and respond to their environment. For example, newborns are able to notice contingencies in their environment, and quickly begin repeating behavior that results in certain events.

Remember, too, that your son has an inborn inclination to respond to movement and contrasts between light and dark. Your face has such contrasts, of course, and you tend to nod your head as you talk to him. He is, therefore, drawn to your face. While your son's early responses to you are reflexive, the patterns of behavior that you are forming with him are important precursors to the more obvious two-way communication that he will soon be practicing with you.

3. *My baby must be extra bright; he's only 4 weeks old, but he already smiles at me when I talk to him.*

Without suggesting that your son isn't exceptional, you should be aware that he probably isn't smiling at you because he is able specifically to recognize your voice. Infants at this age tend to respond with a smile to any gentle stimulation of sound, such as a tinkling bell, the tones of a wind chime, or the tune of a music box. Within the next month or two, however, he will begin smiling in response to a variety of visual or aural stimuli, such as faces, nearby dolls, and spinning mobiles.

4. *My partner and I tend to pick up our daughter fairly promptly whenever she cries. My aunt, however, recently told me that we were spoiling the child.*

The important factor in how a child reacts to its care is largely a matter of how well its needs are being met. If, when you attend to your daughter's cries, you are trying to alleviate her problem, whether by feeding her, changing her diaper, or simply comforting her, there is virtually no chance that you will teach her to be more demanding. Quite the contrary, by responding to her with sensitive care, you are actually teaching her that her signals for help will receive quick and appropriate responses, and that adults can be relied upon. A number of studies show that babies who receive a prompt response cry less than those who do not.

5. *How are temperament and attachment different?*

By temperament, we mean an inborn tendency to behave a certain way emotionally and physically, based on apparent moods and reactions to stress or stimulus; by attachment, we mean the emotional relationships that an individual forms with the important persons in his or her life. In other words, temperament describes the kind and quality of an individual's behavior, and attachment describes the quality of certain relationships. The two are related because they are reflections of the same processes of social and emotional development that the child undergoes in its first year.

Put another way, two infants who are both securely attached to their parents may act quite differently due to their different temperaments. One baby may be temperamentally more active, and tend to be very vocal about his or her needs. Another baby may have a markedly different temperament, and express his or her needs in quite different manners.

6. *Can babies who suffer from failure to thrive syndrome be helped later to develop more normally?*

Because failure to thrive seems to be the result of poor quality care, any attempt to help improve an affected child's development must involve the parents – most importantly, the mother. Mothers of these infants tend to provide generally inadequate care, and are often indifferent or even hostile to their babies. Negative feedback loops develop between mother and child. For example, an anxious or depressed mother, irritated by her baby, cuts the baby's feeding time short, making the baby hungry and frustrated, and further angering the mother.

Programs designed to counteract failure to thrive must therefore focus on improving the relationship between the mother and child. In one program, mothers were given an hour's tutoring per day in how to respond positively to the child's behavior. Another program took a psychoanalytic approach, based on the theory that problems in the mother's own childhood were resurfacing in the current mother and child relationship. In this approach, the mother was helped to remember and come to terms with her own difficulties in infancy. Both programs reported significant positive results for some of the involved infants.

SELF-TEST

The following multiple choice and short answer test questions should help you assess your understanding of the points covered in the text and the video. After answering all the questions, check your answers against the key and use the accuracy of your answers to gauge how well you have met the lesson objectives.

Multiple Choice Questions

1. Studies show that toddlers and preschoolers in full time day care

    a. demonstrate predictable, universal negative effects.
    b. demonstrate positive cognitive and social development.
    c. are more attached to substitute care givers than to primary care givers.
    d. demonstrate initial negative effects that disappear later.

2. A newborn baby is acting in a preadapted social manner when it

    a. begins sucking on a nipple placed in its mouth.
    b. turns its head toward someone's voice.
    c. coos in response to a human voice,
    d. turns its head in the direction of a touch on its cheek.

3. Guiding a child along the developmental path toward true reciprocity is like teaching him or her to

    a. walk.
    b. ride a bicycle.
    c. feed him- or herself.
    d. play ping pong.

4. Sensitive care refers to a type of behavior toward infants that care givers

    a. naturally know how to provide.
    b. can take special classes to learn.
    c. should adopt only when infants are having difficult times.
    d. may form soon after birth during hours spent with their baby.

5. When a baby is surprised its heart beat slows down, which is a sign of

    a. fear.
    b. boredom.
    c. attention.
    d. pleasure.

6. A screenwriter is writing a movie scene about a bank robbery. In the scene, the appearance of a man wearing a mask frightens a baby, who begins crying. To ensure a crying baby, the baby's age should be about

    a. 10 months.
    b. 5 months.
    c. 3 months.
    d. 2 weeks.

7. By attachment, we mean that infants form emotional bonds with

    a. only their biological parents.
    b. only their immediate family, including siblings.
    c. whomever spends any time with them.
    d. their principal care givers.

8. Two mothers are talking about their 1 year olds. "Jamie has always been good-natured," says one woman, "even right after he was born. He barely ever cried, and he just loved taking baths. When I'm shopping for groceries and he's in the cart, I swear he'd let perfect strangers take him away, he's that friendly." Jamie's mother is describing his

    a. fear of strangers.
    b. temperament.
    c. attachment.
    d. attunement.

9. A child is in danger of forming a resistant attachment with his or her mother if the mother

   a. tries to adjust her own responses to the child's actions.
   b. regularly beats or otherwise abuses the child.
   c. is emotionally unavailable to the child.
   d. is inconsistent in her responses to the child's actions.

10. Although the research is inconclusive, some of the available evidence seems to indicate that a significant percentage of infants who are placed in day care before they are 1 year old are at greater risk for

    a. anxious-avoidant attachment.
    b. fear of strangers.
    c. failure to thrive.
    d. disorganized/disoriented attachment.

Short Answer Questions

The following questions should be answered in a paragraph or two. You should identify several key points for each answer and use these to form the framework for your response.

1. The practice of placing young children in day care has been steadily growing in this country over the past several decades. What are some of the effects that developmentalists believe day care has upon children?

2. If babies are preadapted to begin forming social and emotional ties from early infancy, what kind of behaviors are adults seemingly preadapted to practice?

3. In terms of child development, what does reciprocity mean?

8

A Look at the Whole Child: The First Year

LESSON ASSIGNMENT

Completing the following steps will help you master the lesson objectives and achieve the goal for this lesson:

<u>STEP 1:</u> Read the INTRODUCING THE LESSON section to provide a context for what you will learn in this lesson.

<u>STEP 2:</u> Read the lesson's GOAL and LESSON OBJECTIVES so that you will know what you are expected to learn.

<u>STEP 3:</u> Read the text assignment, Chapter 4, pages 131-136, 147-148, and 150-153; Chapter 5, pages 160-164, 167-171, and 174-180; and Chapter 6, pages 191-203, 205-207, 210-213, and 215. Pay particular attention to the key terms and concepts in the Chapter Summaries at the ends of Chapters 4, 5, and 6; they will help you when you watch the video.

<u>STEP 4:</u> Review the VIEWING GUIDE section in the telecourse guide. It lists several points to consider as you watch the video.

<u>STEP 5:</u> Watch the video.

<u>STEP 6:</u> Read the UNDERSTANDING THE LESSON section in the telecourse guide. Make sure you understand the key terms and can answer the focusing questions included there.

<u>STEP 7:</u> Complete the SELF-TEST.

<u>STEP 8:</u> Go back to the LESSON OBJECTIVES and make sure you can respond to each of them.

INTRODUCING THE LESSON

Human beings are record-keeping animals; we can't resist keeping track of our progress through life, both as a species and as individuals. As members of a group, we have painted the walls of the prehistoric caverns in Lescaux, France, erected the Great Pyramid of Cheops, stitched the Bayeux Tapestry commemorating the Norman Conquest of England. Individually, we shoot video footage, compete for sports trophies, file income tax reports.

As conscious creatures, we have a passion for recording our passage through time, and child rearing offers countless opportunities to memorialize significant milestones. Traditionally, mothers have saved locks from their baby's first haircut, preserved their infant's first nightgown and cap, even held on to that first lost baby tooth. Families who reside in one home for several years will often select a wall or door frame on which to measure and record their children's yearly growth. And since the invention of photography, of course, baby pictures have become the joy of parents and the bane of casual acquaintances throughout the world.

One of the great pleasures of parenthood is taking note of the changes that a child undergoes as he or she grows into adulthood. And though most parents will take a lifetime's pleasure in sharing the high points of their offspring's achievements, the first year of life is special. A baby's first year has an emotionally charged air that no later period of development can ever quite match. Within this one year, the child will change dramatically, making remarkable achievements intellectually, physically, emotionally, and socially.

Everyone's first year, after all, starts off with one of life's most memorable events, at least for everyone involved except the infant – birth. And after that exhilarating beginning, the average baby enters into a year of remarkable growth and change. Within the first year, after all, the child's motor skills develop from primitive reflexes to the verge of walking, while its squeals and coos have refined to the point of actually forming a few simple words. From having no awareness of a world existing beyond his or her fingertips, the baby now recognizes that objects exist even when he or she can't see them. And by the time of that first birthday cake with its single bright candle, a baby has formed his or her first emotional attachments. All in all, the first year of an individual's life is an enormously important one in the context of that person's overall development.

In this lesson, you will look at the first year of life as seen from a developmental perspective. To this point, you have studied how the newborn infant develops within his or her first year physically, cognitively, socially, and emotionally; now you will examine the integrated nature of this development, and how the context of each individual's surroundings shapes how development unfolds. And through the lesson's video segment, you will see vivid examples of how developmental change, beginning with the very first year, occurs in an orderly fashion, with each stage building upon the one just before, and moves forward toward greater behavioral complexity.

GOAL

The purpose of this lesson is to provide a comprehensive understanding of the developmental achievements that a child has mastered by the end of its first year – physically, cognitively, socially, and emotionally.

LESSON OBJECTIVES

After reading the text assignment, completing the exercises in this telecourse guide, and viewing the lesson's video portion, you will be able to:

1. Summarize the key developmental changes that occur in the first year of life.

2. Recognize and give examples of the integrated nature of a baby's physical, cognitive, social, and emotional growth.

3. Describe how the context in which an infant is nurtured affects his/her development and how context or environment interacts with genetic potential.

4. Using the video portion of a child's first year as the basis for discussion, show how the child's development illustrated the three general principles of development.

5. Indicate the ways a baby actively participates in its own development.

VIEWING GUIDE

In the video portion of this lesson, you will examine a series of vignettes from the first year of life of a baby girl. At 1 year of age, the child is a remarkably distinctive individual – the result of an integrated series of developmental stages that have occurred within the crucial framework of a familial, social, and economic context. After reading the text material and learning the important terms included there, you are ready to view the lesson's video portion. First, review the questions in the Self-Test at the end of this telecourse guide lesson to give you an idea of important points to watch for in the video. Then, read the following Points to Consider to give you an idea of what the video will cover. Keep these points in mind while watching.

Points to Consider

☐ *Get your motor running*: As you see examples in the video of the motor skills demonstrated by 1 year olds, keep in mind the various developmental stages that the child has already passed through. Recall, for example, how the newborn's reflexes form the basis for later development of motor skills. Notice how individual children experience the various stages and milestones of development in slightly different ways and at varying rates.

☐ *First-year scholars*: As the child matures during its first year, it faces a series of new and increasingly complex behavioral and cognitive challenges. Look for examples in the video of the several types of learning which babies are capable of, including habituation, association, contingencies, and imitation.

☐ *A year-long awakening*: At 1 year old, a child's cognitive capabilities represent an immense quantitative and qualitative leap over its capabilities at birth. Note how a 1 year old's awareness of the world is the result of a series of interrelated physical, mental, and emotional changes.

☐ *The beginning of family and friends*: By his or her first birthday, the baby is an active participant in a web of social and emotional ties. Pay attention to how the baby moves through a number of behavioral milestones, such as the period of stranger distress, to arrive at its emotional and social level at year one.

☐ *A long year's journey into life*: As the video portion's birthday party scenes illustrate, the 1 year old child's overall capabilities are the result of developmental processes that are orderly, sequential, and cumulative. As you view and read, keep in mind how the different stages of development occur in relation to one another, as well as how important a child's environment is to its healthy growth.

UNDERSTANDING THE LESSON

Go into any baby boutique or photography store and you'll find rows of photo albums embossed in silver or gold with the words "Baby's First Birthday." Bound in white calfskin and trimmed with silver, the albums are meant to hold artful photographs of a significant celebration in everyone's life. Of all an individual's birthdays, the first one is arguably the one that most deserves special notice. Certainly for the baby's parents and other family members, if not for the baby itself, it is probably the most poignant. Never again will any of us accomplish so much, in terms of personal growth, as during that first year of life. The beaming, babbling, balancing baby that beats a spoon in erratic time to a chorus of "Happy Birthday" is truly worth celebrating.

Motor Skills at 1 Year Old

As you saw in the video segment, at her first birthday party Lisa Linton performs her duties as guest of honor by moving gracefully among her guests through a combination of crawling and clinging. At 1 year old, most infants are teetering on the verge of walking. And though Lisa doesn't recognize the brightly wrapped boxes as presents, she is able to pick the boxes up and examine them. She also is able to focus on each person at her party, follow their movements, and call out excitedly when she sees her brother or sister grin across the table at her. In all her physical actions, it is evident that Lisa has made great advances in the one year since her birth from the helpless, squinting bundle of uncoordinated reflexes that her family first welcomed.

As you recall from Lesson 5, children begin mastering control over their bodies within the first year. Beginning with preadapted reflexes, the child grows and passes through a series of developmental milestones to an impressive state of coordinated physical abilities. By the end of the first year, the average baby has tripled in weight and grown in length by 10 inches. As the child grows and increasingly practices new motor skills, its capabilities are guided by the developmental principle of *differentiation*, which means that movements that are at first global and poorly defined gradually become precise and specific. For example, when a hand is placed over a newborn's mouth and nose, the infant arches its entire body and flails its arms and legs; one year later, the 1 year old sees the hand coming and intercepts it with its own hand.

From random, searching eye movements at birth, the child's control of its eye movements progresses to the point of being able to track moving objects and to change focus to compensate for their movements upon being carried. At the same time, the infant combines visual capabilities with reaching and grasping movements to develop the skill of reaching and grasping accurately. This process will take more than the first year to develop completely. The 1 year old is able to grasp objects between its fingers and thumb, but the birthday child hasn't yet mastered the thumb-and-forefinger grasp necessary to, say, hold a paintbrush.

As for that developmental watershed of motor skills, walking, the average 1 year old hasn't quite reached there yet. At about 7 months the average child begins writhing or "swimming" along the floor; at 8 months he or she can stand up with help; at 10 months he or she is crawling rapidly along; at 11 months he or she can walk when led; and at his or her first birthday party, the child is pulling him- or herself upright on the edge of coffee tables or chairs and sidling along alone. (Remember, though, that these averages are bracketed by a range of months during which motor skills develop. What the average child can do in a given skill at 8.6 months, other children can do as early as 6 months while some others don't exhibit the same skill until 12 months.)

All of these developmental stages emerge out of initial, inborn reflexes to varying degrees, and unfold depending upon the support and encouragement that the child encounters from its environment. Recall, for example, the examples from Lesson 7 of how poor-quality child care may result in "failure to thrive," which may cause motor development to be delayed. As during all stages of child development, the child's motor skills develop within a framework of other developments, both within and outside the child.

Key Terms

Differentiation

Focusing Questions

1. Hopi Indian infants were traditionally bound to cradle boards for their first year of life, which seems to have had no effect on when the children learned to walk. What might we conclude from this about the importance of practice versus maturity regarding when a child begins walking?

2. Why does physical growth add to the challenge that infants face when mastering basic motor skills?

Learning in the First Year

The motor skills that a child has developed by the end of its first year are a result of both genetic factors and experience. While a child is born with genetic instructions that guide it toward the developmental events of grasping, crawling, walking, and talking, it must learn how to perform each specific chore as it arises in the developmental sequence. In other words, even though an infant will be impelled by increasing maturity toward walking and talking, it must deliberately learn the individual actions necessary to perform each new skill.

Among the earliest types of learning that infants are capable of is *habituation*, which basically refers to the way people eventually become accustomed to any new stimulus. Habituation is a form of learning that we practice all our lives. It ensures that new information, when repeated often enough, soon becomes familiar and thus doesn't distract any longer. Infants are also able from a very early age to practice *associative* learning, by which they learn that certain events are related.

To these early preadaptive types of learning, the child has added *imitative* learning to its repertoire. Through imitation, the child is capable of learning completely new actions or behaviors by watching others. For example, by their first birthday babies are beginning to consciously imitate the sounds of the words they hear around them, and are beginning to shape their babbling in the direction of actual speech.

Imitative learning is an especially significant component in the developmental process, as it depends upon parallel growth of the child's physical and cognitive abilities. For the video's 1-year-old Lisa, for example, to repeat the word "bird" when her father says it to her, the child must be able both to recognize how her father shapes his lips and mouth to say that word, as well as remember what the word sounds like as she tries to say it. But by the end of their first year, most children have progressed through the necessary cognitive and physical stages and are happily parroting the sounds of the language they hear around them.

Key Terms

> Habituation
> Associative learning
> Imitative learning

Focusing Questions

1. Is it accurate to speak of a child "learning" to walk, or is walking just another motor skill that the child more or less grows into along a genetically determined course?

2. Are deaf children able to learn any speech skills through imitation?

Cognitive Development in the First Year

Infants in their first year are unfailing sources of amusement and tenderness to adults because babies possess a continual ability to surprise at this age.

Infants are learning and changing so rapidly in this first year that they constantly confound the expectations of the people around them. In the first year of life, a child's understanding of the world – its cognitive abilities – is steadily reaching out to embrace everything around the child.

Consider, for example, how greatly a baby's ability to actively participate in the world increases during its first year. A newborn baby is entirely dependent upon its reflexes to react in any way with its surroundings. The way a 1 month old seems to actively look at a person as he or she passes by is actually a reflex action, as you learned in Lesson 6. But by the end of year one, the child is actively looking for and recognizing people and things around it, interacting deliberately with them. In terms of social development, the child has learned to return the attention it receives. The 1 year old now sees obstacles in its path, anticipates them, and takes appropriate action to remove or go around them.

As you learned earlier in the telecourse, this ability to do a thing not for its own sake but to achieve another goal is a type of behavior known as "a goal-directed chain." At this stage, a child coordinates simple behaviors – pushing, pulling, shaking – into more complex actions to achieve a goal.

For example, the child may crawl to a low table and pull him- or herself to a standing position in order to shred a newspaper that a parent forgot to put at a higher level. In terms of Piaget's theory of sensorimotor development, the 1 year old has reached stage 4 where his or her ability to combine skills purposefully will depend on the extent of mastery of these skills and the ability to anticipate how well an action will work.

Another vital cognitive hurdle that the 1-year-old child has almost fully cleared is an understanding of *object permanence*, which simply means that the baby understands that objects continue to exist even when the child can't see them. While a 5 or 6 month old will not try to find a toy that it has seen being covered up in front of it, within a few months the same child will be eagerly lunging after the hidden item.

Clearly, by the end of the first year, the child is beginning to exercise a certain degree of memory and is forming an understanding of how different objects may relate to one another. It's important to remember, though, that the child's growing cognitive skills are still based firmly in its developing motor skills; throughout an individual's development, no new skill or capability blossoms in isolation from all others.

Key Terms

Object permanence

Focusing Questions

1. Why do you think it is necessary for a child's memory to improve before it begins developing a true sense of object permanence?

Social and Emotional Development in the First Year

At the same time that children's physical and cognitive abilities have been growing dramatically, so have their social skills. During year one, the infant develops a number of skills or characteristics that create the foundation of a lifetime of social interaction. And as you know from Lesson 6, a 1 year old will have established the first emotional ties of its life in the form of attachment to its primary care givers.

During the first year of life, a child develops not only a sense of object permanence, but also a sense of person permanence. A baby is, therefore, likely to become upset if the primary care taker cannot be found. In the first half of the first year, the absence of the care taker did not lead to this same anxiety on the part of the infant.

At 2 months of age, a crying baby can be comforted by anyone, even a stranger. By 10 months of age, the baby can be comforted by the care giver, but will become more upset if a stranger approaches to give comfort. The development of motor skills also has an effect on attachment behaviors. While a younger baby maintains closeness to the care giver by crying, an older baby is likely to creep across the room to the care giver.

Babies are born with certain preadaptations to form social ties. Crying, for one, serves to establish bonds between infants and care givers. Remember, however, how important it is for an infant's care givers to give the infant sensitive care in response to his or her cries; as always in development, context has a crucial role to play in shaping genetic factors. But given a degree of responsive care, the 1 year old will have developed a strong ability to return attention from others and will be a true partner in social interactions.

An important step along the 1 year old's course of development is the emergence of social smiling. Initially, care givers attend to infant behavior which is innate: crying, reflexive sucking or clutching, spontaneous smiles that arise from stimulation of the lower brain. Next, the child begins to smile when he or she recognizes something as familiar, a step known as *recognition assimilation*. Gradually, by around 4 or 5 months, the child is smiling deliberately at the appearance of certain care givers, and soon after that begins to be wary of strangers.

As you saw in the video portion of this lesson, the 1-year-old child has formed distinct attachments with its primary care givers, either of the secure, anxious, or disorganized/disoriented type. Anyone who has ever seen a baby at a day care center drop its toys and begin crawling happily toward Dad when he enters knows what attachment means. As the first serious relationship of a lifetime, attachment represents the result of many hours of interaction between adult and child, in which the behavior of the adult forms one major context in which the child's innate tendencies will be formed.

Some of the most important learning a child does in the first two years of life is about relationships, including how people relate to each other and what they can expect from care givers. In addition, infants who are securely attached tend to do more exploration in the presence of the care giver, and to work on difficult tasks more persistently as toddlers.

As always in a child's development, the 1 year old's social and emotional skills will be as described here if all the stages leading from birth to that first birthday are met and experienced in a reasonably beneficial environment, and assuming that the child inherited a sound genetic framework.

Key Terms

Recognition assimilation

Focusing Questions

1. What developmental change underlies the young infant's ability to begin practicing reciprocity with its care givers?

2. What are the various types of attachment and what are some of the circumstances believed to cause them?

The General Nature of Development in the First Year

By a child's first birthday, he or she has progressed a long way from birth – physically, cognitively, socially, and emotionally. From early reflexive behaviors that depended upon outside influences, the child is now actively seeking out and exploring his or her world and is initiating actions that lead to anticipated results. The 1 year old, for example, pulls herself up by bookshelf handholds, zeroes in on Volume III of the *Encyclopedia Britannica*, grabs at it – and gapes in amazement when she finds herself seated on the floor with the book spread out on top of her. This little girl may react to the pain with tears, just as she would have at 4 months, but now the child is capable of actively searching out a care giver for solace. The 1 year old is a purposeful, highly mobile individual with rapidly improving motor skills and a wide range of emotional resources.

According to the theories of Jean Piaget, the growing infant modifies its behavior and responses through the twin mechanisms of *adaptation* and *equilibration*. By adaptation, developmentalists mean the way that individuals change their behavior to function better in new situations. For example, as the child becomes more aware that objects have permanence, she adapts her behavior accordingly, and from around 8 to 10 months begins finding hidden objects that previously mystified her. Equilibration comes into play when the child, trying to perform an action, has to adjust her behavior in the direction of increasingly effective adaptations. As you'll recall from the example given in Chapter 5 in your text, equilibration is the process that young Meryl used to learn how to drink out of a cup.

In a cognitive sense, by age 1 the child has adapted a number of initial *schemes*, or mental structures, to structure increasingly complex forms of behavior. Throughout the first year – indeed, throughout an individual's life – developmental change occurs when mental structures are created that coordinate sensory and motor information.

Overall, the developmental changes that the child experiences in all areas of growth during the first year can be considered qualitative, not just quantitative. The excited child blinking at the flame of her first birthday candle is obviously the same being as her year-ago, newborn self – and then again, she isn't. She's a much more capable and complex individual than that wrinkled, flailing, near-sighted baby, and is poised now at the threshold of a lifetime of continuing change and growth – of development.

Key Terms

Adaptation
Equilibration
Schemes

Focusing Questions

1. When Piaget stated that children are active participants in their own cognitive development, what did he mean?

2. Describe some of the qualitative differences between the emotional reactions of the newborn and the 1 year old; between the cognitive abilities of the two.

Questions for Understanding

As you read these questions, often raised by parents, educators, and other child care providers, first answer the questions yourself. Then read the answer following each question and compare your response to it.

1. *Both my husband and I were very excited when our daughter took her first steps just before her first birthday. Are we correct in assuming that, because she walked at such an early age, she's exceptionally bright?*

While it is certainly no cause for alarm, neither does an unusually early start to walking indicate that a child is exceptionally bright. While your daughter did start walking rather early, she still is within the general range of when most children take their first steps. What is important to know is that walking arises out of a sequence of increasingly complex motor skills, which your daughter has clearly mastered.

Also keep in mind that individual infants will differ in just how they progress through the stages of locomotion. When they begin moving around on their own, at month 6 or 7, some babies swim on their stomach by using their arms, while others propel themselves with their legs. Others will get ahead by scooting across floors while sitting upright. But within a broad general range, parents shouldn't worry about whether their child is learning to crawl, scoot, or walk in the "right" way, or upon an exact, biologically-wired time frame.

2. *Vincent has always been a highly vocal child. He has always babbled, usually quite happily, and seems to get great enjoyment from just making sounds. Now that he's about 9 months old, however, more often than not he seems to be deliberately copying our speech, though he can't quite say any words yet. How are his sound-making efforts changing?*

Vincent, who up to now has just been following his biological inclinations to enjoy making noise, is gradually learning how to imitate sounds that catch his ear. So far, Vincent's ability to copy sounds has been restricted to what you echo back at him. In other words, if he squeaks and you repeat it, he might make the sound again. But in his first six months, Vincent wasn't able to imitate sounds that he had never made himself before. The same limitation held true for behaviors, too.

Now, however, Vincent is increasingly gaining control over his mouth and facial muscles, and has a clearer awareness of how a movement of another person's lips can be repeated. His improving memory is also helping guide his concentration on new sounds. Your son is gradually moving toward his first words and the beginnings of speech, a new level of ability which will develop from the sound-making tendencies he has already been practicing. And increasingly, you will notice how your own speech styles and word choices influence what Vincent learns to say.

3. *Until just a few months ago, my 11 month old was completely at ease around people, even those she'd just met. But recently, she seems to become very uneasy whenever she's around strangers. Am I doing anything to make her shy?*

It's unlikely, since the behavior you just described is an example of a normal developmental stage for children of your daughter's age. Known as stranger distress, it just means that sometime between the ages of 7 and 10 months, most children will begin to exhibit unease and wariness whenever they are approached by strangers. Although the degree to which stranger distress affects children varies from child to child, it does occur to some extent for the majority of children.

While nothing you do prompted your daughter to experience stranger distress, there are a few things within your control that could affect how severe your daughter's reaction is. For example, children tend to show less distress when they are in familiar settings, such as their own home, and when they know a care giver is close at hand. Furthermore, if your daughter sees that you are frowning or otherwise somehow signaling possible unease at such times, she is more likely to begin crying or otherwise show signs of stranger distress. Some researchers evaluate these reactions as indications that the child is able to make rudimentary evaluations of the stranger and the degree of possible threat that the person may pose.

4. *Increasingly, our 1-year-old daughter insists on doing things for herself that earlier she was happy to have us do for her, such as feeding herself. How would a child developmentalist account for this growing self-reliance?*

As your daughter grows older, her motor skills are becoming stronger and better coordinated, her memory is improving, her understanding of objects is becoming more sophisticated, and her ability to link cause with effect is expanding greatly. In short, your daughter is in every way a much more capable person today than she was at birth. Daily, as she encounters new situations or re-examines old ones, she is adapting her behavior to better suit the circumstances.

Developmentalists describe this process of adaptation according to its two subprocesses, assimilation and accommodation. In assimilation, the individual applies an already existing capability to a new situation. This tendency explains why young infants like to immediately place everything they can grab into their mouth. But through accommodation, the individual modifies his or her usual behaviors to fit a new situation. For instance, this dual process is one reason why children enjoy throwing things from their high chair tray; once they've mastered this new throwing ability, they assimilate it in often inappropriate ways. Gradually, though, they learn to accommodate their new skill and practice it at more appropriate times.

5. *I recently began working a swing shift instead of a regular daytime job. I was worried that my year-old son would be upset at this change in my schedule. But after a little initial curiosity about the change, he doesn't seem fazed at all. Are all children so adaptable?*

Children do tend to be highly adaptable to changing situations, but how well they adjust to change depends largely upon the quality of the care they receive at the time. If your son is adjusting to your new routine, it is probably at least partly because your overall care of him assures him of continued security.

Babies are also born with certain predispositions to make adjustments to changing circumstances. For instance, even young infants are able to detect contingencies in the environment; that is, they notice how their behavior seems to cause events to happen, and tend to repeat these behaviors. Along with this capacity, infants tend to "fall into step" or synchronize their behaviors with those of their care givers. Based on these two innate abilities, and assuming that you continue to meet his physical and emotional needs in spite of your changed schedule, your son is probably taking your new schedule more in stride than you are.

6. *What are some of the ways children develop socially in their first year?*

Children are born with certain preadaptations that encourage their early social development – if they receive the proper stimulation. As the child becomes more alert for longer periods, he or she will begin taking part in mutual exchanges with others; these exchanges are known as reciprocity. In a context of sensitive care giving, the baby's partner in reciprocity will "frame" interactions with the child and give the baby chances to learn how to control motor responses and how to attend for longer and longer periods. While the older partner will guide the baby's reactions, the child actively participates in his or her own social development from early infancy.

SELF-TEST

The following multiple choice and short answer test questions should help you measure your understanding of the points covered in the text and the video. After answering all the questions, check your answers against the key and use the accuracy of your answers to gauge how well you have met the lesson objectives.

Multiple Choice Questions

1. During the birthday party you saw in the video, it is most likely that 1-year-old Lisa will be able to

   a. walk a few steps unaided.
   b. pick up a teacup using the handle only.
   c. "walk" by holding onto chairs and table edges.
   d. guess that packages contain gifts by rattling them.

2. According to most developmental researchers, the most important factor determining when a child first walks is

   a. maturation.
   b. attachment to care givers.
   c. a well-exercised stepping reflex.
   d. nervous system development.

3. In the video segment, you saw Lisa's older sister impatiently show the younger child how to rip the wrapping off birthday presents. If Lisa then reached for another package and tried to open it herself, she would be showing how she learns through

   a. association.
   b. imitation.
   c. habituation.
   d. accommodation.

4. Eleven-month-old Calvin is eager to grab an antique Malaysian knife that hangs on a wall. The prize, however, is several feet beyond his crawling grasp; further, he isn't able to get a grip on the wall to stand up. So the child crawls over to a nearby couch, hauls himself upright, then sidles along the edge of the couch until he is standing just below the desired item. The cognitive skill that most helps Calvin in his plan of attack is a(n)

   a. sense of object permanence.
   b. ability to imitate actions.
   c. ability to initiate behaviors.
   d. ability to anticipate results.

5. One important cognitive skill which a child must begin to command before she or he can effectively learn to talk is

   a. learning by contingency.
   b. the ability to form concepts.
   c. a sense of object permanence.
   d. long-term memory.

6. A baby is born with certain predispositions toward participating in early social exchanges. These preadaptive mechanisms won't go into full effect, however, unless the baby

   a. receives appropriate stimulation from its care givers.
   b. has regular contact with one consistent care giver.
   c. has achieved a certain level of cognitive abilities.
   d. has formed secure attachments with its care givers.

7. According to Jean Piaget's theories, 1 year olds are capable of forming "goal-directed chains" of behavior. One example of this type of behavior would be

   a. the child who learns to say a curse word because it makes her parents laugh.
   b. standing upright by hanging onto table edges.
   c. using a spoon to eat.
   d. crying for mother when a stranger appears.

8. One example of the orderly, cumulative, and directional nature of development that begins emerging around year one is

    a. a child's imitation of speech.
    b. stranger distress.
    c. attachment.
    d. social smiling.

9. Jane and Pauline are both about 1 year old. Jane is securely attached to her parents, who are financially stable and have lavished great amounts of attention on her in her first year. Pauline, on the other hand, exhibits anxious attachment to her mother, a 16 year old who lives on welfare alone in a studio apartment. Both children, however,

    a. were biologically predisposed to form attachments.
    b. will be permanently affected, both socially and emotionally, by their early attachments.
    c. will seek attachments outside the immediate family at an early age.
    d. will have no memory of these early environmental circumstances when they are old enough to form attachments.

10. Children are participating in their own development when they

    a. show uneasiness when a stranger appears.
    b. turn their heads away from a care giver's excessive stimulation.
    c. begin smiling soon after birth.
    d. first develop object permanence.

Short Answer Questions

The following questions should be answered in a paragraph or two. You should identify several key points for each answer and use them to form the framework for your response.

1. What are some of the qualitative developmental changes that a child has experienced by his or her first birthday?

2. What are some of the developmental stages that the child must successfully negotiate before he or she begins to talk?

3. At 1 week old, Clifton's only way of telling his mom that he's hungry is by fussing or crying. Within a year, however, the little boy is playing with some blocks in a sun-lit patch of living room when he hears the refrigerator door open. Scurrying along on all fours, he heads for the kitchen, where he knows Mom is unwrapping an ice cream bar. What kind of cognitive changes has Clifton undergone to be able to recognize that it is ice cream time again?

MODULE III:

TODDLERHOOD

9

Toddler Language
and Thinking

LESSON ASSIGNMENT

Completing the following steps will help you master the lesson objectives and achieve the goal for this lesson:

STEP 1: Read the INTRODUCING THE LESSON section to provide a context for what you will learn in this lesson.

STEP 2: Read the lesson's GOAL and LESSON OBJECTIVES so that you will know what you are expected to learn.

STEP 3: Read the text assignment, Chapter 7, pages 239-269. Pay particular attention to the key terms and concepts in the Chapter Summary on pages 268-269; they will help you when you watch the video.

STEP 4: Review the VIEWING GUIDE section in the telecourse guide. It lists several points to consider as you watch the video.

STEP 5: Watch the video.

STEP 6: Read the UNDERSTANDING THE LESSON section in the telecourse guide. Make sure you understand the key terms and can answer the focusing questions included there.

STEP 7: Complete the SELF-TEST.

STEP 8: Go back to the LESSON OBJECTIVES and make sure you can respond to each of them.

INTRODUCING THE LESSON

There is a deeply moving scene in the movie *The Miracle Worker*, which is about how Helen Keller learned to communicate. Helen Keller lost her hearing and sight at 19 months, and until she was 7 years old no one was able to communicate with her because she lacked the ability to use language. Her family treated the child as unteachable, allowing her to eat food off people's plates and giving in to her tantrums.

Luckily for Helen, an instructor gifted in teaching language skills to the blind and deaf, Anne Sullivan, was given the job of trying to civilize the child. Ms. Sullivan believed that Helen Keller had normal cognitive abilities and refused to be discouraged by the child's rejection of all efforts to communicate with her. Teacher and resistant pupil fought violent battles as one tried to penetrate the barrier of darkness enfolding the other.

But finally, after great struggles of will, Ms. Sullivan broke through to the child. As dramatized in the movie, Ms. Sullivan is holding Helen Keller's hand under a running pump and, for the umpteenth time, pressing the hand signal for "water" into the palm of her hand. And suddenly the child gets it: the repeated pressure on her hand "means" the sensation of wetness and coolness that she feels. From an expression of blank numbness, Helen Keller's face lights up with exultation. In one ecstatic moment, you see the revelation of what language must be to someone who was previously entrapped within her own mind, with no way of knowing that it was possible to communicate with other people. Helen Keller eventually learned to speak, and in time received a college degree.

Fortunately, children with normally functioning senses come to language in a less spectacular, but still dramatic fashion. Beginning from about the second half year of his or her life, a child is impelled to make increasingly directed efforts to communicate. The child's random babblings begin sounding more and more like actual words. The child is also beginning to make specific signals indicating desires, such as pointing at things or reaching out to be picked up. Then, soon after taking its first steps, the child pronounces that first deliberate word, which thrills his or her parents so greatly. From that moment on, the process of learning to speak proceeds in much the same way as kicking a pebble down a rocky slope starts a landslide.

Learning to talk is a process that will occupy the child and its care givers from the moment of its first word through the next three or four years. As such, it normally isn't the subject of heart-rending plays and movies. But though it occurs gradually for the majority of children, the revelation of meaning that comes with language is no less miraculous for the normal child than it was for Helen Keller.

In this lesson, you will learn just how significant that moment is when baby first says "Mama," or whatever word he or she first utters. Following its preadapted inclinations to make specific types of sounds, the baby is moving steadily in the direction of forming words, with representative speech not far behind. But though it is easy to understand how the mechanism of imitative learning may enable a child to copy the words it hears, how does it go about assigning meaning to them? And how does a child learn to decipher and understand the structure of a sentence? Are the rules of language innate and intuitive, or must we learn everything we know about speaking from our environment?

These are just a sampling of the questions we might ask about how children acquire language during the toddler period, which extends roughly from 12 to 30 months of age. In this lesson, you will follow the child through mastery of language and the transition from baby to child.

GOAL

The purpose of this lesson is to give you an understanding of how a toddler begins learning and using the main means of human communication – language.

LESSON OBJECTIVES

After reading the text assignment, completing the exercises in this telecourse guide, and viewing the lesson's video portion, you will be able to:

1. Describe the characteristics of a child's first words and sentences.

2. Indicate the conventions that toddlers must learn for combining words and the rules for everyday conversations, as well as those for learning specific words.

3. Discuss the developmental changes involved in learning the sound patterns of a language.

4. Summarize theories of how children learn the meaning of words.

5. Recognize the types of syntactic rules children learn during the preschool period and indicate how they are learned.

6. Compare behaviorist, nativist, and cognitive perspectives on language development.

VIEWING GUIDE

In this lesson, the children you have been studying begin gaining their voices. Around the time children begin toddling around 15 months or so, they begin forming their first words and enter a profoundly important phase of their development – that of acquiring language. After reading the text material and learning the important terms included there, you are ready to view the lesson's video portion. First, review the questions in the Self-Test at the end of this telecourse guide lesson to give you an idea of important points to watch for in the video. Then, read the following Points to Consider to give you an idea of what the video will cover. Keep these points in mind while watching.

Points to Consider

☐ *Early messages*: Learning to speak involves much more than being able to say "mama." Be aware of how the toddler's first words are but the introduction to a coherent system of communication rules and structures that the child must master. Notice the ways in which referential and expressive children learn different types of words.

☐ *Language parts*: To learn a language, the child must master an intricate system of rules and structures. Compare the text information about phonology, morphology, syntax, and semantics with what you hear toddlers saying in the video. Keep in mind the difference between *productive* and *receptive* skills as you study the developmental sequence of learning to speak.

☐ *Early language assignments*: In a sense, toddlers begin doing language "homework" long before they ever attend school. Watch the video for early examples of how babies communicate, and notice how the child is preadapted to learn to speak. Look for examples of how toddlers begin assigning specific meanings to words.

☐ *Nature versus nurture again*: Toddlers learn to speak within developmental contexts that are both biological and environmental. Pay attention to the different emphases on development that occur between *nativists* and *environmentalists*. In the video, look for examples which tend to support both positions.

☐ *Let's pretend*: From very early on, children begin learning ways other than words for representing the world and for communicating. Be aware of the cognitive skills that children are displaying and practicing as they pretend to operate cash registers and pump gas. Notice also the role played by the adult form of speech called "motherese" or child-directed speech.

UNDERSTANDING THE LESSON

Sir Thomas Browne, an English philosopher of the 17th century, thought that Hebrew was the original language of Adam and was native to humankind. In Sir Browne's conception, if you took an infant and raised it in total isolation, it would naturally speak Hebrew.

While Sir Browne's explanation of human speech as divine inspiration may seem naive today, his intuition about the miraculous nature of language still rings true. By the time a child is 5 or 6 years old, she or he has acquired a vocabulary of thousands of words and mastered a complex set of rules and conventions about her or his native language that are difficult and sophisticated. And yet the child does this without the benefit of grammar teachers, dictionaries, classes, or testing. The human "gift of tongues" is the toddler's great challenge.

The Nature of Early Language

Have you ever visited a foreign country whose language you didn't know? Perhaps you go to Japan for just a few days, thinking you can get by using a simple pocket dictionary. In a restaurant, you wish to go to the bathroom. Using your phrase book, you look up the word for bathroom – "otearai" – and ask the waitress for help. Later, wishing to buy some aspirin, you look up the word for pharmacy – "kursuri-ya." Again, with just a single word, you're able to get help. Later, back home, you tell your friends that you got around Japan by speaking Japanese "baby-talk."

The one-word sentences described above are similar to what we mean by early language. When a toddler first begins to speak, it uses single words to convey more meaning than what is covered by the word alone. As you learned in the text material, toddlers use single words as *holophrases*, meaning that they seem to be attempting to convey a variety of meanings with the limited vocabulary at their control. Like travelers in a land whose language they don't know how to speak, toddlers seem to be attempting to stretch a few simple words to cover a variety of meanings.

Children who use words to refer to objects and events are known as *referential children* and tend to have care givers who encourage them to ask questions. Referential children seem to learn mainly nouns, some verbs, and adjectives. *Expressive children*, on the other hand, tend to use words mainly to express social routines. These children tend to have care givers who use language to direct their children's behavior.

The next phase of early language occurs at around 18 to 24 months of age, when toddlers begin putting two words together. Although early word combinations are often just two ideas expressed together instead of true sentences, the child soon begins forming true, though compressed, two-word sentences. Toddler speech at this stage is very stripped down, and consists mainly of nouns, verbs, and adjectives. In fact, the bare, pronoun- and article-free sentences of children at this stage are called *telegraphic speech*. Just as telegrams drop unnecessary words to save space, children keep their sentences to the bare essentials. One possible reason they do this is because they do not yet have enough cognitive "room" to create full sentences or to appreciate subtle distinctions.

Key Terms

Holophrase
Telegraphic speech

Focusing Questions

1. When Jason, at 18 months, tries to pick up a kitten, it runs away from him. "Kitty, gone," Jason says. Four months later, when Jason sees the same kitten lying on a chair, he runs toward the cat and causes it to spring away. "Kitty gone!" the child says. Why might you interpret the child's two one-word utterances differently?

2. What is the probable reason that toddlers seem unable to use articles, conjunctions, and adjectives when they first begin forming sentences?

The Bare Bones of Language

In spite of the best efforts of a multi-billion dollar language-teaching industry worldwide, the best linguists and grammarians are not found in U.N. translation booths or the Berlitz Schools of Language – they are found in day care centers and on playgrounds around the world. Toddlers are the quickest studies of language anywhere. All languages consist of a number of agreed-upon conventions or rules that the child must learn. And though the specific rules of each language differ, they all share certain common characteristics.

Linguists divide language into four main parts, phonology, morphology, syntax, and semantics. Phonology is the study of the sounds of a language, and *phonemes* are the smallest units of sound that can change the meaning of the words within a language. Morphology is the study of the smallest meaningful units within a language, which are individually called *morphemes*. *Syntax* refers to the rules that govern how words are organized within a sentence, while *semantics* refers to the rules that govern just what the meaning of a language conveys. A child must begin grasping the basics of these four components of language in order to be able to communicate with others.

But the child must also master the general rules of conversation. One type of concern that shapes conversation is called *pragmatics*, which are the rules governing how people speak in different social contexts. According to the rules of pragmatics, you might brag to your best friend about how much money you made selling home-grown vegetables last year. Your comments on the same subject to the IRS, however, may well be quite different. Children learn very early, for instance, that their parents speak differently to one another than they do to, say, a traffic cop.

Toddlers also develop a pair of mental skills when learning their native language that might be compared to the mouthpiece and the earpiece of a telephone. That is, a child must develop both *productive* and *receptive* skills. A child's productive skills enable it to put ideas into words, whereas receptive skills enable it to understand the words of other people. Generally speaking, toddlers tend to understand somewhat more than they are able to convey as they learn their native tongue.

Key Terms

> Phonemes
> Morphemes
> Syntax
> Semantics
> Productive skills
> Receptive skills
> Sociolinguistics

Focusing Questions

1. Do all languages follow the same syntactical rules?

2. A 2-year-old girl is watching her 7-year-old brother play a video game with a friend. How might the explanations the boys share with one another differ from what they say to the little girl?

Major Tasks in Early Language Learning

Babies prepare to speak by going through four stages of vocalization. While at birth they can only cry to express discomfort, after about 10-12 weeks they begin cooing to express pleasure. This is followed by babbling, which in turn blends into *patterned speech* that begins to replicate the phonemes of the child's native language. This developmental sequence suggests that the child must first master the necessary motor skills to begin speaking, and then learn the phonemes of his or her native tongue, which in essence are the language's raw material.

Toddlers first begin saying a few words without really understanding their meanings. They begin learning new words gradually, then go into a surge of learning new words at about 18 months. As the child begins assigning specific meanings to the new words he or she is learning every day, he or she sometimes applies the wrong meaning to a word. Much more common, however, are errors of under- and overextension. Errors of *underextension* occur when the child applies a word to only a very small category – calling only the goldfish in a bowl "fish," for example. Errors of *overextension* occur when the child applies a name too widely – calling an airplane a "bird," for instance.

Children master the rules of morphology by first acquiring single morphemes – such words as dog, flower, swim, jump, and so on. Then, they gradually learn the rules governing grammatical morphemes, which are suffixes and prefixes that alter the meanings of the words they're added to – "-ing," for example. Developmentalists find the way children learn grammatical morphemes very interesting because it indicates how children learn the rules of language – such as that adding "-s" to a word indicates plurality. They must, of course, eventually learn to handle *overregularizations* – such as using men instead of mans.

As toddlers increase their vocabulary and use new words to communicate, they begin to understand that various words are used differently within sentences. In English, subjects tell "who," verbs tell "how," objects tell "what," and together they constitute the rough syntax of a sentence. As discussed in the text material, toddlers gradually master the forms of passive-voice sentences from about the age of 3 to 5, learning the rules of English syntax as they do so.

Toddlers also demonstrate their growing understanding of their native language by learning how to convert declarative sentences into yes or no questions, which occurs around age 3. Toddlers learn the rules governing the more complex "wh" questions by around the age of 4½, and by about 5 years old are beginning to form negative "wh" questions correctly.

Focusing Questions

1. What is one possible explanation for why young toddlers seem to be able to use some words without having any apparent understanding of their meaning?

2. Why do we say that acquiring the rules for grammatical morphology – such as the rule for indicating the plural of a noun by adding the suffix "-s" – gives the child great "language productivity?"

Learning Language from All Around

Developmentalists have long debated how it is possible for children to learn the complexities of their native language within such a short time. After all, there are no grammar teachers for toddlers, no Berlitz Schools for babies. According to the environmentalist school of thought, children learn to speak mainly through the examples and guidance of the people around them. This is the familiar viewpoint that "nurture" counts the most in a child's development. Others, however, say that biological factors are more important; that school of thought is called nativist. This parallels the "nature" side of the developmental debate. As in other areas of the nature versus nurture debate, children seem to acquire language skills through a combination of inborn capabilities and outside influences, assuming they are around an adult who can speak and will speak to them.

As you learned in Lesson 5, children do show preadaptations to attend to human speech. Furthermore, human language is a species-specific quality, meaning that all humans are predisposed genetically to learn to speak. Current research supports the idea that infants are born with certain strategies and constraints that enable them to learn to speak. These include, possibly, such things as predispositions to pay attention to significant parts of speech, such as stressed syllables and the beginnings and endings of words. A possible example of an inborn constraint on language-learning would be a predisposition to detect broad syntactic categories, such as nouns, verbs, subjects, objects, and so on and to recognize the way each category might behave.

As for factors in their surroundings that influence how toddlers acquire language, other people obviously are of great importance. For one thing, adults tend to simplify their speech when talking to toddlers, using the type of speech known as child directed speech (CDS), or motherese. CDS is grammatically simpler than ordinary speech, repetitive, and spoken in a higher than normal pitch. Adult females and males, as well as slightly older children, tend to follow variations of these forms when addressing toddlers. Research indicates that CDS has the greatest effect on younger toddlers.

Focusing Questions

1. Suppose you wish to raise children who are bilingual. Based on what you know about the biological or innate factors governing how humans learn a language, when would you want to begin teaching your child a second, or even a third, language?

2. Do most researchers believe that a child must hear child directed speech in order to properly learn its native language?

Other Ways Toddlers Learn to Use Representational Thought

In the video portion of this lesson, you saw several examples of toddlers playing house, pretending to drive cars, and acting out popular fantasies such as being Ninja Turtles. Although learning the rules of language is a major task of toddlerhood, words are not the only means that humans have of *representational thought*. Pretend play and the use of gesture are among the other ways that toddlers are beginning to create mental images of objects and concepts.

According to Piaget's theories, toddlers are beginning to form the ability to create symbols – to let a thought, word, object, or action stand for something else. Through symbolic thought and action, a child is able to manipulate things, thus creating new thoughts and words. Piaget thought that children don't develop true symbolic capability until they begin referring to objects and events which are not currently present. This usually occurs between 18 and 24 months of age.

The importance of pretend play in the development of a child's cognitive abilities is obvious from the great increase in time spent in pretend play that occurs between 14 and 19 months. Toddlers first play with replica objects, such as toy horses and cars, then around 24 months or so begin using substitute objects for play, such as using a rock to stand for a garage. Toddlers also demonstrate an ability to form more sophisticated concepts during pretend play with other children than they do alone.

Representational skills begin forming very early with the appearance of gesturing around 9 months, when babies begin pointing and whimpering when they want something. Social gestures such as waving bye-bye and nodding and shaking the head to signal "yes" and "no" appear between 9 and 12 months, and by 13 months, the baby is raising its arms and imploring to be picked up. A toddler's gestures at first increase in frequency, then decline from about 18 to 24 months. Since the decline of gesturing coincides with the child's spurt in vocabulary, some researchers suggest that language is replacing the child's use of gesturing for communication. Other research, however, suggests that gesturing and use of language develop along parallel lines and remain separate even after language has emerged.

Key Terms

Representational thought

Focusing Questions

1. A toddler sees a man approaching him on the sidewalk. The little boy stops and raises his hand, palm up, to the man, and seems to be waiting for something. "He wants you to 'give him five,'" says the boy's mother. How young might the child be?

2. Why does pretend play represent a significant leap in a toddler's ability to understand and adapt to the world?

Questions for Understanding

As you read these questions, often raised by parents, educators, and childcare providers, first try to answer the questions yourself. Then read the answer following each question and compare your response to it.

1. Our 18-month-old daughter spoke her first word about five months ago. At first, she seemed to learn only a few new words every day or so. Lately, however, she seems to be learning a new word every hour or so. Is this possible?

Children of your daughter's age do begin to suddenly learn new words much more quickly than previously. Children who are categorized as referential learners are more likely to experience this learning surge, and predominantly learn new nouns. Referential children have care givers who ask them many questions, encouraging the children to learn the names of things. Children whose care givers tend to use language to direct their behavior, on the other hand, use words mainly to express social routines, saying such phrases as "come here." These children are known as expressive learners. Both types of children learn grammar equally well.

By the way, by the time your daughter is about 3½ years old, she should be able to use about 1,200 words, and about 2,500 words by the time she is 6; this is known as the productive vocabulary. Children also have receptive vocabularies – consisting of words that they recognize – which are much larger than the productive vocabularies.

2. *My baby brother calls everything that has four legs and fur a doggie. He even calls my pet hamster a doggie! How come he does that?*

Your little brother is making a common error of toddlers who are learning to talk, called an overextension error. Because your brother has little experience of animals and doesn't yet possess the necessary concepts for organizing animals into different species, he uses the one word he now knows to identify all furry, four-legged creatures.

The other, related kind of mistakes that toddlers make at this stage are called underextension errors. A child makes these kind of errors when it restricts the meaning of a particular word too narrowly. For example, if your little brother thought that only your dog Maxxie was a doggie, and didn't recognize your neighbor's collie as a dog, he would be making an error of underextension. Notice, though, how much sense there is in both of these kinds of mistakes. Children are learning the rules of how words apply to the objects and actions they describe through a process of making mistakes like these.

3. *How do babies begin learning what words mean?*

One theory of how children learn language holds that they learn part of a word's meaning before they learn all of it. In the example above, the baby brother seems to think that every animal with four legs and fur is a dog. As he makes overextension mistakes and is corrected by others, he will begin to focus on the other specific traits that distinguish a dog.

Another theory proposes that children have a built-in tendency to assume that unfamiliar words refer to objects, features, relationships, or events for which they don't yet have labels. Called the *lexical contrast theory*, this idea suggests that children actively search for words when they realize there are gaps in their vocabulary.

4. *Does a child learn its first words in any special order?*

Yes. For one thing, a child first learns words that are single morphemes, such as Mama, Dadda, bird, kitty. The child next acquires grammatical morphemes, including suffixes, prefixes, and auxiliary verbs.

As the child learns grammatical morphemes, it first learns how to add "-s" to nouns to form plurals and how to add "-ing" to form the participial form of a verb. Next the child figures out how to add the suffix "-ed" to verbs to form their past tense, and how to form the third person singular by adding the suffix "-s" (as in "he drinks"). In the last stage of mastering grammatical morphemes, the child begins forming contractions of the verb "to be" (as in "you're smart").

One theory as to why children learn grammatical morphemes in this order supposes that the grammatically simplest forms are learned first. In other words, a child first learns to combine swim with "-ing" to form swimming because the second, participial form is close to the first, active form. Another theory proposes that the earliest learned forms are syntactically simple. That is, changing an active verb to its participial form by adding "-ing" merely adds the idea that action is ongoing, whereas adding an "-s" to form the third person singular introduces a variety of different ideas.

5. *Why do toddlers have trouble forming passive-voice sentences?*

Syntax refers to how the rules of a particular language create meaning within sentences by word order, and passive sentences are fairly sophisticated examples of how syntax operates. In a passive sentence, the subject receives the action rather than performing it – "The ball was thrown by me" is a passive sentence.

Children seem to have a hard time sorting out the rules for determining who is performing the action in a passive sentence. Early on, children apply semantic rules to decipher sentences; that is, they rely upon the meaning of the words to make sense of sentences. But around 4 years old, children are applying simple syntactic strategies to sentences. If the child has already mastered the simple English sentence structure of subject-verb-object, then he or she may have a hard time sorting out who is the actor and who is the acted-upon in a passive sentence.

In fact, as 4-year-olds pass through this transition period of learning the rules of syntax, they may misinterpret sentences that they previously understood. However, developmentalists consider these to be growth errors, errors caused by the appearance of more advanced thinking; by about the age of 5, most children are using the passive voice correctly.

6. *Both my husband and I change how we speak when talking to our 16-month-old daughter. But while I notice that I tend to ask Monica questions about what she is doing, her father asks her to tell him the names of things. He also uses harder words with her than I do. Which way of speaking will better help our daughter learn to speak?*

Actually, both ways of talking to your little girl are effective, and probably equally so. The way you've described talking to Monica is called motherese, and consists of questions about things mothers and children are doing together, just as you've mentioned. When you speak motherese to Monica, you also probably tend to repeat words, and speak in a high-pitched voice.

Your husband, on the other hand, is speaking a traditionally male version of child directed speech that calls for him to ask your daughter for more labels and explanations than you do, as well as for more clarifications. His tendency to use more sophisticated words with the little girl is another difference in how men speak motherese. While it's neither a better nor worse form of child directed speech, his form of speech is helping your daughter to strive for greater clarity in her speech, as well as preparing her for more complex conversational strategies.

7. *My 2-year-old has recently begun pretending all sorts of things, such as that he is a mail carrier or a checkout clerk. Should I discourage him from living in a fantasy world?*

Quite the contrary; you should be pleased that your son is making normal progress at developing effective strategies for understanding the world. Through pretend play, your son is learning how to use symbolic representation to make sense of the world. By taking on roles and behaviors in his imagination, he is learning about how people interact and rehearsing how he might behave in similar situations. Such symbolic behavior represents a great leap in your son's cognitive skills and shows that he is gaining other communication skills along with his growing language skills.

SELF-TEST

The following multiple choice and short answer test questions should help you measure your understanding of the points covered in the text and the video. After answering all the questions, check your answers against the key and use the accuracy of your answers to gauge how well you have met the lesson objectives.

Multiple Choice Questions

1. Nathan is 16 months old and tends to use phrases related to social actions, such as "shut door" and "drink milk." In other words, he uses what is called an expressive style of speaking. Of the following four children, Nathan is most likely

   a. an orphan who is being raised in foster care.
   b. the first-born child of a two-parent family with high income.
   c. the second-born child of a blue-collar family.
   d. the third-born child of a pair of college professors.

2. The first type of sentences that toddlers begin to make are called

   a. expressive.
   b. telegraphic.
   c. referential.
   d. grammatical.

3. Wilma is playing with her little girl Yvonne when the family's cat jumps up on a nearby chair. "Chair jump kitty," says Yvonne. The type of language mistake which Yvonne made is one of

   a. syntax.
   b. morphology.
   c. phonology.
   d. semantics.

4. Children would be learning pragmatic guides for conversation if they were

   a. always spoken to in commands or criticisms.
   b. told to tell phone salespersons that Mommy is busy with the baby and can't talk to them.
   c. only spoken to in motherese by adults.
   d. always answered, "What do you think it is?" when they asked, "What that?"

5. Before toddlers are able to begin saying words, they must gain physical control over their mouths, lips, tongues, and vocal cords. And although they are not aware of what they are doing, they must also be able to distinguish the parts of their particular language known as

   a. morphemes.
   b. holophrases.
   c. phonemes.
   d. syllables.

6. When she was 16 months old, Sylvia began saying "phone" every time her family's telephone rang. One day when her mother was visiting a friend, her mother rang a doorbell; Sylvia promptly said, "Phone." The little girl's comment about the doorbell is probably an example of

   a. a holophrase.
   b. underextension.
   c. lexical contrast.
   d. overextension.

7. By learning the basic rules of a language's syntax, a child becomes able to produce countless numbers of new

   a. sentences.
   b. words.
   c. questions.
   d. phrases.

8. Four children are showing you their artwork. Jason shows you a painting: "This horse was made by me." Caroline shows you a paper doll: "I cut out the dolly." Clay shows off his fingerpainting: "Me paint." Jaral shows you his pipecleaner doll: "I made it." Based on their level of understanding of syntax, which child do you think is most likely to be 5 years old?

   a. Jason
   b. Caroline
   c. Clay
   d. Jaral

9 According to the environmentalist theory of language development, most of what toddlers learn about talking comes from

   a. genetic factors that all children are born with.
   b. attention from their parents which conditions their understanding of words.

c.   increasing cognitive abilities as they mature.

d.   attention from their parents about the truthfulness of what they say.

10. As an adult, you might practice some of the characteristics of child directed speech if you were

a.   applying for a position at a day care center.
b.   pulled over for speeding by a traffic cop.
c.   trying to give street directions to a tourist who didn't speak English.
d.   trying to learn a foreign language.

Short Answer Questions

The following questions should be answered in a paragraph or two. You should identify several key points for each answer and use these to form the framework for your response.

1. When Elizabeth was about 20 months old, she began saying two words together most of the time instead of just one. Is Elizabeth speaking in real sentences, or is she just stringing words together? If they are sentences, what are some of their characteristics?

2. What are the four basic components of language that every child must master?

3. What types of questions must a child learn to create? In what sequence does a child learn to make questions?

10

Toddler Social and Emotional Development

LESSON ASSIGNMENT

Completing the following steps will help you master the lesson objectives and achieve the goal for this lesson:

STEP 1: Read the INTRODUCING THE LESSON section to provide a context for what you will learn in this lesson.

STEP 2: Read the lesson's GOAL and LESSON OBJECTIVES so that you will know what you are expected to learn.

STEP 3: Read the text assignment, Chapter 8, pages 272-292. Pay particular attention to the key terms and concepts in the Chapter Summary on page 297; they will help you when you watch the video.

STEP 4: Review the VIEWING GUIDE section in the telecourse guide. It lists several points to consider as you watch the video.

STEP 5: Watch the video.

STEP 6: Read the UNDERSTANDING THE LESSON section in the telecourse guide. Make sure you understand the key terms and can answer the focusing questions included there.

STEP 7: Complete the SELF-TEST.

STEP 8: Go back to the LESSON OBJECTIVES and make sure you can respond to each of them.

INTRODUCING THE LESSON

S ome typical scenes from a range of "toddler home videos":

Scene 1: In a supermarket aisle, a child squirms to be let down from his mother's arms. As soon as the woman places the boy on the floor, he dashes off, rocking from side to side. But as he reaches the corner and turns down the aisle of canned goods, he slows and looks back over his shoulder. "Is she following me?" the youngster seems to be wondering.

Scene 2: A man with a harried expression on his face hurries down a sidewalk pulling a little girl behind him by the hand. The child draws a deep breath and bellows, "Give me chockit now! Want it now!" then screams at the top of her lungs as she tries to jerk out of her father's grasp.

Scene 3: In a restaurant, a man and woman sit with two children. The younger child watches closely as her mother cuts a serving of chicken and vegetables into small pieces. "I eat it, Mama," the little girl says as the woman finishes, and spears a slice of carrot on the fork she holds like a sword in her fist. "Like this, Jeanna," says the little girl's older brother, demonstrating a lighter grip on his own fork. The parents smile at one another as they watch the serious look on their daughter's face as she studies her brother's actions and tries to match them.

From a playful bid for independence to the expression of rage at being thwarted to the rapt concentration required to learn how to hold a fork just so – such are the faces and phases of toddlers as they make the transition from infancy to childhood. Toddlers, who are mastering the new skills of walking and talking, are in many ways like someone who has just received a batch of dazzling new toys. They grab hold of their emerging capabilities and plunge into the world, eager to explore the limits of their new powers and insights, demonstrating surprising new attitudes as they do so.

From about the beginning of their first year to around age 5, toddlers are involved in learning how to relate socially with other people, and to handle a flood of new emotions. Along with their first steps, toddlers begin making their first moves toward self-reliance. This begins with the rudimentary development of self, and the dawning realization that others – at first, particularly mother – exist separately from them. And as the child begins to stand on its own without Mom's help, increasingly the child encounters rules, standards, and values. "No" is a word that toddlers soon get used to hearing and using.

With this lesson, the dependent, largely pliant infants of your studies so far begin standing on their own and assuming even more distinctively individual personalities. Toddlerhood is the developmental stage at which personality clearly emerges. As the infant's physical and cognitive abilities continue to improve, the child begins to feel greater urges toward autonomy and is impelled by the urge to "do it myself." Now the child is confronted with pressures toward "socialization" in the form of the rules, standards, and conventions that govern its particular culture. At the same time, the child struggles to maintain the stable and secure relationship it has formed with its care givers.

Toddlerhood is a dynamic time of growing independence and increasing social restraints. Like a row of books held up between the opposing pressures of bookends, the child's personality takes shape between the sometimes conflicting requirements of self-autonomy and socialization.

GOAL

The purpose of this lesson is to show you how the toddler becomes an "I," discovers who others are, and begins practicing the rules for a lifetime of social behavior.

LESSON OBJECTIVES

After reading the text assignment, completing the exercises in this telecourse guide, and viewing the lesson's video portion, you will be able to:

1. Compare the social and emotional capacity of infants and toddlers.

2. Recognize toddlers' need for autonomy and their sociability toward same-age children.

3. Explain the role of care givers in facilitating toddlers' social/emotional/ cognitive growth.

4. Describe how toddlers adopt parental rules and values as part of the process of socialization.

5. Explain how a strong attachment relationship with the care giver can help a toddler reconcile his/her needs for closeness and security with the need to strive toward independence.

VIEWING GUIDE

In this lesson, you examine the processes leading up to the moment when a child can truly say, "I am." During the years of toddlerhood, children must strike a balance between the need to separate from their parents and the need to maintain closeness with them. The time when a toddler agrees to do what a parent wants – without a battle – is an important event. After reading the text material and learning the important terms included there, you are ready to view the lesson's video portion. First, review the questions in the Self-Test at the end of this telecourse guide lesson to give you an idea of important points to watch for in the video. Then read the following Points to Consider to give you an idea of what the video will cover. Keep these points in mind while watching.

Points to Consider

☐ *Socialization from two angles:* One important task of toddlers is to begin learning the rules and values of their culture. Notice how, over the years, society's views have changed on how children should be socialized. Be aware, in particular, of how earlier views of the child as a reluctant member of society have evolved into today's more open attitudes.

☐ *A toddler's many tasks*: During their transition from infants into children, toddlers accomplish several important developmental tasks. Look for examples of the kind of communication between children and care givers known as affective sharing, and be aware of how it illustrates the toddler's move toward sociability. Be aware of the important cognitive steps represented in the toddler's development of a sense of self and an understanding of the separateness of others.

☐ *Keeping up with the whirlwind*: As toddlers explore the limits of their new capabilities, parents face a series of challenges. Focus on the reasons developmentalists stress the need for parents to impose clear and consistent limits on their toddlers. Look for examples of how fathers interact with their children differently from mothers at this stage.

☐ *Every toddler an individual*: As the toddler develops an awareness of "me," he or she is laying down the foundations of personality. As you watch the video portion of the lesson, keep an eye open for examples of how toddlers differ and how differences in attachment are related to children's reactions to the cognitive, social, and emotional challenges of this period.

UNDERSTANDING THE LESSON

The writers of Warner Brothers cartoons must have been parents of young children. Who else could have been inspired to create the Tasmanian Devil, that whirling, jabbering, gesticulating bundle of energy that pursues Bugs Bunny in several cartoons? With his rampant emotions, inquisitiveness, and urge to test the limits, the Tasmanian Devil is a recognizable caricature of the average healthy toddler.

And like the Tasmanian Devil, toddlers must learn to comply with certain rules of behavior. Luckily, toddlers are better prepared for their developmental tasks than any animated figure. The boundless energy and curiosity of toddlers is necessary for the many developmental challenges facing them: becoming self-aware and self-reliant, learning the rules that govern their culture, discovering that other people have separate existences. They also need to begin to make sense of their world and to grasp cause-effect relationships in human behavior and in the world of objects. To accomplish all the cognitive, social, and emotional developments that they will encounter during this stage, toddlers need the energy and enthusiasm of a Tasmanian Devil, and then some.

Socialization: An Inside or an Outside Job?

As the toddler begins moving about with greater agility and regularly "getting into things," parents begin teaching the child the rules of proper behavior of their particular culture. This process, known as *socialization*, is a major developmental task of the toddler. Traditionally, developmentalists have thought of these cultural standards as something that parents and other adults had to impose upon the child from the outside. More recently, however, many experts have moved toward the position that children naturally wish to fall into step with the wishes of their care givers, and hold that socialization largely occurs from within the child as a natural development. It is likely that socialization is a combination of inside and outside influences.

The view of imposing social norms from without was influenced by the theories of Sigmund Freud. In his early work, Freud wrote that babies were a raw bundle of unrestrained biological urges and desires and, as such, required strict control by parents. By blocking children's biological desires through rules and control, the children would redirect their energies toward socially acceptable goals – a process known as sublimation. Because young children wish to maintain the love and closeness of their parents, Freud theorized, they allow their natural urges to be channeled by parental demands. Social learning theorists would later adopt portions of these views for their own theories, suggesting a tendency for children to seek approval and positive reinforcement while avoiding disapproval.

Recently, however, more researchers tend to support the idea that children become socialized as a result of natural inclinations that arise from within them. According to this point of view, because children are raised from birth within a social context, they wish to maintain the harmonious relations with their care givers as they mature. Thus, even when the child begins wanting to do things in conflict with what his or her parent wishes, the child is still going to feel a natural desire to please the parent and will have to learn to deal with the competing impulses in such situations. Current research, in fact, tends to support this theory, at least when the child has received consistently responsive care from care givers. As always, though, the particular reaction of any child to a developmental phase depends greatly upon the context, the situation, and the cumulative effects of prior experiences.

Key Terms

Socialization

Focusing Question

1. According to social learning theory, children learn behavior patterns based on positive versus negative reinforcement. How does this compare with current theories on how children respond to the pressures and processes of socialization?

Major Developments in the Toddler Period

As the very term toddler implies, children at this age are taking their first steps away from their mothers and other care givers. As the toddler relies less and less on physical contact with the mother, he or she increasingly practices forms of psychological contact. Toddlers typically draw the attention of their care givers to the objects they discover, and consistently try to share their pleasures and excitement with their care givers. Known as *affective sharing*, these new behaviors indicate that the child is developing an awareness that other people have points of view different from their own, and that they are becoming able to foresee the reactions of others.

Toddlers are also developing the ability to interpret new situations according to the expression on a care giver's face or by their tone of voice. *Social referencing*, as this developing skill is called, enables the child to benefit vicariously from the greater experience and understanding of its care givers. It also illustrates another of the psychological cues which bind toddlers to care givers.

Another sign of the outward shift of a toddler's focus is the increased interest they show in interacting with other young children. Young toddlers are capable of reacting to one another's actions, and play games which tend to center on objects. As the toddler grows, he or she begins to show preferences for known playmates, and to form the concept of friendship.

Like scientists with new laboratory facilities, toddlers are great experimenters, actively exploring the limits of both their growing capabilities and of the rules imposed by care givers. This pleasure in discovery is fueled by the child's growing sense of self. But though toddlers do rely on others outside their immediate circle to help them through challenging situations, at this stage they still look almost exclusively to care givers for help, rather than to their peers.

As you saw demonstrated in the video portion of the lesson, when children are about 18 months old they begin to notice a dot painted on their forehead while looking in a mirror. When a particular child first develops the awareness of self as indicated by the mirror-image test is closely related to general cognitive development. Children who can recognize themselves in a mirror begin showing embarrassment for the first time, a clear sign of the beginnings of awareness. And finally, toddlers add the word "I" to their vocabularies and begin expressing strong desires to do things themselves. This distinct urge to be self-sufficient, even when not appropriate, is one strong reason for the designation of this period as "the terrible twos." But rather than being a sign of how headstrong or "bad" a child is, the stubbornness and negativity of toddlers is just one more indication of their emerging individuality.

As the toddler develops a sense of the self as separate and self reliant, he or she is also gaining a more sophisticated understanding of other people. At about 1 year old, children are aware that others can do things which the child cannot, but they do not yet understand that other people are independent agents. The toddler next develops an awareness that other people are separate, but still is unclear about how his or her intentions are separate from the other person's. By the end of their second year toddlers are showing that they have a clear understanding of the distinctions between themselves and others, as shown in the video by the skill with which they now play hide-and-seek.

Key Terms

Affective sharing
Social referencing

Focusing Questions

1. What are some of the cognitive advances that a toddler demonstrates through the urge to share emotional experiences?

2. What are some of the behaviors which young toddlers display while playing hide-and-seek that indicate their incomplete grasp of

the separateness of people? Why do we say that being able to play a game of hide-and-seek "by the rules" indicates that a child has mastered the differences between him- or herself and the other players?

3. Is the phrase "the terrible twos" an overly negative holdover from earlier theories of how children react to socialization? What kinds of behavior does it refer to?

Parent-Toddler Relations

When young Randall took his first tottering steps, his mother stood right beside him, her hand ready to shoot out and steady her son should he start to fall. Six months later, however, when Randall slips and lands on his bottom while playing across the room from his mother, she just glances to see that he isn't hurt, smiles, and says "Whoopsy-daisy." As if reassured by his mother's confidence, Randall pushes himself to his feet and returns to his pile of blocks.

Randall's mother is practicing the kind of parental adaptation to a toddler's changing capacities known as *scaffolding*. When a construction crew erects a network of boards, poles, and ropes around a building as it rises, they also dissemble the scaffolding as the structure takes shape. In similar fashion, care givers adjust their help and availability to their growing toddler to accommodate the child's developing abilities. At the same time, care givers provide children with firm and consistent limits on what they are allowed to do, giving them a sense of security while they explore their own capabilities. As you'll recall from Lesson 7, this type of consistent guidance is one hallmark of the sensitive care giver.

During toddlerhood, fathers typically spend more time interacting directly with their children than they did when the children were babies. The attention which fathers give their children tends to be more playful than that of mothers, who are generally more nurturing. These differences have been found in both Western and non-Western cultures, as well as among primates. Apparently, the more playful approach of fathers is well suited to the outgoing, playful style of children at this stage. Furthermore, according to some researchers, the increased time which the father spends with his child at this age may enable the child to more easily separate psychologically from the mother – an important developmental step of this period.

Key Words

Scaffolding

Focusing Questions

1. What are some reasons parents shouldn't be greatly concerned if their child seems to be slow about weaning or toilet training?

2. Why is it important that parents respond sensibly even to their young child's nonsensical vocalizations?

Individual Adaptations

In the Dr. Doolittle books about a doctor who could speak the language of animals, there was a llama with two heads, one on each end of its body. Known as a "Push-Me, Pull-You," the problem with the poor llama was that it didn't have a clear sense of which of its heads was in charge; someone had to push one end or pull the other for the creature to get anywhere.

As the toddler develops an increasing sense of being separate from its care givers – in particular from its mother – it faces a challenge similar to that of the Push-Me, Pull-You. For the infant, there are no clear boundaries between itself and its principal care givers. The process by which the child gradually distinguishes him- or herself from all others is called *separation-individuation*, as you learned in the text material.

Beginning at about 3 months, the baby first recognizes its care givers and begins to distinguish them from unfamiliar people. Later, as it enters the attachment stage, the child is able to signal its own needs and to coordinate its behavior with that of the care giver. Then, toward the end of the child's second half-year, it begins to distinguish the mother as an object separate from the child's direct control. Finally, out of this stage the child develops an awareness of being a separate individual from the mother.

How well toddlers move through the process of separation-individuation from their care givers depends a great deal upon the type of attachment they have formed. Securely attached children are likely to have the assurance that the closeness they have with their parent can be re-established even though they are compelled to increasingly establish their own autonomy. In other words, the nature of this stage of development grows from the foundation of earlier ones.

You saw supporting evidence for the importance of attachment to the child's ability to function autonomously in the video scenes of the experiment based on retrieving candy from a Plexiglass box. As indicated in these and other research findings, mothers who are responsive to their children as infants are likely to support the children's bids for autonomy during toddlerhood.

Other factors affecting how toddlers meet the challenges of becoming autonomous are their individual temperaments which, as you'll recall from Chapter 6, become clear from around the end of the first year. Whether a particular child has shown a markedly amiable or "difficult" personality so far, he or she will continue to act even more so as a toddler. The overall context of the child's family also affects the development of autonomy, by controlling the quality of care which the child receives. The developmental history of the parents can also have a strong impact on parent-child interactions at this stage. In Lesson 11, we will examine the effects that a negative parental developmental history may have on children, and study the dynamics of abusive parent-child relationships.

Key Terms

Separation-individuation

Focusing Questions

1. In what ways does having a sense of trust that his or her parents will continue to provide responsive care encourage the child to move confidently toward autonomy?

2. In the video scenes showing toddlers trying to retrieve a piece of candy from a Plexiglass box, what were some of the interactions between mothers and children who exhibited forms of anxious attachment?

Questions for Understanding

As you read these questions, often raised by parents, educators, and other childcare providers, first try to answer the questions yourself. Then read the answer following each question and compare your response to it.

1. *I was dreading the moment my son entered the "terrible twos." But now that he's 2½, I find him a delight. He's inquisitive, but when I call him back from going too far, he usually listens to me. He also doesn't put up much of a fuss when I leave him, like he used to do when he was a baby. Am I just lucky, or am I doing something right?*

   Probably a little bit of both. Your son's behavior sounds typical of toddlers who have made secure attachments with their care givers and feel assured that their needs will continue to be adequately met. Accordingly, as they enter toddlerhood and begin feeling urges to explore their surroundings and to test the limits of parental restraints, they start from a secure base. Your son, who is now able to talk and thus communicate across distance, feels comfortable separating himself from you and thus developing his independence.

   One reason he seems less anxious when you leave now than when he was a baby is because of his sense that you will re-establish your responsiveness to his needs upon your return. Also, with his improved cognitive abilities and communication skills, he is now able to at least partly understand your reassurances when you leave him.

2. *We all know what it means for countries or political bodies to want autonomy. According to a book I read, my 18-month-old should be striving now to establish her own "autonomy." How does this term apply to young children?*

   By a desire for autonomy, child developmentalists mean that toddlers, who are becoming increasingly skilled at talking, moving around, and dealing with others, wish to practice their new abilities independently as much as possible. Because as a baby your daughter was so completely dependent upon you, now she must separate herself from you in order to gain full benefit from her new emotional and social skills. When the books say that toddlers wish to be autonomous, it just means that they naturally desire to practice their growing powers of self-reliance, not that they wish to break away from you completely.

3. *What is the earliest age at which children begin to have a conception of the self?*

   Generally speaking, toddlers have acquired a basic sense of the self by the age of 24 months. That is, during play, children of this age give plain evidence of being able to distinguish themselves and others as independent agents. Also, most children begin referring to themselves as "I" at about this time.

As for when toddlers first begin to form an awareness of themselves, that is a little harder to say. In an experiment which placed a colored dot on a child's forehead before the child was placed in front of a mirror, it was assumed that children who touched their foreheads with a hand were demonstrating a rudimentary sense of self. In other words, the children recognized themselves in the reflection, noticed the dot as being on their own foreheads, and so reached up to touch it. In one study, three-quarters of the children between the ages of 21 and 24 months touched their own faces. Of children between the ages of 15 and 18 months, only one-quarter touched the dot; below the age of 12 months, none of the children touched their own foreheads.

4. *When I take my 18-month-old to a nearby park, he doesn't play on the sculptured climbing "mountain" that's supposed to be for toddlers. But when my husband takes him, he says that our son plays on it. Why is this?*

One possible reason could be that seeing your son play on this device makes you nervous, which you show by your facial expression. If you frowned and bit your lip while your son explored the sculpture, for example, he might notice your reaction and be affected by your concern. If your husband, on the other hand, reacted more calmly, your son might interpret this calmness as approval. This ability to "read" the facial cues of another person and be guided by their reaction is called social referencing, and it develops when children are about 1 year old.

5. *My son is 16 months old. When will he start to form friendships?*

By now, your son is probably beginning to play with other children in a complementary fashion. In other words, he and another child can play games that follow roughly the same theme. Games like this usually develop between two toddlers when one of them performs an action and the other one imitates it, and they repeat the action back and forth. Children of your son's age also tend to focus on objects such as blocks, balls, dolls, and other toys when they play.

But while your son is old enough to distinguish between several other children, he isn't yet ready to form a friendship. He should be able to begin forming clear preferences among playmates within the next six months or so, and within the year after that will begin learning the concept of "friend" and making other cognitive and emotional advances. For example, over the next year or so you can expect to see your son demonstrating that he is beginning to understand that other children have rights and wishes all their own.

6. *Why do developmentalists stress the need for children to be socialized during the toddler period?*

During the toddler period, the child is becoming much more capable and mobile. It begins to walk, as well as to speak. At the same time, at least in North American society, it is weaned from the bottle and breast and will soon begin toilet training. The toddler is also naturally becoming more social, and feels a great interest in meeting other children and exploring interactively with them. As the toddler increasingly goes off on its own, getting into things and learning to play with others, parents are compelled to begin establishing rules for the child to follow, to set limits. These rules and limits, generally, are ones that are commonly shared by our culture: a child shouldn't grab a toy from another child's hand, for example, and the child can't have ice cream or candy whenever it desires. Through setting clear, firm, and consistent rules regarding what kinds of behavior are and aren't acceptable, parents are helping the child move toward greater self-reliance, as well as to learn the particular rules and values of its society.

SELF-TEST

The following multiple choice and short answer test questions should help you assess your understanding of the points covered in the text and the video. After answering all the questions, check your answers against the key and use the accuracy of your answers to gauge how well you have met the lesson objectives.

Multiple Choice Questions

1. In a booklet called "Infant Care" published by the U.S. Department of Labor's Children's Bureau in 1914, mothers were told that babies are born with strong and dangerous impulses and would "rebel fiercely" when these impulses were thwarted. How does today's research relate to this philosophy?

   a. Parents now expect children to learn proper behavior mainly by the good examples of other people.
   b. Today's parents capitalize on children's natural desires to please their parents.
   c. Today's research shows that parents should punish children for "bad" behavior and reward them for "good."
   d. Today's research considers negative behavior an indicator of problems between the parents and the child.

2. If you place a colored dot on the forehead of children aged 12 months, 18 months, and 24 months and placed each child in front of a mirror, you would most likely expect

   a. all three children to touch the dot.
   b. only the 24-month-old to touch the dot.
   c. perhaps both older children to touch the dot.
   d. none of the children to touch the dot.

3. You are a worker in a day care center in charge of Jane, age 16 months; Karen, age 18 months; Sam, age 24 months; and Amy, age 30 months. When playing hide-and-seek with your charges, you find that one child consistently runs away from you as you get closer to its hiding place. That child is most likely to be

   a. Jane.
   b. Karen.
   c. Sam.
   d. Amy.

4. Kevin and Melinda are both 20 months old. They spend time together one afternoon while their mothers meet to go over the books for their catering business. When the mothers look in on them, the children are most likely to be

   a. playing pretend "house."
   b. stacking and pushing over blocks.
   c. playing independently.
   d. sharing a box of crayons to draw pictures.

5. When Kevin and Melinda (question 4) first meet, their mothers put them together in Kevin's bedroom. Melinda looks around, sees a two-foot-high, fuzzy green dragon. Seeing what her daughter is looking at, Melinda's mother smiles, and says, "Ah, what a cute monster." Melinda then walks over to the doll and reaches out to it. This interaction between mother and daughter is an example of

   a. scaffolding.
   b. affective sharing.
   c. autonomy.
   d. social referencing.

6. When a child developmentalist says that one task of the toddler is to establish autonomy, the developmentalist means that toddlers

   a. naturally resist doing what their parents want.
   b. are naturally compelled to practice self-reliance.
   c. must break free of the restrictions imposed by their parents.
   d. will benefit from having limits that constantly change.

7. The different ways in which fathers tend to interact with their children during toddlerhood in comparison with how mothers interact

   a. reflect the dominance of males in our culture.
   b. generally take up about the same amount of time.
   c. may help the child separate psychologically from the mother.
   d. indicate that men are less capable of nurturing than women.

8. As toddlers become more mobile and their improving cognitive skills encourage them to become more independent of their parents, they tend to fear losing the closeness they have established with their parents. The tension that results from this conflict, however, will be least for children who

   a. are securely attached.
   b. are anxious-avoidant attached.
   c. are anxious-resistant attached.
   d. are given firm limits.

9. According to *People* magazine, *The National Enquirer*, and other popular sources, Prince Charles of England is not very involved in his children's upbringing. He is said to be aloof and emotionally unresponsive to the two young princes, William and Harry. Supposing this is so, and presuming that the two boys form insecure attachments with their father, probably the ways they will treat their own children

   a. will be much the same.

b. depends on the full context of their emotional relationships.
c. will probably not be affected.
d. is impossible to predict.

10. By the term separation-individuation, the developmentalist Margaret Mahler meant

a. to suggest that children are socialized mainly because of internal impulses.
b. the overall process by which toddlers become independent, self-aware individuals.
c. to describe the moment at which toddlers first begin to say "I."
d. the urge that toddlers feel to practice autonomy

Short Answer Questions

The following questions should be answered in a paragraph or two. You should identify several key points for each answer and use these to form the framework for your response.

1. What are the differences between the processes of socialization from the outside and socialization from the inside?

2. Why is the term "the terrible twos" not a very accurate way to describe toddlerhood?

3. What are some of the behaviors that indicate toddlers are becoming more sociable?

11

Abuse and Neglect
of Children

LESSON ASSIGNMENT

Completing the following steps will help you master the lesson objectives and achieve the goal for this lesson:

STEP 1: Read the INTRODUCING THE LESSON section to provide a context for what you will learn in this lesson.

STEP 2: Read the lesson's GOAL and LESSON OBJECTIVES so that you will know what you are expected to learn.

STEP 3: Read the text assignment, Chapter 8, pages 286-300. Pay particular attention to the key terms and concepts in the Chapter Summary on pages 297-300; they will help you when you watch the video.

STEP 4: Review the VIEWING GUIDE section in the telecourse guide. It lists several points to consider as you watch the video.

STEP 5: Watch the video.

STEP 6: Read the UNDERSTANDING THE LESSON section in the telecourse guide. Make sure you understand the key terms and can answer the focusing questions included there.

STEP 7: Complete the SELF-TEST.

STEP 8: Go back to the LESSON OBJECTIVES and make sure you can respond to each of them.

INTRODUCING THE LESSON

The topic is a common theme of newspaper headlines: "Newborn baby found stuffed in garbage can . . . Mother of burned 3-year-old arrested . . . Stepfather found guilty in death of toddler."

At school, a kindergarten teacher sees the shirt ride up on the back of a withdrawn little boy, and notices a row of long, thick scabs. When the teacher asks him how he hurt himself, the child drops his head and mutters something the teacher can't hear.

In Santa Cruz, California, police answering a complaint about a domestic disturbance look through a window and see several potted marijuana plants. When they enter the dwelling, they find piles of rotting garbage, food, and unwashed dishes – and three sisters aged 2, 4, and 6 who are malnourished and don't know how to speak. The police had been called to the apartment by neighbors who reported that beatings in the home were making the pictures on their walls rattle.

Every year, thousands of children in this country suffer from child abuse. The injuries they suffer range all the way from "just" bruises to fractured skulls. Children are regularly burned, beaten, raped, and kicked by people responsible for their care. And for a number of reasons, including their lack of experience, physical vulnerability, and tendency to "misbehave," the majority of these children are toddlers. Tragically, abuse and maltreatment are among the possible contexts which may shape a toddler's development.

In previous lessons, you have learned how adults are seemingly prepared biologically to respond to the helplessness of infants. Think of the urge you have to lean down close to an infant's face and talk in high-pitched baby talk, for instance. Similarly, infants are born with pre-adaptations which are apparently intended to encourage interaction between them and care givers and to stimulate supportive attachments. How then is it possible for development to go so far off track that a mother would burn her own child with an iron, or starve it, or shake it until it suffers brain damage? Is child abuse a result of adults' mental illness, or are care givers who abuse or neglect their children simply "bad" people?

This lesson explores some of the darker possibilities that may influence a toddler's development. If a toddler's mother was herself abused, if the mother has no one to help her raise the child or if she can't pay the rent or buy food, if either parent suffers from a debilitating depression – all of these may contribute to a situation of child abuse or neglect.

When a sprouting seed sends its roots down into stony, parched, or toxic soil, the resulting plant may be stunted or deformed – it may even die. Similarly, children who are abused may develop along sadly warped lines. In the text material and the video portion of the lesson, you will see how the toddler adapts to the experience of an abusive context, perhaps becoming a potential future abusive parent him- or herself.

GOAL

The purpose of this lesson is to give you a general understanding of the causes, extent, and dynamics of child abuse and neglect, particularly among toddlers, as well as some ideas for how it might be prevented or remedied.

LESSON OBJECTIVES

After reading the text assignment, completing the exercises in this telecourse guide, and viewing the lesson's video portion, you will be able to:

1. Describe the parental characteristics, child characteristics, and contextual factors that may influence the child/care giver relationship.

2. Recognize the broad range and incidence of behaviors that characterize child abuse and neglect.

3. Indicate why toddlers are particularly vulnerable to abuse.

4. Relate the consequences of child abuse or neglect to the particular form of mistreatment.

5. Summarize research related to the causes of child abuse.

6. Discuss intervention approaches that have been successful in diminishing the incidence of child abuse and neglect.

VIEWING GUIDE

This lesson takes up the topic of what happens when child care becomes child abuse. While the majority of children are born into families which want them and do their best to raise them in healthful and supportive environments, some children enter abusive situations. After reading the text material and learning the important terms included there, you are ready to view the lesson's video portion. First, review the questions in the Self-Test at the end of this telecourse guide lesson to give you an idea of important points to watch for in the video. Then, read the following Points to Consider to give you an idea of what the video will cover. Keep these points in mind while watching.

Points to Consider

☐ *Unhappy attachments*: Previous lessons have established the importance of attachment in the framework of a child's development. In the video section of this lesson, look for examples of disorganized-disoriented attachment. Notice how toddlers perceived as "difficult" may become caught in negative cycles of parental discipline.

☐ *Abuse in context*: Like all other types of relationships, abusive ones occur within specific, unique contexts. Be aware of the larger environments in which child abuse takes place, including the economic, social, cultural, and past developmental. Listen for comments from people in the video that help to explain specific cases of maltreatment.

☐ *An epidemic of abuse*: While children are abused at every age, most are under the age of 3. Try to discover the reasons why young children are most prone to maltreatment. Take special note of the various effects that different types of abuse have on children. Pay attention to the various theories which have been put forth to explain abusive relationships, and see if there are any special characteristics that generally define abusive parents.

☐ *Hopes for change*: In spite of the disheartening nature of the subject of child abuse, the results of current studies do offer hope for both prevention and intervention. Look for indicators of potentially abusive parents and be aware of how identifying such individuals may suggest ways they can be helped.

UNDERSTANDING THE LESSON

Children probably have always been maltreated among human societies. Even quite recently, so-called primitive cultures have practiced infanticide as a means of population control. In Biblical times, the Ammonites and Phoenicians are said to have tossed live children onto the flaming altars of the god Moloch as sacrifices. During the early years of the Industrial Revolution, children as young as 7 years old were employed in coal mines and cotton mills.

In modern societies, however, we can hardly justify the pain and terror of our abused children on ecological, religious, or economic grounds. Children are abused today as a result of a combination of such factors as poverty, stress on care givers, parental history, poor education, and social isolation. In the palette of colors that compose the picture of child development, child abuse makes up the darker hues – and toddlers are the most frequent victims.

Parents and Toddlers

As the child encounters the exciting but complex challenges of the toddler years, the ease and skill with which it moves through these developmental phases depends greatly upon its relationships with care givers. As you have already seen, the quality of children's attachments affect how they handle such milestones of the period as learning to talk, becoming self aware, and beginning to interact with others. In Lessons 9 and 10, you saw many examples of how secure toddler-parent attachments help provide the necessary basis for the child to continue developing toward self-sufficiency.

Unfortunately, parent-child relationships do not always unfold in a constructive manner. For a variety of reasons, care givers are sometimes abusive or neglectful of toddlers, creating developmental problems of varying types and degrees. As mentioned in Chapter 6, one recent researcher has even developed a specific category of anxious-attachment for infants who have been abused, referred to as disorganized-disoriented attachment. During encounters with strangers, these infants exhibited maladaptive behaviors such as becoming motionless or slow moving and appeared dazed or disoriented. Other researchers have found a relationship between avoidant attachment and physical abuse.

If an infant has already formed maladaptive behaviors as a result of abuse or neglect, then probably it will continue to practice them as a toddler. Sadly, maladaptive behavior such as lethargy or confusion can be interpreted by the care giver as "dumbness" or "not minding," setting the stage for further abuse. As pointed out in the text material, the very need that some toddlers have at this stage for more support and sensitive care may prevent them from getting what they need from their care givers.

Particularly at risk are such children as those who have been born with physical or cognitive handicaps, and especially those born to drug-abusing mothers. As they become toddlers, the traits that these children exhibited as babies, such as lethargy and irritability, tend to become more pronounced. If their care givers perceive these children as "difficult," the potential is particularly real for abusive behavior.

Focusing Questions

1. What are some of the attachment behaviors which you might expect an abused infant to show as a toddler?

2. In what ways might the distinctive styles of behavior which toddlers exhibit contribute to abusive behavior from their care givers?

The Family Context

Three-year-old Sarah clutches her Care Bear and hunkers down between her bed and the wall. A few minutes ago, the yelling between her mother and her mother's boyfriend had climbed to a crescendo, then been cut off by the sound of a slap and a thud. A door slammed and car tires squealed away; now the sound of her mother's weeping and cursing drifts down the hallway from the kitchen to the little girl. "Shh, Mr. Bear," the child cautions her toy. "Be quiet, or Momma spank."

As you saw in the video portion of this lesson, the relationship which develops between a parent and child takes place within larger webs of relationships, all of which affect how parents behave toward their children. During times of stress, parents may have less patience or emotional resources with which to handle the needs of toddlers. Poverty, unemployment, lack of education, and poor medical care are among the social and economic stresses that parents encounter. Single mothers are particularly hard pressed during times of stress to handle the demands of young children. Studies have shown that women who are involved in supportive relationships are better able to respond affectionately toward their child.

The parents' own developmental history also helps shape the quality of child-parent interactions. Women who had abusive childhoods are at particular risk of being abusive mothers, for example. June, the abusive mother profiled in the video, was herself an abused child. She is also divorced and unemployed, which are additional stressful factors. According to the theories of Bowlby and others, a mother who had an unsatisfactory early history is unable to form positive images of parent-child nurturing and feels unworthy of care herself. This is another example of the potential that exists for negative cycles of behavior to develop between parents and children.

A history of abuse, however, does not guarantee that a woman will herself be an abusive mother. While previous stages of development do affect later ones, the current context also always plays a part. In one study, researchers found mothers who had themselves been maltreated as children were able to overcome their backgrounds and interact positively with their own children. These women had all formed a stable, supportive relationship with some adult during childhood and were currently involved in a stable partnership. In addition, many of them had been involved in extensive therapy. The important lesson here, obviously, is that the negative cycle of abusive behavior can be broken.

Focusing Questions

1. In what ways might being in a positive relationship help a low-income mother cope with the stresses of poverty?

2. Will children who have been abused always make less effective parents than people who had "happy" childhoods?

Parental Abuse and Neglect

The enthusiasm, energy, and assertiveness of toddlers makes them especially beguiling to adults. These same characteristics, on the other hand, can also make toddlers an overwhelming burden to overstressed, inadequately prepared parents. The old Biblical warning to "spare the rod and spoil the child" is sometimes too literally interpreted by well-meaning parents who feel that physical punishment is necessary to produce a well-behaved child. Children below the age of 3 are at the greatest risk of abuse or neglect.

A number of categories fall under the general label of abuse or neglect. Maltreatment covers a multitude of behaviors, including the physical fact of not meeting the child's needs for food, warmth, cleanliness, and so on. Neglected children often suffer severe health problems and have trouble dealing with the world of objects. Children who are physically abused, on the other hand, often have behavioral and emotional problems and lack social sensitivity and empathy. And if the child's parents are depressed and withhold all emotions from the child, they may become apathetic and lose any ability to experience joy or pleasure. Children who have been sexually abused may later experience anxiety, dissociation, and psychopathology.

While early investigations into child abuse sought specific child behaviors that might have contributed to abuse, little linkage was found. An ill or "difficult" child may add to the stresses of a family, increasing the chances of abuse, but in that case it is the overall stress of the family's situation that causes the abuse, not something in the child's nature. Neither is mental illness a common contributing factor among abusing parents; only one in ten abusing parents is thought to be emotionally disturbed. In one study of abusive mothers, researchers found an inability to cope well with the doubts and stresses of a first pregnancy, plus little understanding of what caring for a baby required. Partly as a result, these women had a negative and fearful view of their new babies.

1. Is there any one social, ethnic, or religious group which is less likely than any others to produce child-abusing parents?

2. If you were organizing a research project to study parents who are more likely to abuse their children, would you want to focus more on the parents' individual personalities, or on their particular attitudes and emotions about child rearing?

Prevention and Intervention

When Kevin's mother was arrested for drug abuse, he was the one who spent time in the hospital. In addition to being malnourished and small for his age, the 4-year-old had several broken ribs and unhealed welts on his back. "She didn't want him," says Kevin's aunt, "but if she kept him, she could still get welfare checks. She never stopped doing crack while she was pregnant, either. She used to say she'd whip Kevin if she wanted to, just like her Mama did to her."

Professionals in child welfare programs, hospitals, and law enforcement agencies are depressingly familiar with cases like Kevin's. In the video portion of this lesson, you have seen a brief glimpse of the horrifying effects of abuse on young children and heard the comments of child psychologists and other developmentalists as to which parents are at risk of being abusers. As terrible as these scenarios are, child care professionals can take heart from the fact that certain mothers can be identified as potential child abusers, and perhaps helped. Among the danger signs are mothers who do not want their child, who did not plan the pregnancy, or who did not make any preparations for its birth, such as attending childbirth classes or setting aside a special room for the baby. Furthermore, women who abused their children originally held unrealistic ideas about raising an infant. Other general indicators of possible abusive problems include poor education, poverty, social isolation, and a personal history of abuse.

If potentially abusive parents can be identified early, then perhaps they can be offered help in learning how to care for their children. Early intervention programs exist which strive to help at-risk parents by educating them in proper child care as well as providing emotional support. Groups such as Parents Anonymous have a significant impact on abusive behaviors if their intervention occurs at an early stage in the abusive situation. As you saw in the video segment featuring June and her little boy Tim, parents are not abusive out of a desire to be cruel or because they are "bad" or "crazy." Rather, child abuse is the result of a combination of factors that include the parent's social and economic background, their attitude toward the child, and their own developmental history. Any effort to prevent abuse or undo its effects must take place within the context of a host of related factors.

Focusing Questions

1. In a Lamaze natural birthing class, what percentage of the participants are likely to be single, teenage mothers? Why is it important that mothers have supportive partners when raising children?

2. What are some of the characteristic indicators of a mother who might maltreat her children? Are there similar indicators for men?

Questions for Understanding

As you read these questions, often raised by parents, educators, and other childcare providers, first try to answer the questions yourself. Then read the answer following each question and compare your response to it.

1. *From media reports, I get the impression that child abuse is a growing problem in this country. Is that true?*

   It is difficult to say for sure. Certainly the incidence of reported child abuse has risen dramatically over the past two decades or so. For example, the number of cases of reported child abuse in the U.S. rose from 515,000 in 1977 to 1.9 million in 1985. And even though this is a great increase, experts believe that it still does not represent the actual numbers of children being abused in America at that time. In other words, even though more cases of child abuse are being reported to authorities, there are still many children being abused who are never reported – or helped.

   At the same time, we do not know if the reported cases represent an increase in the actual amount of child abuse or if more cases are just being reported. During the 1970s and early 1980s, due to an increase in awareness among the general public of the prevalence of child abuse, people became more willing to report it. Teachers and others in schools, for example, are being better trained to detect the symptoms of child abuse and, in some places, are required by law to report cases of suspected abuse. So we do not know whether child abuse is becoming more common or if it is simply being detected and reported more often.

   Incidentally, the problem of child abuse and how to deal with it is not a new one. In 1874, there was a famous case involving a young girl named Mary Ellen who was being overtly abused. But because there were no laws at the time against abuse, some concerned people went to court and had the child declared an animal so she could be protected under the laws of the Society for the Prevention of Cruelty to Animals. This case helped call attention to problems of abuse and initiated change in the laws.

2. *As a day care worker, I sometimes see children with bruises, cuts, and scrapes and wonder if they are victims of abuse. At the same time, I know that toddlers are very active and often fall and hurt themselves. Is there any way I can be sure when a child is being abused?*

   There are certain behavioral signs that abused children tend to exhibit; in other words, it's unlikely that physical clues are the only indication of abuse. Some of the signs are somewhat obvious to the observer; for example, children who suffer from neglect and do not receive adequate food or bodily care tend to suffer from severe health problems. Later, they may have problems in school.

   Children who are physically abused, on the other hand, often show the characteristics of avoidant and disorganized attachment and may interact aggressively with their peers. Battered children may display blunted emotions and a lack of empathy with their playmates. And children who experience emotional unavailability of a parent are often severely affected and become apathetic and generally lacking in joy or pleasure. Such children are also easily upset and frustrated.

Remember, anyone who suspects that a child is being abused or neglected is required by law, in almost all jurisdictions, to report their suspicions to local authorities. Such authorities have been trained to spot abuse.

3. *Is it possible for some children to be so badly behaved that they almost force their parents to mistreat them?*

While there have been some researchers who have proposed that some children may have inherent characteristics that elicit abuse from adults, results from their research generally hasn't supported this idea. For one thing, the studies which have looked into the influence that prematurity, physical defects, and infant irritability might have on abuse all studied abuse after it had occurred. In prospective studies which assessed children in advance of any abuse, researchers failed to find any link between prematurity or irritability and later abuse, though there may be a tendency for an already overstressed parent to mistreat an infant who is ill and therefore fussy and difficult.

4. *The number of reports that I read in the press of parents beating or brutalizing their children shocks me. I can't understand how parents could ever hurt their child. Are most child abusers mentally ill people?*

No. Quite the contrary; abusing parents are generally as "sane" as the rest of the populace. By and large, most abusing parents wish to do well by their children but are overwhelmed by a variety of pressures and stresses.

Generally speaking, parents who abuse their child or children tend to share a range of circumstances and attitudes that seem to pre-dispose them to abusive behavior. One study found that abusing mothers dealt poorly with the ambivalent feelings and stressful emotions produced by their first pregnancy, and furthermore had little understanding of what to expect in caring for a baby. Typically, such an unprepared mother responds poorly to the difficulty of caring for a newborn – waking up early in the morning to feed the baby, changing diapers, responding to the baby's crying – and becomes hostile toward her baby. From this position it is a short step to abusive behavior, especially when outside pressures such as financial problems, poor housing, and lack of partner support add to the woman's stress.

5. *Is it inevitable that parents who have been abused as children will abuse their own children?*

While there is a distinct link between being abused as a child and later abusing one's own children, it is not an inevitable cause-and-effect relationship. Many people who were abused as children provide healthful, loving homes for their children.

Researchers have found that the most important factor for such successful parents is to have had a supportive alternate relationship with an adult while they were children. In other words, such children had a chance to see examples of positive adult role models in addition to their own parents' examples. In addition, a highly supportive spouse or partner can be an enormous help in making a parent with a poor developmental history into a good parent.

But it is true that having a history of abuse is common among abusing parents. One theory is that abused children learn maladaptive ways of handling the pressures of child rearing; abuse, such parents seem to have learned, is the normal response to crying, disruptive, or noisy children.

6. *Low-income housing projects seem to have a high proportion of child abuse situations. What kinds of programs are available for parents in cases such as these?*

Because the stresses of poverty, isolation, and lack of education are all known to be contributing factors to abusive situations, any programs that can help lessen these problems would be helpful. Abusive parents, and especially single mothers, often feel isolated with the burden of parenting and lack support in dealing with the problems that come with raising young children. A neighborhood support group could definitely be helpful in preventing child abuse.

Care-sharing arrangements would enable children to come home from school to a waiting adult. Simply getting involved in a community organization would act against the syndrome of isolation and inadequacy that tends to promote abuse in many parents. Studies have shown that community pride, cohesiveness in the family, and involvement in the neighborhood all help prevent child abuse in low-income neighborhoods.

Respite child care is an excellent alternative. For example, in Lansing, Michigan, Child Abuse Prevention Services offers a place where parents can leave their children for a few hours at a time. Overstressed parents can run errands without having to deal with their children at the same time or enjoy the company of other adults in relative quiet.

SELF-TEST

The following multiple choice and short answer test questions should help you measure your understanding of the points covered in the text and the video. After answering all the questions, check your answers against the key and use the accuracy of your answers to gauge how well you have met the lesson objectives.

Multiple Choice Questions

1. Last week the Alpha Computer Factory laid off 700 assembly line workers. Counselors at the town's human resources center are bracing for a wave of attempted suicides, episodes of depression, and domestic problems. In particular, counselors expect to see an increase in child abuse among laid-off workers who are

   a. single mothers who live near their parents.
   b. married men with more than one child.

    c. single fathers with no immediate family and no close friends.

    d. divorced men who see their children once a week.

2. Several women are waiting to be called at the human resources center. Their toddlers play together around a low table in a corner. While most of the children occasionally call out to their mothers, either to show her a new toy or to fuss about some irritation, one little girl consistently ignores her mother. In fact, when her mother is called to an office and calls for her child, the little girl hunkers down over a stuffed animal and refuses to come; the mother has to come over and drag the child off with her. The little girl is giving evidence of the type of attachment known as

    a. anxious-avoidant.

    b. anxious-resistant.

    c. secure.

    d. disorganized-disoriented.

3. A child whose single mother suffered from severe depression and was unable to express any emotion to the child would be most likely to show signs of

    a. excessive aggression toward peers.

    b. being very clumsy with objects.

    c. uncontrollable anger.

    d. extreme apathy.

4. According to a child developmentalist, an 18-month-old child unstrings her mother's favorite beads and drops them down the toilet because she is exploring her capabilities. To an abusive mother, however, the child is

    a. "Trying to be a plumber."

    b. "Just fooling around."

    c. "Seeing what will happen."

    d. "Trying to drive me crazy."

5. Children who have experienced physical abuse have a tendency to

    a. do all of the following.

    b. be aggressive with their peers.

    c. become apathetic.

    d. have major problems in school.

6. Some years ago, researchers conducted studies to find out if there might be children with certain characteristics that made them especially vulnerable to abuse. However, the results of these studies have mostly been invalidated because

    a. their conclusions were based on evidence after the abuse.

    b. the studies were prospective in nature.

    c. not enough parents agreed to discuss their problems.

    d. too few children participated in the study to place confidence in the results.

7. In a study by Brunnquell, Crichton, and Egeland, involving mostly single mothers, researchers found that those who abused their infants shared two similar characteristics: (1) they coped poorly with the ambivalent and stressful emotions of a first pregnancy, and (2) they

    a. came from low-income homes.
    b. had been abused themselves.
    c. had serious mental problems.
    d. did not make any preparations for the arrival of the baby.

8. You are a child developmentalist who is trying to create a questionnaire for women pregnant with their first child that will help identify potentially abusive mothers. Which one of the following statements suggests that the woman who answers "yes" will be most likely to abuse her child?

    a. I expect my husband to help me care for the baby.
    b. I plan to attend natural child birth classes.
    c. I don't expect to get much sleep for the first few months of my baby's life.
    d. I'll find a place for the baby's bed after the baby is born.

9. Jeanna is a 32-year-old mother of two children, aged 7 and 3. "I was slapped around pretty badly as a kid," she says. "My father left my mother when she was pregnant with me, and she had to go on welfare. I guess she felt pretty hopeless sometimes, and she'd take it out on me when things got tough. But I've never so much as slapped either of my girls, even though I've really felt like it sometimes. The one thing that helped me, though, was the

    a. college courses I took in child development."
    b. abusive parent's support group I found."
    c. support and understanding of my husband, Gene."
    d. knowledge that my mother hadn't intentionally been cruel."

10. If intervention programs designed to prevent child abuse are to work, it is important that

    a. at-risk parents be identified before they begin having problems with their children.
    b. children who are being abused be taken away from their parents as soon as possible.
    c. at-risk mothers be informed of the benefits of having a partner to help them raise their child.
    d. anonymous programs be set up for volunteers to provide positive adult role models for abused children.

Short Answer Questions

The following questions should be answered in a paragraph or two. You should identify several key points for each answer and use these to form the framework for your response.

1. Not every child who is abused grows up to be an abusive parent. What are some of the reasons for this?

2. Amanda is 16 and pregnant. Her parents wanted her to have an abortion; they said they couldn't afford to feed another mouth. Her boyfriend also thought she should have an abortion. But Amanda wanted to keep her baby, and her family told her she had to leave. She applied for welfare and is now living in a subsidized housing unit. "Sometimes I'm furious at myself for getting pregnant," Amanda says, "and other times I can't wait to have my baby. But at last I'll have somebody who will love me just as I am and who I can tell what to do." Assess this situation in terms of the potential factors for Amanda's becoming an abusive mother.

3. According to current theories, simply blaming parents who abuse their children without examining the context of the total family will not change the behavior pattern and help solve the problem. What are some of the factors which researchers have found to result in a parent mistreating a child?

12

A Look at the Whole Child: Age 1 to 2½

LESSON ASSIGNMENT

Completing the following steps will help you master the lesson objectives and achieve the goal for this lesson:

STEP 1: Read the INTRODUCING THE LESSON section to provide a context for what you will learn in this lesson.

STEP 2: Read the lesson's GOAL and LESSON OBJECTIVES so that you will know what you are expected to learn.

STEP 3: Read the text assignment, Chapter 7, pages 239-269, and Chapter 8, pages 271-292 and 297. Pay particular attention to the key terms and concepts in the Chapter Summaries; they will help you when you watch the video.

STEP 4: Review the VIEWING GUIDE in the telecourse guide. It lists several points to consider as you watch the video.

STEP 5: Watch the video.

STEP 6: Read the UNDERSTANDING THE LESSON section in the telecourse guide. Make sure you understand the key terms and can answer the focusing questions included there.

STEP 7: Complete the SELF-TEST.

STEP 8: Go back to the LESSON OBJECTIVES and make sure you can respond to each of them.

INTRODUCING THE LESSON

As his dad speaks to a neighbor, George marches up to the neighbor and holds out two small books. "Books," he says. Then, pointing at a picture on one book's cover, he says, "Ducks."

"Do you have ducks?" the man asks George, knowing that the child's parents don't own any pets.

"Yes," George says solemnly. Then, looking across the street, George sees several crows alighting on the roof of a house. "Ducks," the boy screams, pointing excitedly. "Ducks!" he says again, and laughs happily.

"Those look like crows to me," says the neighbor.

"Ducks," George replies. "Go backyard now," George then says, walking away from his dad. "Go backyard," the boy says again, looking back over his shoulder at his dad as he walks.

"George, no, we're going to the pool now. Come on, not the backyard." But George has turned the corner of the house and headed toward the swing set and other attractions which the backyard holds. Finishing his conversation, George's dad follows his son toward the rear of the house, calling out, "George, let's go now, come on."

At 2 years, George is a toddler in full bloom; as such, he displays several of the characteristic traits of this period. By speaking with his adult neighbor, George shows the sociability that is natural to children at this age. When he holds out the book for the neighbor's admiration, George is practicing affective sharing, as he also does when he points out the crows across the street. Even the mistake that George makes when he identifies the crows as ducks marks him as a toddler, when children are learning to speak and making a number of typical mistakes about which objects, animals, people, and emotions go with which words.

And George's interactions with his father are typically those of a toddler. By noticing his father's posture, tone of voice, and facial expression, George observes that this is a safe situation and that he can approach his neighbor with confidence. By moving off on his own toward the backyard, looking backward as he does so to check out his dad's reaction, George also demonstrates the urge to independence that toddlers feel. As the result of a range of emotional, physical, and cognitive advances in development, the average toddler is a subtle, complex, energetic – and often demanding – individual.

With this lesson, you focus on the overall developmental stage which toddlers have reached and examine the nature and extent of the changes that it includes. You take a look at how the very dramatic, qualitative growth that the toddler undergoes – taking his or her first steps and then walking, for example, and beginning to talk – unfolds along an orderly path and occurs within a network of social and economic contexts. In the video portion, toddlers at three different ages – 14 months, 21 months, and 28 months – will be followed through the similar activities of one day in order to show how the child's capabilities and skills expand during this period.

As a toddler, the child's individuality begins to emerge under the pressure of numerous influences. With this lesson, you are able to condense some two years and more of growth into a single, representative "day in the life" of a typical toddler.

GOAL

The purpose of this lesson is to present an overall picture of toddlers and to give you a clear understanding of how they develop into unique walking, talking, endlessly curious small individuals.

LESSON OBJECTIVES

After reading the text assignment, completing the exercises in this telecourse guide, and viewing the lesson's video portion, you will be able to:

1. Describe some of the major physical changes that occur during toddlerhood.

2. Give examples of representational and symbolic language and/or thinking skills that emerge during the toddler years.

3. Recognize how emotions are affected by the toddler's developing awareness of self, understanding of others.

4. Describe the changes that tend to occur in the parent-child relationship during toddlerhood.

5. Recognize how the various changes that occur during the preschool period – physical, cognitive, and social – relate to each other and to the orderly, cumulative, and directional aspects of development.

VIEWING GUIDE

The theme of this lesson is that the toddler is the product of an impressive array of cognitive, emotional, and physical changes and emerges as a distinct, unique individual by about the age of 30 months. After reading the text material and learning the important terms included there, you are ready to view the lesson's video portion. First, review the questions in the Self-Test at the end of this telecourse guide lesson to give you an idea of important points to watch for in the video. Then read the following Points to Consider to give you an idea of what the video will cover. Keep these points in mind while watching.

Points to Consider

☐ *Physically ready*: Toddlers are much more capable physically than are infants. Notice the differences in coordination, walking ability, and poise among the three children of different ages in the video portion of this lesson.

☐ *Words for things*: The sudden eruption of words that flows from the toddler is the visible manifestation of profound changes in the child's cognitive abilities. Try to distinguish the numerous ways that toddlers indicate their growing ability to think symbolically. Be aware of the cognitive advances that are required for each advance in language ability.

☐ *Becoming an individual*: The discovery of the self is a monumental accomplishment for the child. Keep an eye out for examples of how the child begins distinguishing between itself and its mother; between itself and other people. Notice how the urge toward autonomy sets up tension between toddlers and their care givers.

☐ *Changing roles and rules*: In toddlerhood, children and parents for the first – but not the last – time significantly change their relationships. Be aware of how important the quality of the child's attachment relationship is at this time. In the video, look for ways mothers and fathers begin interacting differently with their challenging toddler.

☐ *A medley of contexts*: The numerous and profound changes that turn infants into toddlers are the result of the child's total cognitive, emotional, physical, and social developments to this point. Keep in mind the different contexts that affect the toddler's impressive accomplishments; remember that the toddler grows out of the previous stages of infancy.

UNDERSTANDING THE LESSON

Pull the string coiled around a wooden top; the top shoots off the tip of the string, wobbles in a circle for a moment, then settles down to a steady, upright spin. Then, if it rides on a smooth, solid surface and doesn't collide with any obstacles, the top will spin for a long time.

In similar fashion, toddlers get up on their own two feet, stagger a bit, and then zoom off on a period of exploration and growth of dazzling speed and complexity. And much like the course of a spinning top, the direction and quality of the toddler's development depends upon how he or she is "launched" and the nature of the surface he or she "spins" on. As the toddler enters the period of self discovery, learning to talk, increasing mobility, and blossoming sociability, he or she is continuing along a course already determined by the influences of biology, family, and personal history. The particular "spin" each toddler takes depends upon everything that has gone before in his or her development.

The Fast-growing Toddler

The video portion of this lesson gives a vivid example of the swift physical growth that children experience during the toddler years. At 14 months, the child waits more or less patiently for her mom to lace up her sneakers; a year later, the same child is pushing mom's help aside and trying to "do it myself." While the urge to accomplish things on her own represents cognitive and emotional development, the toddler's physical abilities must first be sufficiently developed to allow her to accomplish the goals she has set. The many impressive skills that toddlers acquire are based firmly on the physical developments which are occurring at this stage.

Take walking, for example. This new skill enables the child to begin exploring the limits of its rapidly expanding capabilities. Most children begin walking soon after their first birthday; in fact, the shaky, side-to-side gait typical of this period – "toddling" – gives it its name. This motor skill has grown from the early reflexive steps and frog kicks of the infant, through crawling and standing upright with assistance, to full-fledged walking. Each of these stages occurred as the child's bones strengthened, muscles developed, nerve endings connected, and coordination improved. Then, as the result of a cumulative progression of improving motor skills, the child was off and toddling.

Learning to talk likewise depends upon a number of physical developments. Before the child can form that first word, he or she must be able to control the complicated apparatus involved in producing words – the mouth, lips, tongue, and vocal cords, along with a range of muscular movements required to send puffs of air out of the lungs and through the trachea.

Another sign of the toddler's improving motor capabilities is the skill with which he relies on gestures to communicate. When young George spied the crows across the street, he pointed at the birds and simultaneously looked up at the man, a coordination skill that a year earlier he wouldn't have been able to perform. As a result of orderly and directional physical growth, toddlers are well prepared to accomplish the many cognitive, social, and emotional tasks which they tackle during this period.

Focusing Questions

1. You are shopping for a birthday present for a 2-year-old girl. Will you buy her a frisbee, a kite, or a plastic-dome "corn popper" that pops loudly when pushed by a stick?

2. "You have to crawl before you can walk" is a well-known cliche. How might you rephrase it to suit the ability to talk?

New Thinking Skills

It has been a busy week at Silver Lining Day Care Center. Fourteen-month-old Kareem spoke his first word – "dude." Eighteen-month-old Diana walked into the kitchen in the afternoon and told a worker, "No fish." For the first time, 2-year-olds Kelly and Brian were able to take on a role in a pretend game of beauticians and customers, even though they just did what the older children told them. And 28-month-old Bob had a crying fit because he got stuck under a table during a game of hide-and-seek, and became afraid.

Toddlers are obviously making great strides physically as they begin to walk and explore their surroundings. What may be less apparent is the great increase in cognitive abilities that accompanies their halting steps and mispronounced words. Take learning to talk, for example. As the child begins speaking a limited number of words, he or she is encouraged by care givers to begin using them in meaningful patterns; the child quickly begins practicing the particular patterns of its language. The child begins to form associations of meaning with words, and begins forming concepts: a kitty has four legs and fur, birdies cheep and jump into the air, pulling on the phone cord makes Mama shout "no" real loud. And as you learned in Lesson 9, the toddler must discriminate among an enormous number of rules to be able to use language intelligibly – phonology, morphology, syntax, and semantics must all be grasped intuitively for the toddler to begin communicating.

Most of these cognitive achievements can be described under the heading of symbolic thought. Words, after all, are nothing but sounds that symbolize things – objects, emotions, people, ideas – for the purpose of communication. In fact, Jean Piaget thought that the emergence of the ability to think symbolically was the main cognitive development of toddlerhood. In Piaget's view, toddlers are demonstrating the ability to think symbolically both when they speak and when they engage in pretend play. Piaget thought that toddlers began developing true symbolic capability at about 18 to 24 months of age, which would mark the end of his six sensorimotor stages.

With the growth of its vocabulary, the child gains an increasing store of symbols to manipulate and learns to use words imaginatively to refer to objects and events which aren't actually present. The growth in cognitive abilities which attend these new skills are especially evident during the latter part of the toddler period, when the child begins pretend playing.

Focusing Questions

1. Much to his mother's embarrassment, Kevin's first word was "King," which the child seemed to have picked up from Burger King commercials on television. Can Kevin's first word be counted as a true example of representational thought?

2. Why did Piaget believe that the child has reached the end of the sixth and final sensorimotor phase when it begins using words to refer to objects and events that aren't currently present?

Learning to Think About "Me"

Sometime during the toddler period, children make one of the most important discoveries of their lives: they learn the difference between "I" and "not I." Developing a sense of self is one of the most significant milestones of a child's cognitive development; it signals a dramatic change in how the child relates to the rest of the world.

For one thing, as you saw demonstrated in the video portion of the lesson, toddlers begin asserting themselves in many areas. As children's awareness of their own existence solidifies, so does their need to find out what the limits of their capabilities are. "I do it," says the suddenly determined 20-month-old when it comes time to take the dog out for a walk. At the same time, the child is striving to establish its own autonomy, and so often attempts tasks beyond its capabilities. Jamie, excited at the prospect of being able to control his family's labrador retriever, isn't easily dissuaded from his desire just because the dog outweighs him by 15 pounds. As a result, the toddler period is a time of frequent contests of will between parents and children.

In addition, as children's understanding of their own existence takes seed and begins to grow, so does an awareness of the separateness of other people. The delightful sociability and openness of toddlers is a reflection of this developmental change. As the child increasingly appreciates the differences in his or her actions and intentions from those of other people, the possibilities for play, communication, emotional sharing, and learning by imitation expand immensely. While the toddler is not yet mature enough to appreciate the concept of friendship, he or she is beginning to coordinate play with other children and to interact in more complex ways with playmates.

As described in Lesson 10, the child's second year is a period of establishing autonomy from its care givers, while at the same time maintaining a sense of intimacy and security with them. In the space between these conflicting claims of the need to be independent and the need for security, the child's personality begins to take shape.

Focusing Questions

1. When Brian's dad begins unpacking and assembling the family's new tent, Brian plunges in. "Me help," the child says, grabbing the folding aluminum tubing and attempting to lock the legs into place. What major developmental change of the toddler period is Brian demonstrating?

2. Suppose you are a worker in a day care center. What kinds of activities might you organize to occupy a group of 18 month olds? A group of 30 month olds? How would the focus or capabilities of the two groups vary?

Changing Relationships Between Parents and Children

Mike Jones is an investment banker who used to get some of his best ideas while shaving. Lately, however, his shaving time is more likely to be spent talking with his 2-year-old daughter Sally than in brainstorming.

"Juice," Sally says, pointing at the can of shaving foam her father has in his hand.

"This, honey?" Mike says. "No, this is shaving foam, not juice . . . foam. It's in a can, too. Watch," he says, and sprays a ball of foam into his hand. The little girl stares, apparently fascinated.

"Daddy eat foam," Sally says, making a statement. Mike laughs, and continues telling his daughter what he's doing as he shaves.

The change in Mike's usual morning routine is just one example of how toddlers affect the lives of their care givers as they become increasingly active participants in their families. As children exercise their growing language skills, parents coax and guide their responses, teaching them new words and language rules. Parents also change their behavior in response to the child's expanding mobility and urge to explore, creating a secure arena in which the child can experiment with its new abilities. As you learned in Lesson 10, Jerome Bruner referred to this concept as scaffolding.

And as you saw in the video portion of the lesson, fathers interact more often with their toddlers than they did when the children were infants. Fathers tend to interact differently with their children than do mothers, too. Typically, researchers find that fathers tend to engage their children in play, whereas mothers engage more in nurturing activities. Recall also that fathers speak a slightly different form of child directed speech, or motherese, to children than do mothers. Fathers tend to ask their toddlers to label objects and to explain what they are doing, as well as using a slightly more sophisticated vocabulary than do mothers.

Both mothers and fathers, however, find their relationship with their child changing during the toddler period. As the child's sense of self grows and his or her mobility, cognitive powers, and urge to physically explore the world increase, so does his or her need to achieve autonomy. Parents, who previously were the secure center of the infant's universe, now may find themselves becoming obstacles to the child's wishes. To a degree, toddlers discover what they are capable of by matching their wishes against their parents. At the same time, toddlers have a need to maintain the security and intimacy they've established with their parents, and so need clearly defined limits to continue feeling secure. While the relationship between toddlers and parents is changing, it is vital to the child's development that its parents behave consistently toward it.

Focusing Questions

1. In the video portion of the lesson, you saw examples of how toddlers behave at three different ages. How do toddlers and parents interact during meal times, for example, during the three ages depicted? How do parents and toddlers play together differently during those three ages?

2. The toddler years are popularly known as "the terrible twos." Specifically, what aspect of the child's awareness is changing that sometimes makes them so hard for adults to deal with?

Toddling through Development

Mothers of toddlers are a staple of cartoons and television ads, and are usually depicted as exhausted custodians of tireless, three-foot-high whirlwinds of energy. For many mothers, it's a recognizable exaggeration. Especially once they begin walking on their own, children are inquisitive, challenging, sometimes exasperating vortexes of activity. To a care giver worn out by the seemingly boundless energy of her 2-year-old, it's almost as though her child has abruptly gone from being a simple three-channel TV set to one equipped with cable. Where the infant was programmed with the standards of sleeping, eating, and waking, toddlers are tuned in to bigtime wrestling, 24-hour sports channels, news reports, science specials, commercials, and weather stations.

Most parents, of course, greatly value these years when their children are experiencing such an explosion of cognitive, social, physical, and emotional growth. As the child's sense of self develops and his or her personality unfolds, the care giver takes great pleasure in watching the child's rising self reliance. Seemingly, every individual development which takes place at this stage reinforces or affects other areas of development. As parents respond to a child's efforts to communicate, for example, they are also encouraging his or her urges to be sociable. Likewise, by providing clues about the safety or unreliability of individuals during certain situations through social referencing, parents guide their children toward greater sociability.

At the same time, as the child explores and gets into things, the parent sets limits on its behavior. This, in turn, begins teaching the child about the rules of its society and how to behave around other people. Even the type of words you use around a child and how you speak to it, convey messages about proper social behavior. As you learned in Lesson 9, discourse of this kind is called pragmatics.

The type of attachment which a child has with its care givers also greatly affects the course of a toddler's development. How confidently a child approaches the tasks of separating itself from its mother, for example, and beginning to strive for self-reliance depends largely upon the type of attachment the child has formed. As described in the text's story of Karen and her daughter Meryl, an anxiously attached child may have difficulty balancing its urge to gain autonomy with a sense of uncertainty about how its mother will react to its demands. The dramatic, qualitative transformations that the toddler undergoes are to a large part constrained and nourished by the previous stages of development which the child has already gone through.

Focusing Questions

1. Think of ways in which cognitive development is affected by physical development during the toddler period. For example, does the fact that toddlers have generally begun walking when they begin talking affect the way in which they learn to speak?

2. What are some of the ways in which being securely attached to its care givers prepares a child to confidently handle the challenges of toddlerhood?

Questions for Understanding

As you read these questions, often raised by parents, educators, and other childcare providers, first try to answer the questions yourself. Then read the answer following each question and compare your response to it.

1. *Until recently, my 14-month-old daughter could only make a few gestures, such as waving bye-bye and shaking or nodding her head yes and no. But over the past month or so, she has begun pointing at things – the salt shaker on the table, our fish in their tank, my earrings – and whining or crying. Shouldn't she be talking by now, instead of just pointing and making noises?*

From the behavior you describe, your daughter is developing just fine. The gestures you describe, which are clearly efforts at communicating her desires, are precursors of the start of talking. Another common gesture that emerges in children of your daughter's age is the common "pick-me-up" plea with the arms held upward. You can next expect your daughter to begin practicing more complex gestures, such as pretending to stroke the fur on a cat.

Developmentally, these gestures are quite normal and do not take the place of beginning to speak. In fact, gestures seem to increase in frequency in parallel with the beginnings of language development. After she has begun talking, your daughter will go through a stage where her vocabulary seems to explode; at that point, which occurs around the 18th month, her amount of gesturing will most likely decline. Some researchers suggest that this switch takes place as language replaces gesturing as the more effective means of communication.

2. *My son Clarence is just past 2 years old. Most of the time, he's an absolute joy. But he just can't seem to keep his hands off of things. Nothing within his reach is safe, and lately he's begun scooting chairs around and climbing on them to reach things on shelves. Today I came into the living room and found him pouring a bowlful of roasted peanuts into my collection of Dresden china cups. Is it normal for kids to be so mischievous?*

To be fair, your son isn't necessarily being mischievous. As hard as it may be to believe, he isn't deliberately setting out just to perform actions that he knows will irritate you. As Clarence's physical abilities are improving and he is able to walk, move chairs around, and coordinate his grasp better, so too are his cognitive abilities expanding. He is becoming increasingly aware that he is a separate being from you and other people, that objects have an existence all their own, and that he can have effects on people and objects. One characteristic of toddlers is that they are becoming aware of themselves and developing distinct intentions to do things, and are increasingly able to match their wishes with action.

At the same time, though your son is beginning to think symbolically and to be able to manipulate the concepts mentally, he still is greatly limited in his cognitive abilities. For example, toddlers are still unable to think logically and rely upon a lot of physical contact to test their ideas. As he makes the transition from the sensorimotor period, when all information comes to the child through his senses and physical actions, he often puts his thoughts into immediate action. Thus, you get roasted peanuts in your china cups.

3. *My sister is raising her daughter by herself, and sometimes I'm afraid that she isn't doing a very good job. For one thing, she has trouble being firm; if my niece cries long enough, my sister gives in. But now that the child has started to walk, is there any chance that my sister will begin being more consistent with her?*

Certainly your sister could begin practicing more consistent discipline with her daughter, but she isn't likely to just because the little girl begins walking. Usually, the patterns that care givers and infants establish during infancy are the ones they'll continue as the child begins to walk, unless some aspect of the care giving context changes. For example, a child who has formed an anxious-resistant type of attachment, which is characterized by ambivalence, confused emotional messages, and poor communications between child and care givers, will continue to act in a similar fashion during toddlerhood. As with other stages of development, the actual course of any given phase is set by the outcome of the previous stages.

Having said that, however, it is true that individuals can alter their behavior and attachments can be changed. If the mother of an anxiously attached child were to change her own behavior toward the child – by establishing firm rules of behavior for the child, for example, and sticking to them consistently – then it's quite possible for the child to change its attachment to a secure one. Also, single mothers who establish stable partnering relationships have reported improvement in the behavior of their children.

4. *I've seen parents who kept track of their young children by attaching them to leashes. Are toddlers likely to run away from their parents once they begin walking?*

While it would be very unlikely for a toddler to deliberately run away from its parents, children of that age are very inquisitive and adventurous and can easily wander far from their care givers. Toddlers also vary in their degrees of self-assurance and independence; while some tend to keep very close to their care givers even in familiar surroundings, other, bolder children delight in dashing off on their own at every chance. Probably you've seen mothers of such children, keeping one hand on their squirming offspring while navigating the aisles of a store.

Impulsive toddlers can be especially hard to keep an eye on in crowds. For harried parents of active youngsters, the leashes that you describe may be a way of providing a temporary secure attachment during times of distraction.

5. *Can toddlers play games together?*

Yes, though the games are not of great complexity. Younger toddlers are able to respond to one another's behavior and often get quite a kick out of matching one another's actions. Two toddlers in a park will often take turns running at a flock of pigeons, for example, screaming in delight as the birds flurry up and then settle down. Play at this period often centers on objects such as balls and blocks. As toddlers advance into their third year, they begin playing around shared themes and begin playing pretend games together. Their increasing ability to coordinate their actions and intentions reflects both cognitive and physical growth.

6. *When my son first began talking, he didn't always seem to know just what the words he used meant. For example, under the influence of his 7-year-old brother, he tended to use the word "awesome" fairly indiscriminately. When do children begin using words meaningfully?*

At least from the child's point of view, most of their early words are meaningful. They just may not be using them in ways that you and I understand, as in your example of your son's fondness for "awesome." But even when he applied the word to situations where it didn't apply – a typical early toddler language error known as over extension – he still was using the word to express meaning. He just hadn't yet learned the rules needed to give the word the same meaning as other people.

Young toddlers are also often hard to understand because they try to use single words to convey complex meanings. As the child's vocabulary expands, he or she begins speaking in simple two-word sentences and then in the condensed style called telegraphic speech.

But the important thing to recognize about your child's efforts to speak is that they represent a major change in his ability to think. By using words, for the first time your son is showing an ability to form concepts and, in the form of words, use them to have an effect upon his environment. Learning to speak involves the child in a major qualitative developmental change.

SELF-TEST

The following multiple choice and short answer test questions should help you assess your understanding of the points covered in the text and the video. After answering all the questions, check your answers against the key and use the accuracy of your answers to gauge how well you have met the lesson objectives.

Multiple Choice Questions

1. Since her daughter Heather turned 2 years old last month, Shirley has been having more and more trouble getting the child ready to go to child care in the morning. The most plausible reason for this is probably that Heather

   a. needs more sleep now.
   b. wants to put on her own clothes by herself.
   c. is going through a difficult stage.
   d. hates going to day care.

2. You are in charge of a group of 2-year-olds at a day care center. Physically, the one activity that they're capable of playing together is

   a. Nintendo.
   b. tag.
   c. catch.
   d. velcro darts.

3. Of the following choices, the only one that is NOT part of a toddler's increasing ability to think symbolically is

   a. playing with pretend animals.
   b. understanding the word "no."
   c. petting a cat.
   d. nodding the head for "yes."

4. You are caring for four children, ranging in age from 14 to 36 months old. While you are walking with the kids along the sidewalk, a woman drives up and parks a shiny red Porsche. You point at the car and say to the children, "See that car? That car is red. Can you say that? That car is red." One of the children is only able to say, "Car red." That child is the

   a. 36-month-old.
   b. 28-month-old.
   c. 20-month-old.
   d. 14-month-old.

5. Marge is getting exasperated; Jake, her 28-month-old, insists on tying his own shoelaces. In fact, he throws a tantrum every time his mother tries to take over the chore. But ten minutes after he's "tied" them, the laces are flopping loose, and again Jake has to tie them. Marge is trying to be patient with her son because she understands that his actions are

   a. Jake's way of asserting his sense of self.
   b. necessary for Jake to learn how to tie his shoes.
   c. typical behavior of highly gifted children.
   d. just his attempt to wear out her patience.

6. Two-year-old Jennifer is playing with a miniature xylophone. Eighteen-month-old Caroline approaches and tries to pry the xylophone from Jennifer's hands. A care giver intercedes between the two children and Jennifer retains her toy. Moments later, another 2-year-old, Blake, comes over to Jennifer. Instead of grabbing the xylophone, Blake tries to trade Jennifer a miniature race car for it. By his action, Blake demonstrates awareness of

   a. Jennifer's feelings.
   b. a sense of fairness.
   c. the concept of taking turns.
   d. the possession rule.

7. As their children become toddlers, fathers tend to interact more with them than they did earlier. This may help the child

   a. develop its motor skills and coordination.
   b. more easily separate psychologically from its mother.
   c. become more confident socially.
   d. develop a wider range of language skills.

8. Understanding the rules of how to use language in different social contexts is referred to as

   a. semantics.
   b. morphology.
   c. pragmatics.
   d. phonology.

9. An example of how parents instill the rules and values of their particular culture in their children would be a

   a. mother spanking her son's hand when he reaches for a candle flame.
   b. father shooing his child away from the street.
   c. father stopping his son from stripping off his clothes while playing in the front yard.
   d. mother stopping her child from pulling their cat's tail.

10. The rapid speed at which children learn to speak shows that they are

    a. genetically prepared to learn language.
    b. clever mimics.
    c. anxious to communicate with others.
    d. well adapted to a social existence.

Short Answer Questions

The following questions should be answered in a paragraph or two. You should identify several key points for each answer and use these to form the framework for your response.

1. What are some of the special types of interactions that occur between toddlers and adults as toddlers begin learning to speak?

2. How do the ways mothers and fathers interact with their children differ during the toddler period?

3. What are the four main types of attachment and how do they affect the challenges of development faced by the toddler?

MODULE IV:

EARLY CHILDHOOD

13

Early Childhood
Cognitive Development

LESSON ASSIGNMENT

Completing the following steps will help you master the lesson objectives and achieve the goal for this lesson:

STEP 1: Read the INTRODUCING THE LESSON section to provide a context for what you will learn in this lesson.

STEP 2: Read the lesson's GOAL and LESSON OBJECTIVES so that you will know what you are expected to learn.

STEP 3: Read the text assignment, Chapter 9, pages 310-343. Pay particular attention to the key terms and concepts in the Chapter Summary on pages 342-343; they will help you when you watch the video.

STEP 4: Review the VIEWING GUIDE section in the telecourse guide. It lists several points to consider as you watch the video.

STEP 5: Watch the video.

STEP 6: Read the UNDERSTANDING THE LESSON section in the telecourse guide. Make sure you understand the key terms and can answer the focusing questions included there.

STEP 7: Complete the SELF-TEST.

STEP 8: Go back to the LESSON OBJECTIVES and make sure you can respond to each of them.

INTRODUCING THE LESSON

The Brazilian movie *Black Orpheus* is a beautiful retelling of the Greek myth of Orpheus, the legendary hero with superhuman skill in music and song. In his modern movie incarnation, Orpheus (called Orféo) is a cable car conductor who lives in the slums overlooking Rio de Janeiro. Every morning three neighborhood children come to Orféo before dawn and beg him to play his guitar so that the sun will come up. Later, at the end of the movie after Orpheus has been killed, the three children return to his hut before dawn. One of the children – also named Orféo – finds Orféo's guitar and picks out his own simple version of the dead hero's song. As a 5-year-old girl dances, the sun rises over Rio de Janeiro.

The three children of Black Orpheus are not just acting out a poignant parallel of the ancient belief in the power of human beings to affect the physical world. On the contrary, the belief that the children have in Orféo's ability to make the sun rise by playing his guitar is a good example of both the cognitive abilities *and* limitations of preschoolers. As they emerge from the toddler stage, children continue to reach out actively to understand their world. During the preschool period, which lasts from about 2½ to 5 years old, children develop increasingly advanced concepts of how things work and why events take place.

While preschoolers are much more advanced in their cognitive skills than are toddlers, they are still far from a full understanding of such concepts as cause and effect, as shown by the children's belief that human beings can affect the rising of the sun. Preschoolers are still restricted by a number of important cognitive limitations as they struggle to make sense out of the world. Among other things, preschoolers have trouble distinguishing between appearance and reality – a shortcoming that seems to be at work in the scenes described above. Preschoolers also have not yet developed the memory skills that they will later acquire.

But even with their cognitive limitations, preschoolers make impressive progress toward a greater understanding of reality and the ability to communicate effectively. By the time they are ready to enter school, children are applying consistent rules to solving problems – even though they are still often wrong in their answers. Their growing cognitive abilities also enable them to interact more effectively with their environments and in particular to take part in social activities at increasingly sophisticated levels. At the same time, the improved communication that they experience with others now encourages their cognitive development.

In this lesson, you will examine the various stages that children go through during the preschool period on their way to an understanding of such things as causation, the behavior of fluids, classification, and seriation. You will learn why young preschoolers often exhibit "magical" thinking, and how they gradually acquire a variety of conceptual tools that help them make sense of the world. You will see how a preschooler's powers of attention and memory grow and compare some of the theories that researchers have applied to these developments.

Along the way, you'll find out why 3 year olds often give adults such gifts as dolls, fire trucks, and packets of gummy bears. And you'll understand why it probably isn't far-fetched to imagine that every day, a trio of 5 year olds gathers to play and dance the sun up over Rio de Janeiro.

GOAL

The purpose of this lesson is to provide a picture of the cognitive advances that occur during the preschool period and to show how advances in memory and the central nervous system in general contribute to this cognitive development.

LESSON OBJECTIVES

After reading the text assignment, completing the exercises in this telecourse guide, and viewing the lesson's video portion, you will be able to:

1. Explain the ways in which preschoolers are active participants in their cognitive development.

2. List and describe the important conceptual tools children begin to acquire in early childhood.

3. Indicate how preschoolers select information to respond to stimuli in their environment.

4. Identify three limitations in thinking that the majority of preschoolers exhibit.

5. Recognize the preschooler's social communication abilities and limitations.

6. Describe the preschooler's memory abilities and limitations.

7. Define egocentrism, and suggest the cognitive factors and social experiences necessary for children to overcome egocentrism.

8. Discuss the effects of preschool intervention programs on school performance.

VIEWING GUIDE

Preschoolers usually create their own reality with an abundance of self-confidence. But because of certain cognitive limitations, their early explorations sometimes seem to be done through the wrong end of a telescope. During this time, children acquire new cognitive skills and continue to operate with a number of limitations. After reading the text material and learning the important terms included there, you are ready to view the lesson's video portion. First, review the questions in the Self-Test at the end of this telecourse guide lesson to give you an idea of important points to watch for in the video. Then read the following Points to Consider to give you an idea of what the video will cover. Keep these points in mind while watching.

Points to Consider

☐ *Early toolkits*: The preschool period is when each of us began acquiring many of the basic conceptual tools we will use to interpret the world throughout our lives. Notice how preschoolers struggle to make sense of how things work according to a number of strategies. Be aware of the various cognitive limitations that restrict children at this stage.

☐ *Adding to the collection*: Among children's growing conceptual tools are ones that enable them to classify, arrange by order, and compare. Keep an eye out for instances of the difficulties younger preschoolers have when arranging something by categories. Notice when youngsters begin making inferences about relationships from related information.

☐ *Remembering to remember*: Being able to pay attention and think consciously of ways to remember important information are big steps forward for children. Be aware of the information-processing model of attention and short-term memory. Notice how preschoolers begin awakening to the benefits to be gained from having an efficient memory.

☐ *Centers of their universe*: To the preschooler, figuring out someone else's mind is a simple matter of listening to his or her own thoughts. Take note of how often preschoolers fail to consider the wishes and thoughts of others. Be aware of the stages of cognitive development that preschoolers attain at this time.

UNDERSTANDING THE LESSON

Most people grasp intuitively that a great gulf exists between the way they understood things as a child and the way they understand things now. As adults, we understand that the conceptual frameworks by which we now explain the workings of the universe – physics, chemistry, religion, economics, philosophy – once had a simple, altogether neater label in our young minds: magic.

To a child of 3 or 4, existence is much less of a mystery than it is to a Nobel Prize-winning cosmologist. Instead of accounting for stars by such arcane theories as the Big Bang and the concept of waves of light arriving 20,000 years after they were emitted, a child may "explain" starlight as bright marbles glittering just overhead.

During the preschool period, children develop many of the conceptual tools that will enable them to understand the workings of cause and effect; they also learn to distinguish between appearance and reality. They make great leaps toward understanding another person's point of view and at being able to communicate effectively – but they also gradually lose their faith in magic.

Causal Reasoning and Conceptual Tools

As children emerge from the toddler period, they are actively searching for reasons why things happen. Piaget developed a four-stage description of how we develop an understanding of causation. At level 1, we say that things happen because we cause them: "I make the sun come up." At level 2, we say God or a powerful force makes things happen: "God makes the sun come up." At level 3, we explain happenings as caused by nature: "The sun comes up because the wind blows it." And by level 4, we are beginning to approach adult levels of understanding: "The sun comes up because the world turns."

Preschoolers develop a number of important conceptual abilities that aid them in understanding how the world works. One important concept is that of *conservation*, which means that a substance may be of the same quantity even though it takes on a new form. The knowledge that a pint of water is still a pint whether it's in a quart jar or a gallon jar is one that early preschoolers do not have. They are misled by the *appearance-reality problem*. As you saw demonstrated in the video, this essentially means that young children think that "what you see is what you get." Another reason that young preschoolers don't grasp conservation is because they tend to focus on only one aspect of a situation at a time, a concept known as *centration*. In Piaget's view, children have achieved a level 4, or adult understanding of conservation of liquid volume, by about age 7.

Although Piaget believed that children were unable to understand conservation until about the beginning of middle childhood, later researchers have disputed this. As you learned in Chapter 9, some 4 to 6 year olds have been taught to understand conservation at an earlier age; either they have been helped around the appearance-reality problem or have sidestepped problems of centration. The results seem simply to have speeded up these children's development along its normal course.

Preschoolers must also develop an understanding of the conservation of numbers. Young preschoolers will get confused if you take a line of six dolls and stretch it out longer. They will think that the longer line now contains more dolls. Not surprisingly, young children have an easier time understanding problems of quantity when they have to consider sets of numbers. Even 2 and 3 year olds apply a "primitive rule" to questions of more or less, saying that adding a number makes more of a group and subtracting makes less. Slightly older children adopt a more sophisticated "qualitative rule" to problems of number, basing their judgments on whether two groups were equal before changing in number. And by adopting a "quantitative rule" that always takes into account the actual numbers of two changing groups, 6 to 7 year olds consistently begin making correct assessments of number.

Although preschoolers do not yet have a solid conceptual grasp of conservation, they are still able to make many correct measurements intuitively. For example, even young preschoolers can evenly divide up a large pile of blocks by separating them two at a time. What children lack at this stage is a systematic way of thinking about quantity, which requires an understanding of the concepts of order.

Key Terms

Causation
Conservation
Appearance-reality problem
Centration

Focusing Questions

1. Why do developmentalists look upon wrong answers that children give about natural phenomena, such as "It's raining because Mommy bought me a new umbrella," as signs that children actively participate in their own cognitive development?

2. Before children can thoroughly understand the concept of conservation, what two types of cognitive growth must occur?

Other Conceptual Tools of Preschoolers

When Megan got home from shopping, her 30-month-old son Bruce insisted on helping her put things away. "Okay," she said, handing him a can of stewed tomatoes. "Do you know where this goes?"

"Uh huh," said the boy – and made a bee line for the recycling box for metal and tossed the full can in with all the empty ones.

As Bruce shows, young preschoolers have a glimmering of how objects or events can be classified according to their shared characteristics, though at first only in a rough manner. At first, children can *classify* objects only along one dimension, such as shape or color. This is another example of how the cognitive abilities of preschoolers are limited by centration. Bruce, for example, was able only to focus on the fact that he had a tin can, without being able to further categorize it as empty or full. On the other hand, preschoolers find it easier to organize objects that belong to collections, which are naturally occurring groups of similar things. For example, a child would be more likely to identify a school of fish or a field of flowers rather than an individual salmon or tulip.

Another important conceptual tool that develops now is *seriation*, which is the ability to organize items according to a logical progression, such as from shortest to longest. While younger preschoolers have trouble with seriation, most of them will have mastered it by about age 6 or 7. Again, the main obstacles which a child must overcome to understand seriation are the appearance-reality problem and centration.

Young preschoolers are also unable to make comparative judgments about something by comparing it to two related items – a skill known as *transitive inference*. Suppose, for example, that you tell a 3 year old that a guinea pig is bigger than a rat, but a rat is bigger than a hamster. If you ask the child which is bigger, a guinea pig or a hamster, she may guess the right answer, but she won't be able to infer that animal A is bigger than animal C. One probable reason that preschoolers have a hard time with transitive inference until they reach school age is that they find it hard to coordinate all the required information.

As you have noted in the previous section and observed in the video segment, preschoolers often make mistakes when judging quantity or classifying items because they confuse appearance with reality. To a young preschooler, looking through rose-colored glasses isn't a way to escape reality, but to truly change it. At the same time, even 3-year-olds exhibit the beginnings of understanding the difference between appearance and reality, as indicated by the example in your text of the children who turned down a drink of roach-tainted juice. Generally speaking, though, preschoolers seem to possess only the bare outlines of such cognitive skills as conservation, classification, seriation, and transitive inference. As you will see with the chapters on middle childhood, these are the cognitive skills which begin unfolding as children enter school.

Key Terms

>   Classification
>   Seriation
>   Transitive inference

Focusing Questions

1. If you ask a 4-year-old boy to line up a stack of pencils from the shortest to the longest, he will be more likely to succeed if you give him just four or five pencils instead of a larger number. Why?

2. If you gave the boy in the question above the same larger stack of pencils and asked him to order them like a family – oldest to youngest or biggest to smallest – what do you think he would do? Why?

3. Piaget believed that children couldn't solve problems by using transitive inference until middle childhood. Has his conclusion been supported by subsequent research?

Paying Attention and Remembering Among Preschoolers

Anyone who has ever babysat for a 3 year old knows how much work it can be to keep a preschooler's attention focused if he is not interested in the topic or the event of the moment. Young children have immense amounts of energy, but they don't yet have the necessary cognitive means to follow specific directions given by an adult if the subject isn't interesting to them, or if something more interesting is happening within the immediate area. As an adult, you are able to keep a child occupied by imagining what the child might like and then using your greater mental abilities to direct the child's attention toward some interesting stimuli – if you're lucky.

According to information-processing theory, we receive information in the form of a stimulus that enters our sensory registers and is stored there for less than a second. Whatever catches our attention out of that stimulus then passes into the short-term memory, where it may last 10 seconds. Finally, any event or sight that really stands out may then be moved into long-term memory, where it will make up a fragment of our lifetime's store of knowledge and experience.

As you'll recall, infants comprehend the world by acting upon it. Then, with toddlerhood, we begin to develop language skills and to form concepts. In the preschool stage, children begin acquiring the ability to direct their attention more and more, though they do not at first have much ability to use their natural attention skills strategically. Remember, for instance, the study noted in your text of how preschoolers approached the problem of discovering which of a series of pictures of houses were similar. Compared with older children, the preschoolers did poorly because they looked at the windows of the houses in a haphazard fashion. Furthermore, the younger children tended to look first at the focal point of the picture and scan downward, missing important information.

Related to the difficulty preschoolers have in controlling their attention skills is the way they use their memories. Preschoolers have little conscious awareness of the need to practice using their memories. While even 3 year olds have acquired some memory ability, they won't begin forming specific plans to remember things until about 9 years of age. During preschool, a child's memory strategies tend to be limited, context-specific, and inconsistently used.

Focusing Questions

1. You probably wouldn't expect a 4 year old to be able to remember a 7-digit phone number. Why not? How about the child's chances for memorizing the emergency number, 911?

2. Suppose a group of preschoolers in day care are given pumpkins just before Halloween. During the day, the children must leave the center. What kind of strategies might the children use to help them remember which pumpkin they'd chosen when they return?

Social Cognition

Carol is slightly behind schedule as she tries to get out the door on her way to work. As she pours herself a cup of coffee, she shouts through the doorway of her 3-year-old daughter's room: "Mary? What pants are you putting on?"

From around the corner and out of sight comes the answer: "These ones."

"Which ones are those, honey?" Carol replies.

"These ones I like," answers the little girl.

This mother-daughter interaction demonstrates one of the limitations preschoolers face in their ability to interact with others. Mary acts as though her mother can see everything she can, a cognitive mistake known as *egocentrism*. With egocentrism, the child either thinks another person perceives an event with the child's senses or else that the other person shares the child's thought processes. Egocentrism is a common way of thinking among preschoolers and seems closely related to the problems they often have with the difference between appearance and reality.

Obviously, being unable to separate your own thoughts and feelings from those of other people will affect your ability to interact socially. Over time, the child will move past egocentrism by beginning to realize that other people have motivations, thoughts, and viewpoints that may differ from theirs. Children will also begin to grasp that they can get along better with people if they try to consider the other person's point of view. And getting beyond egocentrism means being able to "read" another person's actions and to imagine their point of view. But for preschoolers, these skills must await further cognitive growth.

As the preschooler matures, he or she will gradually think less and less egocentrically. Three year olds, for example, will commonly chatter away happily to themselves, carrying on solitary conversations. Even when playing with other children, young preschoolers will actually be carrying on parallel, self-involved monologues. At this early stage, children seem to have difficulty realizing what another person needs to know to foster clear communication. Preschoolers also must learn to adapt their vocabularies and style of speech to suit the age and understanding of their audience, a communication skill at which they generally seem poor. While preschoolers are forming the basics of social cognitive skills, they are still best at communicating in simple, undistracting situations. Some researchers also theorize that better communication must wait until children master the appropriate *scripts*, which are conceptual frameworks or "game plans" of how to behave during certain situations. A common and early example of a script would be how to talk on the telephone.

Key Words

> Egocentrism
> Scripts

Focusing Questions

1. Is egocentrism a cognitive limitation that affects only infants and preschoolers?

2. What are some of the types of information that children need to have in order to be able to participate in conversations?

Questions for Understanding

As you read these questions, often raised by parents, educators, and other childcare providers, first try to answer the questions yourself. Then read the answer following each question and compare your response to it.

1. *Why does my 3-year-old son have such a difficult time seeing that even though I use different glasses, I'm giving each child the same amount of juice?*

   The reason may be due to a lack of conservation skills. Jean Piaget proposed a three-stage process for mastering conservation. In stage 1, from about age 3, children are nonconservers and judge the amount of a liquid by the height it reaches in a container. Children at this stage consistently use the wrong rule to judge the volume of the liquid. In stage 2, from about age 5 to 6, children still make wrong answers, but are beginning to wonder if the answers really are right. In this transitional stage, children are beginning to be able to get around centration to concentrate on more than one side of the problem. By stage 3, mature conservation, children consistently make right judgments about the volume of liquid in various containers. By now, the child has also surmounted the appearance versus reality problem and so is able to understand that the shape of a liquid's container does not change its volume. This point, which most children reach at about age 7, is one of the cognitive markers for transition into middle childhood.

2. *I am interested in helping my 4-year-old daughter get a head start on school. Is it possible for her to begin learning things that kids don't usually pick up until kindergarten or first grade, such as simple counting?*

   Certainly it is possible for preschoolers to master certain cognitive tasks earlier than usual, though you need to be aware of the realistic limits to their abilities at this stage. For example, researchers have found that children of your daughter's age have difficulty mastering the concept of conservation of liquid, even in tests designed to overcome their limitations of centration and the appearance-reality problem. But with children in Piaget's transitional stage 2, researchers were able to dramatically improve the children's performance. They did this by asking children questions about water in different containers that were hidden from the children by a screen. Apparently this kept the children from being confused by the conflict of appearance with reality and to concentrate on the underlying concepts. Similar results have been found with problems of number conservation. It is probably possible to speed up the ability of older preschoolers and young elementary school children to grasp some concepts by about a year.

3. *Why do preschoolers have difficulty with such problems of organization as lining up a series of sticks according to their length? Can't they see the differences among the sticks?*

Certainly young preschoolers can see the various lengths of a group of sticks, but organizing them in a series requires the ability to perform several cognitive chores that may be beyond them. For one thing, to perceive that a series of sticks can be lined up from shortest to longest, you must first understand the concept of seriation, and preschoolers typically do not. Instead, preschoolers try to arrange the sticks by trial and error, which is likely to succeed only with small numbers of sticks – say, three or four.

Preschoolers are limited in this task because they confuse appearance with reality. In this case, children cannot conceive of the reality of an ordered series without having one before them. Children at this stage are also limited by centration and may well successfully line up the top ends of the sticks in ascending order, but leave the bottom ends in ragged disorder. Apparently, children cannot focus on two things at one time, which in this case would mean simultaneously coordinating the information about both ends of the sticks.

4. *Why do preschoolers have such short attention spans?*

For one thing, preschoolers do not yet have the necessary cognitive skills to select the appropriate information related to a specific goal or desire from the wealth of stimuli clamoring for their attention. Suppose, for example, that you and your 3-year-old daughter are in the park and you suggest looking for four-leaf clovers. The child is enthusiastic and bends her nose close to the lawn. In the grass, however, she spies a lady bug crawling along and picks it up for your approval. Then, when she tosses it into the air so it can fly off, she notices a blue jay perched on the branch of a tree. Since the four-leaf clover hunt wasn't her idea in the first place, she may want to explore the events she finds more stimulating and interesting.

5. *I recently took a 3 year old shopping for a birthday present for his mother. It was all I could do to keep him from heading for his favorite toy store to get his mom a Garfield doll. Why are young children unable to imagine what someone else might want as a gift?*

It's largely because of egocentrism, which is the inability to distinguish your own point of view from someone else's. Cognitively, your 3-year-old friend is unable to put himself into his mother's place, so he thinks that what he would like as a present is also what she would like. Egocentrism is normal among preschoolers; they will gradually come to realize that other people may have desires different from their own and begin to take another person's perspective in trying to figure out what that person's wishes might be. You can expect your youngster to be able to select a present for his mother from the point of view of what she might like by the time he's about 6 years old.

6. *Why do preschoolers ask "why" so much?*

As children advance out of the toddler stage, they are building upon their new skills of representational thought, which in turn are influenced by their growing language skills. Preschoolers are now able to imagine the consequences of actions and to take a lively interest in how things work and why things happen. Preschoolers are both actively exploring their world and constructing an explanation of the world as they perceive it. As part of this active attempt to understand reality, they search for general patterns and clues. They understand that there are problems to solve, and, increasingly, they are developing new cognitive skills that enable them to successfully consider these problems. In a sense, the "whys" of young preschoolers are the verbal sparks thrown off by the friction of their new cognitive skills rubbing up against the nature of reality.

SELF-TEST

The following multiple choice and short answer test questions should help you assess your understanding of the points covered in the text and the video. After answering all the questions, check your answers against the key and use the accuracy of your answers to gauge how well you have met the lesson objectives.

Multiple Choice Questions

1. A 3 year old's telling you that she can make birds move from tree to tree by looking at them is an example of how preschoolers

   a. are limited by centration.
   b. actively participate in their own development.
   c. don't understand conservation.
   d. imagine that everyone thinks as they do.

2. According to Jean Piaget's levels of developing understanding of causation, children are most likely to be confused by problems of appearance versus reality during

   a. level 1.
   b. level 2.
   c. level 3.
   d. level 4.

3. A preschooler sees a set of six hollow wooden dolls in the shape of Russian peasant women disassembled on a table. Working slowly and using trial and error to put the appropriate doll inside its next-largest partner, the child finally gets all six dolls back into the largest doll. The child's action is an example of the conceptual tool called

   a. conservation.
   b. transitive inference.
   c. centration.
   d. seriation.

4. Seriation, classification, conservation, and transitive inference are all examples of

   a. cognitive limitations.
   b. attention strategies.
   c. conceptual tools.
   d. mistakes caused by egocentrism.

5. When asked to arrange a series of sticks of different length in ascending order, 3-year-old Neil managed to place one end of the sticks on an even line; the other ends were arranged completely randomly. Neil was able to accomplish this much only by

   a. overcoming the limitations of centration.
   b. adopting the point of view of the person asking him to do the task.
   c. specifically selecting certain stimuli from his environment to respond to.
   d. correctly solving the appearance-reality problem.

6. The longest number of digits the average preschooler can memorize is about

   a. three.
   b. four.
   c. five.
   d. six.

7. You can be sure your preschool-age daughter is thinking egocentrically when she

   a. gives you a bright yellow plastic lunchbox for your 30th birthday.
   b. tells you that the clouds move when she does.
   c. asks you why the sun doesn't burn up completely.
   d. thinks you've lost some of her juice when you pour it from a bottle into a glass.

8. If you are trying to get a preschool-age child to converse with you in a way that decreases his egocentrism, you might try to

   a. use hard words to focus his concentration.
   b. make sure that you have eye contact with him.
   c. be careful to speak in sentences no longer than seven words.
   d. allow the child to look away while speaking so he can concentrate.

9. Two 4-year-old girls are playing "grocery shopping" together. One pushes a shoebox as a shopping cart, while the other girl picks up blocks and puts them into the box. "Get some corn flakes," the girl pushing the cart says. "Okay, and milk," answers her friend. The behavior of the girls demonstrates that they have mastered

   a. at least one script.
   b. transitive inference.
   c. the difference between classes and collections.
   d. ordering.

10. By teaching them a strategy of counting as a way to judge the number of items in each of two groups, researchers have been able to teach preschool-age children the principles of conservation. By doing this, they were able to train the children to succeed with tasks about a year earlier than they normally would have. These training procedures will probably

    a. enable the children to skip a few grades in school.
    b. produce extremely stable results for almost all children.
    c. have little effect in the long run.
    d. have nothing to do with the children's other cognitive abilities.

Short Answer Questions

The following questions should be answered in a paragraph or two. You should identify several key points for each answer and use these to form the framework for your response.

1. What are some of the limitations that continue to restrict the cognitive abilities of children during the preschool period?

2. What are scripts and how might they contribute to a child's ability to communicate more effectively with others?

3. What are the three stages that Piaget believed children must pass through before reaching a full understanding of conservation?

14

Social and Emotional Development in Early Childhood

LESSON ASSIGNMENT

Completing the following steps will help you master the lesson objectives and achieve the goal for this lesson:

STEP 1: Read the INTRODUCING THE LESSON section to provide a context for what you will learn in this lesson.

STEP 2: Read the lesson's GOAL and LESSON OBJECTIVES so that you will know what you are expected to learn.

STEP 3: Read the text assignment, Chapter 10, pages 346-380. Pay particular attention to the key terms and concepts in the Chapter Summary on pages 379-380; they will help you when you watch the video.

STEP 4: Review the VIEWING GUIDE section in the telecourse guide. It lists several points to consider as you watch the video.

STEP 5: Watch the video.

STEP 6: Read the UNDERSTANDING THE LESSON section in the telecourse guide. Make sure you understand the key terms and can answer the focusing questions included there.

STEP 7: Complete the SELF-TEST.

STEP 8: Go back to the LESSON OBJECTIVES and make sure you can respond to each of them.

INTRODUCING THE LESSON

I t is mid-morning at the Green Turtle Day Care Center, and several children are playing in the yard. At first glance, three toddlers seem to be engaged in a joint building project in a sand box. Closer inspection, however, reveals that each child is engrossed in his or her particular section of sand, piling up small hillocks in happy disregard of the other children's activities. At one point, Wes decides that the yellow bucket Vivian is filling up is much nicer than his red one. No sooner has he had the impulse than he is reaching across and grabbing, trying to wrench it from Vivian's hands. Vivian's indignant wails soon bring the mediation of a day care worker.

Nearby, meanwhile, another group of older children interact in a much different manner. Friends Allen, Brenda, and Jake dash back and forth between the trunks of two trees, playing a game of "airport."

"I'm making a landing," Allen shouts, spreading his arms and running toward his companions.

"Do you have any bags?" Brenda asks. "Now we'll drink some coffee."

"This truck is in this place," Jake says, moving a toy truck around the base of the tree. "Crash into him."

"KABOOM! Crash landing!" Allen says, kicking the truck and falling over on the ground.

"Now we need the amb'lance," Brenda says.

Both sets of youngsters are playing and interacting, but the difference in their styles is immediately apparent. While the younger children do play in the same area, they can hardly be said to be playing together on a reciprocal basis. And when Wes and Vivian both want the same toy, they have few strategies other than force to settle their dispute.

In contrast, the children who are two or three years older exhibit considerably greater degrees of social and emotional skills. Their interactions are truly reciprocal, with each child responding to the other. The older children are engaging in much more sophisticated levels of peer exchange and are capable of using negotiation to settle their disputes. Because they have much greater cognitive abilities than the toddlers, the older children are able to engage in mutual fantasy and role-playing and to draw upon greatly expanded concepts of the world around them. In comparison with the younger children, the preschoolers are reaching out to explore a much broader world.

In this lesson you will examine the developments in social and emotional behavior that occur during the preschool period, a time of growing individual autonomy and self-reliance. Children of this age are developing new powers of self-control and are learning how to inhibit actions, delay gratification, and tolerate frustration. This is also a time of increasing peer interaction. Children at this stage are beginning to gain the social skills and adaptability that they will need to become socially competent later in life. Social competence in early childhood involves developing empathy and friendship, learning to cooperate and to be generous and sharing, understanding why it feels good to help others, and discovering that everyone has rights. And for parents, it is an idyllic period when children are beginning to mind what they're told and to identify with their parents. For children and parents alike, early childhood is a time of deepening relationships and understanding.

GOAL

The purpose of this lesson is to demonstrate the numerous advances in social skills and emotional understanding that preschoolers make as they begin forming peer friendships, developing a sense of empathy, establishing smoother relationships with parents, and moving actively into their expanding worlds.

LESSON OBJECTIVES

After reading the text assignment, completing the exercises in this telecourse guide, and viewing the lesson's video portion, you will be able to:

1. Indicate how a child's level of curiosity, exploration, and movement toward self-reliance contribute to social competence.

2. Discuss peer relationships in early childhood and their role as components of social competence.

3. Describe ego-resiliency and the behaviors associated with it in early childhood.

4. Relate advances in self-regulation to the emergence of aggression, empathy, and altruism.

5. Explain the process by which children adopt their parents' rules and values as their own.

6. Describe the development of gender roles and sex-typed behavior.

7. Indicate how preschoolers develop a sense of self-constancy and self-esteem.

8. Summarize parenting practices that support preschoolers' social development.

VIEWING GUIDE

As social animals, we find ourselves truly joining the flock in early childhood. Among the advances in social and emotional development that occur between the years 2½ and 5 are the beginning of friendships, a dawning awareness of the feelings of others, a grasp of gender, and growing skills for interacting with others. After reading the text material and learning the important terms included there, you are ready to view the lesson's video portion. First, review the questions in the Self-Test at the end of this telecourse guide lesson to give you an idea of important points to watch for in the video. Then read the following Points to Consider to give you an idea of what the video will cover. Keep these points in mind while watching.

Points to Consider

☐ *Curiouser and curiouser*: In the preschool period, the child's curiosity and desire to understand the world is growing rapidly, pushing him or her forward into new situations and toward new levels of understanding. Notice how preschoolers are well-prepared for the increased stimuli and interaction that their expanding world will offer. Be aware of the various forms that parent-and-child relationships take on as preschoolers develop new levels of self-awareness.

☐ *Getting a grip on the self*: As children emerge from the toddler stage, tantrums become less frequent. Pay attention to the numerous emotional skills that now enable children to muster increasing degrees of self-mastery. Look for examples of how children begin understanding the feelings of others.

☐ *Like Mommy or Daddy*: New social skills can transform children at this age into delightful companions for their parents. Look for instances that demonstrate the child's developing awareness of gender. Notice how much pleasure children get now from fantasy play. Be aware of the ways in which self-awareness also changes during this period.

☐ *Changing children, changing parents*: The growing powers of self-management that preschoolers develop require adjustments on the part of their parents. Keep track of the various tasks facing parents at this stage. Compare the varying effects that different parenting styles have on development and remember the importance of attachment as children grow and mature into later stages.

UNDERSTANDING THE LESSON

Flip through any parents' album of their children, and you'll probably find several pictures of their preschoolers playing "dress-up." Impish smiles beam from under outsized hats, draping dresses, cavernous jackets. These are pictures of children exploring their new understanding of how other people act, feel, and look; they are also pictures of offspring practicing the roles they see their parents fulfilling.

During early childhood, youngsters are boundlessly curious and pursue their interests through a range of exploration, fantasy play, peer interactions, role-playing, and identification with parents. Their expanding social interactions are propelled by a new sense of empathy, which is often expressed as unselfish acts of altruism. At the same time, the growing emotional capacities and social skills of preschoolers also enable them to exhibit true aggression for the first time.

The Child's Expanding World

As the light changes from red to green at a downtown intersection, two young women scurry their group of 3- and 4-year-old day care charges over the crosswalk. The seven children all clutch a strand of yellow nylon rope stretching between the women. The children's eyes are big as they stare at the automobiles, towering buildings, steam seeping from manhole covers.

The rope that the children hold as they cross a busy street is probably a good idea. Preschoolers are increasingly exposed to the world outside their homes, and their natural curiosity often drives them to explore new settings in ways that may not be safe. But at this age, "getting into things" is a sign of healthy development. With their growing language and cognitive skills, as well as greater physical capacities, preschoolers are moving toward greater *self-reliance*. In particular, their new capacity for fantasy play allows them to explore a new sense of power in ways that can't be restricted by adults.

It is important now for children to strike a balance between self-reliance and over-dependence upon their care givers. Some children are unable to leave the security of infantile dependence and are said to show too much *emotional dependency*. These children typically crave physical contact with care givers even when not upset. Children who are developing a balanced sense of self-reliance, on the other hand, tend to seek attention from care givers only when they are upset or need help with a difficult problem. This is known as *instrumental dependency* and is appropriate for children at this stage of development. Not surprisingly, children who have formed secure attachments with their parents are more likely to show signs of self-reliance. In John Bowlby's view, such children have developed an *inner working model* of rules and values that gives them confidence in their own ability to make things happen.

Preschoolers are also capable of much richer relationships with peers now than they were only a short time before. This is the age when children begin making friends and engaging in mutual fantasy play. How well a child gets along with others is described as *social competence* and is a measure of how a child interacts with others. Judgments about a child's status within a group depend upon how often he or she is accepted or rejected by the group.

A child's degree of social competence is an important part of development, as the peer group is a major learning area for concepts of fairness, reciprocity, and cooperation. The peer group is also a context in which children begin learning how to handle interpersonal aggression, as they continue to absorb lessons about cultural norms and values. Developmentalists judge an individual's social competence by the way other children evaluate them and by the judgments of their teachers.

Key Terms

Self-reliance
Emotional dependency
Instrumental dependency
Inner working model
Social competence

Focusing Questions

1. When Angela's mother drops her off at the day care center, the little girl howls and cries; she spends much of the day whining to be picked up by the day care workers. What kind of attachment do you think Angela has with her mother? What kind of dependency?

2. What kind of behavior would you look for to assess a preschooler's social competence?

Self-Control and Self-Management

The order and discipline that Japanese kindergartners exhibit when leaving a classroom is impressive. At a teacher's command, each child solemnly picks up his or her chair, carries it to a wall and stacks it. Then they exit the room in an even, quiet row – and burst into squeals and spasms of unrestrained energy upon reaching the corridor outside.

As a result of a number of developmental changes, preschoolers are able to practice an increasing degree of self-control. They are able to foresee possible consequences of their actions and to delay some pleasurable activities. They can think of ways around obstacles and can better control their emotions when frustrated. They can do more than one thing at a time and can concentrate better than their younger brothers and sisters. All these abilities are necessary advances for the child to be able to interact effectively with others.

While a toddler will generally grab at anything attractive it sees, the 4 and 5 year old is learning how to inhibit his or her impulses. Another tool of self-control that develops now is *delay of gratification*, which means the ability to put off some pleasurable action until later. By about the age of 2, children begin developing the ability to tolerate frustration. Researchers speculate that this advance occurs as the child becomes capable of suppressing his or her emotions, as well as learning strategies for avoiding the build-up of frustration in the first place. All these new abilities lead to improved relations with parents, such as fewer tantrums when the child's wishes are thwarted, for example.

At the same time that preschoolers are becoming more skilled at managing their impulses, they are also becoming better able to tailor their responses to the circumstances. The kindergartners described earlier file out in orderly rows, but explode happily upon leaving the classroom. Preschoolers are developing the ability to modify their self-control depending upon the circumstances, a skill known as *ego resiliency* because the ego is showing flexibility in its control over behavior.

Fortunately, these powers of self-control arise soon after the child begins feeling urges of aggression, which is the intent to harm someone else. During preschool, aggressive behavior between children becomes common, as anyone who has ever separated two battling 3 year olds knows. In older preschoolers, fighting over objects, known as *instrumental aggression*, begins to decline as children become more skilled at negotiating. On the other hand, aggression aimed at hurting someone else, known as *hostile aggression*, begins rising in early childhood.

Interestingly, the same cognitive advances that lead children to tease one another also lead them to acts of unselfishness. Preschoolers are becoming capable of imagining another person's feelings, or experiencing *empathy*. If, instead of wanting to hurt someone else, the child is moved to unselfishly help that person, we say they are acting *altruistically*. As children begin to grasp that their actions can affect other people and that they are independent, responsible agents, they become capable of acts of aggression, empathy, and altruism.

Key Terms

> Delay of gratification
> Ego resiliency
> Instrumental aggression
> Hostile aggression
> Empathy
> Altruism

Focusing Questions

1. If a 4-year-old girl is consistently impulsive, what chance do you think she has of growing out of it?

2. Why would a high degree of ego-resiliency enable a child to get along better with other children and adults in a variety of situations?

From Imitation to Identification

At age 2, Roslynne amused her father by following him around as he worked in the garden, digging enthusiastically in the flowerbeds with a spoon. Now that the girl is 5 years old, however, he welcomes her attention on seed-buying trips to the local garden center. "How about these, Daddy?" she says as she removes a packet of marigold seeds from a rack. "Didn't you say these make the bugs stay off our plants?"

While toddlers often imitate the actions of their parents, preschoolers begin to *identify* with them, meaning they adopt their values and preferences. Identification, empathy, and aggression develop about the same time, along with increased powers of self-control. Just as a child must attach with someone, so must he or she identify with care givers. Children with secure attachments are likely to have a positive identification with family values and to be open to socialization; those with insecure attachments are likely to face emotional conflict.

Children learn about the proper roles of males and females within their society largely through identification with the parent of the opposite sex. A sense of being male or female is known as *gender role concept* and is absorbed by the child from parents, siblings, teachers, television, and other segments of the culture. Sex-typed behavior increases during the ages of 3 and 4 and is reinforced by parents, peers, and others. A sense of *gender constancy* also develops during this time, meaning that the child understands that gender doesn't change as a result of superficial alterations in appearance.

Children explore many of their changing roles and views of the world at this time through play. As was illustrated in the video portion of the lesson, children work through conflict as they play, and they use play to practice identification. Pretend-play also offers an important format for practicing various social roles that the child is exposed to. Again, the complexity, flexibility, and elaborateness of a child's fantasy play is richer and more productive for children with secure attachment histories.

Preschoolers also develop important new levels of self-understanding. For one thing, they can "uncouple" themselves from experience, enabling them to pretend and be aware of it at the same time. For another, they can move cognitively between the past and the present. Children now are also developing a sense of self-constancy, which means that they understand that the self continues despite disruptions in relationships. All of these different concepts of the self contribute to and are shaped by the child's sense of *self-esteem*, which is his or her self-view as shaped by past experiences. Again, just as the nature of a child's attachment affects his or her ability to play productively, previous stages of development help shape current ones.

Key Terms

> Identification
> Gender role concept
> Gender constancy

Focusing Questions

1. What are some of the ways in which a child's identification with the parent of the opposite sex may affect his or her developing sense of gender?

2. Suppose you are a day care worker who notices that one of the children at your center seems unable to play effectively with the other children, and seems oddly uncurious. Why should you be concerned about this child?

Parental Roles and Individual Differences

During the preschool period, the need that children have to strive for new levels of understanding requires new roles for parents. Preschoolers are attempting to master the world in many ways and need sensitive guidance. Parents need to present clear roles as their children seek to identify with them. During infancy and toddlerhood, the parent tends to regulate the child's behavior in a two-way relationship. With the growing abilities and autonomy of early childhood, however, the child increasingly becomes capable of self-management. It is important for the child's development that parents now consistently affirm that their relationship with the child remains intact, even after the child has become angry or destructive.

Among the tasks of parents during early childhood are those of nurturance, training, and channeling the child's physical needs, helping the child develop interpersonal skills, and transmitting cultural values. As you saw in the video portion of the lesson, parents who want their children to comply with their wishes have the best results when they rely on reasoning rather than the assertion of power. With responsive care and the use of firm limits, parents are able to encourage self-confidence, autonomy, and positive feelings toward others.

At this stage of development, children exhibit a coherent sense of self as they work through many developmental tasks. For example, children who are socially competent show more social play and higher positive affect, while those who show hostility do not show much prosocial behavior. And though children behave differently in different circumstances, being quiet in church, for example, and boisterous on the playground, this merely indicates consistent patterns of self-control. Again, children with secure attachment histories tend to cope successfully with the challenges of early childhood. Children with secure attachment, for example, tend to have high self-esteem, are popular with peers, and show little hostile aggression. They are also more likely to be empathic and have a greater capacity to form friendships. Children with a history of anxious attachment, on the other hand, tend to have lower self-esteem, lower peer acceptance, and lower capacity for self-management.

Focusing Questions

1. What are some of the differences in how the parents of preschool children must guide their children toward autonomy as compared with similar tasks when the children were toddlers?

2. What are the possible effects of an avoidant attachment when a child faces the early childhood tasks of learning to deal with aggression, to get along with other children, and to form friendships?

Questions for Understanding

As you read these questions, often raised by parents, educators, and other childcare providers, first try to answer the questions yourself. Then read the answer following each question and compare your response to it.

1. *How is my preschooler's level of social competence assessed?*

   Researchers often ask teachers to evaluate such things as how well their students get along with others and are regarded by them. While these reports are valuable, there is the possibility that teachers may sometimes be reporting the child's social competence with the teacher instead of their peers. To offset this possibility, researchers supplement teacher assessments with the judgments of the child's peers. This procedure, known as *sociometrics*, involves asking children questions such as whom they "especially like," and whom they "do not especially like." Researchers also observe children in social groups themselves, watching for such behaviors as solitary, parallel, and cooperative play. Other techniques include noting which children are dominant in groups or receive lots of attention from other children.

2. *When can I expect my 2-year-old son to begin obeying when I tell him "no."*

   Generally speaking, your son should be able to stop doing whatever it is you wish him to by about the time he's 4 years old. The ability that he needs to develop first is self-restraint, which is very difficult for children of his age. At his stage, he finds it hard even to physically resist taking an action once it has occurred to him. To paraphrase Wordsworth, the thought is father to the action for a 2 year old – as any parent who has ever said "Don't touch that" to a toddler lunging at a VCR control will recognize. When commanded not to do something he or she wants to do, the response of a 2 year old is likely to be a tantrum.

But you can expect your 2 year old to have much better powers of self-control by the time he's 30 months old, as his ability to inhibit his own actions improves. And by the age of 4, most children are able to suppress their own impulses when they know they should, even in cases when an adult is not present to encourage them.

3. *The other day, my son and I were watching an old Western movie on television. In one scene, the cowboys rounded up some cattle and were branding them. When I explained what they were doing to my son, who is 5, he got very upset. "But that must hurt the cows," he said. "Why do they have to hurt the cows?" I've never known him to be so sensitive to someone else's pain, and here he is agonizing over cows. What's going on?*

Your son is just showing signs of a developing sense of empathy, that's all. This is perfectly normal for children of his age. During infancy, when he has only a fuzzy grasp of the separation between himself and those around him, the child is incapable of understanding that some-one else feels pain. As the child's cognitive powers grow during toddlerhood to include a stronger sense of the self, the child begins to sense when another child feels pain. During this phase, however, the child still cannot fully comprehend the needs of another person and tends to interpret their cries of distress according to what he himself would like.

By about your son's age, however, the child's conceptual abilities and sense of self have expanded to the point of being able to imagine both how another person feels and to think of how they might like to be comforted. This new ability to empathize is often accompanied by acts of altruism, offering help to someone in an unselfish manner. Your son's distress at the sight of cattle being branded is just a sign of appropriate social development for his age.

4. *What is the psychoanalytic view of how preschoolers identify with their parents?*

During early childhood, children strive to become like their parents through the process of identification. Identification involves acting like one or both parents, as well as adopting their feelings, thoughts, and values. According to psychoanalytic theory, identification is how chil-dren adapt to the conflicts that arise at this time between the growing need for autonomy and the limitations imposed by parents. As chil-dren move out of the dependency of infancy, they feel increasingly powerful. However, as their wishes collide with those of their parents, they discover that they aren't as powerful or free as they'd thought.

To resolve this conflict, children identify with their parents, incor-porating the parents' attributes into their own selves. Preschoolers are capable of these conceptual adjustments as a result of the cognitive growth that they are experiencing now. As a result of identifying with their parents, children show greater confidence and security, cooper-ate more with their parents, and generally get along with them better than ever. For many parents, this is an especially enjoyable stage of parenthood.

5. *My wife and I are parents of a 1-year-old boy and are interested in raising him to have as open a mind as possible. We're especially concerned that he not have a sexist attitude toward women. What can we do to be sure he develops positive values toward women?*

Probably the surest way you can instill the kind of values you admire in your son is to model them yourselves. Through the process of identification, your son is likely to form a good part of his attitudes toward other people, including the opposite sex, by striving to be like his parents and to please them.

Keep in mind, however, that gender issues are a mixture of environmental and biological forces, with influences other than your own at work. For example, your son will see examples of both male- and femaleness on television shows or in magazine advertising. Playing with other children will also affect how he views his own gender and relates to the other.

Generally speaking, sex-typed behavior and development of gender role concept are linked to a child's cognitive growth. By about age 2, children are already showing gender-related preferences in toys. At the same time, children of this age are not yet aware that they share a gender with one of their parents. Sex-typed behavior has greatly increased by about age 3 or 4, by which time children know that they are either a boy or a girl. In addition, 4 year olds also know what is appropriate behavior and attire for their sex and will know that their peers will react negatively to them if they violate these standards.

6. *Parents use different styles to raise their children. What are some of the different effects that some of these styles have?*

The developmentalist Diana Baumrind has studied the personalities of preschoolers and assessed them according to how their parents related to them. Baumrind's Group 1 consists of children who are energetic, self-reliant, and highly curious, as well as being emotionally positive toward peers and self-controlled. The parents of these children typically were consistently nurturant and responsive and set firm limits without being punitive – the type of parenting known as authoritative. They were also flexible in their attitudes and supported their children's move to independence.

Children in Group 2, on the other hand, were moody, apprehensive, easily upset, passively hostile, and either negative in their relations with peers or socially withdrawn. Baumrind found that the parents of these children did not respond to their wishes and controlled their behavior strictly, even harshly. These authoritarian parents tended to follow inflexible rules. Studies have indicated that Group 2 children stand a high risk of developing aggressiveness or other behavioral problems later in life.

Children in Group 3, while exhibiting cheerfulness and a general sense of resilience, tended to be impulsive, undercontrolled, and not particularly self-reliant. Their parents turned out to be somewhat nurturant, but didn't set firm limits on their children's behavior, a parenting style known as permissive. By also failing to require appropriately mature behavior from their children, Group 3 parents failed to encourage their children to develop self-control.

SELF-TEST

The following multiple choice and short answer test questions should help you assess your understanding of the points covered in the text and the video. After answering all the questions, check your answers against the key and use the accuracy of your answers to gauge how well you have met the lesson objectives.

Multiple Choice Questions

1. Among a group of 4 year olds in a day care center, the child you would assess as being most socially competent is the one who

   a. regularly hits other children to get toys.
   b. spends a lot of time whining for the workers' attention.
   c. regularly shows great curiosity over new toys or people.
   d. spends a lot of time avoiding the other children.

2. When two preschoolers form a friendship at about age 4, the two children can be expected to

   a. disagree with each other more often than with other children.
   b. treat each other just the same as they do other children.
   c. develop difficulties in cooperating with each other to solve problems.
   d. show little interest in maintaining the friendship on their own.

3. One good way of evaluating a preschooler's level of social competence is by

   a. counting the number of contacts he or she has with others.
   b. asking the child how he or she gets along with others.
   c. having the child's teacher assess him or her.
   d. observing which children are seldom rejected by others.

4. Lorraine is driving on the freeway with her 5-year-old son Justin, teaching him the words to one of her favorite songs. But when a highway patrolman pulls them over for a missing bulb in a tail light, the boy becomes quiet and watchful. After talking with the patrolman and re-entering traffic, Lorraine explains to Justin that they weren't in any trouble and soon has him singing again. Justin's behavior is a measure of his

   a. impulsiveness.
   b. ego resiliency.
   c. poor self-control.
   d. emotional overdependency.

5. When 2-year-old Susan grabs at the stuffed bear a friend is clutching, she isn't acting aggressively because she doesn't understand the consequences of her actions. However, when Susan's 5-year-old sister

Gwen grabs a candy bar away from a friend, she is acting aggressively because now

a. she is bigger than the other girl.
b. she understands the self as agent and the concept of fairness.
c. she should be able to know how to divide the candy bar evenly.
d. she should be past the stage of being interested in other people's objects.

6. Recently, Brad's 4-year-old son Brandon has been playing "airplane builder," based on his father's job as an aerospace engineer. Furthermore, the boy has been drawing lots of pictures of airplanes, saying they are "just like the ones Daddy builds." A child developmentalist would identify Brandon's behavior as a sign of

a. identification.
b. delayed gratification.
c. instrumental aggression.
d. emotional overdependency.

7. Children who are able to incorporate the values of their families without much conflict or turmoil during early childhood probably have

a. experienced resistant attachment.
b. little sense of curiosity.
c. experienced secure attachment with their parents.
d. a good chance of having developmental problems later.

8. During the preschool period, children who act in ways that aren't considered gender-appropriate by their peers and parents will probably

a. receive negative feedback from both groups.
b. receive no feedback from these two groups.
c. develop a sense of altruism faster than children who act gender-appropriately.
d. have trouble developing a sense of self-reliance.

9. Jim gets a big hug from his mother for helping her fold clothes. Fifteen minutes later, however, the 3 year old is getting scolded for making random phone calls after being told not to. And yet at dinner time, both mother and son are interacting as though they'd never had a moment of conflict. For Jim, his ability to defy and then make up with his mother indicates that he has achieved

a. self-reliance.
b. gender concept.
c. identification.
d. self-constancy.

10. Parents should not worry too much that disciplining their child might compromise the child's healthy development if they

a. are careful never to show emotion to the child.
b. make sure they let the child know how angry they are.
c. make every effort to let the child develop without restraints.
d. are careful to restore harmonious relations after a disruption.

Short Answer Questions

The following questions should be answered in a paragraph or two. You should identify several key points for each answer and use these to form the framework for your response.

1. What are some characteristics of emotional dependency and how does it differ from instrumental dependency?

2. What are the four main abilities that a child must master in order to achieve self-control?

3. What is gender constancy? Have researchers changed their views on it in recent years?

15

Play and Imagination

LESSON ASSIGNMENT

Completing the following steps will help you master the lesson objectives and achieve the goal for this lesson:

STEP 1: Read the INTRODUCING THE LESSON section to provide a context for what you will learn in this lesson.

STEP 2: Read the lesson's GOAL and LESSON OBJECTIVES so that you will know what you are expected to learn.

STEP 3: Read the text assignment, Chapter 10, pages 346-380. Pay particular attention to the key terms and concepts in the Chapter Summary on pages 379-380; they will help you when you watch the video.

STEP 4: Review the VIEWING GUIDE section in the telecourse guide. It lists several points to consider as you watch the video.

STEP 5: Watch the video.

STEP 6: Read the UNDERSTANDING THE LESSON section in the telecourse guide. Make sure you understand the key terms and can answer the focusing questions included there.

STEP 7: Complete the SELF-TEST.

STEP 8: Go back to the LESSON OBJECTIVES and make sure you can respond to each of them.

INTRODUCING THE LESSON

Hanging in the Cultural History Museum in Vienna, Austria, is a huge painting by the 16th century Flemish master, Pieter Bruegel the Elder. The scene depicted in this painting is of a peasant village filled entirely with young children, every one of whom is playing a game. The children in "Children's Games" spin tops, chase one another blind-folded, hide from one another behind buildings, shoot marbles, and act out the roles of soldiers, riders, and farmers. Everywhere you look on the surface of this massive painting, which measures about eight feet across and six feet high, are groups of children – three, four, five – engaged in the universal business of childhood: playing.

Imagine now that you use modern motion-picture techniques to fade Bruegel's painting out, revealing beneath it a picture taken from above of a contemporary elementary school playground. The long dresses, head scarves, and leather jerkins of the 16th century peasant children dissolve into the T-shirts, blue jeans, and baseball caps of contemporary American kindergartners and first-graders. Though the clothing and background change, the groupings and postures of the children remain nearly identical. In the 20th century, children still bend down toward bunches of rocks or glass in the dirt, extend their hands toward one another, chase after each other across open fields, or take turns trying to toss a ball a certain distance. In other words, then as now, play is a central aspect of the developing child's life.

And probably, the resemblance between child's play in a 16th century Flemish peasant village and a 20th century schoolyard continues in another way. As they make up games of their own and pretend to be mothers and fathers, policemen, and mail carriers, the modern children are probably echoing similar activities of their predecessors in play – who undoubtedly had their own games of being the baker, or the village priest, or the hunter of wolves. Then, as now, play allowed the young child a safe way of getting a handle on some of the confusing or frightening aspects of the world and bringing them down to the child's scale. Play is one of the main ways that children make sense out of the world and begin to figure out their own places in it.

In this lesson you will take a look at the importance of play in the unfolding development of the preschool child. During early childhood, children face a number of developmental challenges, which include establishing peer relationships, mastering self-control, expanding their involvement with the world, and forming new relationships with their parents. The child approaches all of these tasks, and others, through play. You will study how children use fantasy, role play, and pretend play to come to grips with the pressures and dilemmas that they face now. You will get an understanding of what a powerful tool play can be for children as they move through the cognitive, social, and emotional changes of the preschool period.

And you may well gain an appreciation of the similarities between 5 year olds in a modern schoolyard and their counterparts of 400 years ago.

GOAL

The purpose of this lesson is to show how preschoolers use play to come to grips with and master a number of the developmental challenges which they face.

LESSON OBJECTIVES

After reading the text assignment, completing the exercises in this telecourse guide, and viewing the lesson's video portion, you will be able to:

1. Recognize the role of play in a child's social, cognitive, emotional, and physical development.

2. Give examples of what children learn when they experiment with their environment in play.

3. Indicate the various functions fantasy play can serve.

4. Recognize that some play is more productive than other play, and discuss ways in which play can be managed or directed.

5. Discuss the role of play therapy and when and how it is conducted.

VIEWING GUIDE

Many of a child's stages of development require assistance. Learning to walk, to talk, to follow our society's particular rules of behavior – all these require help from parents, other adults, and siblings. But no one has to explain to the healthy child the benefits and pleasures of playing. Just as surely as the newborn is pre-conditioned to reflexively suck in its first breath, so is the normal preschooler prepared to explore the world in play. After reading the text material and learning the important terms included there, you are ready to view the lesson's video portion. First, review the questions in the Self-Test at the end of this telecourse guide lesson to give you an idea of important points to watch for in the video. Then read the following Points to Consider to give you an idea of what the video will cover. Keep these points in mind while watching.

Points to Consider

☐ *Development through play*: For normally developing preschoolers, play is a tool for working through and coming to grips with many of the tasks of this period. Notice how children use fantasy and role playing to act out their new concepts of others and the self. Be aware of the importance of play in forming early friendships.

☐ *Playing for social skills*: During early childhood, the child's emerging social skills are often expressed in play. Watch for examples of how new concepts of aggression, empathy, and altruism are all expressed in play. Look for examples of how children explore their concept of gender through play.

☐ *Changing ways of playing*: Pretend play offers preschoolers a safe way of confronting and mastering many of their fears. Keep in mind that children are now seeking to identify with their parents and may practice this through play. Remember the various advances in self-awareness that now underlie the child's new skills of pretending.

☐ *Playing at school*: Educators are well aware of the value of using play in teaching children during early childhood. Notice how teachers assess their pupils' social competence by observing them during play. Pay attention to the ways educators can structure play to help disturbed children function more normally.

UNDERSTANDING THE LESSON

"In our play we reveal what kind of people we are." Ovid, the Roman poet who said that around 10 A.D., was expressing an insight worthy of a modern child developmentalist. From the developmentalist's point of view, however, the aphorism might more truly read that in play as children, we reveal what kind of people we are likely to become.

During early childhood, children begin playing together in groups, acting together to create elaborate fantasy games through which they both explore and express their views of the world. Preschoolers also spend long hours in solitary play, entertaining themselves and exercising their new concepts of the self. Throughout early childhood, when young children play, they are doing much more than just having a good time: they are preparing themselves for a lifetime of social involvement.

The Role of Play in Development

For preschoolers, the Fisher-Price Playlab in East Aurora, New Jersey, is a taste of heaven. Here, in front of one-way mirrors, children between the ages of 2 and 7 romp unsupervised among the brightly colored miniature schoolbuses, saxophones, and stacking rings created by this toy manufacturer. Using the riches of specially designed props, the young toy testers pretend to put out fires, sell groceries, drive cabs, cook meals, and raise families. As they stack blocks, push around dump trucks, and arrange the furniture in the rooms of miniature condominiums, the children are having fun – and providing a wealth of data to observing company staff members.

Unlike their adult counterparts in consumer surveys, however, children don't need any monetary encouragement to participate in such research. Like a kitten confronted with a ball of yarn, the normal 3 year old has one response when presented with replicas of the adult world scaled to his or her size: to play. And just like the developing young animal, the young human is gathering information about the world and practicing responses to it by playing. If curiosity is the natural fuel that supplies a preschooler with the energy to explore the world, then play is the vehicle that the children drive in search of its answers.

One important form of play that children begin adopting in early childhood is that of fantasy, or role playing. With the development of new powers of conceptualization and language ability, the child becomes able to imagine him- or herself as being someone else and acting that out. By pretending to be a parent or teacher or some other adult with control over him or her, the child is able to promote his or her own self-confidence and sense of autonomy without having to defer to someone more powerful. Furthermore, by sharing fantasies, agreeing on the elaborate rules for a game, and coordinating their behaviors, 4 and 5 year olds actively build up their levels of social competence.

Clearly, playing together is an important way for children to form early friendships and then to maintain them. As was shown in the text example of Mikey and his friends playing on the schoolyard climbing structure, mutual play offers children opportunities for developing communication and interaction skills, as well as for exercising their imaginations. Child developmentalists have used observations of such playground activities to measure the social competence of children – focusing, in particular, on whether children engage in solitary, parallel, or cooperative play.

Playing together also enables children to absorb important lessons from their peers about fairness, reciprocity, and cooperation. In pretend games such as "Mommy and Daddy," "going to work," and "police," children learn a great deal about cultural norms and values, such as the roles associated with being male and female and the rules of their particular society. And within the structure of the family, siblings will interact in play in special ways. For example, one study has shown that young preschoolers enjoy fantasy play with nurturant older siblings in ways that they can't with their mothers. Again, these types of play allow the children safe ways of examining feelings about their parents.

Focusing Questions

1. Early childhood is a time when the child's social world is greatly expanding. What are some of the new opportunities that preschool children will typically have to encounter other children and play with them?

2. In the Alaskan fishing port of Dutch Harbor, a group of 5-year-old boys gets together at recess to play "crabber." By consent, Danny is chosen captain of the children's imaginary vessel because his father is in real life a crab boat captain. What are some of the possible lessons about life and getting along with one another that the boys are demonstrating here?

Practicing New Social Skills Through Play

Four-year-olds Emily and April are having a tea party with their stuffed animals in the backyard of Emily's house. Emily's 5-year-old brother John, who is unhappy because his mother won't buy him a RoboCop gun and holster set, wanders over to the two girls.

"Wanna play with us?" Emily asks her brother. "You can have some good cakes," she says, pointing at the pine cones lying on the platters in front of Mr. Bear and Mrs. Raccoon.

"Uh uh, I don't want to play with your dumb bear," John answers. Darting forward, he grabs a pine cone from a plate. "It's my hand grenade," he says, tossing the transformed slice of "cake" over the backyard fence. "Kaboosh!" he yells, mimicking the sound of an explosion.

"Mommy!" Emily wails as her brother runs off. "John's bein' mean."

With their growth in the understanding of the self as an agent and of the concept of fairness, children also become capable of more sophisticated forms of aggression. John, for example, is now able to channel some of his anger at his mother toward his sister in an act of hostile aggression, which indicates that he understands the effects his actions will have on the girls' feelings.

As any parent will recognize, children of John's age are influenced by movies and television in their subjects for play. Understandably, researchers have concentrated on what effects such exposure, especially to television, has on the behavior of children. Although the results have been inconclusive, watching violent TV programs does appear to increase the amount of aggression shown by children in a nursery school classroom, at least within the short term. And since children typically act out in play their responses to important influences or events, you can expect to see children modeling fantasy play on the themes of TV shows and movies they see.

Another important issue which children approach through play during early childhood is that of gender. Through role playing, children are able to practice the roles they see adults of their own sex acting out in society, as well as to learn to relate to the opposite gender. And although young preschoolers often enjoy toys regardless of their gender, parents and other adults usually steer them toward toys that their culture considers gender-appropriate. Researchers at Fisher-Price's Playlab, for instance, note that both boy and girl 3 year olds sought out the company's water-squirting fire pumper – but parents bought it only for boys.

Focusing Questions

1. Why would you expect preschoolers to have the most opportunities to express hostile aggression during play?

2. What are some differences in how boys and girls play during early childhood?

Changing Ways of Playing During Early Childhood

While feeding the geese in the park one afternoon, 4-year-old Beth had her fingers bitten by an especially voracious bird. Though her skin was unbroken, the little girl was badly scared by the incident. A few days later, Beth's mother noticed her little girl acting out a scenario of the incident in which she was in control of the situation. Holding out her hand to a stuffed panda that was meant to be a goose, Beth acted out being bitten and flinching back. The child then shifted into the role of her mother, pushing the toy away and saying, "Bad goose! Don't bite Beth! Be nice, eat the nice bread." Then, to her "little girl," Beth said, "Don't cry, Beth. The bad goose is go away."

Beth's solitary pretend play demonstrates one important function of play in the preschooler's development. By imagining a frightening situation and taking over the part of her more-powerful mother, Beth is able to work out her anxieties from being bitten and thus master them. Through play, she is able to directly confront fears that would otherwise be too much for her.

This type of pretend play offers the child a chance to work through her emotions over a number of developmental challenges that arise now. Recall, for example, the task of identification with parents that children must accomplish in early childhood. Although in real life the child faces conflict when she realizes that in fact her parents are much more powerful than she is, through play she can switch places with her parents and make them submit to her powers. As described in Chapter 10, through play the child can scold or discipline her parents and get away with it. By pretending, the child can express feelings and behaviors that are otherwise forbidden and even escape feeling guilty for it. The solutions to problems that the child now begins to actively discover through play become prototypes for more mature solutions in later years.

Fantasy role playing also helps children gain practice in a number of social roles at this time. By the judgments of their teachers, in fact, students who most often engage in social fantasy play are the most socially competent. In classroom settings, those children who are most popular are the most skilled at social play and vice versa.

It is important to recognize that the preschool child becomes so adept at play-pretending now because of a number of related developmental advances. As noted in Lesson 14, the child is now capable of detaching herself from her immediate experience. When a 4 year old dresses up as her mother and preens before the mirror, part of her pleasure comes from knowing that she is a little girl acting as an adult; she has the ability to observe herself acting. Likewise, the child is now able to move back and forth from previous to present experiences and compare then and now. Once again, a new level of developmental skill grows out of previous stages.

Focusing Questions

1. What makes pretend play such an attractive way for children to deal with their fears and other emotional problems?

2. While driving around in a deserted parking lot on a weekend, Barry places his 3-year-old son on his lap and lets the boy "steer" the car. What kind of activity is the father encouraging with this type of play?

Productive Play and Therapy Play

For many years schools and youth centers have set up special play centers to keep kids busy during the summer months, much to the relief of mothers and fathers everywhere. But at Seattle's Pacific Science Center in the summer of 1991, some lucky preschoolers got a chance to play their way toward an early understanding of technology. At the Center's Technology Academy, children between the ages of 3 and 6 designed outer-space toilets and practiced pushing buttons on robots. As part of a University of Washington project to promote technological expertise in children, the young explorers were expected to do just what they would normally do – to play.

As this example shows, play can be structured to give children new information and practice in developing skills. Indeed, improving eye-hand coordination, learning to take turns, and furthering the socialization process are major goals of such kindergarten games as bean-bag toss, the Hokie-Pokie, and blindman's bluff.

Of course, teachers will be familiar with the importance of play to early childhood learning. As noted in the previous lesson, teachers recognize that children who lack curiosity or enthusiasm, or fail to play well with other children, may have developmental problems. Teachers also rate those children who show more social play as being more socially competent. Remember also that teachers and researchers assess a child's degree of flexible self-control by how he or she behaves in a variety of situations.

Fantasy play is also a good indication of what kind of expectations or working models children have about the social world. When researchers use dolls to set up pretend situations that address the child's separation from the parent, they find that children with secure attachment histories tend to show that they expect parents and other adults to respond positively and reliably to them. On the other hand, children with histories of anxious or avoidant attachment tend to have difficulties playing with their peers. In the text, for example, you saw an instance of how a child with anxious attachment shows little resilience or facility in playing with other children.

The power of play as a learning and developmental tool, however, is further demonstrated by recent research. In one study, children who were emotionally withdrawn were put into special play sessions with younger children. Their interactions with the younger children seemed to have the effect of enhancing their social skills and confidence in peer relations. Upon return to their regular classrooms, the formerly withdrawn children then became more outgoing toward their peers.

Focusing Questions

1. Why would you expect a child who had high self-esteem, good self-confidence, and strong curiosity to be more appreciated as a playmate by peers than a child who was deficient in these areas?

2. Suppose you are a kindergarten teacher. Among your students, would you probably call on children with a history of secure attachment or anxious attachment to lead games?

Questions for Understanding

As you read these questions, often raised by parents, educators, and other childcare providers, first try to answer the questions yourself. Then read the answer following each question and compare your response to it.

1. *I've noticed that our 4-year-old son has recently begun playing more difficult games with other children. For instance, he's now able to play hide-and-seek without popping out before the kid who is "it" finds him. What is it that now enables my son to play more sophisticated games?*

For one thing, children of your son's age are gaining the ability to inhibit their actions, which is something they can't do as toddlers. As he grows older, your son can control his excitement when he's hiding during hide-and-seek and wait until the coast is clear to run back to base.

In general, your son will now be showing other signs of growing self-control as he plays. For example, you can expect your son to throw fewer tantrums when you ask him to put off playing with a toy until a later time. As you've already noticed, your son's growing powers of self-control enable him to take part in more involved games with his peers, as well as making him more enjoyable for you to be around.

2. *How does an increased ability to tolerate frustration affect a child's play during early childhood?*

As the ability to tolerate frustration increases, children become capable of handling more complicated toys. For example, you probably wouldn't give even a child's simplified cassette player to a child younger than 4 or 5 because they wouldn't have the patience to master the necessary buttons. Giving sophisticated toys or gadgets to toddlers is inappropriate because they get frustrated easily and tend to deal with the situation by throwing tantrums. By about the age of 3, however, the child's ability to handle frustration has greatly improved, as has the range of games he or she can play, both alone or with other children.

3. *What is ego resiliency and how is it expressed in play?*

Ego resiliency simply refers to the child's ability to adjust his or her level of self-discipline appropriately in different situations. As children move out of the toddler period, a time when they more or less act upon their impulses as they feel them, they begin adapting behavior to circumstances. The child is learning that in some cases it is okay to run unrestrained across a room, screaming loudly, while in different circumstances, he or she will have to stand quietly in that same room. Likewise, the child with appropriate ego resilience knows that some games, such as Red Rover, require an effort of maximum physical strength, whereas a game of hopscotch takes a finer concentration of physical skills.

As another example, consider the behavior of a pair of 5-year-old cousins at their grandfather's funeral. During the service at the funeral parlor, the two boys sit together behind their parents, keeping quiet with only an occasional nudge in one another's ribs or a stifled giggle. After the service, when the family gathers in front of the casket for a few words, both boys stand solemnly alongside their parents. But a half hour later, as the adults receive condolences at graveside, the two boys are happily dodging one another between the headstones. The flexibility with which the boys move from self-restrained attention to exuberant play demonstrates their appropriate ego resilience.

4. *My 4-year-old daughter loves playing with her 7-year-old brother's collection of model trucks and trains – at least she tries to when he isn't looking. But I've noticed that when she attends day care, she plays with the more traditionally female toys such as dolls, kitchen equipment, and play houses. Does this apparent confusion in preference for types of toys indicate any problems?*

Probably not. Your daughter is at an age when sex-typed behavior greatly increases, particularly in settings such as day care. There, she is surrounded by little girls her own age who are quick to enforce what they already sense are the "correct" toys for them. Adults are also important sources of what toys boys and girls should play with, beginning with parents during the toddler period. But these gender roles also seem to have some biological basis, as shown by the greater amount of rough-housing among young boys and the tendency of girls to nurture babies.

At home, your daughter apparently feels safe playing with the toys that she prefers, which in her case include trucks and trains. That her tastes aren't necessarily unusual is backed up by evidence from the Fisher-Price Playlab: a favorite toy of preschool boys at the lab was a line of kitchen toys that included a child-size stove, but parents bought the stove only for their daughters.

5. *I've noticed that my 4-year-old son spends a lot of time in pretend play by himself. That didn't bother me until one afternoon I listened in to what he was saying as he played. He was pretending that he was the mommy, as well as himself. He imagined scolding himself because he wanted to go see the new Arnold Schwarzenegger movie, but as "Mommy" he kept saying it was "too violent" – just as I'd explained to him last week. But then, I heard him pretending that he sneaked out of a back window and went to the movie anyway. Is playing like this a sign that my son is unhappy?*

Not necessarily. On the contrary, what you describe sounds like a normal preschooler imaginatively working through a disappointing real situation to a more positive one. During early childhood, children often resort to pretend play to assess and come to grips with problems or frustrations. In fact, researchers have found that children with histories of secure attachment are more likely to imagine negative themes and bring them to successful resolution than children who do not have such histories. In other words, by pretending to have gotten what he wanted out of you, your son is actively seeking to discharge his frustration with you. Even the solitary play you describe is usually a healthy outlet for children your son's age. After all, in his imagination he is recognizing a problem and trying to solve it, rather than denying it. Chances are good that this kind of behavior will serve as a model for his later, more mature decisions.

6. *When I listen to my 4-year-old son play by himself, I'm amazed at how complicated his play scenarios are. Sometimes he'll act out the parts of three or four figures in an imaginary scene – pretending to be an ambulance driver, an emergency room nurse, and a surgeon, for example. I sometimes fantasize about his becoming a fine actor some day. Is my son exceptionally gifted?*

Frankly, the behavior that you describe is that of a very normal preschooler of your son's age. Like other normal children of his age, your son is now able to "uncouple" himself from the various aspects of an experience. For example, when he is in his room playing hospital, he is fully aware that he is playing the various parts of the hospital personnel and that he is a small boy playing in his room. Likewise, children your son's age can alternate among several different "voices" in play. That is, he can be simultaneously an actor in his dramas, a narrator, and a stage manager.

A related development is the ability to understand that he has consistent dispositions, or ways of acting, that remain the same over time. All of these abilities and skills represent new growth in the preschooler's sense of self.

SELF-TEST

The following multiple choice and short answer test questions should help you assess your understanding of the points covered in the text and the video. After answering all the questions, check your answers against the key and use the accuracy of your answers to gauge how well you have met the lesson objectives.

Multiple Choice Questions

1. Among the 25 or so kindergartners lined up to get on a school bus, there is relatively little jostling – except for one little boy who keeps darting away from the line and trying to get over to the playground. Although the teacher snags him and tries to talk to him several times, he struggles and fights to get away: "I just want to play on the swings, that's all!" he keeps shouting. Apparently, this child does not have

   a. a high level of curiosity.
   b. a history of avoidant-anxious attachment.
   c. ego resiliency.
   d. any siblings.

2. Ed and Laura agree to play a make-believe game of "gas station." "Okay," says Ed, "I'll drive the car; you take the money." The game the children are playing is an example of

   a. social incompetence.
   b. denial of reality.
   c. identification.
   d. fantasy play.

3. You are observing the children in a kindergarten class. You know you've found an example of socially competent play when you see

   a. four children cooperating in a game of cops and robbers.
   b. a single child playing with a stuffed doll in a quiet corner.
   c. two children busy coloring but not talking.
   d. one boy punching another boy in the stomach.

4. In the same kindergarten classroom, you listen to the four boys organize their game of cops and robbers: "I'll be the motorcycle cop," says one boy. "No, I wanta ride the bike," says another. "You been using it all recess now." "Okay," says the first boy, "you take a turn, and I'll use this dynamite to blow up the bank." Among other things, these boys are clearly learning about the concept of

   a. instrumental aggression.
   b. banking hours.

   c. fairness.
   d. hostile aggression.

5. "Baby boomer" parents Jeff and Diane Jones are very upset when their 4-year-old son Winston picks up a single chopstick from the dinner table, points it at his father, and says, "Pow, pow! I shot you." Since the Jeff and Diane have never allowed Winston to play with guns, they ask him where he learned his new trick. "At day school," the boy says. "All the guys have guns. Will you buy me one?" Winston's gun play shows one way that children use play to

   a. antagonize their parents.
   b. learn to delay gratification.
   c. learn to tolerate frustration.
   d. learn gender-appropriate behavior.

6. Four-year-old Helen is playing alone with her dolls. She drops a doll into a pretend lake that she has made by spreading a cloth on the floor. "Oh, oh, look out, the little girl's in the water, she'll get drownded. Poor little girl, boo hoo. Look, here comes her mommy; she's crying too. Come here, Mr. Policeman, get the little girl out of the water. Okay, she's not drownded anymore – hooray!" Helen's play is a way for her to practice using her newly developing sense of

   a. emotional dependency.
   b. empathy.
   c. self-control.
   d. ego resilience.

7. Suppose, in the play scene described above, that Helen had pretended that she was the policewoman who rescues the little girl. Further suppose that Helen's mother herself is a policewoman and that Helen imagines herself as a policewoman doing good deeds. In that case, Helen would have been practicing her newly developing sense of

   a. identification.
   b. gender-appropriate behavior.
   c. instrumental aggression.
   d. delayed gratification.

8. In both of the fantasy play scenes described above, the one area of development that Helen would have learned the *least* about would have been

   a. empathy.
   b. altruism.
   c. hostile aggression.
   d. identification.

9. As a kindergarten teacher, you would be interested in the most effective ways of teaching your children about how to behave in certain situations. Suppose, for example, that you wish to impress on the children the importance of not talking to strangers. You decide that the best way to do this is to have

   a. a policeman come in and talk to them about how to behave when approached by a stranger.
   b. them view a videotape about how to behave when approached by a stranger.
   c. them draw pictures of what they should do when approached by a stranger.
   d. the children act out a role play of how to behave when approached by a stranger.

10. In a special play session, children who were emotionally withdrawn were able to be drawn out of their shells somewhat by interacting with

    a. younger children.
    b. much older children.
    c. adults.
    d. pets.

Short Answer Questions

The following questions should be answered in a paragraph or two. You should identify several key points for each answer and use these to form the framework for your response.

1. What are some of the cognitive, social, emotional, and physical developments that must take place before children can begin enjoying some of the more advanced forms of play during early childhood, such as fantasy and role play?

2. What are some of the signs of social competence that you would expect a normally developing child to show during play?

3. During an afternoon at day care, several 3 and 4 year olds, both boys and girls, get together for a game of "Mommy and Daddy." What are some of the gender-related issues that you would expect the children to be addressing through this game?

16

A Look at the Whole Child:
Ages 2½ through 5

LESSON ASSIGNMENT

Completing the following steps will help you master the lesson objectives and achieve the goal for this lesson:

STEP 1: Read the INTRODUCING THE LESSON section to provide a context for what you will learn in this lesson.

STEP 2: Read the lesson's GOAL and LESSON OBJECTIVES so that you will know what you are expected to learn.

STEP 3: Read the text assignment, Chapter 9, pages 310-343, and Chapter 10, pages 346-380. Pay particular attention to the key terms and concepts in the Chapter Summaries; they will help you when you watch the video.

STEP 4: Review the VIEWING GUIDE section in the telecourse guide. It lists several points to consider as you watch the video.

STEP 5: Watch the video.

STEP 6: Read the UNDERSTANDING THE LESSON section in the telecourse guide. Make sure you understand the key terms and can answer the focusing questions included there.

STEP 7: Complete the SELF-TEST.

STEP 8: Go back to the LESSON OBJECTIVES and make sure you can respond to each of them.

INTRODUCING THE LESSON

As Pat Ellison walks her son Walt to kindergarten on the first day of school, she wonders who is more nervous, herself or her 5 year old. He'll be just fine, she thinks; he doesn't have any trouble getting to know other kids. Besides, at least two of his playmates – Cammie Jones and Doug Fraser, both from the neighborhood – are starting school today too.

"Mom," Walt says, interrupting Pat's reverie. "How come I can't have a lunch box too?" referring to an older boy across the street on his way to school, toting a lunch box with a picture of a popular cartoon character on it.

"Because you'll be coming home at noon, honey, in time for lunch with me. You'll get to take your lunch next year, when you start first grade."

"I wish I could take my lunch now," says the boy.

"Why? Because you'd like a lunchbox like that boy?"

"Uh huh. But mostly 'cause Daddy takes his lunch sometimes too, doesn't he? Going to kind-a-garden's kinda like going to work, isn't it? If Daddy gets to take his own sammwich's, I want to, too."

"Well, you can do that next year, when you start first grade."

"Hey, neat, they stop the traffic for the kids," says Walt as he and his mom reach the crosswalk in front of the school. Fifth- and sixth-graders in caps and sashes hold up STOP signs to help the children cross the street. "It's easy to get across. This is going to be fun, Mom."

Later, as Walt's mother walks back home, she'll admit to herself that she's more sad to see her son start kindergarten than she is anxious about his experience there. She'll miss the boy, who is continually asking her questions about how things work and why people behave the way they do. Over the past couple of years, Walt has become increasingly self-reliant and capable. He spends hours playing, both alone and with neighborhood children near his own age. He has even begun showing much greater patience when he has to wait to get some help or receive something from his parents. He's more willing to accept the limitations that his parents put on him than he was as a toddler, and he seems particularly close to his father. And he's starting to read, Pat thinks. Yes, he's definitely ready to step out a little further from his mom.

With this lesson, you review the numerous developments that occur during early childhood. As you have seen in the previous three lessons, children experience qualitative change at this time, becoming much more sophisticated thinkers and actors than they were as toddlers. As a result of their improved skills of conceptual thought and their new social abilities, the child at the end of the preschool period stands ready to embark on a new level of involvement in the world. In self-control, powers of thought, communication skill, and self-awareness, the 5-year-old child is far more capable and skilled than he was just two or three years earlier.

GOAL

The purpose of this lesson is to present you with a comprehensive picture of the many developmental changes that preschoolers experience.

LESSON OBJECTIVES

After reading the text assignment, completing the exercises in this telecourse guide, and viewing the lesson's video portion, you will be able to:

1. Review the major physical changes that occur during early childhood.

2. Give examples of how the preschooler's more advanced capacity for mental representation and for using and manipulating symbols facilitates communication and learning.

3. Summarize the ways in which the cognitive advances a child achieves between the ages of 2½ and 5 help to foster social and emotional development.

4. Discuss the intimate connection that exists between different aspects of development and how temperament and experience are incorporated into the total child by the preschool period.

5. Recognize that early childhood experiences may manifest themselves later in life and that continuity in development proceeds beyond the preschool period.

VIEWING GUIDE

Children cross a number of important developmental boundaries during early childhood. They master new conceptual tools, begin making friends, further establish their identities, and accelerate their search for knowledge. By the end of the preschool period, the child is in many ways closer to adulthood than to toddlerhood. After reading the text material and learning the important terms included there, you are ready to view the lesson's video portion. First, review the questions in the Self-Test at the end of this telecourse guide lesson to give you an idea of important points to watch for in the video. Then read the following Points to Consider to give you an idea of what the video will cover. Keep these points in mind while watching.

Points to Consider

☐ *A new grasp of concepts*: During the preschool period, children develop many new cognitive skills that are reflected in improved levels of communication and understanding. Look for examples of how the conceptual tools that arise now make the child a better communicator. Be aware of how preschoolers' limited memory and attention affect their development.

☐ *Getting better at getting along*: The way that preschoolers' thinking is changing affects how they get along with others, both peers and adults. Pay attention to the effect that egocentrism, self-reliance, empathy, and aggression have on the social relations of preschoolers. Note the connection among cognitive, social, and emotional development.

☐ *The ways we are*: As in all other stages of development, preschoolers are affected by the various cognitive, emotional, and social changes in individual, unique ways. Be aware of how earlier stages of development mold the preschooler's search for self-reliance, a sense of gender, and new ways of relating to parents. In the video portion, see if you can detect clues that reveal the levels of self-esteem of the children profiled there.

☐ *Another layer on the foundation of the self*: Children enter early childhood from the direction they've been pointed by earlier stages of development, and what they experience between the ages of 2½ and 5 will affect their future growth. Be aware of how a child's history of attachment influences a wide range of developmental tasks now. Look for examples of how the preschooler's evolving sense of self-esteem, gender, and self-reliance will in turn shape future growth.

UNDERSTANDING THE LESSON

If human development were structured like government programs, then early childhood would be a gargantuan bureaucracy. If civil servants ran childhood, each of us would contain Bureaus of Conceptual Tools, Departments of Self-Esteem, Self-Reliance, and Self-Resilience, and Agencies of First Friendship and Identification with Parents. And probably, if internal development paralleled government programs, each of us would find it easy to get "funding" for feelings of aggression, but not for a sense of empathy.

Fortunately, however, individual development follows coherent and directional lines during early childhood and all other periods. The growth in cognitive abilities that preschoolers experience will be reflected by their emotional and social growth. Likewise, their abilities to learn will be affected by their expanding social horizons and colored by their new emotional outlooks. In a very real sense, the preschooler is the fortunate focus of a fully-funded, coherently structured program of personal growth.

Preschoolers' Advances Toward Communication and Learning

As Tom Neville got ready to paint the trim around his living room door, he called his two young children into the room. "Daddy's going to paint this part," he told the children. "Now don't touch it, okay?"

"Okay," answered 5-year-old Martin.

" 'Kay," answered 2½-year-old Melanie. But 20 minutes later, while her father wasn't looking, Melanie sidled up to the fresh paint and planted a palm on its sticky surface. Martin noticed his sister's act and called to his father, "Daddy, Melanie's touching the paint!"

Martin and Melanie are both preschoolers, but they stand at opposite ends of that period's range of development. Though Tom thought both his children understood his warning about the paint, each obviously meant something different when they said "okay." As a young preschooler, Melanie is not nearly as physically mature as her older brother. She isn't as steady on her feet or as skilled at using her hands as her brother is. And, most importantly for Tom's fresh paint, she has yet to gain the ability to inhibit her actions. Although he delivered the same warning to both children and got a similar reaction, Tom failed to recognize that his children had different cognitive abilities to understand and respond to his words.

Over the previous three lessons, you have followed the significant cognitive growth that preschoolers experience. By about age 5, children are beginning to grasp the concept of cause and effect, though they lack an abstract understanding of what can constitute a cause. They are beginning to master the basics of several vital conceptual tools, including conservation, classification, seriation, and transitive inference. By the time children enter elementary school, many (but certainly not all) of them have gained the capacity to deal with simple questions of "how much," "how big," "how often," and "how fast." Their growing ability to handle concepts of quantity and volume also enables them to better communicate with one another when they need to negotiate sharing food and toys, tasks that arise frequently as they more often interact with their peers.

You have seen how the preschooler's capacity for learning expands as he or she grows beyond centration. During this period, children become able to consider more than one aspect of a problem at a time. The older preschooler's powers of communication also improve as centration declines.

Preschoolers' ability to pay attention is also becoming more controlled than it was during infancy. As you saw in the comparison of conversations between toddlers and 5-year-olds in the video portion of this lesson, the preschoolers are much better able to stay with one another's remarks and are communicating on a much higher level. And with their improved memories, preschoolers are able to keep track of the lessons that they're absorbing now from parents and peers in what is "correct" behavior for their gender. Across the board, preschoolers' better understanding of how things happen or work, of other people's feelings, and their ability to concentrate and pay attention to what they're being told make them better conversationalists and, increasingly, insatiable learners.

Focusing Questions

1. Why would centration make it difficult for a preschooler to learn to play many of the games older children enjoy?

2. What are some of the main cognitive skills that children must begin to grasp before they can benefit from a structured school setting?

Cognitive Growth and Social and Emotional Development in Early Childhood

Maurice Sendak, the writer and illustrator of children's books, once described, in a National Public Radio interview, an interaction between himself and a 4 year old. Sendak was signing copies of his book, *In the Night Kitchen*, and the little boy roughly tossed his copy of the book on the table.

"He must have seen a look of hurt on my face," Sendak remembered, "because he came around and laid his head in the crook of my arm. Then he looked up at me with a sly grin, and said, 'Is your name Maurice?' "

"And I said, 'Yes.' "

" 'Do you hate your name, Maurice?' "

"And again I said, 'Yes.' "

"Then he said, 'Are you a tough guy, Maurice?' I have no idea of what he was thinking when he said that, but he just leaped right into my head and started playing."

Sendak's reported conversation with a preschooler illustrates a number of the cognitive skills and limitations that affect a child's social and emotional interactions at this time. For one thing, the preschooler often thinks everyone thinks and feels as he or she does. For this little boy, having the name Maurice would have been unpleasant, so of course the adult had to hate the name too. But at the same time, by noticing the expression of hurt on the author's face and responding to it, the little boy is showing powers of empathy. Within these limits and abilities, the child is able to carry on a truly two-way conversation.

During the preschool period, children develop the ability to grasp another person's point of view, though often imperfectly. You saw this in the text example of how older preschoolers begin picking appropriate gifts for other people, something younger children have trouble doing. You saw how the growth of empathy leads to acts of altruism and improved relations among peers. At the same time, the preschooler develops within the confines of the limitations of this period. For example, by acting out role plays that often reflect the child's egocentric point of view, the child is able to resolve conflicts during solitary play that might otherwise be overpowering.

The preschooler's growing sense of self-reliance and awareness that his or her self is constant over time contributes to more numerous peer relations now also. By the age of 5, children are capable of interacting with other children, of sharing, of negotiating differences – all in parallel with their increasing cognitive abilities. With increased social and cognitive strengths come greater social competence and accelerated learning. With their better memories and wider range of experience, preschoolers have a variety of scripts that they can use to effectively play together and to master their environment. As you saw in the examples of the children in the video portion of this lesson, the interplay between cognitive, emotional, and social growth during early childhood is deeply symbiotic.

Focusing Questions

1. What are some of the conceptual abilities that a child must acquire before being able to leave egocentrism behind and begin to have a sense of empathy?

2. You have learned that teachers and researchers measure a child's level of social competence in part according to how well they get along with other children. What are some of the social and emotional advances that contribute to a child's level of social competence?

Incorporating Temperament and Experience During Early Childhood

In the opinion of many critics, the characters in fairy tales take on symbolic meaning that is applied to the developmental tasks that children face. For example, the two young girls who are the heroines of the story *Snow White and Rose Red* are better behaved and sweeter-tempered than any real children have ever been. "They were more pious and kind, more hardworking and diligent than any other two children in the world," the tale insists. So sweet and good are these two that hares eat out of their hands and deer leap around them; when they stray too far from their home in the forest, they lie down on the moss and go to sleep, unafraid.

But even the tellers of fairy tales gave a nod to the variety of human personality. According to the story, even these two paragons of virtue differed slightly: "Snow White was more quiet and gentle than Rose Red, who preferred to run around in the meadows and fields, look for flowers, and catch butterflies. Snow White stayed at home with her mother, helped her with the housework, or read to her when there was nothing to do." Even under exactly similar circumstances, individual children will have different temperaments and so react differently to the cognitive and social developments of early childhood.

You have seen examples of how the curiosity that preschoolers exhibit about their environment will tend to be fairly consistent over time and across situations. Likewise, the self-reliance that children develop in early childhood will help shape their future growth, just as it has been affected by previous stages of development. For example, some children have trouble with the move toward greater independence and develop emotional overdependence on their care givers. This appears to be a result of not having achieved a secure attachment relationship with care givers in an early stage of development. The inner working model that such a child is likely to develop will affect his or her growth throughout later stages of development.

Similar issues of temperament and prior experience are at work as preschoolers begin forming peer relationships, developing greater self-control and ego resilience, and changing their relationships with parents. As you have learned, social competence in early childhood will be affected by children's levels of self-esteem, which hinges in part on whether or not children feel they can have an effect on their environment. Children who have had parents who modeled prosocial behavior, empathy, and helpfulness toward others are more likely to develop these traits themselves. In contrast, children of parents who are either unresponsive and inflexible or else insufficiently firm in setting limits developed problems of behavior that affect their social competence, both now and in later phases of development.

1. Suppose you are a kindergarten teacher. In planning activities for your pupils, you have your choice of a range of games and activities: finger-painting, hide-the-thimble, beanbag toss, storytelling, block building. If you have a large number of self-reliant, actively curious children in the class, how might it affect your choice of activities? If you have a large number of emotionally dependent children in your class, how might that affect your plans?

2. What kind of characteristics would you expect from children whose parents are nurturant and responsive and set firm limits?

The Continuity of Development Through Preschool Onward

Kindergarten teacher Connie Jones would be shocked and hurt if you suggested that she gives preferential attention to some children over others. As she puts it, "I bend over backwards to be fair to these children. I know how important an influence I am on them."

But if you asked Ms. Jones which are the "difficult" children in her class, she would have no trouble pointing them out. "Probably the hardest to get along with is Margaret – she's a real troublemaker, always picking on the weaker children. I really have to keep an eye on her." Likewise, the teacher finds it easy to pinpoint her "prides and joys," those children who get along with the other children and show an active interest in all classroom activities. "Both Angie and Bobby are little angels; all the other kids like them. Whenever I set up an activity, I know they'll be right in the middle of it and won't need to be looked after. But Margaret has some real behavioral problems – I spend more time dealing with her than with any other child."

Individual characteristics grow or are modified at each stage of a child's development. As you have seen already in this course, each stage of development unfolds from the previous one and sets the stage for what follows. During the important years of development between 2½ and 5, children experience a number of qualitative changes that form a foundation for the rest of their life's development. Or, as clergyman Henry Ward Beecher once put it, "That energy which makes a child hard to manage is the energy which afterward makes him a manager of life."

For example, the success or failure with which children master self-control or the ability to tolerate frustration will affect their abilities to adjust to situations throughout later stages of development. Furthermore, preschoolers must also develop a degree of ego resiliency for coping with the changing demands in behavior of a variety of social circumstances. But as you saw in the example in Chapter 10 of preschoolers who practiced deliberate hostile aggression against other children, negative histories can produce negative results. Children with avoidant-resistant histories of attachment acted in ways that reflected their developmental histories. In other words, a child's behavior, whether prosocial or aggressive, tends to be coherent and understandable over time. And many patterns of action and response, of expectation and fulfillment, are established during early childhood.

Among the other important steps that children go through at this time are identification with parents, mastering a concept of gender, learning how to play productively with others, developing a sense of empathy, and forming a sense of self-esteem. And as shown by the example above of how even a well-intentioned teacher reacts to children according to their "good" or "bad" behavior, it is clear that the responses children have to the challenges of early childhood can have a profound effect on how others relate to them.

Focusing Questions

1. Most of us have at some time met people who could be described as "clingy" and who tended to need emotional support from their relationships. What kind of attachment relationships would you expect these people to have had as children?

2. What are some of the important elements of a parent-child relationship that will help a child develop a sense of high self-esteem?

Questions for Understanding

As you read these questions, often raised by parents, educators, and other childcare providers, first try to answer the questions yourself. Then read the answer following each question and compare your response to it.

1. *I have heard that 2 or 3 year olds are much closer to infant than adult in how they think. However, by the time children are 5 or so, they are closer in ways of thinking to an adult than an infant. Is this so? And if it is, why?*

   By the end of the preschool period, yes, children have acquired many of the ways of thinking that are recognizably "adult." For example, they have begun to understand the concept of cause and effect, to be very skilled at a variety of ways of organizing the information that they are now rapidly absorbing, and to have some understanding that their thought processes can be managed. Preschoolers are also gaining the ability to understand that other people have feelings, or a sense of empathy. And with the mastery of a growing number of scripts, the older preschooler has gained a basis for interacting with others in a number of situations.

   Among the cognitive skills that enable the preschooler to develop a more sophisticated understanding of the world are a number of conceptual tools. These include a new understanding of quantity, ordering, classes and collections, and conservation. Though these abilities will remain limited for some time by such difficulties as centration and confusion between appearance and reality, they still point the preschooler toward a higher grasp of abstraction and more complex symbolic thought.

2. *I have in my family room a realistic-looking "boulder" made of spongy polystyrene. Though it is about the size of a basketball and looks quite heavy, it actually weighs only a couple of ounces. Once, when my sister came over with my two nieces, I tossed the object at the older girl, who's 5. She threw her arms up, surprised, then laughed when it hit her arms and bounced off. But when she, in turn, tossed it at her 3-year-old sister,*

the younger girl cried, even though she'd already seen the "rock" bounce off her sister. Why was there such a difference in how the girls reacted?

Probably because your older niece has a greater ability to distinguish between appearances and reality than her younger sister. Children at about 3 years of age consistently interpret what something looks like to be what it really is, no matter what you may tell them. This cognitive limitation is part of the reason young preschoolers have difficulty solving problems of conservation or arranging items by length, for instance. By about the age of 5 or 6, however, the child's cognitive development will have advanced to the point that she is no longer easily fooled by superficial appearances – hence, the laughter of your 5-year-old niece and the tears of her 3-year-old sister.

3. *I've noticed that when I visit friends with my 4-year-old son, he makes no attempt at all to remember his outdoor clothing when we leave. Even if it's fairly cold outside, he's just as likely to skip merrily outside without putting his jacket back on. And heaven forbid that I ask him where his jacket or hat is: "I don't know," is all he'll ever say. Is such a poor memory normal for children of his age?*

Definitely. While 4 year olds will have considerably greater powers of recognition and recall than toddlers, they are not yet very aware of the memory demands of a particular situation. In other words, when your son flings off his coat in your friend's house, he doesn't realize he needs to make an effort to remember where he left it. As far as he is concerned, the jacket is your problem. He's used to having someone there to think of such things for him. If he has some involvement in an object, such as a favorite toy, he may be willing to make more of an effort to remember it.

4. *What are some of the developmental changes that take place during early childhood that make it easier for children to begin interacting with children of the same age and even to begin forming friendships?*

Among other things, children are now developing the ability to play on a more sophisticated level. For example, they can pretend to be a race car driver, say, while simultaneously knowing that they are pretending. Also, they are improving their vocabularies and language skills and so are better able to communicate with other children. Children are now increasingly able to control themselves, enabling them to better coordinate their activities with other children. For example, preschoolers begin to be able to inhibit their actions, enabling them to enjoy games that require greater physical control, such as hide-and-seek, or freeze tag.

At the same time, preschoolers are gaining a greater tolerance for frustration, which broadens the range of activities they can share with others. In fact, learning to share and to take turns are both important skills that children are now beginning to acquire, and which help them to relate with other children. And don't forget that the greater involvement with others which children now have also promotes their cognitive and social growth.

5. *I am aware of the concept of secure attachment and have a good idea of the kind of behaviors you would expect to see in a kindergartner with that kind of developmental history. But my county's social worker says that the 5-year-old foster son who just came to live with me had a history of anxious-avoidant attachment; how might you expect this child to act, both with other children and with his teacher?*

Children with a history of anxious-avoidant behavior are very likely going to have difficulty interacting with other children. They may act with hostile aggression toward other children, which in turn would tend to make the other children dislike them, creating further isolation. Or they might tend to stay away from the other children, preferring to play alone rather than in groups, which would also have the effect of further alienating them from the other children. These children often lie, blame other children in disagreements, and act defiantly.

Toward their teachers, these children often act erratically, at times seeking a great deal of attention and at other times rejecting it. On average, they require more support and discipline from their teachers than other students. All of these actions, while perhaps appearing inconsistent, are in fact coherent reactions to previous patterns of neglect or lack of nurturance and reflect low self-esteem and general mistrust.

6. *If all preschoolers face the same general tasks of development – becoming self-reliant, identifying with parents, forming a concept of gender, making friends, and so on – then why are there so many different types of children?*

The simple answer, of course, is that each individual is the result of different genetic combinations and developmental history. We all come from different families, different economic and social backgrounds, and have varying temperaments. And, in fact, even children within the same family can be as different from each other as individuals in any group of strangers. Then, the rate at which any one child will begin dealing with a particular stage of development – forming a sense of empathy, understanding that boys and girls are different, developing self-control – will vary from person to person.

Boys and girls vary in their development too, though no one can say for sure why. For instance, boys are more aggressive than girls, while girls tend to show evidence of more nurturing skills. Some researchers emphasize the role of biology in individual differences, while others lean more toward the role of experience. However, today probably most researchers favor a blend of both inborn factors and experience to explain the course of development that particular children take.

SELF-TEST

The following multiple choice and short answer test questions should help you assess your understanding of the points covered in the text and the video. After answering all the questions, check your answers against the key and use the accuracy of your answers to gauge how well you have met the lesson objectives.

Multiple Choice Questions

1. If you try to organize a foot race among several 3 year olds, you may have trouble getting them to start at the same time because of the difficulty they have

    a. running.
    b. inhibiting their actions.
    c. understanding the concept of a race.
    d. paying attention for even short periods of time.

2. Recently, Victor has been playing Memory with his 4-year-old daughter, Samantha. To play the game, they lay out all 52 cards face down in rows on a table. Then they take turns picking up two cards and putting them down. If they match two cards, they remove them and get another turn. When all the cards are off the table, the player with the most cards wins. Samantha is now able to play this game because of her growing ability to

    a. classify objects.
    b. understand conservation.
    c. distinguish between appearance and reality.
    d. learn a script.

3. Suppose you are babysitting a set of 3-year-old triplet girls and their 5-year-old brother. Further suppose that you are able to keep their attention long enough to ask them the question, "Why are polar bears white?" The answer of the 5-year-old brother is most likely to be,

    a. "Because they're painted that color."
    b. "Because they wear white blankets."
    c. "Because God makes them that way."
    d. "Because that way, the hunters can't see them."

4. At Halloween, 3-year-old Brenda's older sister Emily dressed up as a Roaring '20s bank robber, complete with a pencil-thin moustache. When Brenda saw her, she said, "Are you going to be a boy now, Emily?" Before the 3 year old will understand the concept of gender constancy, she must first

    a. identify with her parents.
    b. be able to delay gratification.
    c. overcome the appearance-reality problem.
    d. master the concept of conservation.

5. When children begin choosing birthday presents for people based on what they think the recipient might actually want instead of just what the child would like, it is in part because they have

    a. outgrown centration.
    b. begun to understand social inference.
    c. mastered the script of gift giving.
    d. developed good social competence.

6. Before preschoolers can effectively describe something that they're holding in front of them to someone who can't see them – over the phone, for example – they must first

   a. develop a sense of altruism.
   b. be able to handle abstractions.
   c. develop stronger powers of attention.
   d. begin to outgrow egocentrism.

7. During early childhood, children must repeat, in a somewhat different degree, a task of the toddler period. That developmental task is to

   a. form their first friendships.
   b. learn to inhibit their actions.
   c. establish a new level of autonomy.
   d. learn to delay gratification.

8. In developmental terms, 5-year-old Peter would rate a high level of social competence. Other children enjoy playing with him, his kindergarten teacher finds him full of energy and curiosity, and he generally seems to have high self-esteem. During an earlier stage of development, Peter probably

   a. formed an anxious attachment with his parents.
   b. was spoiled by his parents.
   c. didn't get sufficient nurturing.
   d. formed a secure attachment with his parents.

9. Among their students, preschool teachers tend to be very controlling of one particular category of child, though they are also very nurturing of these students. As a rule, these children tend to have

   a. a history of secure attachment.
   b. a history of anxious-avoidant attachment.
   c. a history of anxious-resistant attachment.
   d. never formed attachments with anyone.

10. At the age of 5, Christine is much more timid than most of her peers. Getting her to go to kindergarten every day is a struggle; once she's there, she whines to get her teacher's attention. With these characteristics as a 5 year old, which indicate she has a history of anxious-resistant attachment, by the time she is an adult, Christine will probably

    a. be shy and withdrawn regardless of the quality of her care in the future.
    b. be shy and withdrawn unless the quality of her care improves.
    c. be an entirely different person whose characteristics we can't foresee.
    d. have strong behavioral problems.

Short Answer Questions

The following questions should be answered in a paragraph or two. You should identify several key points for each answer and use these to form the framework for your response.

1. What are some of the cognitive developments which children must experience before they can begin feeling a sense of empathy?

2. During early childhood, children work through a number of the developmental challenges that they face through play. For example, they act out fantasies that enable them to resolve fears and conflicts and to help them identify with their parents. What are some of the cognitive advances of the preschool period that promote these types of play?

3. What are some of the cognitive limitations that still affect children as they come to the end of the preschool period?

MODULE V:

MIDDLE CHILDHOOD

17

Cognitive Development in Middle Childhood

LESSON ASSIGNMENT

Completing the following steps will help you master the lesson objectives and achieve the goal for this lesson:

STEP 1: Read the INTRODUCING THE LESSON section to provide a context for what you will learn in this lesson.

STEP 2: Read the lesson's GOAL and LESSON OBJECTIVES so that you will know what you are expected to learn.

STEP 3: Read the text assignment, Chapter 11, pages 395-435. Pay particular attention to the key terms and concepts in the Chapter Summary on pages 433-435; they will help you when you watch the video.

STEP 4: Review the VIEWING GUIDE in the telecourse guide. It lists several points to consider as you watch the video.

STEP 5: Watch the video.

STEP 6: Read the UNDERSTANDING THE LESSON section in the telecourse guide. Make sure you understand the key terms and can answer the focusing questions included there.

STEP 7: Complete the telecourse guide lesson's SELF-TEST.

STEP 8: Go back to the LESSON OBJECTIVES and make sure you can respond to each of them.

INTRODUCING THE LESSON

As he walks by his son's room, William pauses and pokes his head in. Seeing 9-year-old Andrew seated at his desk writing on some large sheets of paper, he asks, "Doing homework, Son?"

"Uh uh," says Andrew, without looking up from his work. "Inventing."

"What's the project?" the father asks, stepping into the room.

"Missiles," the boy says. "I'm gonna make models of Patriot missiles." As his dad leans over his shoulder, the boy looks up. "See," he says, pointing at the cylindrical outlines sketched on the paper, "This is the fuel chamber. I'm gonna use 16-ounce frozen orange juice cans for the body; I figure about half that'll be for fuel and the other half for the guidance system. But I can't figure out yet how to attach the stabilizer fins. I'd solder 'em on, but the cans are too thin. Maybe liquid solder?"

"That's a thought," says the father. "What are you going to use for fuel?"

"Oh, either the charcoal lighter stuff you use to barbecue or liquid nitrogen. Probably lighter fluid, 'cause I think liquid nitrogen's hard to keep; it melts off at room temperature."

"Um, yeah, I guess so. But before you try using any charcoal lighter, talk to me first, okay?"

"Sure, Dad."

Because he trusts his son, William doesn't worry that Andrew might actually attempt to fuel an orange-juice-can Patriot missile with charcoal briquet lighter fluid. Instead, his reaction is one of amusement at his son's multilevel mix of knowledge about missile systems, fractions, metallurgy, and explosive fluids. He feels proud at his son's apparent brightness and yet indulgent toward the obvious limits on his son's understanding. Mostly, though, he is pleased to see Andrew grappling with problems of mathematics and planning.

Although he probably doesn't think of it that way, the father has just witnessed an example of his son's continuing cognitive development. During the years of middle childhood, children make great strides in their ability to comprehend and analyze information. Between the ages of 7 and 10, children continue to expand the fundamental cognitive skills which they first began exhibiting in the preschool period – skills such as an understanding of conservation, classification rules, and metacognition.

At the same time, children in this age group are still constrained by certain cognitive limitations, as shown by Andrew's obvious misunderstanding of the volatility of flammable liquids. Children in middle childhood have not yet acquired a broad base of knowledge to draw upon, nor have they had much chance to practice their expanding cognitive abilities. Andrew, for example, recognizes that an orange juice can is too flimsy to support soldering, but doesn't realize that it also wouldn't make a suitable container for rocket fluid.

This lesson explores the gains in cognitive abilities that children make during middle childhood and sets out some of the constraints on cognition that still limit them. The text material will examine the range of cognitive skills of children at this age, the ones they improve in and the new ones they gain. It will also show how their memories continue to develop. You will briefly study the history of intelligence testing and learn the difference between formal and informal concepts of intelligence itself. And in the video portion of the lesson, you will see examples of grade-school children demonstrating their emerging cognitive abilities.

GOAL

The purpose of this lesson is to introduce you to the cognitive advances which children make during middle childhood and to examine the concept of intelligence and how it is measured.

LESSON OBJECTIVES

After reading the text assignment, completing the exercises in this telecourse guide, and viewing the lesson's video portion, you will be able to:

1. Compare the cognitive advances and limitations of middle childhood to those of the preschool period.

2. Explain the concept of conservation as it relates to cognitive development in middle childhood; indicate how Piaget and information-processing theorists differ in their view of how children acquire conservation.

3. Describe two kinds of classification skills children attain during middle childhood and the ages at which these skills generally become evident.

4. Differentiate between the basic processes of memory, constructive memory, mnemonic strategies, and metamemory and show how they are related to memory development in middle childhood.

5. Recognize the relationship between peer interaction and cognitive development.

6. Compare informal and formal concepts of intelligence.

7. Examine issues related to IQ testing including predictability, reliability, and cultural bias.

VIEWING GUIDE

This lesson takes a look at the rapid and broad growth in cognitive abilities which children undergo between the ages of about 7 and 10. During middle childhood, children show great improvement in the fundamental thinking skills they already have and become much more sophisticated at solving problems. After reading the text material and learning the important terms included there, you are ready to view the lesson's video portion. First, review the questions in the Self-Test at the end of this telecourse guide lesson to give you an idea of important points to watch for in the video. Then, read the following Points to Consider and keep them in mind while watching.

Points to Consider

☐ *Skills of conservation and classification*: During middle childhood, children make great cognitive advances by building upon skills they have already developed. Notice how elementary school children improve in comprehending the principles of conservation of number, weight, and liquids. Be aware of the differences between the hierarchical and matrix classification skills which improve at this time.

☐ *Remembering to remember*: As children begin the structured tasks of elementary school, their skills in remembering what they've learned are growing in a number of ways. In the video segment of the lesson, look for examples of how children remember through the four methods of basic process, knowledge, mnemonic strategies, and metamemory.

☐ *Using group interaction for learning*: Children are grouped together in elementary school classes for reasons besides convenience. Be aware of the various ways children develop their cognitive skills through interaction with their peers. Look for examples of children learning in didactic and cooperative situations.

☐ *Measuring young minds*: Individual intelligence, like art, is easy to recognize but hard to define. Pay attention to the distinctions between formal and informal conceptions of intelligence and be aware of the disagreements among psychologists about the nature and value of intelligence testing. Try to form an idea of the roles played by culture and education in IQ measurement.

UNDERSTANDING THE LESSON

In the late 1700s, a Viennese doctor named Franz Josef Gall introduced a system of determining an individual's personal characteristics and mental abilities by studying the contours of the skull. Phrenology, as the system was called, gained wide popularity in Europe and America.

Although we tend to smile at the idea of being able to judge intelligence through measuring the bumps on someone's head, interest in gauging individual cognitive abilities is still great. In Western societies, interest in measuring individual intelligence becomes especially important when children begin formal education. During the years of middle childhood, children are both developing rapidly across a wide range of cognitive skills and being assessed by peers, parents, and society at large as to their intellectual capacities.

Cognitive Development in Middle Childhood

Rebecca, the babysitter, finishes blending frozen yogurt and fresh peaches into a "smoothie" and pours the liquid into glasses for 5-year-old Larry and 9-year-old Janice. Larry looks at the smoothie filling his short, squat glass and then glances at his sister's smoothie, which fills a tall, slender glass.

"Janice got more than I did, Rebecca," says the Larry. "That's not fair."

"I did not," says the girl. "You got as much as me; your glass is just fatter."

"Your glass is taller," says Larry. "You got more."

"No she didn't," says the babysitter. "Look: the blender holds exactly 24 ounces; I gave each of you guys 12 ounces. You've both got the same amount."

Rebecca's explanation, while sufficient for Janice, probably will not satisfy Larry. This is because he has not yet gained an understanding of conservation, which makes it clear that an amount of liquid remains unchanged even though it is poured into different-sized containers. Also, Janice is able to understand her babysitter's example of necessary truth: 12 ounces plus 12 ounces equals 24 ounces, no matter how much the two glasses may vary in shape. Larry, however, is basing his perceptions on what he can understand using his senses – and he can "see" that his amount of smoothie is less than his sister's.

Jean Piaget thought that the same logic skills underlaid a child's understanding of all the applications of conservation, which include conservation of number, weight, and displaced liquid. Information-processing theorists, on the other hand, hold that children apply a variety of rules to conservation problems, modifying them according to the type of problem under consideration.

During middle childhood, children also improve in their abilities to learn information by strategies of classification. Although children are capable of classification during infancy and the toddler years, now they become able to understand the interrelationships among categories and sub-categories in complex systems. According to Piaget, children develop these improved abilities during the *concrete operational period*, which begins somewhere around age 6 or 7.

At this time, children develop the ability to categorize items according to *hierarchical classification*, the principle of organizing groups by adding to classes. We use hierarchical classification whenever we include one item of a smaller group under the umbrella of a larger, related group – saying, for example, that Mt. Saint Helens is a volcano in the Cascades Range. If a researcher then asked you whether there were more mountains or volcanoes in the Cascade Range, that would be a problem of *class inclusion*. The other major categorizing skill that emerges during middle childhood is *matrix classification*, which groups items according to two different qualities. If you were stocking an auto parts store, for example, you might first sort out all the headlights into one bin, and then subdivide them into regular, fog, and halogen lamps. In doing so, you would be using a matrix classification.

While the classifying skills that children possess in middle childhood are refinements of ones they've already developed, during this period they become much more capable of effectively establishing relationships among classes. They also overcome the preschooler's limitation of *centration*, which is the tendency to focus on only one aspect of a subject at a time. At the same time, children at this stage tend to be able to apply their classifying skills mainly to concrete objects and situations; the solution of abstract problems must await further cognitive development.

Key Terms

>   Hierarchical classification
>   Matrix classification
>   Class inclusion
>   Concrete operational thinking
>   Formal operational thinking

Focusing Questions

>   1. Why does the development of an understanding of necessary truth represent a great improvement in the ability of children to solve number problems?

Development of Memory Abilities in Middle Childhood

During the middle childhood school years, children are introduced to a number of fairly complex learning challenges, including mathematics. In the video portion of the lesson, you have seen the brows of 8 and 9 year olds knitting up as they concentrate on problems of division and multiplication and the mysteries of fractions. One reason that children are now ready to tackle these problems is the development in memory ability which they experience at this time.

By about the age of 7, children have mastered the basic processes of memory, including the routine acts of storing and retrieving information. While children in middle childhood make only minor refinements in their basic processes of memory, they do improve greatly in their ability to remember things better as a result of their increasing knowledge. Because children at this age have already accumulated a certain quantity of knowledge, they are often better able to store and recall new items of information based on inferences made on the basis of knowledge already stored in memory. This ability is called *constructive memory*.

Elementary school children also have more efficient memories than preschoolers because they are now capable of comprehending and using memory "tricks" or aids, called mnemonic strategies. The range of mnemonic devices is wide and could include repeating the name of a new acquaintance under your breath when you're introduced or tying a string to your finger as a memory-jogger. As you learned in the text material, children at the beginning of the middle childhood period may have a desire to remember something but lack an awareness of the strategies they might employ to aid their memory. By the end of the period, however, children show a general understanding of most of the major mnemonic strategies – rehearsal, organizing information, and summarizing, among others – and have begun using them regularly. In the video portion of the lesson, you saw scenes of how researchers measure memory efforts by having children tap their fingers while working through memorization tasks.

The other great aid to memory which occurs at this stage is *meta-memory*, which refers to your awareness of your own memory system's strengths and weaknesses as well as mnemonic strategies appropriate to *certain memory tasks.* Metamemory improves greatly during middle childhood.

Focusing Questions

1. How does constructive memory differ from just making things up? How does constructive memory enable children to use inference to answer questions based on information they have learned previously?

2. Can you think of some examples from your own experience of how you apply metamemory to problems of memory?

Social Interaction and Cognitive Development

The middle childhood years are also the elementary school years. Normal cognitive development is intricately interwoven with the interactions children have with others, both peers and adults, at this stage. Developmentalists refer to direct learning such as an explanation or a demonstration from a teacher, whether the teacher is an adult or another child, as a *didactic situation*. When two children of about the same level learn more or less equally from each other through working together toward a solution, it is known as a *cooperative situation*. You saw numerous examples of both styles of learning in the video portion of the lesson.

Research has shown that two conditions must exist for children to show cognitive improvement from peer interaction: first, at least one child has to possess certain prerequisite skills and, second, there must be sustained give-and-take between the children involved. In didactic situations, on the other hand, children learn best from teachers who use an adaptation of the concept of *scaffolding*, which you first encountered in Lesson 10. With scaffolding, the teacher aids the learner by giving hints, guidance, and advice about the learner's progress in mastering a task. Apparently, the ability to use scaffolding to help others learn is a cognitive skill that emerges during middle childhood.

Children practice a variety of styles of learning during middle childhood. They may choose to work on tasks alone or by observing while others perform a task. They may work together side-by-side, exchanging information, or they may cooperate in guiding one another to accomplish goals. And they may choose to collaborate in a power-sharing style that allows them to shape the flow of the interaction mutually.

During the early years of middle childhood, children tend to practice more symmetrical collaborations in learning situations. Younger children also rely more on physical demonstrations to teach others and tend to leap quickly to simple solutions. Older children, on the other hand, are better able to engage in longer and more extended arguments over problems and to bring more advanced metacognitive skills to bear on shared problem solving.

Key Terms

Scaffolding

Focusing Questions

1. Nine-year-old Brian is showing his 6-year-old sister how to load and play tapes on his portable cassette player. Are the two children involved in a didactic or a cooperative situation? Why?

2. Why do you think that having increased skills of metacognition would enable older elementary school children to be more effective teachers than children a few years younger?

Individual Differences in Intelligence

Perhaps at some point in your elementary school years, you had to take a kind of intelligence test. If so, in about the third or fourth grade you and your classmates took a test consisting of a variety of questions. For example, you might have had to answer mathematical or logic questions of varying degrees of difficulty. And if your teacher told you that the tests were to measure your *intelligence quotient* – your IQ – you thought you knew what that meant: the tests measured how "smart" you were.

As you learned in the text material, school children tend to think of intelligence as the ability to process information and to accomplish tasks. Then, as they age, children begin to view intelligence as the ability to acquire information and to learn. Finally, as adults, we synthesize the two earlier views and see intelligence as a blend of abstract problem solving and reasoning skills using such attributes as verbal skills and accumulated information.

Traditional intelligence tests predict school performance. As described in the text, the first modern intelligence tests were developed by French psychologist Alfred Binet around the beginning of the twentieth century. When Binet's tests were later adapted into English, the concept of measuring intelligence in terms of an individual's mental age – determined by comparing test scores to norms obtained from testing large numbers of children of various ages – was introduced. Then, by dividing an individual's mental age by their chronological age and multiplying the result by 100, researchers came up with that person's intelligence quotient – their "IQ." This is a unitary approach, which assumes that intelligence is a single, measurable characteristic.

However, not all modern psychologists agree that intelligence is measurable in the unitary sense. Indeed, as researcher Jane Mercer's comments in the video portion of the lesson made plain, some psychologists reject the very idea of intelligence as a useful scientific concept. In the view of many people, traditional intelligence tests just measure the ability of examinees to perform well in school settings or the amount of knowledge which a person has accumulated, instead of indicating any real mental abilities. They say these school-limited findings indicate "academic intelligence," as opposed to "practical intelligence" – the ability to function in everyday, "real-world" situations.

Be that as it may, developmentalists continue to debate the role of heredity and environment in the origination of intelligence. Much of the evidence for the role of genes in individual IQ development comes from studies of twins and adopted children. The data seem to show that while genes do account for the initial differences between individuals' IQs, how a person's IQ develops over time depends greatly on environment. Scientists use the concept of the *reaction range* to account for the interplay between genes and environment. According to this concept, genes set the lower and upper limits on a person's potential IQ, but the environment they are raised in determines what their IQ will actually be. The developmental truism that context, heredity, and individual history interact to shape individual growth appears to be true for the growth of intelligence as well.

Key Terms

Intelligence quotient
Reaction range

Focusing Questions

1. Why do you suppose that Dr. Mercer feels strongly negative about "intelligence" as a scientific concept? What are some of the ways in which academic intelligence testing may harm individuals? What are some advantages of such testing?

Questions for Understanding

As you read these questions, often raised by parents, educators, and other childcare providers, first try to answer the questions yourself. Then read the answer following each question and compare your response to it.

1. *I volunteered to care for a group of children recently. To keep the kids busy, I organized a game of "twenty questions." But not all of the kids were able to keep up; specifically, those who were under 6 or 7 never seemed to get the point. Why is that?*

The reason that the younger children in your group weren't very good at playing "twenty questions" is that they haven't yet developed the necessary cognitive skills. To be effective at a game of twenty questions, a player must be able to narrow down the possibilities defining a secret object or theme with just twenty yes/no questions. The players' fun comes from thinking of logically exclusive questions to narrow the possible answers down before using up the allotted twenty questions. Older children do this through a form of matrix classifying called "constraint seeking."

Younger children, however, do not yet have enough cognitive development to be able to use matrix classification schemes. Instead, they tend to practice "hypothesis scanning." They tend to think of every possible alternative for the answer and ask it. Up to about age 6, most children use hypothesis scanning; by age 11, however, they've switched to a constraint-seeking strategy about 80 percent of the time.

2. *During a parent-teacher conference, my daughter's third-grade teacher mentioned my child's "constructive memory." What did she mean?*

Constructive memory refers to a cognitive ability which develops in most children during elementary school. The idea is that as a child accumulates knowledge, he or she is better able to remember new information. For example, if someone is giving you directions on how to get to their house and they say, "Go north on 12th Street," you'll be likely to remember their directions in part because you already know which direction north is. With constructive memory, we build up new patterns of recall based partly on previously learned information.

The skills of constructive memory also allow us to infer new information based on previously learned information. Suppose your daughter goes to a friend's birthday party. When she comes home, she asks you to guess what they ate at the party. You will probably guess something like cake and ice cream, inferring the answer from your own experience of birthday parties.

Research indicates that this capacity begins to develop during middle childhood, although it may begin to appear during the preschool period. By the age of 11, most children use constructive memory the same way adults do.

3. *Recently, I've read of several court cases in which young children were important witnesses. How reliable is the testimony of children?*

A child's reliability as a witness depends largely upon his or her age. As the child grows older, his or her cognitive skills – including memory – improve. Generally speaking, by about 9 or 10, a child can recall whether an event actually occurred and can pick someone out of a police lineup. Their recognition memory is well ahead of recall.

On the other hand, children seem more susceptible to being directed by leading questions than are adults. A lawyer may ask an 8- or 9-year-old child, "Was the tattoo on the man's right or left arm?" when the man actually had no tattoo at all. According to one study, children in middle childhood were almost twice as likely as adults to be confused by such a question. So while children can remember events fairly accurately by middle childhood, their recall is also more easily influenced by the questions they're asked.

4. *I'm going to work at a camp this summer, and I'd like to organize the children in crafts groups. How should I structure their projects so that the kids can help one another learn?*

For two children to effectively learn something together, one of the two must already possess certain prerequisite skills. If you're going to ask two children to learn together how to follow a map, for example, at least one of the children should be able to find north. Another condition for cooperative learning is that the two should trade opinions back and forth, without one child's ideas overwhelming the other. Some researchers suggest that the children should have a concrete task to work on and that it not have just one "right" answer. Finally, the children should agree on reaching a consensus as the goal of their interaction.

5. *My son took an intelligence test in his third grade class. Although the school wouldn't tell me his exact IQ, they did say that he tested in the upper segment of his age group. Do IQ test results imply anything for his future?*

IQ tests do appear to indicate how well a child will do in school. This seems reasonable since, traditionally, intelligence tests have measured the skills and information one learns in school; thus, intelligence tests have really measured "academic intelligence," or a person's ability to perform well in school.

On the other hand, IQ testing may not necessarily do a good job of measuring "practical intelligence," which some psychologists have described as an individual's ability to ably perform tasks in ordinary, day-to-day settings. Some research has indicated that the skills measured by academic intelligence tests don't correlate with more practical skills.

6. *What are some of the problems which children from different cultures might have when they begin school?*

Children who attend schools that reflect a different cultural background from the one in which they have grown up are the most likely candidates to experience problems adjusting to formal education. Because these children don't match the teachers' expectations for interaction in the classroom, they are perceived as slow or unresponsive, setting up a pattern of frustration and potential failure.

In addition, academic skills of children are influenced by parental expectations, economic resources, and educational background. Children from cultural backgrounds where education is highly valued will more than likely do much better in school than children from other backgrounds – even if the cultural match is acceptable for all groups.

SELF-TEST

The following multiple choice and short answer test questions should help you measure your understanding of the points covered in the text and the video. After answering all the questions, check your answers against the key and use the accuracy of your answers to gauge how well you have met the lesson objectives.

Multiple Choice Questions

1. At the age of 8, children are able to enjoy jokes which they didn't understand at age 5 because now they

    a. have mastered conservation skills.
    b. have gained the required cognitive skills.
    c. have developed a sense of humor.
    d. use humor to lessen anxiety.

2. When Jenny was 4, she liked to let a bowl of ice cream melt before she'd eat it because, as she put it, "it makes more." However, now that she's 8, Jenny eats her ice cream unmelted. By doing this, Jenny demonstrates her improved understanding of

    a. centration.
    b. contingent truth.
    c. conservation of number.
    d. conservation of liquid volume.

3. At a Japanese garden, Aaron sees bullfrogs, carp, and turtles. When his dad asks him if there are more fish or creatures in the pond, the 7 year old replies, "Fish." By his answer, Aaron shows that he has not yet mastered the cognitive skill of

   a. hierarchical classification.
   b. matrix classification.
   c. inference.
   d. hypothetical questions.

4. Suppose you are a research scientist developing a test of the cognitive skills children develop during middle childhood. To test their abilities at sorting items according to matrix classification, you might ask them to

   a. complete a grid which classifies circles, triangles, and squares according to three different colors.
   b. sort out a collection of different animals, fish, and insects.
   c. play a game of tic tac toe.
   d. answer a series of questions about the different sizes of containers into which a certain volume of liquid would fit.

5. Which of the following is NOT a way in which cultural background can influence a person's score on an IQ test?

   a. Familiarity with the language of the test
   b. The cultural background of the test giver as related to that of the test taker
   c. The ability to construct a mental image of something
   d. Familiarity with the general information on the test

6. In his fourth-grade math class, Jamal is learning about fractions. Under his breath, he is muttering, "Numerator above, denominator below; numerator above, denominator below," over and over. Jamal is practicing

   a. scaffolding.
   b. inference based on knowledge.
   c. metamemory.
   d. a mnemonic strategy.

7. An example of a child using metamemory would be one who

   a. repeats to herself the spelling rule, "I before E except after C."
   b. says, "I'd better write down the time for swimming practice, 'cause I'm bad about remembering time."
   c. says, "The answer has to be C, 'cause the Panama Canal doesn't connect the Mediterranean Sea and the Indian Ocean."
   d. puts out the clothes she wants to wear to school the next day before she goes to bed at night.

8. In a third-grade class, after demonstrating how to solve some problems in division, the teacher gives the children a free work period and allows them to choose their own way of studying. Colleen and Yuriko pull their chairs together and begin sharing impressions of what they've just heard from their teacher. The learning style the girls are using is

   a. solitary.
   b. onlooking.
   c. parallel-coordinate.
   d. guidance.

9. Some psychologists feel that traditional ways of measuring intelligence are inadequate and should be modified to include measurement of "practical intelligence." Among other things, the kinds of problems people solve with practical intelligence

   a. contain sufficient information to determine a solution.
   b. are well-defined.
   c. have one correct answer.
   d. may have more than one way to find the answer.

10. Which one of the following basic intelligences, as identified by Gardner, is NOT tested in traditional IQ tests?

    a. Linguistic
    b. Logical-mathematical
    c. Intrapersonal
    d. Spatial

Short Answer Questions

The following questions should be answered in a paragraph or two. You should identify several key points for each answer and use these to form the framework for your response.

1. What are some of the cognitive changes that children go through during the middle childhood years?

2. What are some of the important memory skills that children develop during middle childhood?

3. What are some of the ways in which heredity and environment are believed to contribute to the development of individual IQ?

18

Social and Emotional Development in Middle Childhood: Self and Peers

LESSON ASSIGNMENT

Completing the following steps will help you master the lesson objectives and achieve the goal for this lesson:

STEP 1: Read the INTRODUCING THE LESSON section to provide a context for what you will learn in this lesson.

STEP 2: Read the lesson's GOAL and LESSON OBJECTIVES so that you will know what you are expected to learn.

STEP 3: Read the text assignment, Chapter 12, pages 437-457 and 468-470. Pay particular attention to the key terms and concepts in the Chapter Summary on page 471; they will help you when you watch the video.

STEP 4: Review the VIEWING GUIDE section in the telecourse guide. It lists several points to consider as you watch the video.

STEP 5: Watch the video.

STEP 6: Read the UNDERSTANDING THE LESSON section in the telecourse guide. Make sure you understand the key terms and can answer the focusing questions included there.

STEP 7: Complete the SELF-TEST.

STEP 8: Go back to the LESSON OBJECTIVES and make sure you can respond to each of them.

INTRODUCING THE LESSON

It's lunchtime at Garfield Elementary School. Over by the two-square outlines, 10-year-old Jimmy has had the misfortune of being smiled at by classmate Diane. Now Jimmy's buddies, Duane and Stefan, are razzing him mercilessly: "Jimmy and Diane, sitting in a tree, K-I-S-S-I-N-G."

Across the playground, two fourth-graders, Laura and Doranne, usually best friends, are hurling insults at one another.

"Yeah, well your ideas about what's fun to do are garbage," Laura says.

"You should know what garbage is," Doranne responds, "since that's what your brain is made of."

Across the baseball field from the playground, buddies Sid, Jeff, and Yusef are engaged in a round of intense bargaining over baseball cards.

"Look, man, I'll give you one Shane West and a Gary Gaetti for your Ken Griffey Jr.," says Jeff.

"Are you kidding?" responds Sid. "Gaetti's such a turkey; Griffey's a way better hitter, any day."

"Why don't you give him one of your Desert Storm cards, Jeff," suggests Yusef. "You've got two T-72 Main Battle Tanks, and Sid doesn't have any."

Lunchtime at an elementary school, in other words, provides a microcosm of some of the main developmental skills and advances of children during the years of middle childhood. From the intricate rules governing behavior between the sexes to the intense emotions that accompany friendships, children at this stage are building upon the cognitive and social abilities of infancy and toddlerhood. During this stage, however, they consolidate and expand upon their abilities, reaching almost-adult levels in some areas.

Developmentalists once viewed middle childhood as a time of little change, developmentally. Sigmund Freud, in fact, dubbed this a latency period, meaning that children of this age have little curiosity about sex. In contrast, developmentalists now see middle childhood as an important period of development in its own right, apart from its role in the study of children in school and with peers. During the years of middle childhood, children form their first true friendships, begin competing with others, and learn how to behave as members of larger social groups.

In this lesson you will study how a child's self-image is confirmed and altered during the middle childhood years by a variety of new factors and challenges. These years, covering roughly from ages 6 to 12, are the years when children must adapt to the demands and opportunities of school and when, for the first time, children must measure themselves against their peers. In the video portion of the lesson, you will see several children commenting on the "rules" and routines that govern their behavior at this time, particularly insofar as it concerns the opposite sex. You will also hear the opinions of children of various ages about what it means to be a friend and develop an appreciation of the gains in self-understanding that are both a prerequisite for having, and a result of being, someone's friend.

GOALS

The purpose of this lesson is to give you an understanding of the developmental changes which a child undergoes as he or she enters school, develops friendships, becomes a member of various groups, and discovers how "creepy" all members of the opposite sex are – all normal stages of middle childhood.

LESSON OBJECTIVES

After reading the text assignment, completing the exercises in this telecourse guide, and viewing the lesson's video portion, you will be able to:

1. Describe the advances in self-understanding that occur during middle childhood.

2. Discuss how self-esteem and a sense of locus of control emerge in middle childhood.

3. Examine the role of peer groups in middle childhood in terms of gender differences, group norms, socialization, and status and popularity within the group.

4. Describe the social skills that are important for group acceptance and the formation of friendships.

5. Compare the strategies that are used by popular and unpopular children to gain group acceptance.

VIEWING GUIDE

In this lesson, the children you will encounter are increasingly members of groups. During middle childhood comes the development of friendship, greater social involvement, deeper awareness of the self and others – and a complete boycott of all voluntary contact with members of the opposite sex. After reading the text material and learning the important terms included there, you are ready to view the lesson's video portion. First, review the questions in the Self-Test at the end of this telecourse guide lesson to give you an idea of important points to watch for in the video. Then, read the following Points to Consider to give you an idea of what the video will cover. Keep these points in mind while watching.

Points to Consider

☐ *Fine-tuning the self*: Elementary school children are developing increasingly sophisticated self-images. Notice how children at this stage begin describing themselves by how they feel, think, and behave, as opposed to just their physical appearance. Be aware of the child's social self that emerges now.

☐ *Getting along with peers*: Spending an increasing amount of time with children of the same age is important in the middle childhood years. Look for ways in which children begin to resolve their differences in ways other than they did as preschoolers. Be aware of the growing need to make friends and the cognitive changes which take place that make deep friendships possible.

☐ *Seeking out the crowd*: Middle childhood is the time of belonging to groups. In the video portion of the lesson, pay attention to how children tend to define themselves as members of groups. Take note of the various ways children in groups enforce group norms, teach one another the rules for dealing with the opposite sex, and promote socialization. And be aware of the various factors that influence each child's acceptance – or rejection – by their peer group.

☐ *School days*: By sheer volume of time spent there, the school is a major developmental context for children. Look for ways that children are influenced, both deliberately and inadvertently, by their teachers. Be aware of the subtle ways children are taught "proper" gender roles by teachers and peers within the school context.

UNDERSTANDING THE LESSON

A massive, double-doored, copper-enameled refrigerator is the center of the Brewer household. It isn't the refrigerator's contents that regularly draws the attention of 11-year-old Brooke and 8-year-old Lyndon, though, but rather the week's schedule of activities that is attached to its exterior by magnets.

"Monday: 3:45, swimming practice, Brooke; 3:30, Cub Scouts, Lyndon; Tuesday: 3:30, Girl Scouts, Brooke; Thursday, 3:45, soccer practice, Lyndon; Friday: slumber party, Brooke's friends; Lyndon to John's."

With the beginning of the school years, children spend more and more time with their peers, both in groups that center on activities and in smaller units of friends. As their self knowledge grows and deepens, children are becoming more skilled members of peer groups and are learning the rewards and trials of one of life's great compensations – friendship.

Development of the Self

As an adult, you have a fairly well-developed image of your own self. You understand that "you" are in one sense a number of different individuals, since your personality is shaped by many characteristics, skills, attitudes, and experiences. While you may at times speak of "finding yourself," you are a distinct individual who within him- or herself "contains multitudes," as the poet Walt Whitman once put it.

During the early elementary school years, children tend to think of themselves in a strictly physical, body-defined sense. Many of the characteristics which now make up "you," however, took solid shape during these years. With the early childhood years, children begin thinking of themselves in psychological terms and defining themselves by how they feel and act, rather than by just how they look. With middle childhood, children begin separating mental from physical acts and begin to think more effectively because they can associate separate but related categories. While preschoolers also have a sense of stable identity, now it becomes based on an understanding of inner uniqueness.

Middle childhood is also when children begin forming a *social self*, an awareness of individual traits which depend upon others for existence or expression. As children enter school, they increasingly join groups – Girl and Boy Scouts, Little League, swimming teams, and so on are the choices of at least some socio-economic groups – and begin forming impressions of themselves in comparison with others. This process of comparison becomes especially important when children enter grade school and attempt to perform tasks in groups of their peers. Unlike younger children, older children typically define themselves in terms of their special abilities.

Along with the importance of individual performance in comparison with that of other children comes a greater emphasis on self-esteem. As you saw in the video portion of the lesson, children with high self-esteem value themselves. Generally speaking, children who value themselves in middle childhood tend to have a history of secure attachment in infancy; now they approach problems with self-confidence in their own abilities, which naturally enables them to succeed often. As you learned in the text material, Erik Erikson referred to this positive state of mind as *sense of industry*, by which he meant having a basic self-confidence in one's own abilities and a tendency to seek out new learning opportunities and to work hard to accomplish goals.

An important component of self-esteem is a sense of individual effectiveness. Developmentalists refer to this as a *locus of control*, and speak of children as having either an *internal* or an *external* locus of control. Individuals with an internal locus of control feel that they have power over their actions, that they can master their circumstances and succeed on the basis of their internal abilities. People with an external locus of control, on the other hand, see themselves as having little power over the circumstances of their lives and tend to think of such things as social success as being out of their control. Both attitudes emerge gradually during the middle childhood period and are greatly affected by past experience.

The development of a deeper psychological understanding of the self is just one social-emotional change which occurs during the middle childhood period. Current views of the importance of this developmental period are in contrast with the views of Freud, who considered this a time of *latency*, with little of significance taking place for the child either physically, cognitively, or socially. While earlier developmentalists didn't go so far as Freud in saying that *nothing* of importance happened during these years, they did focus on learning and peer relationships to the exclusion of social-emotional development.

Key Terms

Sense of industry
Social self
Internal locus of control

External locus of control
Latency

Focusing Questions

1. What are some of the different ways that elementary school children view differences between the mind and body as compared with preschoolers?

2. How does school influence children to begin comparing their performance on tasks with that of their peers?

Developmental Changes in Peer Relations

Anne stands at the kitchen window, looking out at the backyard. Her daughter Dee and three friends have been playing for hours in a treehouse about 40 feet away. Anne has come to the window not because of what she can hear, but because of what she can't; after a long bout of shrieking, bumping, and giggling, the girls have been quiet for over an hour. All Anne can see are the tops of four 10-year-old heads, bent over in apparent close conversation.

If Anne were to ask a child developmentalist what the girls are learning from their interaction, she'd get some very specific answers. That's because children of her daughter's age are spending a great deal of time together in *peer groups*, where they deal with each other on equal terms. As a result, children learn a great deal from one another about reciprocity, cooperation, and aggression. What children learn from adults, on the other hand, is of a different nature partly because the relationships between children and adults are unequal: adults tend to command children; children are expected to obey. With peers, on the other hand, children must learn to be persuasive and flexible in order to get their points of view across.

One result of the equal nature of peer relations is that children begin understanding another person's point of view. In other words, learning to deal with children of the same age encourages feelings of empathy. This in turn leads them, for the first time, to think of other children in psychological rather than just physically descriptive terms. A disliked neighbor child becomes that "stuck-up Melissa" rather than the girl "who lives in the big house."

One consequence of this improved understanding of the feelings of other children is an increase in prosocial behavior. Another noticeable change in how children of this age relate to one another involves aggression. Compared with preschoolers, elementary children are less likely to use force, called instrumental aggression, to get a desired object away from another child. Now children are more likely to try to talk each other out of a desired toy, or to barter for it, or to encourage another child to share. At the same time, as they better understand other people's feelings, children engage more often in hostile aggression, particularly in the form of name calling and insult trading.

But along with "new and improved" forms of aggression come the pleasures and rewards of friendship. The deeper, more intense friendships that children form in middle childhood are built upon their cognitive advances, particularly in how they can better understand another person's feelings. Children are simultaneously more aware of the complex nature of their own emotions, as well as the possibility that other children may have feelings they don't express. For perhaps the first time, children are learning not always to take someone's word unquestioningly. They begin to understand close friendship as a relationship which can contain and withstand conflict between two people, and to appreciate the complexity and mutual benefits inherent in friendships. Among other important concepts and social skills which friends learn from one another at this time, children develop a sense of fairness, which they use as a gauge to judge the actions of both adults and their peers.

Key Terms

Peer groups

Focusing Questions

1. Why are children more likely to learn about compromise, give and take, and concepts of fairness and sharing from each other than from adults?

2. When Kevin, in a moment of anger, tells his friend Chuck that Chuck really can't draw well at all, or else he would have scored higher in the art contest, what does his comment reveal about his understanding of his friend's self-image?

Peer Groups in Middle Childhood

In the movie *Stand By Me*, four preadolescent boys race to find and report to police the body of an accident victim before a group of older, tougher boys can do so. Along the way, the younger boys have a number of adventures that both deepen their understandings of one another and intensify their feelings of being a group. And as the movie's title implies, the boys mainly learn that standing by your friends – the quality of loyalty – is a major part of friendship.

As you know now after reading and viewing the material for this lesson, the movie's underlying depiction of how elementary school children develop a sense of "groupness" is an accurate one. Middle childhood children typically form groups and develop a group identity distinct from other, often competing, groups. Through participation in a group, children begin to form the concepts of shared values and goals and to develop a sense of "we." Intergroup competition, along with a heightened sense of "us" versus "them," is typical of this period.

Through their participation in groups, children are learning peer group *norms* – the specific rules of behavior and belief important to their age and class. Among the norms or rules that children master at this time is a sense of equity, or fair rules for the distribution of rewards. Within the group, norms such as equity tend to contribute to peer group harmony and cohesiveness; outside the group, they help to teach children the principle that performance may determine the extent of rewards.

Peer groups are also important arenas of socialization for children. Among other things, same-age children are the strictest enforcers of appropriate gender roles. Undoubtedly you can recall the danger of getting "cooties" from the opposite sex during your own childhood; as shown by L. Alan Sroufe's comments on the video, boy or girl cooties remains an especially virulent disease of middle childhood. To maintain the proper distance, middle childhooders master an elaborate set of "rules" governing contact with the opposite sex. Developmentalists theorize that gender separation, which is a feature of this age group worldwide, may act to protect children from premature sexual contact.

An individual child's status or popularity within a group at this time is determined largely by such personal characteristics as a sense of self-esteem, kindness, and an ability to make friends. Children now tend to judge one another according to trait terms, which may in turn reinforce the negative self-images of children who have been rejected or neglected by their peers. Such children tend to act in ways that cause them difficulty in interacting with other children – by standing on the sidelines and just watching during play, for example, or by acting aggressively with others. In turn, such behavior tends to make them unpopular, further reinforcing their negative self-images. Again, we see the importance of previous stages of development in their influence upon later growth.

Key Terms

Norms

Focusing Questions

1. What are the differences between *conforming* and *adhering* to group norms?

2. Who sets the "rules" governing the circumstances under which children may legitimately encounter the opposite sex? Who enforces the rules, and how?

Children in School

Many of the scenes which you saw in the video illustrated how middle childhooders develop social selves, form friendships, learn group norms, and master gender differences. These views were taken from school rooms and playgrounds. This is appropriate, because a large proportion of the events that mark the phases of development during middle childhood take place between the morning starting and the afternoon closing bells of school. School is a major arena for development during middle childhood.

For one thing, the experience of school may encourage cooperation among children, make them behave more prosocially, and give them chances to meet children of different ethnic groups whom they might not have met otherwise. At the same time, schools also reinforce the dominant cultural norms and values of mainstream society. With the start of school, the process of socialization that first begins in toddlerhood gets a large boost.

Schools have an especially strong influence on a child's understanding of gender roles. By separating students into lines by sex, by assigning chores according to gender, by dividing games into boy's and girl's teams, educators help train children to understand and accept what society considers to be their "proper" sex roles. And as your text material points out, not all the lessons about sex roles which children absorb at school are consciously intended ones. In one study, for example, girls who achieved high marks on assignments actually got less praise from their teachers than any other group.

The role played by the school experience in a child's development, however, is just one part of the overall picture of growth during middle childhood. Children who have behavioral problems in school, for example, often come from households with parental stress caused by economic or other problems. An individual child's performance in school, as well as his or her popularity among classmates, is strongly affected by the child's sense of self-esteem – which, in turn, is nurtured or warped according to earlier stages of development. In short, the challenges of middle childhood – firming up a sense of self, establishing membership in peer groups, adjusting successfully to school – will be met by each child according to an entire range of previous experiences and development and within a specific context.

Focusing Questions

1. What are some of the specific mainstream values that children will learn at school along with reading, writing, and mathematics?

2. What are some of the criticisms an elementary school teacher might apply, probably subconsciously, to a girl's classwork in contrast to a boy's?

Questions for Understanding

As you read these questions, often raised by parents, educators, and other childcare providers, first try to answer the questions yourself. Then read the answer following each question and compare your response to it.

1. *Over the past year or so, my 9-year-old daughter seems to have grown up a lot; she just seems much more level-headed and self-confident. Is this a typical change for children of her age?*

   Certainly it is common for children of your daughter's age to make significant emotional and social advances at this time. For one thing, children are now switching from the fantasy play typical of preschoolers and instead are setting objectives for themselves based on real-world possibilities. Children are also pulling together the several images of themselves which they previously held separately and are starting to form a single, coherent self-image.

   At the same time, however, the kinds of self-image and social skills which a child develops during middle childhood will depend partly upon the child's history so far. Children who have had negative developmental experiences to date may have difficulty mastering the tasks of middle childhood and subsequently feel inferior and incompetent. So, while your daughter's reactions are typical of her age, they also reflect her prior developmental experience.

2. *I was pleased last year when Bridgette, our 9 year old, wanted to try out for the swim team. I was even prouder when she won several races. This year, however, she seems completely absorbed by swimming. Her*

friends – all girls – are also swimmers. Should I worry about her becoming too competitive?

Of course you should be concerned if your daughter becomes so caught up in one activity that she neglects other aspects of her life. As an adult, you may be in a better position to provide a balanced perspective for Bridgette's involvement in swimming than she is.

On the other hand, your daughter is at an age when her social self is developing. She is starting to think of herself in terms of traits that she exhibits toward others. Children her age are beginning to define themselves as members of groups and to compare themselves against other children. Bridgette's activities with her swim team, as well as her growing competitive urge, are typical and normal expressions of her cognitive and social growth at this time.

3. *As a fourth-grade teacher, I have long noticed that some children have good self-control about deferring rewards, while others have none or very little. What accounts for the differences among children?*

One difference in how much patience children have when awaiting a reward is related to their locus of control. Children with an internal locus of control tend to think of themselves as being in control of their lives to a certain degree and to believe their actions have consequence. These children have been shown to be capable of deferring gratification, mainly by keeping themselves busy during the waiting period. Probably the main reason they are able to exercise such patience is that they are convinced their actions matter, so choosing to wait for a reward is an active, empowered decision.

Children who have an external locus of control, on the other hand, view themselves as helpless to affect the circumstances of their lives and adopt a more passive attitude. These children tend to be poor at deferring gratification, perhaps because they are convinced that they are to a great extent the victim of forces beyond their control. As a result of this fatalism, they are more likely to live in the here-and-now and take what the moment offers. In their view, you may as well live for the moment, because the future is not only unknowable but unchangeable.

4. *These days, my 11 year old seems to spend most of her time with her friends. Not only are the three best friends "thick as thieves," they're as secretive, too. Is this normal?*

Yes, it is. Children your daughter's age are learning how to get along in social groups, and one of the best places for them to learn this is among small groups of close friends. One reason that peer group relationships are so important to children is that they are relationships of equality. When one child wants something from another, she must negotiate and bargain for it. Through peer interactions, children begin learning the principles of reciprocity and equity. The rules and expectations about how to behave are among those which will guide their behavior toward others all their lives.

Between adults and children, however, relationships are always unequal; adults have power and children do not. Adults can tell a child what to do and the child must do it, or suffer the consequences.

This being the case, it's hardly surprising that children begin spending so much time with their chums at about the age of 9 or 10 (though that, of course, isn't the *only* reason).

5. *Why do two friends seem to argue together more than two other children who aren't friends?*

The ability to establish intimate friendships is a major cognitive and emotional development of middle childhood. In forming friendships, elementary school children develop a more sophisticated understanding of friendship than they possessed previously. Among the principles of friendship that children come to understand is that conflict is a part of friendship, and it may even deepen a friendship.

Friendships involve a deeper investment of self and more emotional intensity than casual relationships. As children gradually come to understand this, their grasp of how other people feel and behave also deepens. The emotional intensity between two friends may also lead them to compete even more strongly with one another at times.

6. *What are some of the differences between boy and girl friendship groups during middle childhood?*

While the friendship networks which both boys and girls gravitate to during middle childhood tend to be stable, friendship groups of girls tend to be smaller. Girls cluster in threesomes, which best enables them to nurture the intimacy, confidence sharing, and mutual support that is important to them. Boys, on the other hand, congregate in larger groups, concentrating on shared activities and on issues of loyalty to the group.

7. *While working at my son's grade school as a volunteer playground assistant, I noticed some children just don't seem to fit in. On every playground, there are always a few kids who hover around the edges of games, apparently incapable of joining in. Why is this?*

Although elementary school is when it becomes important for children to establish positions of popularity or status, the basis of individual acceptance by peers is established earlier. For example, children who have difficulty adjusting to earlier stages of development or have been abused or neglected may have low self-esteem and poor self-confidence. Often, such children are ill-prepared for the social challenges of the new group activities of middle childhood. In consequence, these children fail to form effective ties within groups and may be rejected by the other children. This in turn gives the children even more negative messages, reinforcing their originally poor self-image. These children tend to be isolated from others, are more likely to behave aggressively, and often speak out inappropriately in groups. These are the children you've seen standing on the playground sidelines.

SELF-TEST

The following multiple choice and short answer test questions should help you assess your understanding of the points covered in the text and the video. After answering all the questions, check your answers against the key and use the accuracy of your answers to gauge how well you have met the lesson objectives.

Multiple Choice Questions

1. By a "sense of industry," Erik Erikson meant to indicate that during middle childhood, children are developing

    a. a strong ability to stick to tasks.
    b. a basic belief in their own competence.
    c. an appreciation of the world of work.
    d. a tendency to want to earn money.

2. If you were to ask a group of children of varying ages how they are not like a dog, which of the following are you most likely to get from an 11-year-old?

    a. "I don't have fur."
    b. "I can't bark."
    c. "I can think."
    d. "I don't have four legs."

3. Children who give signs of high self-esteem during middle childhood were probably, as toddlers,

    a. unusually bright.
    b. early talkers.
    c. prematurely born.
    d. securely attached to their care givers.

4. One day Glenn commits the sin of lacing his high-top tennis shoes all the way up. But that, he's told by his buddies, "is how girls wear them," so he goes back to leaving the top two holes unused. By giving in to his friends' pressures, Glenn is following the process of

    a. group norms.
    b. cross-gender interaction.
    c. latency.
    d. identification.

5. According to the "rules" of middle childhood, in which of these circumstances would it NOT be permissible to have contact with the other sex?

    a. When you think you would like being with the other person
    b. When a teacher instructs you to do so
    c. When you have a friend of the same sex with you
    d. When you are trying to be insulting

6. One cognitive ability which children develop during middle childhood that helps pave the way to forming friendships is a

   a. sense of competition.
   b. tendency to compare one's self with others.
   c. deeper understanding of other people's feelings.
   d. tendency to want to resolve conflicts.

7. When asked to describe herself, 10-year-old Mary Beth starts off by saying, "Well, I'm a Girl Scout . . ." Mary Beth's answer is an indication of her need to

   a. practice her sense of industry.
   b. share in a collective identity.
   c. form close friendships.
   d. avoid contact with boys.

8. Roger is a very popular fourth grader. When the teacher asked Roger's friend Spencer the reason for Roger's popularity, he replied,

   a. "Roger's good at getting games started."
   b. "Roger's the tallest in the class."
   c. "Roger's dad owns the ice cream shop."
   d. "Roger's so smart at math."

9. When same-age cousins Darrin and Eloise used to get together as preschoolers, the two children were constantly whacking one another; related or not, the cousins couldn't stand each other. Now that they are 10 years old, however, their meetings are characterized by

   a. mutual curiosity.
   b. apparent indifference.
   c. verbal insults.
   d. sharing of secrets.

10. Nine-year-olds Cheryl, Dale, and Debra are all members of the same Girl Scout troop. In preparation for their annual cookie sale, the girls are poring over a map, carefully dividing up neighborhoods where each will go door-to-door. The girls argue over which neighborhood is likely to be easiest or toughest for sales and debate which girl should get which block. The girls' strict attention to fairness is an example of

    a. conformity.
    b. their sense of industry.
    c. peer group norms.
    d. socialization.

Short Answer Questions

The following questions should be answered in a paragraph or two. You should identify several key points for each answer and use these to form the framework for your response.

1. What are some of the differences between the perceptions of the self that are held by youngsters in middle childhood and those of preschoolers?

2. Imagine you are observing four children, one pair of 4 year olds and one pair of 9 year olds. Strictly in the interest of science, you give each pair an intriguing toy that only one child can enjoy at a time – a battery-powered robot, say, for the younger children and a hand-held video game for the older pair. In what ways might the pairs differ in how they go about deciding who will play with the toy first?

3. Why are some children more popular among their peers than others?

19

Social and Emotional Development in Middle Childhood: Family Influence

LESSON ASSIGNMENT

Completing the following steps will help you master the lesson objectives and achieve the goal for this lesson:

STEP 1: Read the INTRODUCING THE LESSON section to provide a context for what you will learn in this lesson.

STEP 2: Read the lesson's GOAL and LESSON OBJECTIVES so that you will know what you are expected to learn.

STEP 3: Read the text assignment Chapter 12, pages 433-450 and 457-471. Pay particular attention to the key terms and concepts in the Chapter Summary for Chapter 12 on page 471; they will help you when you watch the video.

STEP 4: Review the VIEWING GUIDE section in the telecourse guide. It lists several points to consider as you watch the video.

STEP 5: Watch the video.

STEP 6: Read the UNDERSTANDING THE LESSON section in the telecourse guide. Make sure you understand the key terms and can answer the focusing questions included there.

STEP 7: Complete the SELF-TEST.

STEP 8: Go back to the LESSON OBJECTIVES and make sure you can respond to each of them.

INTRODUCING THE LESSON

Probably, if you stop and concentrate for a moment, you can tap into one of childhood's most common memories: the mix of emotions a child feels after being disciplined by his or her parents. Sulking in your room or nursing a bruised ego while seated on a swing, you muttered the aggrieved child's mantra of consolation and defiance: "When I grow up, I'm never going to be mean to my kids."

Or maybe you'd been in a fight with a brother or sister and gone off by yourself to nurse your grievance. "Why did Mom and Dad have to have two kids?" you might have pondered in your anger. "Why couldn't I have been an only child?"

With adulthood, such memories bring only a wry, understanding smile, especially if you've since become a parent yourself. Now you understand the reasons behind your parents' seeming strictness and can sympathize with the difficulty they faced in raising you. With maturity, you can even accept – maybe – that a younger brother or sister wasn't really a constant pest, or an older one such a bully. With growth and experience comes an appreciation of the complexity and emotional depth of the ties within one's family and even a certain fondness for memories of arguments and power struggles. Now, with luck and time, you have come to accept the individual foibles and quirks of your family and probably regard them with a mixture of love and resignation. Families, for most of us, are for keeps.

But whether recollections of our family are fond or furious ones, the family is where our memories begin. The first other person that the infant becomes aware of is its mother, followed by other family members. Toddlers learn to walk by staggering toward a parent's outstretched arms; and preschoolers often tag along in the wake of an adored older brother or sister. And the growing self-confidence and social skills of school-age children are rooted within the framework of each individual's family. From birth onward, the family is a major influence upon individual development.

Mothers and fathers, for example, provide models of gender roles as their children enter school and begin sorting out the differences between boys and girls. By their parenting "styles," parents help shape their childrens' outlook on the world and influence their basic personalities. Through interaction with brothers and sisters, children learn negotiation skills and the consequences of conflict, as well as the comforts of filial affection. Like the trademark stamped into the bottom of a pottery mold, a person's family leaves its mark on the individual for life.

With this lesson we focus on the specific ways in which the family shapes individual development during the middle childhood years. As the child negotiates the emotional, cognitive, and social twists and turns of adapting to school, forming peer relationships, and forming a firm gender identity, the family is the frame surrounding the larger picture of development. During middle childhood, the family exerts a continuing influence on individual development.

GOAL

The purpose of this lesson is to demonstrate the strong influence that the family has on individual development, with an emphasis on the role that parents and siblings play in the cognitive, social, and emotional changes that occur during middle childhood.

LESSON OBJECTIVES

After reading the text assignment, completing the exercises in this telecourse guide, and viewing the lesson's video portion, you will be able to:

1. Compare the influence of the family during middle childhood to its importance during toddlerhood and early childhood.

2. Describe the different dynamics that take place within peer and sibling relationships.

3. Discuss the complex emotional ties that exist between brothers and sisters and the factors that influence these relationships.

4. Indicate the ways in which siblings learn from each other.

5. Relate parenting styles to patterns of child behavior and the personality characteristics which children acquire.

6. Indicate the ways in which families influence the gender roles that children acquire.

7. Discuss the possible effects of marital conflict and divorce on school-age boys and girls.

VIEWING GUIDE

In this lesson you will relive childhood arguments with brothers and sisters and re-examine what you learned from your parents about being a boy or a girl. The effect on children of family styles, teachings, histories, and beliefs are especially important during middle childhood. After reading the text material and learning the important terms included there, you are ready to view the lesson's video portion. First, review the Self-Test questions at the end of this telecourse guide lesson to give you an idea of important points to watch for in the video. Then read the following Points to Consider to give you an idea of what the video will cover. Keep these points in mind while watching.

Points to Consider

☐ *Matters of style*: The ways in which parents raise their children continue to be of great importance during middle childhood. While viewing the video segment, note how differences in parental style affect children differently. Keep in mind the distinguishing differences between "authoritative" and "authoritarian" parenting styles.

☐ *Broken families*: The influence on children of a broken family can be a major one. Notice the importance of how parents deal with conflict between them in helping their children handle a divorce. Look for comments by developmentalists on how parents can lessen the impact of a family breakup on children.

☐ *Moms and Dads as role models*: During middle childhood, children absorb important lessons from their parents about what it means to be male or female. Notice the great subtlety with which parents offer themselves as role models to their children for proper gender behavior – often quite subconsciously.

☐ *Brotherhood, sisterhood*: For many children, siblings are their first friends, competitors, allies, and enemies. Pay attention to the ways in which siblings both learn from and teach one another, and notice the negotiating skills they practice with one another. Be aware of the complexity of sibling relationships and how feelings of ambivalence are common features of a brother's or a sister's affections.

UNDERSTANDING THE LESSON

The "situation comedy" has been a staple of television programming in this country since broadcasting first began in the late 1940s. Hundreds of comedies since then have had a common focus. "The Donna Reed Show," "Ozzie and Harriet," "The Dick Van Dyke Show," "The Beverly Hillbillies," "The Partridge Family," "The Bill Cosby Show," "The Simpsons" – all have featured the antics and adventures of a family.

In the real world, families are not always scenes of hilarity and neatly summarized weekly plots. But even without script writers, big budgets, and the benefits of national broadcasting, families exert immense influence upon the children growing up within them. During middle childhood, as boys and girls join peer groups, make friends, sort out gender roles, and master the cognitive challenges of school, they are simultaneously being affected, in ways both obvious and unseen, by their families. Family life – sometimes comedy, sometimes drama, sometimes live-coverage news from a war zone – is a prime-time feature of the middle childhood years.

Parenting Styles

As you learned in the previous lesson, middle childhood is a time of great camaraderie. School-age chums plan long hikes into the countryside; boys and girls – in separate groups – plan overnight parties at one another's houses. Children band together in baseball teams, scout groups, and hobby clubs. But one thing doesn't change as children form friendships and become more sophisticated socially: they still have to ask parental permission for many of the activities they're now interested in. "Mom, can I go to John's/Jane's?" is a common question of the middle childhood years.

The way parents respond to their child's requests during this period may offer clues to the child's future development. Some parents are quite permissive, while others are more controlling; some parents talk to their children and try to understand their needs, whereas others are more abrupt, interested mainly in having the child "behave." In the text material, you saw how these different parenting styles are expressed in terms of the types of affection parents show their children, as well as how the parents handle issues of autonomy versus control. By using this framework, researchers are able to make some predictions on how a child will develop as they grow older. For example, the children of parents who are warm and loving tend to grow into socially responsible and cooperative individuals. But the children of parents who are dominating and don't offer much physical warmth tend to be more aggressive and noncompliant.

One researcher, Diana Baumrind, tried to clarify some of the ways children are affected by different parenting styles by dividing parents into authoritative and authoritarian types. In Baumrind's description, authoritative parents are nurturing, set firm limits for their children's behavior and then explain the reasons for any discipline, and respect the child's point of view. Children raised by such parents tend to be friendly, energetic, and self-reliant. Authoritarian parents, on the other hand, tend to set rigid rules of behavior and enforce them harshly, without much concern for how the child sees the situation. The children of such parents tend to be irritable and conflict-ridden. Further study indicates that children of authoritative parents have a more highly developed sense of "agency," the ability to seize the initiative and accomplish one's own goals, than do children raised by authoritarian parents.

Not surprisingly, the relationships between parents and children during the middle childhood years follow the lines laid down in earlier stages of development. Overall, positive parent-child relationships are those with relatively infrequent conflicts over goals and a certain amount of fairness in how parents and children resolve their differences. In healthy families, parents make some demands, while at the same time they sometimes give in to the child's desires. According to one theory, such reciprocal parent-child relationships are based upon the child's confidence in the parent's judgment, which has been established from infancy onward. Now, however, children are increasingly able to understand just how much more experienced and capable their parents are and to trust the parent's judgment accordingly.

Focusing Questions

1. As a child's cognitive abilities develop during middle childhood, how does his or her understanding of the parent's rules of behavior or sense of values change?

2. Which parents are more likely to expect a certain amount of maturity from their children as they enter the school years, those with authoritative or authoritarian parenting styles? Why?

Parental Conflict and Divorce

Until quite recently, divorce was perceived as not only a difficult and expensive legal proceeding, but also an event creating only negative effects for any children involved. And one of the arguments in favor of a mismatched couple staying together was that preserving the family was "better for the kids" than separating. In popularly accepted articles about juvenile delinquency written in the 1950s and '60s, problem children were generally assumed to be the products of "broken homes."

Now, however, as you can surmise from the video segment, our view of divorce and its effect on children isn't so uniform or inflexible. For one thing, a divorce is easier to obtain and more common. For another, researchers have concluded that the simple fact of divorce doesn't send all children spinning into spirals of low self-esteem, uncertainty, and confusion. As with other aspects of child development, just how a specific child is affected by the divorce of his or her parents depends upon a variety of factors, including the child's age, history, temperament, and relationship with both parents, as well as the parents' level of post-divorce hostility.

Violence in the family, on the other hand, does have a negative impact on children, whether directed at them or between their parents. The effects of violence on children include low self-esteem, aggression toward others, and withdrawal. Developmentalists now generally agree that divorce has the greatest effect on children when the conflict between the parents is highest and especially when it involves violence. In light of these findings, most experts today believe that children may benefit if their parents separate, when the separation results in a lessening or end of conflict.

Another widely held assumption about the effect of divorce on children is its different effects on boys and girls, but that assumption is contradicted by recent research. It used to be thought that boys were more affected by the divorce of their parents than were girls. Experts now assert that both sexes have equal chances of suffering ill effects. Boys tend to exhibit their reactions more directly through aggression and impulsive behavior, and girls tend to show their reactions more through withdrawal, anxiety, and inhibition.

Overall, however, researchers now view the effect of divorce on children as the result of numerous interrelated factors; the most important may be the attitudes of both parents toward the child. Especially important to the child's development is a good relationship with the custodial parent. While the family break-up cannot help being stressful for children, its long-term effects upon development depend greatly upon the specific relationship of the child with both parents, as well as the level of conflict between the parents during and after the divorce.

Focusing Questions

1. Which child is likely to be more upset by the divorce of their parents, 4-year-old Jill or her 10-year-old brother Vincent? Why?

2. What are some of the important factors that promote a good outcome for children when their parents divorce?

Learning About Gender Roles from Parents

After dinner, parents Les and Terri begin clearing away dishes. Les picks up a bowl and hands it to his 10-year-old son, saying, "Kevin, start loading the dishwasher, okay?"

But Kevin makes a face. "Aw, Dad, couldn't you let Mom and Celia clean up? Jason and his dad never have to do housework; they say that's woman's work." As Kevin comments, his mom and dad look at one another, eyebrows lifted; each knows the other is thinking, "Okay, how do you want to handle this one?"

Kevin's comments about the "proper" kinds of chores a male should do around the home come as a surprise to his parents. The couple has tried to raise Kevin and his 7-year-old sister without stereotypical notions of what kinds of things boys or girls should or shouldn't do. Despite the great influence parents have on a child's gender identity, during middle childhood they are likely to discover the strong influence a child's peers have on his or her socialization.

From infancy, much of what children learn about being a boy or a girl comes directly from their parents. Mothers may select pink booties for their baby girl and wrap their baby boy in a blue blanket. As toddlers, boys get noisy push-trucks; girls get cuddly dolls. And even when they start to roam, boys tend to be given more freedom than their sisters. The role of biology in gender differences, while real, is subject to controversy and is hard to establish; the importance of parents and family in teaching gender roles, however, is indisputable. It is usually parents, after all, who first tell a child that little girls are a mixture of "sugar and spice and everything nice," while boys, on the other hand, are composed of "snakes and snails and puppy dog tails." As the text points out, even such insightful fairy tales as *Jack and the Beanstalk* and *The Princess and the Pea* convey subtle messages about gender roles.

Focusing Questions

1. What are some of the ways gender-role stereotyping might prepare children for assuming broader social roles as they grow older?

2. Are all children just naturally likely to become conservative about gender roles during middle childhood? If so, will they maintain their attitudes as they grow?

Siblings: Rivals and Allies

Certain figures of speech attest to the fact that emotional ties between siblings are often deep and strong. Negotiators working toward peace between warring parties commonly plead for a sense of "brotherly" emotions from all concerned; women struggling for their rights call upon a sense of "sisterhood;" and in the vocabulary of Christianity, church members are often called brothers and sisters, nuns are referred to as sister, and monks as brother.

These strong emotional ties are natural; by middle childhood, children consider both parental and sibling relationships to be more durable and reliable than those with people outside the family. Sibling relationships are complex, ranging from the nurturing feelings that an older sibling feels for a younger one to the sense of competition that often develops between siblings. Sibling conflict is common, as is rivalry for parental affection. At the same time, younger siblings perceive older brothers and sisters as facilitators and often use them as models for their own developing cognitive and social skills.

Among the lessons that siblings learn from one another is how long-term relationships can survive anger and conflict. From dealing with each other, siblings learn coping skills such as how to negotiate, get along, and play a variety of roles. Older siblings may develop nurturing and teaching skills, while younger siblings may have to grapple with issues of dependency. Though little research has been done in this area, some researchers think the kind of skills which siblings learn from one another should transfer to their relationships with peers.

Focusing Questions

1. Siblings often express ambivalent feelings about one another. Why do you think this is so?

2. What are some of the differences in how a child must deal with a serious argument or fight with a friend as opposed to one with a brother or sister?

Questions for Understanding

As you read these questions often raised by parents, educators, and other childcare providers, first try to answer the questions yourself. Then read the answer following each question and compare your response to it.

1. *My 11 year old, Tricia, is outgoing, self-confident, and a real "jock." Her 7-year-old brother Marty, on the other hand, is reserved, a little shy, and doesn't really enjoy sports. How can two children of the same family be so different?*

    While it is true that your children do come from the same gene pool, remember that each has a unique blend of dominant and recessive genes. Each individual also has their own unique temperament. And while your son and daughter share the environment of your home, remember that they also have non-shared environments that are affecting them separately – their friends and different classes in school, for example. By virtue of being born second, your son has been influenced by his older sister, giving him a different set of developmental circumstances. And she, in turn, has been affected by having to adapt to the arrival of a baby brother. In short, the varying aspects of the family, genetics, and their separate environments have all contributed to the differences between your son and daughter.

2. *My older sister and her husband have raised their daughter, who is now 10, very strictly. They've never let my niece do anything on her own and always punished her very harshly. How will my niece be affected by this upbringing?*

    According to several studies, the children of very domineering and restrictive parents tend to be inhibited as they grow up. Very frequently, such children are shy, self-conscious, and unusually dependent. They may also be very self-controlled, polite, and obedient when parents are present, but in other situations they have been found to be aggressive and non-compliant, demonstrating a tendency to project blame for negative results.

It is important to remember, however, that it is extremely difficult or even impossible to predict a person's future behavior on the basis of one aspect of their overall development. For example, when parents are not only very strict but also lacking in affection toward their children, the children run the risk of withdrawing from social contacts and developing neurotic problems. But when an overly protective style of parenting is combined with love and affection, the children often lean toward being dependent upon and submissive to others. So it's really impossible to make any specific predictions about how your niece will "turn out," beyond saying that she is at higher risk for developing problems typical of children from authoritarian families.

3. *Do developmentalists have any suggestions for parents about the best way to handle conflict with their elementary school-age children?*

According to one recent model of parenting styles, the best situation for children is one in which conflicts over goals between parents and child are relatively infrequent. This is likely to occur when parents are supportive of their child and are willing to listen to the child and negotiate with him or her. Likewise, children benefit when they perceive fairness in the resolution of disagreements with their parents; sometimes the parents get their wishes, and sometimes so does the child. There is room for give-and-take in such relationships. At the same time, the parents are consistently firm in their expectations so that the child respects the parents' views.

The creators of this model, Eleanor Maccoby and John Martin, emphasize that this outcome is most likely for those parents who have been responsive to their child's needs since infancy. Now, when children must at times defer to their parents' greater experience and understanding, they are likely to do so because their parents have already demonstrated their reliability. Maccoby and Martin refer to this reservoir of trust as emotional "money in the bank" on which the children can now draw.

4. *At what age is divorce hardest on children?*

Generally speaking, the breakup of family tends to affect younger children most strongly. Very young children of divorced families may manifest how upset they are by having trouble with their peers and problems in school. But of course, divorce is difficult for children of all ages. When a divorce involves a high degree of conflict, children are very likely to be affected – no matter how old they are. If the divorcing couple can end or greatly reduce the conflict between them, the children tend to benefit accordingly.

5. *Children in grade school seem to have a variety of "styles" of friendship. Some kids are able to have both "best friends" and a wider range of friends and to mix pretty smoothly with their classmates. Other children*

form tighter, more exclusive friendships and don't mix well with others. Does family background influence a child's relationships with peers?

Yes. On the positive side, this influence can be as direct as the emotional support and encouragement that parents give a child who is establishing a friendship. On the negative side, a child's ability to get along with peers may be lessened by such pressures as a depressed or alcoholic parent or conflict between the mother and father. Not surprisingly, children with positive and affectionate parents are most likely to be able to cope successfully with the challenges of peer relationships and to form stable, mutually rewarding friendships. It cannot be conclusively proved, however, that early attachment patterns affect all of the later characteristics of peer relationships.

But family influences on children at this time are a direct result of many years of development. Researchers have found that children who are skillful at peer relationships tend to have histories of secure attachment with their parents. Children who were securely attached as infants tend to be self-confident, less dependent, socially skilled, and capable of forming friendships. These children tend to form reciprocal friendships with other securely attached children.

If two children with histories of avoidant attachment, on the other hand, become friends, they tend to exclude others and to play apart from them. Children with resistant histories form similarly exclusive, unstable relationships. As you can see, the family influence on a child's style of relating with peers is both immediate and historical.

6. *Is there some kind of biological "trigger" that makes siblings fight?*

While there is no built-in biological requirement that siblings, whether of the opposite or the same sex, must fight, conflicts between them may seem inevitable at times – to their parents, anyway. Sibling relationships are complex and emotionally intense; in contrast to relationships with their peers, children cannot cut off all contact with brothers and sisters after an emotional blow-up. In addition, siblings – especially of the same sex – often compete with one another for their parents' affection, which in turn may lead to antagonism between the siblings. Siblings who are close together in age report greater feelings of ambivalence toward one another than those further apart. Conflicts between siblings are the most frequent cause of parental discipline, and most of these disagreements are about possessions. Finally, it should come as no surprise that in families where one or both parents show preferential treatment to one child, there is greater competitiveness between the children.

SELF-TEST

The following multiple choice and short answer test questions should help you assess your understanding of the points covered in the text and the video. After answering all the questions, check your answers against the key and use the accuracy of your answers to gauge how well you have met the lesson objectives.

Multiple Choice Questions

1. Generally speaking, and assuming all other conditions are the same, the child who is probably going to be the most upset about the parents' divorce is

   a. 4-year-old Lorraine.
   b. 7-year-old Dean.
   c. 11-year-old Bob.
   d. 14-year-old Chris.

2. Ten-year-olds Barbara and Collette are best friends, which for them means not having any other friends. On days when one girl is sick from school, the other one plays by herself during recess and refuses to join in any games. It is possible that both girls have a history of

   a. premature birth.
   b. avoidant attachment.
   c. divorce in the family.
   d. secure attachment.

3. Eleven-year-old Brandon has an 8-year-old sister, Celeste, with whom he often fights. Just as often, however, he spends time watching TV with his sister or playing the license-plate game with her on family trips in the car. Compared to relations with friends his own age, Brandon's dealings with his sister

   a. allow him to dominate her.
   b. are usually hostile.
   c. can be avoided at his choice.
   d. allow him to cross gender barriers.

4. Brandon and his sister (item 3) sometimes have arguments, just as he sometimes does with his best friend, Harry. But one thing that Brandon can do when he is angry with his best friend that he cannot do with his little sister is

   a. hit her.
   b. avoid her completely.
   c. insult her.
   d. make up with her.

5. Siblings commonly have feelings of both anger and affection for one another. These feelings of ambivalence are greatest when siblings are

   a. close in age.
   b. the opposite sex.
   c. the same sex.
   d. far apart in age.

6. One of the most common lessons that children learn from having siblings is that

   a. boys and girls can get along with each other.
   b. sharing is a useful way to solve some problems.
   c. expressing anger doesn't have to end a relationship.
   d. life doesn't end when parents divorce.

7. Among the children in a particular fourth grade class, Joe is one of the biggest discipline problems. Though Joe is very friendly and sociable with the other kids, he is also disobedient, easy to distract, and irresponsible. When thinking about the boy and his possible home environment, his teacher forms a mental picture of parents who are probably

   a. very authoritarian.
   b. very authoritative.
   c. abusive of Joe.
   d. overly permissive.

8. Children who are raised by authoritative parents tend to be

   a. irritable and conflict-ridden.
   b. energetic, friendly, and self-reliant.
   c. shy and self-critical.
   d. aggressive, domineering, and frenetic.

9. Brenda's parents prided themselves on rearing their daughter with a mix of firmness and affection and in always trying to accompany any punishment with an explanation. But as Brenda progressed through grade school, her parents noticed that Brenda became more argumentative with them, and especially with her dad. According to the theories of Diana Baumrind, Brenda's argumentativeness

   a. may help boost her later self-assertiveness.
   b. indicates a deep confusion about her sense of self.
   c. is a temporary development of no lasting importance.
   d. indicates her need to establish a clear sexual identity.

10. Suppose a husband and wife are not getting along and consider divorce. Their friends and family, however, advise them to stay together "for the sake of the children." To sort out their options, the couple talk with a child development expert, who tells them that

   a. divorce upsets only very young children.
   b. their parents and friends are right.
   c. high levels of parental conflict are often worse for kids than divorce.
   d. they should focus only on their own needs in this matter.

Short Answer Questions

The following questions should be answered in a paragraph or two. You should identify several key points for each answer and use these to form the framework for your response.

1. What are the two different styles of parenting that were defined by Diana Baumrind, and how do children raised by these types of parents differ?

2. It used to be commonly assumed that divorce was harder on boys than on girls. Why did people think this? Do they still?

3. Some siblings seem to be forever fighting; other siblings, are one another's best friends. What are some of the possible reasons for such different outcomes?

20

Prosocial and Aggressive Behavior

LESSON ASSIGNMENT

Completing the following steps will help you master the lesson objectives and achieve the goal for this lesson:

STEP 1: Read the INTRODUCING THE LESSON section to provide a context for what you will learn in this lesson.

STEP 2: Read the lesson's GOAL and LESSON OBJECTIVES so that you will know what you are expected to learn.

STEP 3: Read the text assignment, Chapter 10, pages 358-362 and 373-379; Chapter 12, pages 447-448 and 458-462; and Chapter 15, pages 556-583. Pay particular attention to the key terms and concepts in the Chapter Summaries for Chapter 10 on pages 379-380, for Chapter 12 on pages 471, and for Chapter 15 on pages 583-584; they will help you when you watch the video.

STEP 4: Review the VIEWING GUIDE section in the telecourse guide. It lists several points to consider as you watch the video.

STEP 5: Watch the video.

STEP 6: Read the UNDERSTANDING THE LESSON section in the telecourse guide. Make sure you understand the key terms and can answer the focusing questions included there.

STEP 7: Complete the SELF-TEST.

STEP 8: Go back to the LESSON OBJECTIVES and make sure you can respond to each of them.

INTRODUCING THE LESSON

It happens to most of us fairly often: as you approach an intersection in your car, a vehicle coming from the opposite direction turns left, crossing in front of you. You have to slam on your brakes to avoid hitting it.

"You idiot!" you shout – or, possibly, you utter something much more colorful and less polite, as your heart pounds and your adrenalin soars. In your mind's eye, a .50-caliber machine guns pops out of its fender mount and fires off a burst at the offending car. Instead of passing unharmed and unpunished out of your life, you imagine the offender vanishing in an eruption of sheet metal and fire. You mutter about the dangerous clowns driving cars as you move on, shaken and irritable.

Now consider another chance meeting: You pull into a supermarket parking lot. As you get out of your car, you notice that the hood of the car alongside yours is up and a man is bending into the engine compartment. He looks up at you, and you ask him what the problem is.

"Won't start," he replies. "Looks like my battery's dead."

After quick reflection – you're in no hurry, you're in a good mood – you decide to be a Good Samaritan. You say, "I've got jumper cables; I'll give you a jump." The man gratefully takes you up on your offer; after hooking up the cables and starting his car, you go on your way, mentally patting yourself on the back for being such a nice person.

As an adult, you understand that the average individual is subject to a number of powerful and often contradictory impulses. When our feelings are hurt or our pride slighted, we react: we want revenge, justification, some kind of satisfaction, no matter how irrational the wish may be. We know that we have urges of aggression and have learned to control them – though occasional reports of gunfire during arguments and traffic jams prove, unfortunately, that this isn't true for everyone.

At the same time, you know that sometimes you can offer help to a stranger, for no reason other than that it's a nice thing to do – it feels right. Because you can understand another person's feelings and put yourself "in their shoes," you sometimes enjoy lending a hand.

The great majority of adults deal with these often conflicting impulses without giving them much thought because they've been balancing them since childhood. Very early on, you learned that whacking playmates isn't a "nice" thing to do, no matter how much you may want to. As you grew, parents, teachers, and other adults taught and modeled ways in which you could channel your feelings of hostility toward others in positive, prosocial ways.

In this lesson, we explore how children begin acting in both aggressive and prosocial ways during middle childhood and how they learn to control their behavior appropriately. You will examine arguments about the influence television has on children and learn how parenting styles contribute to the child's behavior toward others. And in a chapter examining some of the ways development can go wrong, you will study an overview of some possible childhood disorders. By the end of the lesson, you will understand how the impulse to beat up a bad driver may actually share some characteristics with your more altruistic feelings.

GOAL

The purpose of this lesson is to examine the ways in which children learn to control their impulses and how this affects both their aggressive and prosocial behaviors during middle childhood.

LESSON OBJECTIVES

After reading the text assignment, completing the exercises in this telecourse guide, and viewing the lesson's video portion, you will be able to:

1. Differentiate between prosocial and aggressive behavior.

2. Trace the developmental changes in aggression that occur from toddlerhood through middle childhood.

3. Compare the developmental course of empathy and altruism to aggression; recognize the cognitive factors that underlie these behaviors.

4. Indicate the ways in which a parent's style of care giving influences a child's prosocial behavior.

5. Summarize the research related to the influence of television on a child's prosocial and aggressive behavior.

6. Discuss the factors that contribute to childhood disorders.

7. Recognize how genetic/biological differences contribute to differences in prosocial and aggressive behavior.

VIEWING GUIDE

The focus of this lesson is on how a child's behavior toward others develops during middle childhood, in both positive and negative ways. In the course of normal development, children learn to control their aggressive urges and to enjoy the benefits of prosocial behavior. But a variety of genetic, environmental, and historical contexts may lead to psychopathology for some children. After reading the text material and learning the important terms included there, you are ready to view the lesson's video portion. First, review the Self-Test questions at the end of this telecourse guide lesson to give you an idea of important points to watch for in the video. Then, read the following Points to Consider to give you an idea of what the video will cover and keep them in mind while watching.

Points to Consider

☐ *To hit or not to hit*: From toddlerhood on, children struggle for a balance between aggressive and prosocial behavior. In the statements of middle childhood children, look for signs that they understand the consequences of aggressive behavior on other children. Be sure you grasp the difference between instrumental and hostile aggression.

☐ *Just like Mom and Dad*: Parents have a powerful influence on their children's behavior, both in how they parent and as models of behavior. In the video portion of the lesson, notice how children learn – or do not learn – the virtues of self-control from watching their parents. See if you can detect any clear connections between how children are disciplined and how they behave toward others.

☐ *Broken models*: Psychopathology is the study of ways in which normal development can go seriously wrong. Keep an eye out for the ways in which various models of psychopathology explain aggressive or antisocial behavior among children. Be aware of how differing theories try to explain psychopathology and whether a particular disorder's etiology is considered genetic, organic, or environmental.

☐ *Maps of disorder*: The list of possible childhood disorders is long and perplexing. Notice the numerous models of psychopathology that researchers have created to explain such diverse developmental problems as severe withdrawal, depression, anxiety, and law-breaking. Be alert to how various disorders may affect a child's ability to form a unified self image, develop self restraint, and establish peer group relationships.

UNDERSTANDING THE LESSON

The 1991 action movie, *Terminator 2*, features a killer robot played by Arnold Schwarzenegger. The robot has been sent back from the future to save the life of a 12-year-old boy. But the boy won't let the robot kill anyone in its efforts to protect him. "You can't just go around killing people," the boy tells the robot.

As far-fetched as the movie's basic plot may be, this one device is based on solid developmental fact. During middle childhood, children grapple with the conflicting urges of aggressive and prosocial feelings and strive for a successful balance in their behavior. And luckily, given normal circumstances, most children are ably guided toward prosocial behavior by parents, teachers, peers, and other role models. By the age of 12, most children are able to control their aggressive impulses and behave in prosocial ways – and even, conceivably, act as role models themselves.

Aggression and Prosocial Behavior

In the classic psychological horror story, *Strange Case of Dr. Jekyll and Mr. Hyde* by Robert Louis Stevenson, the normally kind-hearted Dr. Jekyll becomes the vicious Mr. Hyde after drinking a personality-altering drug. Mr. Hyde feels no self-restraint whatsoever; whatever he sees that he wants, he grabs; any impulse that he feels, he immediately acts upon. Eventually, Mr. Hyde's complete lack of control leads him to commit murder and results in his own destruction – as well as the end, of course, of the "good" Dr. Jekyll.

Stevenson's fable is a sensitive metaphor for the struggle which children undergo as they learn to exercise self-restraint over their impulses and emotions. As children pass through infancy and toddlerhood, they increasingly face pressure to control their actions. With cognitive growth, toddlers become capable of aggression, which is the conscious intent to harm another person. At first, toddlers are limited to fighting over toys and other objects they desire, a behavior known as instrumental aggression. With middle childhood, children less often fight over objects, but begin trying to hurt other children because of slights to their emotions, known as hostile aggression.

Underlying the shift from instrumental to hostile aggression is the child's increasing awareness of how other people feel. With this understanding comes the flip side to childhood aggression, prosocial behavior. The same child who knows how to shape an especially effective insult now also understands the pain of another child's scuffed knee, or can sympathize with a child whose parents have divorced. In other words, the child can now empathize with another's feelings. And as a result of this new cognitive awareness, the child also becomes capable of acts of altruism – trying unselfishly to help someone else.

As Stevenson recognized in his fable of Jekyll/Hyde, the human capabilities for aggression, empathy, and altruism spring from the same wells. As you saw demonstrated in the video portion of the lesson, children are greatly influenced in prosocial behavior by parents who model empathy and altruism for the child. Secure attachment is also associated with a high level of empathy and prosocial behavior in the preschool years.

Less clear is the role played by television in affecting the aggressive and prosocial behaviors of children. Some studies have shown an increase in short-term aggressive behavior among children who watch violent TV shows. These studies are inconclusive, however, since they did not establish whether the content of the shows made the children more aggressive, or whether aggressive children tended to seek out such shows in the first place. Most researchers agree that the content of TV shows can have an effect on a child's behavior, at least over the short term, though the extent of such effects remains difficult to define.

Focusing Questions

1. What are some of the cognitive advances a child demonstrates when calling another child "a stupid jerk"?

2. What purpose does empathy serve during middle childhood for the child who begins making friends, joining peer groups, and establishing a firm sense of gender?

Parental Roles

When Charlotte asks her 10-year-old daughter Bev what's new at school, she is surprised at the child's answer.

"Oh, we've got this creepy new kid in our class. Her mom's a bum; she lives in a car. She doesn't even have nice clothes," says Bev.

"Hold on," says Charlotte, looking intently at the girl. "Just because somebody doesn't have a home doesn't mean they're a bum. There are lots of people who lose their homes because maybe they got sick or lost all their money and couldn't pay rent. People don't like to live on the street. Think how awful it'd be to not have a home of your own. You should try to be a little more understanding, honey."

Charlotte knows that many of her daughter's attitudes and values stem from her own. When she has to punish Bev, she takes the time to try to make clear to the girl why she does. Now, she's concerned about her daughter's lack of empathy for the other child's situation and wants to make the child more aware of how someone else might feel. In this case, since the mother and child have a trusting and secure relationship, her daughter is likely to absorb some of her mother's compassion.

The way parents convey messages about the child's prosocial and aggressive behavior is important. Among the parenting styles you studied in Lesson 19, the authoritative approach has the most positive effects. In one study, children raised by nurturing and responsive parents – the authoritative style – held positive feelings toward their peers and showed good self-control. Children of parents who were strict and inflexible disciplinarians – the authoritarian style – tended to be impulsive and under-controlled and were inclined to act aggressively toward others. A warm and nurturing parenting style helps children develop the self-confidence and strong sense of self that is necessary to appreciate and understand another person's feelings. At the same time, providing consistent and firm limits for children helps them develop appropriate self-restraint and learn to delay gratification.

Focusing Questions

1. What are some of the important factors a parent should keep in mind when trying to encourage a sense of empathy in their child?

2. John's father's idea of discipline is a "belt across the seat of the pants and a good hollering." On his way to the ice cream truck one afternoon, another boy runs up at the same time as John and jumps in front of him. What might John's reaction be?

Models of Psychopathology

Earlier, we described the parable of Dr. Jekyll and Mr. Hyde as being symbolic of the potential all individuals possess for both aggressive and prosocial behavior. But Stevenson relied upon the device of a powerful drug to remove all the moral restraints and sense of compassion from Dr. Jekyll. In real life, what are some of the reasons people grow up lacking empathy or self-control?

Any characteristic, behavior, or circumstance that may contribute to later pathology is called a risk factor. Childhood aggression is one risk factor for a number of later problems. Whether a child later develops pathologies depends on a variety of genetic, environmental, and socioeconomic factors. For example, circumstances that tend to offset negative influences in individual development are called protective factors and include the presence of at least one loving parent. Developmentalists look for warning signs such as aggression, lying, and stealing among children when trying to predict later pathology.

One school of thought about the cause of developmental problems follows biological explanations. For example, the traditional medical model tends to explain conduct problems as forms of mental illness and looks for underlying physiological causes. Neurological models posit the lack or imbalance of neurotransmitters in the brain as the cause of conduct problems, while genetic models seek to find answers within inheritable characteristics.

Environmental explanations of conduct disorders, on the other hand, include sociological models, which search for the cause of pathology within the social context. Behavioral models focus on the ways disruptive behaviors are reinforced, while psychodynamic models assume that prior stages of development are causing current problems. Family models, on the other hand, examine the family structure from which disruptive children come, assuming that the entire family dynamic is disturbed.

As you know by now, the developmental perspective presented by this course integrates certain principles of all these models. For example, developmentalists assume that genetic, environmental, and historical factors are all probably at work in an individual who develops schizophrenia. Within the developmental model, problematic behavior such as aggression and antisocial behavior is seen as one component within the context of a variety of contributing factors.

Key Terms

> Biological explanations for developmental disorders
> Environmental explanations for developmental disorders

Focusing Questions

1. It is common for preschoolers to lie. Likewise, many preschoolers will walk off with candy bars from stores even though they know it is stealing. Taken by themselves, why wouldn't these behaviors be considered risk factors?

2. Suppose an eight-year-old boy is discovered setting a grass fire and admits to having started several other fires. How might a psychologist following a medical model try to understand the child? A psychologist following a family model?

Childhood Disorders

As pointed out in Chapter 15 of your textbook, aggression or antisocial behavior in childhood may be indicative of serious developmental problems. One of the most serious childhood disorders is early childhood autism, which you may recall if you saw the movie *Rainman*. Researchers believe that autistic children are unable to sort out their sensory input; they are overwhelmed by their perceptions. Most researchers agree that autism is caused at least in part by genetic or organic malfunctions.

Children who exhibit a variety of problem behaviors that include extreme restlessness, impulsiveness, short attention span, and difficulty concentrating are grouped under the category of attention deficit/hyperactivity disorder. A common problem of school children, hyperactivity afflicts children of at least normal intelligence; researchers disagree on whether its causes are organic or environmental.

Children who suffer from general worry or fear to the detriment of normal behavior for their age are diagnosed as having an anxiety disorder. Such children may be overanxious generally or become excessively agitated when they are separated from a parent or other loved one. Researchers believe most anxiety disorders stem from the child's environment.

Anorexia nervosa is an extreme eating disorder that affects mainly adolescent girls and young women. Victims of anorexia nervosa restrict their eating so severely that they drastically lose weight and may even starve to death. Many researchers now consider anorexia to be based in environmental causes and treat patients within the context of their families.

Depression may occur during middle childhood or even earlier, though the research on the subject is controversial. One problem in diagnosing early depression is that children have difficulty expressing feelings of despair. Also, such symptoms of depression as lethargy and loss of appetite may be covered up by other problems. Some researchers assume that depression is genetically linked, while others look for psychological causes.

While not all childhood disorders cause children to behave aggressively or antisocially, they all greatly affect the child's ability to meet the normal tasks of development. An autistic child can barely function, let alone worry about being popular; a hyperactive boy may get a reputation as volatile because he has little impulse control. Childhood disorders represent one possible aspect of the overall context in which many children develop.

Key Terms

Autism
Hyperactive
Anxiety disorder
Anorexia nervosa

Focusing Questions

1. In which of the disorders described in this section would you expect to find the highest level of aggressive behavior? Do you think any of these disorders would NOT affect prosocial behavior?

2. Thinking of children in middle childhood, what are some of the differences between a normal level of energy and concentration and the behaviors of children who are hyperactive?

Questions for Understanding

As you read these questions often raised by parents, educators, and other childcare providers, first try to answer the questions yourself. Then read the answer following each question and compare your response to it.

1. *My 8-month-old son delights in pulling moustaches and hair, no matter how many times we scold him. Should I worry about raising a sadist?*

You should hardly conclude that your son is going to grow up to be "sadistic" just because he enjoys pulling people's hair as an infant. It is perfectly natural for children of his age to explore their world physically and to enjoy the reactions they get. But at this stage, your son has no awareness of the effects of his actions upon you; he has no comprehension that you have feelings. Even as he becomes a toddler and gets involved in grim tugs-of-war over toys with other kids, he still isn't deliberately being mean. We don't attribute personal negative intent to the behavior of toddlers.

With the cognitive advances of the preschool period, however, children can comprehend the self as an agent and begin intentionally practicing aggression toward other children. This is called instrumental aggression because it usually centers on objects. As children reach the end of the preschool period and begin forming an idea of the feelings of others, instrumental aggression declines and is replaced by hostile aggression. With the beginning of the elementary school years, children increasingly understand how others feel and thus are able to know how to hurt them. If a child is going to develop aggressive or "bullying" behaviors, it will probably show up then.

2. *How do empathy and altruism develop?*

According to experts, children develop a sense of empathy in three stages. Even as infants, the crying of one child may make another one cry or seek out its mother. At this point, however, the child doesn't clearly distinguish between its own feelings and those of another.

Next, during early toddlerhood, children begin offering help to children who are distressed. But the child as yet can only think of the other child's feelings in terms of his or her own feelings; the toddler isn't yet able to take the cognitive leap into another's emotions.

With the third stage, in early childhood, children make dramatic advances in the ability to empathize with others. This parallels the cognitive growth that toddlers demonstrate as they develop skills of fantasizing and role playing. At this point, though, the child's ability to empathize and act altruistically is still fairly rudimentary; the examples and guidance of adults will greatly determine each child's behavior toward others.

3. *Should I let my son watch TV programs about "super heroes," like The Flash? Sometimes they're awfully violent.*

The evidence on how the content of television shows affects children has been mixed. On the one hand, several studies have shown a short-term rise in the aggressive behavior of children who watched shows such as Superman and Batman cartoons. The problem with these studies is that the children who became more aggressive after watching TV had already rated high in aggressiveness before watching TV. While violent TV programs do appear to have some influence, any increase in aggression occurs within a context of other factors.

In short, studies on the effects of TV violence on children have been inconclusive. Keep in mind, however, that parental behavior and attitudes are among the most powerful influences on a child's behavior and that you control, to a certain extent, what your child is exposed to. If you are uncomfortable with the shows your child wants to watch, you should probably consider either controlling the shows he watches or negotiating a change in his viewing habits.

4. *I live in a duplex; a man and woman with two grade-school kids live in the next unit. The kids pretty much do as they please; the mother and father are hardly ever home. When they are home, I often hear them screaming at the children. I'm worried about these kids; how will an upbringing like this affect them?*

Unfortunately, given the situation you've described, these children may be negatively affected. According to one study of families that rated parents by how much warmth and control they directed toward their children, your neighbor's children stand a chance of becoming aggressive individuals who don't readily control their destructive impulses. This outcome is one predicted by parenting styles that combine hostility with permissiveness, as it sounds like your neighbors do.

Keep in mind, however, that numerous factors other than parenting style contribute to individual development. Individual temperament, prior developmental history, genetic makeup – these and other factors will have an effect on the formation of each individual. Parenting styles, in short, may make up just one possible risk factor that must be taken into account with all other aspects of an individual's development.

5. *In my son's day care center, one little boy is always causing problems. He's something of a bully; he seems to seek out weaker children and pick on them. And yet he seems to need more attention from the day care workers than other children. Isn't such behavior sort of contradictory?*

Not really. Remember that the behavior of any individual is always coherent, at least within the overall context of that person's development. Actions which, taken by themselves, seem to make no sense will usually add up when considered with other factors. In the situation you've described, for example, the little boy's different behaviors toward his peers and adults are both guided by the same developmental profile. By your description, this child sounds like he may be showing the effects of avoidant attachment in infancy. Typically, avoidant attached children are aggressive and hostile toward other children. They also may be emotionally isolated. At the same time, such antisocial children have strong dependency needs. Their aggressive behavior, in fact, may be their way of coercing guidance and discipline from adults.

6. *What are some specific risk factors that may affect a child's future development? What are some specific protective factors?*

Among possible risk factors are familial ones such as having parents who are going through a difficult divorce, biological ones such as having a parent with a disorder known to be genetic, and socioeconomic ones such as being raised by homeless parents. Children who exhibit childhood aggression, experience harsh parenting, are brought up in lower socio-economic conditions, have parents with low education, and who themselves have a low IQ are at risk of criminal activities later, for example. According to several studies, children who experience three or more such risk factors stand a three-in-four chance of developing problem behavior.

But if a child with such a triple whammy has the good fortune to be exposed to at least one protective factor, then their chances of developing a later disorder fall to just one in four. Among the most positive of possible protective factors is having at least one parent who is loving and dependable. Being in a stable economic environment would also be a protective factor. The degree to which a single protective factor in a child's background can ameliorate a number of risk factors just points up the importance of all the aspects of a child's overall development.

SELF-TEST

The following multiple choice and short answer test questions should help you assess your understanding of the points covered in the text and the video. After answering all the questions, check your answers against the key and use the accuracy of your answers to gauge how well you have met the lesson objectives.

Multiple Choice Questions

1. When 9-year-old Kelly stops by to visit her best friend Mavis, she finds her friend in tears. "What happened?" Kelly asks. "Mr. Budgie died," Mavis says, referring to her pet parakeet. Within moments, Kelly is crying just as hard as Mavis, demonstrating her ability to

   a. be altruistic.
   b. act contagiously.
   c. act aggressively.
   d. empathize.

2. An example of hostile aggression would be

   a. a toddler pulling books off a low shelf and tearing pages from them.
   b. two 8 year olds engaged in a name-calling contest.
   c. two preschoolers trying to yank a hand-held video game from each other's hands.
   d. an autistic child's refusal to interact with other children.

3. The main cognitive ability that children must develop before being able to act aggressively or feel empathy is a(n)

   a. sense that they are independent agents responsible for their own actions.
   b. ability to tolerate frustration.
   c. awareness of the parent of the same sex as a role model.
   d. strong sense of gender.

4. At the end of the day, children are hurrying along a hallway on their way out of school. One 7-year-old girl drops a pencil case. Without even pausing, a passing 8-year-old boy kicks the plastic case down the hall, smiling at the girl as he does. The boy's past developmental history might include

   a. avoidant attachment.
   b. secure attachment.

    c. autism.
    d. anxious detachment.

5. A first-grader is helping his mother by pushing a shopping cart along the aisles of a drug store. At one point, he doesn't watch where he's going and knocks several bottles of mouthwash onto the floor, breaking them. His mother reaches out and hits the boy hard on his ear. "Damn it Charles! I told you to pay attention to what you're doing. Can't you do anything right?" The boy's mother is modeling the style of parenting known as

    a. authoritative.
    b. permissive.
    c. overinvolved.
    d. authoritarian.

6. To date, the research on the effect of violence in television shows upon children has

    a. demonstrated a clear negative impact.
    b. demonstrated there is no impact at all.
    c. proved that aggressive children like aggressive shows.
    d. shown ambivalent results.

7. A child psychologist is conducting a survey of a range of elementary school students. After going over her data, looking for behavioral signs that might indicate the child will later develop a form of conduct disorder, she is most concerned about the

    a. first grader who is finicky about her diet.
    b. third grader who wets her bed.
    c. fourth grader who has nightmares.
    d. kindergartner who lies a lot.

8. Fred is having problems in the fourth grade. He's bright but can't seem to sit still. His teacher complains that he seems unable to concentrate on his lessons and is always interrupting the other children while they work. Fred's parents take him to a child psychologist, who tells them their son is hyperactive. To help the boy adjust, the psychologist asks Fred to meet with him regularly for what he calls "slowing-down" lessons. In their sessions, he teaches the boy how to control his behavior and gives him a series of messages to repeat when feeling impatient. The psychologist approaches Fred's problem from

    a. the traditional medical model.
    b. the behavioral model.
    c. the psychodynamic model.
    d. the family model.

9. Of a variety of pathologies which children develop, the one which some researchers agree is most likely affected by genetic factors is/are

    a. depression.
    b. anorexia nervosa.
    c. anxiety disorders.
    d. conduct disorders.

10. When making predictions about later behavior, developmentalists consider childhood aggression to be one of many possible

   a. risk factors.
   b. genetic markers.
   c. protective factors.
   d. environmental influences.

Short Answer Questions

The following questions should be answered in a paragraph or two. You should identify several key points for each answer and use these to form the framework for your response.

1. What are some of the cognitive abilities which a child must gain before beginning to develop empathy, and what can parents do to encourage its development in their children?

2. What are some of the ways in which a child's aggressive behavior develops?

3. Suppose a 10-year-old boy consistently gets in fights at school and has a long history of being unable to control his anger. The boy is frequently violent and is considered a bully by the other children. How might several psychologists who followed different scientific models of psychopathology approach the boy's problem?

21

A Look at the Whole Child:
Ages 6 through 12

LESSON ASSIGNMENT

Completing the following steps will help you master the lesson objectives and achieve the goal for this lesson:

STEP 1: Read the INTRODUCING THE LESSON section to provide a context for what you will learn in this lesson.

STEP 2: Read the lesson's GOAL and LESSON OBJECTIVES so that you will know what you are expected to learn.

STEP 3: Read the text assignment, Chapter 11, pages 395-422 and 431-435; and Chapter 12, pages 437-457 and 468-471. Pay particular attention to the key terms and concepts in the Chapter Summary for Chapter 11 on pages 433-435, and for Chapter 12 on page 471; they will help you when you watch the video.

STEP 4: Review the VIEWING GUIDE section in the telecourse guide. It lists several points to consider as you watch the video.

STEP 5: Watch the video.

STEP 6: Read the telecourse guide chapter's UNDERSTANDING THE LESSON section in the telecourse guide. Make sure you understand the key terms and can answer the focusing questions included there.

STEP 7: Complete the SELF-TEST.

STEP 8: Go back to the LESSON OBJECTIVES and make sure you can respond to each of them.

INTRODUCING THE LESSON

Ed, age 11, is in his room packing for a Boy Scout campout the following weekend. As he assembles his gear, he sorts the various items by different criteria.

"Okay," he says to himself, "this is the stuff for my first-aid kit. The bandages, tape, and gauze all go in this compartment. Bottles and ointments, like Mercurochrome, zinc ointment, and mosquito repellent, go in this compartment. Snake-bite kit next to the card for CPR . . .What else?"

Looking around the cluttered room, Ed notices a flashlight sticking out of a pair of high-top sneakers. "Oh yeah," he says, "gotta get batteries for the flashlight. I almost forgot. Good thing I thought to stick the flashlight where I'd be sure to remember it needs batteries."

Just then there is a knock on the door, and then the door pops open. Ed's 7-year-old sister, Wendy, sticks her head into the room. "What're you doing?" the little girl asks, looking around the room. "You're not taking my jump rope camping," Wendy says as she notices a coil of rope beside Ed's bed.

"Don't be so dumb," Ed replies. "That's my rope, for mountain climbing and using as a clothesline. I wouldn't use your stupid jump rope, anyway. Only little kids jump rope – I'm a Boy Scout, and we do cool stuff in the woods."

"What's this?" Wendy asks, pointing to a compass lying on top of Ed's unrolled sleeping bag.

"That's a compass," Ed says. "You use it in the woods to tell you which direction you're going."

"Like a map?" the younger child asks.

"Not exactly; you use it with a map. Here, see this needle," he says, pointing at the quivering blue needle of the compass. "See how it stays in just about the same place even when I turn the compass? That's 'cause it's always pointing north – or anyway, magnetic north, which is a little different."

Probably, Ed's little sister understands little of his discussion of magnetic and true north. And while she does grasp the idea that the compass needle always points in one direction, she's less sure about why that natural phenomenon is important information to a Boy Scout. Her brother, on the other hand, not only uses a compass to help him interpret a map to navigate through the woods, but also might know a little of the history of how compasses were used by ancient mariners to circumnavigate the globe. Although both Ed and his younger sister are within the limits of the developmental stage of middle childhood, their cognitive capabilities differ widely.

Wendy, for example, probably would not have thought to put the flashlight in her shoes as a reminder to herself to get more batteries. She likewise would have found it more difficult to pack the items of a first aid kit according to category of use. And even Ed's participation in Boy Scouts represents a degree of social behavior that Wendy is probably not yet ready for.

In this lesson you will see an overview of the numerous developmental changes children undergo during middle childhood. As you have learned in previous lessons, middle childhood is the time when each child consolidates his or her self-image, forms intimate friendships, begins to associate with peers, and learns the complicated rules for dealing with the opposite sex. The array of cognitive, social, and emotional changes that children undergo during middle childhood is subtle and far-ranging and creates the solid foundation of self which children will need as they enter the tumultuous period of adolescence.

GOAL

The purpose of this lesson is to present a comprehensive picture of the various cognitive, social, and emotional advances which children make during middle childhood.

LESSON OBJECTIVES

After reading the text assignment, completing the exercises in this telecourse guide, and viewing the lesson's video portion, you will be able to:

1. Compare the rate of physical development and growth occurring in middle childhood to those of infancy and toddlerhood.

2. Describe the qualitative cognitive changes that occur during middle childhood.

3. Indicate the major social advances that are achieved during middle childhood.

4. Discuss the interconnection between cognitive and social development and how they influence each other.

5. Recognize the "unevenness" of development and indicate why such occurrences make sense in terms of what is happening to the child at a particular time.

VIEWING GUIDE

In this lesson, the various "pieces" of development during middle childhood – better classification skills, improved memory, growing friendships and associations in groups, increased empathy – all come together ideally, under the right conditions to form a coherent picture of individual development. By about the age of 12, children have been formed by a combination of developmental contexts that interact with one another to produce a distinct individual, poised to tackle the challenges of adolescence. After reading the text material and learning the important terms included there, you are ready to view the lesson's video portion. First, review the questions in the Self-Test at the end of this telecourse guide lesson to give you an idea of important points to watch for in the video. Then, read the following

Points to Consider to give you an idea of what the video will cover. Keep these points in mind while watching.

Points to Consider

☐ *What school kids know*: The cognitive advances children make during middle childhood are based upon changes which begin in the toddler and preschool periods. Look for examples of how much better a child understands the concepts of conservation and classification after three or four years of school. Notice how the child's improved memory grows out of previous stages of development.

☐ *Who schoolkids know*: Middle childhood is when children seek out other children of the same age. In the video segment, pay attention to the different ways in which the children relate to their peers. Be aware of the changes in self-awareness which children demonstrate at this time.

☐ *The sum of their parts*: The combination of cognitive and social developments during middle childhood has definite feedback effects on the child's overall development. Look for examples of children teaching others through scaffolding. Try to distinguish the results of social changes from cognitive ones on the children shown in the video segment.

☐ *Between average and unique*: The course of any child's development during middle childhood depends on their history of growth so far. Use the examples of the three children shown in the video segment to compare the results of different developmental histories on individual children. Be aware of how development during middle childhood continues to be coherent and orderly for all children when conditions are optimum. Otherwise, there can be developmental consequences.

UNDERSTANDING THE LESSON

Children going through middle childhood experience some very important changes. The beginning of school, discovering a first "best friend," learning to strike out verbally instead of physically, establishing the attributes of their own gender, joining a network of one's peers – these are the developmental milestones of middle childhood.

The 11 or 12 year old stands on the verge of adolescence with an array of social, cognitive, and emotional skills that were only hinted at in the preschool period. By the end of middle childhood, the average child has mastered an impressive range of developmental challenges and is prepared for the next stage of growth. And, Sigmund Freud notwithstanding, he or she hasn't gotten there without effort or revelation.

Cognitive Changes of Middle Childhood

As children develop physically during the preschool years, they become capable of mastering an ever greater number of games and tasks. Within the space of a few years, the preschooler who required adult help to clamber out of a snowsuit will be handling the bindings of skis all alone. The child who stood on the sidelines enviously watching an older sibling play hopscotch now takes up the game, along with the playground staples of tetherball, two- and four-square, and dodgeball. Gains in height, weight, and coordination abilities ensure that children will be able to take part in and enjoy the many group-based games of elementary school.

Equally important as the physical developments of middle childhood, however, are the many cognitive changes which children experience between the ages of 6 and 12. As you learned in Lesson 17, middle childhood is when children master the concepts of conservation of number, weight, and displacement of liquid volume. Furthermore, children in middle childhood begin to base their understanding of conservation on the concept of necessary as opposed to contingent truth. Attending these cognitive advances in the elementary years is an increase in the child's ability to monitor his or her own thought processes – an ability known as metacognition.

The child's classification skills are broadening and deepening at this time as well, aiding each child in the task of imposing structure on the world. Classification skills are also important in learning language and communication. With hierarchical classification, the child organizes a body of knowledge by assigning each of its members a place within an ordered sequence. Within the structure of animal classification, for example, this would mean classifying a certain marine animal as a vertebrate, mammal, cetacea, whale, and sperm whale. With matrix classification, children sort out related items according to two dimensions. One example of matrix clarification would be sorting a stamp collection according to country and denomination.

Memory abilities continue to grow during these years. With the start of their school years, children greatly increase their fund of knowledge, which forms the basis of the expanded cognitive ability known as constructive memory. During middle childhood, children become better able to integrate information from verbal material and pictures, and to integrate information more rapidly – important skills for succeeding in school. Children in middle childhood are also mastering a number of memory "tricks" which aid them in recalling and coordinating the mass of information and skills which they are building upon and adding to. These memory tricks, known as mnemonics, include visual cues such as Boy Scout Ed used to remind him to get new batteries, rehearsing things in order to remember them, and even the simple act of writing things down. And the school-age child is increasingly aware of his or her memory strengths and weaknesses, an awareness known as metamemory.

With the end of middle childhood, most children will have filled in and solidified his or her competencies in a number of cognitive abilities which the child began to acquire at the end of the preschool period. Much as a finished paint-by-number painting represents the completion of an outline that already existed, the cognitive skills of 11 and 12 year olds are the refined and elaborated results of capabilities which they inherited from the previous stage of development. At the same time, the cognitive abilities of older children in middle childhood are definitely constrained by a general lack of knowledge and practice in using new skills.

Focusing Questions

1. What changes occur in memory abilities between the ages of 6 or 7 and 10 or 11?

2. In what ways do you think the middle childhood child's increasing powers of metacognition enable him or her to consolidate and improve the cognitive skills which they have already acquired?

Social Growth During Middle Childhood

In terms of individual development, middle childhood could easily be dubbed the "period of joining." Repeatedly throughout the past three lessons, you have seen examples of children acting as members of groups: as students, as Boy and Girl Scouts, as members of camera clubs, swim teams, and chess clubs. Most of the communicative and experiential skills that each person will need for a lifetime of social interaction are honed and consolidated during middle childhood.

As you learned in Lesson 18, a child's sense of self undergoes several important changes during this time. Whereas preschoolers tend to define themselves in physical terms, with the start of elementary school children increasingly think of themselves in psychological terms. Children are now beginning to think in more general terms and to combine previously separated categories of thought. The middle childhood youngster develops a more sophisticated understanding of how other people think and feel and further develops a sense of empathy. Children begin to grasp that another person's feelings may be different from what the person actually says and can make inferences based on that knowledge.

Along with this deeper understanding of self comes a new awareness of the self as a social being. Increasingly, school-age children describe themselves in terms of the personality traits other people notice or are affected by: "I am friendly; I'm good at math; I like singing." Also, children begin defining themselves as members of certain groups, such as scouts, sports teams, or church groups. Comparison with others, especially peers, is an increasingly important part of self-awareness.

As children enter school and begin spending long periods of time with other children of the same age, they develop socially in several ways. Along with their growing powers of empathy and altruism, children are now improving in their ability to communicate, especially with one another. Children are thinking of one another in more complex psychological ways, reflecting their improved cognitive abilities. Prosocial behavior begins to supplant the instrumental aggression typical of toddlers and preschoolers, while at the same time hostile aggression is on the rise. As you saw in earlier video segments, this means that now children hit each other less, but taunt and tease each other more.

Children also now tend to associate with one another in peer groups; by the age of 11, the average American child spends as much time with peers as with adults. The elementary school age child joins a network of friends, with girls forming smaller, more intimate circles than boys do. As you'll recall from numerous examples, boys and girls form separate groups and create and observe a number of rigid though unwritten "rules" for enforcing this gender separation. Within their peer groups, children are gaining valuable experience in cooperation and communication, as well as learning lessons in socialization. In particular, the equal-status relations of peer groups give school-age children valuable lessons in fairness, reciprocity, and equity.

Focusing Questions

1. During middle childhood, youngsters begin combining various concepts of the self into a coherent self-image. What are some of the ways in which elementary school age children define themselves differently from the way they thought of themselves as preschoolers?

2. In what ways do peer groups act as agents of socialization?

The Combined Influences of Cognitive and Social Changes

In medicine, the term *synergism* refers to the action of two drugs which, combined, have a greater effect than the sum of their effects if the drugs are taken individually. For example, doctors treat migraine headaches with a combination of caffeine and ergotamine; the caffeine constricts blood vessels in the brain and thus lowers the blood flow, while the ergotamine stifles the painful pulsations of cranial arteries. Taken together, the two drugs treat the pain of migraine headaches much more effectively than would either one taken alone.

In similar fashion, the cognitive and social advances which children make during middle childhood both stimulate and reinforce one another. As children move from the settings of preschool, where they have limited contact with others, into the social context of elementary school, children find that their cognitive knacks for understanding others and themselves are now being shaped by their new peer relationships. The interplay of cognitive and social challenges produces synergistic results for most children.

For example, in learning situations where one child who understands the concept of conservation works on a question with a child who doesn't understand the concept, the more knowledgeable child is often able to teach the other child. As you'll recall from Lesson 17, this particular peer teaching relationship is called a didactic situation. Likewise, when children interact to solve problems which neither fully comprehends, they often are able to show improved understanding over what they learn alone. The improvements which children realize from working together on problems, called a cooperative situation, often are generalized to related tasks. In other words, the children's cognitive performances are improved through their social interactions.

Piaget thought that children were able to learn well when grouped with other children because social interaction allows them to experience conflict between their ideas and those of other people. Social groups help children to learn through the type of progressive guidance known as scaffolding. Remember that scaffolding is a teaching strategy that is used not only by adult teachers to help their young students, but also by older children with younger ones. When older middle childhood youngsters practice scaffolding, it is an example of their growing metacognitive skills.

Another impact on a child's cognitive growth comes when children enter school and find themselves being compared with their peers. Research has shown that children begin evaluating their own performances in relation to others at around the age of 7 or 8. This change in style of self-assessment seems to be a result of both the child's advancing cognitive development and increased instances of being compared in performance to others at school.

Focusing Questions

1. What are some of the cognitive skills which children have already begun to develop when they start elementary school?

2. Suppose you ask a 5 year old to describe herself. What attributes would her answers mention? If you ask the same child a similar question four or five years later, what might she say then?

Individual Variations

As always with issues of development, the general outlines of change and growth during middle childhood as sketched out in this course may vary from child to child. A host of contexts, including previous development history, the family context, genetic history, and the economic environment will affect each child's individual development in unique ways.

Take, for example, the area of self-esteem and how it affects cognitive and social development during middle childhood. Not surprisingly, studies have shown that children with high self-esteem tend to do well in school, are self-confident, and tend to trust their own reactions and conclusions. Such children have good expectations of successfully forming peer friendships and positively influencing other children, which in turn will encourage positive treatment from other children. In other words, such children have a good chance of being viewed as well-liked by their peers. As could be expected, high self-esteem equates with positive attachment in infancy, as well as from secure patterns of adaptation during the preschool period.

Conversely, a host of negative factors can impact a child's ability to master the cognitive and social challenges of middle childhood. Jerry, the troubled boy in the video segment, is one example of some of the difficulties that children can face as they deal with the cognitive and social requirements of the elementary school years. When Jerry blames his behavior problems on others, we see how social interactions both channel and are shaped by individual cognitive abilities, in this case Jerry's degree of self-awareness.

Another area where individual development may vary comes when children of varying cultures enter the mainstream school system. As you studied in earlier lessons, children from lower economic brackets and minority groups may have difficulty making the shift from using their language, problem solving, and other cognitive skills in the home to using these skills in the classroom. Furthermore, the social interaction expected in school may be unfamiliar to some children.

Overall, however, development in middle childhood is coherent and orderly – as in all other stages of development. The children who best master the various challenges of middle childhood – consolidating a sense of self, gaining confidence in their own abilities, forming peer friendships, joining peer groups, and successfully adjusting to school – are those who have gotten off to a good start in earlier stages. Generally speaking, self-confident, securely attached children present themselves to others in positive ways that elicit favorable reactions, further enhancing their self-confidence. Likewise, any variations from the positive course of average development may elicit negative reactions from peers and teachers.

Focusing Questions

1. When children enter elementary school, they must make a shift from solving problems on a strictly verbal level to dealing with problems in written form. What are some of the cultural backgrounds which might make this transition more difficult for some children than for others?

2. What are some of the attitudes children who have high self-esteem use to approach the challenges of school and interacting with peer groups?

Questions for Understanding

As you read these questions, often raised by parents, educators, and other childcare providers, first try to answer the questions yourself. Then read the answer following each question and compare your response to it.

1. *It seems that children around the world begin their education between the ages of 5 and 7. How did this become a universal starting point and is it really the right one?*

Somewhere between the ages of 5 and 7, children have informally mastered certain skills which are important to the kind of learning they will be expected to do in school. For example, they can speak and understand their native language, and they can understand something of the concepts of quantity and number. In addition, they have some logical reasoning skills.

Still, for some children the transition to school may be difficult because "formal education" requires working with abstract problems and the ability to handle problems in written form. The early childhood learning experiences of some cultures make this transition easier to make than the practices of other cultures. Thus, some children experience success in school more quickly and easily than others though the starting age is fairly universal.

2. *What are some of the limitations which still constrain the cognitive abilities of older middle childhood youngsters?*

For one thing, children do not as yet have a wide range of knowledge and stored experience upon which to draw when trying to solve problems. As a result, their reasoning about certain situations may be immature and incomplete. And even when elementary school age children have acquired a new reasoning skill, they haven't as yet had much chance to practice it. As a result, they may have trouble bringing it to bear on a real-life problem.

A child who has just successfully passed a test on the multiplication tables, for example, may not be able to look at a room containing 9 rows of 7 chairs and tell you that it could seat 63 people. Furthermore, even 10 and 11 year olds have difficulty reasoning maturely about abstract and hypothetical problems. Memorizing multiplication tables is certainly a skill, but understanding what the process of multiplication is and how to use it is a very different skill. It is a mistake to assume that a child who has memorized his math tables understands the process of multiplication.

3. *Our 10-year-old son seems to be very uneven in how he learns in school. In subjects like social sciences and history, he has to struggle to remember every new fact or date. And yet in areas he's interested in, such as biology and dinosaurs, he knows a great deal and has no trouble learning and retaining new information. What accounts for the difference in how well he learns in different subjects?*

On a general level, all individuals are gifted differently in different areas. Some children are math whizzes, others seem naturally to assume leadership roles; this one picks up clarinet effortlessly, that one has a knack for Spanish. But in your son's case, it sounds like he assimilates new information about biology and dinosaurs mainly because he already knows a lot about these subjects. We are all better able to remember new information when we can fit it into what we already know.

If, for example, your son has to learn about a new species of amphibian in his biology class, he'll be able to incorporate the new information into what he already knows about animal classification systems. Chances are also good that he will be able to make inferences about the new information based on what he already knows, a type of memory which is called constructive memory. This ability is one which expands throughout the middle childhood years and, indeed, one's entire life.

4. *What are some of the ways in which a child's concept of the self changes from preschool into middle childhood?*

Perhaps the most significant change is that with middle childhood, children begin forming the concept of the "psychological self." Whereas toddlers have formed the concept of the self and have begun to distinguish themselves from others, they do so largely in physical terms. In other words, preschoolers think of their "self" as something concrete, as an object, usually located in the head or brain. They also tend to describe themselves by their physical characteristics or abilities: "I have blonde hair; I can roller skate."

With middle childhood, however, children begin thinking of themselves in more general terms, often using emotional categories to describe themselves: "I don't get mad very often; I feel sorry for homeless people." And although older children do define themselves by their physical traits, they are now more likely to do so in comparison with others.

5. *My 10-year-old daughter hardly ever seems to want to spend time with her family any more – she's always with her two best friends. Can school kids spend too much time with their friends?*

Deciding if a child is spending "too much" time with friends of the same age depends on the child's behavior, performance in school, family relations, and a variety of other factors. But it may reassure you to know that spending a great deal of time with peer group friends is normal for children of your daughter's age. If your daughter seems to prefer being with her friends to spending time with you, it's not because she likes them more or loves you less.

At this age, your daughter is experiencing a need to explore her feelings and thoughts with others of her own age; in fact, researchers have found that peer groups rival the family at this time as the child's major setting for development. By spending time with her friends, your daughter is learning valuable lessons in getting along with others, cooperating, and coping with feelings of aggression. And precisely because she and her friends are close in age and status, they behave with one another in ways that they cannot with adults – which includes their parents.

6. *During middle childhood, what are some of the changes that children will undergo in how they relate to their peers?*

Because they are now making cognitive leaps in their ability to understand how other people feel, children develop better skills in communicating with others. At the same time as they are getting better at getting their ideas across to others, children are also improving their prosocial abilities. And the aggression which children now feel toward one another is likely to be expressed verbally in the form of taunts and insults instead of the physical aggression more common among younger children. Individual friendships become important to children at this age, as does the need to belong to a group of peers.

SELF-TEST

The following multiple choice and short answer test questions should help you assess your understanding of the points covered in the text and the video. After answering all the questions, check your answers against the key and use the accuracy of your answers to gauge how well you have met the lesson objectives.

Multiple Choice Questions

1. According to most developmentalists, the major cognitive advances which children make during middle childhood are

   a. in new areas of development.
   b. in areas of previous development.
   c. sudden and dramatic.
   d. unrelated to later developments.

2. Ed, Kevin, and Jered are working on a Boy Scout map problem. When they realize that they will have to use a little algebra to figure out the distance between two points, Ed and Jered immediately turn to Kevin because, as Kevin puts it, he is able "to just see in my head what

the numbers mean, kind of." Kevin's comment about his math capabilities is an example of the awareness known as

a. constructive memory.
b. necessary truth.
c. contingent truth.
d. metacognition.

3. The students in a fourth grade geography class are taking a test. One of the questions gives a list of cities around the world and asks the children to group the cities according to their continents and then rank them by the size of their populations. To answer this question correctly, the students must use the cognitive skill of

a. hierarchical classification.
b. matrix classification.
c. constructive memory.
d. metamemory.

4. While passing through a city while on a trip, you pay a visit to friends whom you haven't seen in 10 years. Your friends have three children, aged 5, 7, and 11. While talking to the kids, you ask each one to tell you a little about him or herself. Of the four answers below, the one that the 11 year old is most likely to give you is

a. "I've got the best time for the 100-meter butterfly."
b. "My hair is the same color as my Dad's."
c. "I've got a truly awesome stamp collection."
d. "I like animals – want to see my hamster apartment?"

5. During middle childhood, youngsters increasingly base their self understanding on how they perceive or relate to the people around them. This cognitive advance is referred to as the development of a

a. psychological self.
b. sense of mastery.
c. social self.
d. locus of control.

6. A researcher asks a group of children to describe what "a friend" means to them. The comment which is most likely to have been made by a child at the end of middle childhood is

a. "A friend is someone I like, that's all."
b. "A friend is somebody I play with all the time."
c. "A friend is somebody who you can trust to keep your secrets."
d. "A friend is somebody with neat toys."

7. Many elementary school teachers regularly praise the students in their classes who achieve high grades and test scores. As one result, by the age of 9 and 10 children routinely assess themselves at least partly in comparison with others. This outcome is a result of

a. cognitive development only.
b. cognitive and social factors working together.
c. social development only.
d. culturally-based IQ scores.

8. As compared to toddlerhood, the rate of physical growth during middle childhood

   a. occurs at about the same rate.
   b. becomes slower.
   c. varies so much from child to child that a comparison cannot be made.
   d. increases more for boys than for girls.

9. When children begin formal schooling, one of the main differences between how they have been learning and how they will learn in school is that now they must

   a. answer questions.
   b. communicate with others.
   c. deal with problems in written form.
   d. talk to strangers.

10. During the elementary school years, children do NOT face the developmental task of

    a. developing a sense of autonomy.
    b. consolidating a sense of self.
    c. joining peer groups.
    d. successfully adjusting to school.

Short Answer Questions

The following questions should be answered in a paragraph or two. You should identify several key points for each answer and use these to form the framework for your response.

1. What are some of the ways in which children learn from one another during middle childhood?

2. What are some of the differences between how children learn at home and at school?

3. What are some of the ways that a child's sense of self-esteem will affect his or her cognitive and social growth during middle childhood?

MODULE VI:

ADOLESCENCE

22

Physical and Cognitive Development in Adolescence

LESSON ASSIGNMENT

Completing the following steps will help you master the lesson objectives and achieve the goal for this lesson:

STEP 1: Read the INTRODUCING THE LESSON section to provide a context for what you will learn in this lesson.

STEP 2: Read the lesson's GOAL and LESSON OBJECTIVES so that you will know what you are expected to learn.

STEP 3: Read the text assignment, Chapter 13, pages 485-510. Pay particular attention to the key terms and concepts in the Chapter Summary on pages 510-511; they will help you when you watch the video.

STEP 4: Review the VIEWING GUIDE section in the telecourse guide. It lists several points to consider as you watch the video.

STEP 5: Watch the video.

STEP 6: Read the UNDERSTANDING THE LESSON section in the telecourse guide. Make sure you understand the key terms and can answer the focusing questions included there.

STEP 7: Complete the SELF-TEST.

STEP 8: Go back to the LESSON OBJECTIVES and make sure you can respond to each of them.

INTRODUCING THE LESSON

It is Saturday afternoon at Southland Community Mall, and the broad corridors of the enclosed structure are filled with strolling people. Couples with small children move purposefully from shop to shop, accumulating purchases. At dozens of tables in the food concourse, shoppers take a break over fast food. Pairs of well-dressed young women walk along, talking and occasionally stopping to gaze in store windows.

And everywhere among the throngs of people are teenagers, shopping, eating, just hanging out. Just as a large marsh along a migratory flyway attracts flocks of birds, a contemporary suburban shopping mall attracts adolescents. Outside of a high school, a mall is probably one of the best places for observing adolescent behavior.

Take the four young teenage boys carrying skateboards who are draped over a bench near a reflecting pool. As they talk, they keep an eye on a security guard who's passing by. As the guard turns a corner, one boy says, "Awright, man, let's do it." Laughing loudly, the boys place their skateboards atop the bench, race along it, and then kick and jump their boards several feet across a gap to the low wall rimming the pool. The boys propel themselves down one side of the pool and jump down, scattering several shoppers as they go. Then, they grab their boards and run off, pushing one another and shouting.

Over in the food concourse, three girls, all 15 years old, sit over bowls of frozen yogurt and talk. "This is so beautiful," says one, propping open a copy of *The Prophet* by Kahlil Gibran. "Listen to this, what he has to say to parents about children: 'You may give them your love but not your thoughts, For they have their own thoughts. You may house their bodies but not their souls.' Wow, that is so true. But do you think my mom could ever understand that? No way."

"Neither could my parents," replies her friend. "They'd never read anything heavy like this; all they ever read is TV Guide. It's like they can't believe I could have any thoughts of my own, you know, that they didn't give me first."

In another part of the mall, another young teenage girl leaves a clothing store, followed by her mother. "Nancy, slow down," the girl's mother says. "What's the matter now? Why'd you storm out of there like that?"

"Because I don't have to be laughed at by some dumb clerk," says the girl, her cheeks flushing. "You saw how she looked at me, when I couldn't fit into those jeans. It's not my fault the stupid companies make everything for beanpoles. She thinks she's better than me because she has skinny thighs."

"That's ridiculous," says the girl's mother. "That girl was very nice. And there's nothing wrong with your thighs. You're just not growing as quickly as your sister did; you'll stretch out soon enough."

During the developmental stage of adolescence, which is roughly from about age 10 or 12 through the late teens, children experience dramatic physical and cognitive growth. As the above examples illustrate, adolescent behavior ranges from self-centered and rowdy to thoughtful and idealistic. Caught up in an often bewildering period of "fast-forward" physical and cognitive change, adolescents can be both exasperating and inspiring. In the view of many developmentalists, overall adolescence marks a period of transition from middle childhood to adulthood.

In this lesson, we begin our study of adolescence by concentrating on how children change physically and cognitively during this period. Adolescence marks the arrival of puberty, when the child's body begins reacting to the sex hormones which will stimulate his or her sexual development. Cognitively, the adolescent begins to master new abilities of handling abstract thought and to adopt more psychological, sophisticated views. And increasingly, the adolescent is aware of how he or she thinks, which leads to new forms of self-absorption.

GOAL

The purpose of this lesson is to present the major physiological and cognitive changes of adolescence and to survey some of the developmental theories which have been proposed for this stage by Jean Piaget and other developmentalists.

LESSON OBJECTIVES

After reading the text assignment, completing the exercises in this telecourse guide, and viewing the lesson's video portion, you will be able to:

1. Contrast the biological changes and physical transformations experienced by girls during puberty with those experienced by boys.

2. Cite the evidence which suggests that changes in brain structure and function may also result from hormonal changes during adolescence.

3. Briefly describe the range of thinking skills that emerge during adolescence and Piaget's theories regarding how these skills develop.

4. Discuss the various criticisms that have been leveled at Piaget's theory of formal operations.

5. Define and give examples of adolescent egocentrism.

6. Summarize Kohlberg's and Piaget's theories regarding the development of moral reasoning.

VIEWING GUIDE

While studying this lesson, you may find yourself remembering the strong emotions of adolescence, when your body underwent such great change and your emotional outlook may have seemed as unpredictable as the stock market. For most adults, the passages of adolescence remain vividly alive in our memories – as well as being expressed daily in our adult values.

After reading the text material and learning the important terms included there, you are ready to view the lesson's video portion. First, review the questions in the Self-Test at the end of this telecourse guide lesson to give you an idea of important points to watch for in the video. Then read the following Points to Consider to give you an idea of what the video will cover. Keep these points in mind while watching.

Points to Consider

☐ *The return of biology*: Adolescence is a time of profound biological change, including sexual maturation. Keep track of how the hormones which initiate puberty also contribute to a variety of other physical changes. Be aware of how broad a range there is in when individuals begin puberty and of how development within an individual may be uneven. Consider the problems this creates for both adolescents and teachers in age-graded schools.

☐ *Changing minds*: Adolescence is also when the mind's ability to grasp abstractions expands greatly. Look for examples of how adolescents are able to comprehend previously obscure concepts. Pay attention to how Piaget's three experiments were designed to assess the ways in which adolescents are now better able to solve problems.

☐ *Evaluating Piaget's theories*: Piaget's ideas about the nature and course of cognitive development in adolescence have come under criticism by subsequent experts. Take notice of charges that formal operational thinking may be culture-bound.

☐ *"Everybody's staring at me"*: The range of cognitive developments which adolescence brings include changes beyond improved logical abilities. Notice how the blinders of egocentrism once again shape individual points of view. Pay attention to how adolescents develop powers of moral reasoning, and compare how Piaget's and Kohlberg's models of moral development differ.

UNDERSTANDING THE LESSON

In his fairy tale of *The Ugly Duckling*, Hans Christian Andersen created a metaphor for some of the feelings of adolescence. As a result of the sudden growth of their limbs, the startling changes in their sexual organs, the activity in their sweat glands, and the upheaval in their thinking processes, teenagers often feel like outsiders among more "normal" people – like ugly ducklings, in fact.

Also like the misplaced swan of the story, teenagers often feel misunderstood, as though only they had ever experienced the feelings of doubt and confusion that often accompany the changes of puberty and adolescence. But as strange and unsettling as the changes of adolescence may seem to teenagers, they are all rooted in the individual's previous developmental history. Though it doesn't feel that way to them at times, the "Ugly Duckling" stage of their growth is just a stage, and not a final destination.

Biological Changes During Adolescence

Some of the changes which children undergo during middle childhood are so gradual that they go almost unremarked, both by the children and their care givers; the same thing can hardly be said of adolescence. For one thing, adolescence is the time of *puberty*, when children attain reproductive maturity and experience dramatic physical change.

Puberty is actually a cycle of development of primary and secondary sex characteristics which takes place over a period of four or more years. For girls, the most striking change is *menarche*, the beginning of menstruation – followed, several months later, by ovulation. In America, girls begin menstruating sometime between the ages of 10 and 16. For boys, the critical change during puberty is the ability to ejaculate sperm. Generally speaking, boys enter puberty about two years after girls do. Puberty for both sexes is triggered by the secretion of hormones, though researchers are unsure why the body begins secreting hormones when it does.

In both sexes, the pituitary gland is influenced by hormones from the hypothalamus to release pituitary hormones called gonadotropins, which stimulate growth of the genitals. In boys, the male hormone androgen sets off the development of the genitals and the production of live sperm and leads to the growth of broader shoulders and facial hair, as well as the deepening of the voice. For girls, the female hormones called estrogens begin menstruation and breast development, among other changes. Both genders do produce androgen and estrogen, however. Androgens in girls are responsible for pubic and body hair growth and for increased activity of the sweat glands.

Adolescents experience a variety of physiological changes as a result of these hormonal stimulations, known as *secondary sex characteristics*. These changes affect the size of the skeleton and its proportions, redistribute fat and muscle tissue, and bring about the growth of hair on certain parts of the body. As with the onset of puberty, girls begin developing such characteristics as pubic hair about two years ahead of boys the same age; by the end of puberty, however, boys are behind girls in the development of pubic hair by only about six months. Keep in mind, though, that individuals within an age group will vary widely in when they begin certain phases of puberty. Indeed, a given individual may develop more rapidly in one part of the body than another; a boy, for example, may find his scrotum and testes growing before he develops pubic hair.

The skin of both boys and girls becomes rougher and more oily during puberty, and the sweat glands of both become more active, especially in the underarm and genital areas. This increased oiliness and sweat gland activity are the cause of that common bane of teenagers, acne. Generally speaking, stronger body odor and acne are more of a problem for males than for females.

Adolescence is also the time of the last great growth spurt, which again starts about two years earlier for girls than for boys. As described in your text, growth now occurs at the ends of bones in cartilage called epiphyseal growing plates and ends when this cartilage begins to calcify – again, a result of increased secretion of sex hormones. Growth patterns for boys include broader shoulders, narrower hips, and longer legs relative to torso, and for girls narrower shoulders, broader hips, and shorter legs relative to torso.   Girls also develop fat deposits on the thighs, hips, buttocks, and upper arms.

Both sexes become considerably stronger during adolescence.   The hearts and lungs also develop further at this time, enabling adolescents to take part in demanding physical sports.   Overall, this growth spurt reaches its peak after about a year and a half, and generally reaches a higher peak for boys than for girls.

There is also some evidence that the brain changes substantially during adolescence.   Some researchers have reported a slight increase in brain weight around puberty, while others have reported that the number of synapses in the brain may decrease at this time.   Behavioral evidence for neurological changes includes a decline in the amount of deep sleep that adolescents now need and the fact that young children recover from brain injuries more quickly than adults do.   Although these observations are debated by researchers, it does appear that the brain becomes more efficient at some operations at this time, with a certain accompanying decrease in flexibility.

Key Terms

> Puberty
> Menarche
> Secondary sex characteristics

Focusing Questions

1. What are some of the obvious physical changes that adolescents experience as a direct result of puberty?

2. Children have an apparently greater ability to learn new languages than do adults.   How does this relate to the possibility that the brain may undergo change during puberty?

Adolescent Thought

Adolescence is the time of awakening to great ideas, when teenagers discover the power of idealism and begin forming passionate opinions on the issues of injustice, world peace, and fair treatment for all types of people.   These new concerns reflect the cognitive changes that adolescents experience following puberty, which result in more mature reasoning and problem-solving capabilities.

For one thing, adolescents begin applying their logical abilities to what might possibly exist, as opposed to just what does exist.   Adolescents also begin using *hypothetico-deductive reasoning*, by which one is able to imagine hypothetical solutions to a problem and then think systematically about which of these solutions best suits a specific case.   The third big cognitive advance at this time is the ability to think about the relationships among abstract concepts, which is a reflection of the adolescent's improved meta-cognitive abilities.   And finally, the fourth cognitive advance of adolescence is a willingness to be more flexible in reaching conclusions or a capability to understand that things can be other than they are.   In other words, adolescents can accept a less-than-final answer on a given question.

As was explained in Chapter 13, Piaget accounted for these cognitive changes of adolescence by his theory of *formal operations*.   In developing his theory, Piaget created three experiments. In the first of these, known as the law of floating bodies study, children of varying ages were questioned on their ideas about why different objects either float or sink in water. Piaget used this experiment to demonstrate how adolescents now are able to reason about proportions and to grasp how two abstract concepts can produce a third, more abstract concept. Piaget's second experiment, known as the pendulum study, asked youngsters to figure out which of four different factors determines the period of a pendulum. In this study, adolescents demonstrate a new ability to isolate one aspect of a problem from its surroundings and make correct conclusions based on logical deduction. And Piaget's third experiment, the all-possible-combinations study, which required children to determine which combinations of five clear liquids made a yellow liquid, shows how adolescents now adopt a systematic approach to solve problems of combinations.

From the results of these experiments, Piaget developed the concept of formal operations, which he characterized as new kinds of mental transformations that adolescents can perform. In Piaget's theory, formal operations are used to manipulate abstract mental formations to form a more sophisticated understanding of things. Piaget also thought that formal operations are organized to form a unified logical system that can be used together to solve problems. And, finally, Piaget thought that the cognitive skills that make up formal operations represent new and qualitatively advanced abilities, though he did view these skills as being created by the same processes of adaptation and equilibration that produced earlier cognitive structures.

Researchers since the time of Piaget have discovered that formal operations are of the most use in scientific and mathematical fields. It seems, therefore, that many adolescents and adults who are capable of formal operations do not use them or use them only in areas where they have some special interest or ability.

Key Terms

Hypothetico-deductive reasoning
Formal operations

Focusing Questions

1. Why are we able to say that adolescents are less dependent upon notions of contingent truth in solving some problems than are younger children?

2. Suppose you are using a computer and the screen goes blank. How might you apply the concept of hypothetico-deductive reasoning to figure out what is wrong?

Evaluating Piaget's Views of Adolescent Thought

Piaget's views on adolescent thought consisted of two parts, a description of how an individual's ability to solve problems changes at this time and an explanation of how these new abilities occur. Of the two, Piaget's description of adolescent thought processes has fared better over the years. Later researchers have repeated Piaget's experiments and found that their subjects did exhibit similar age-related performance changes in the tasks as Piaget described.

Piaget's theories about how an adolescent's new cognitive skills develop, however, have received greater criticism. For one thing, later researchers question how widespread the use of formal operations to solve problems actually is among adolescents, or even among adults; in tests of older subjects, only about one-third used formal operations. However, it does seem to be true that adolescents with higher levels of scholastic ability are more likely to use formal operations. In addition, formal operational thinking appears to be culture-bound and is most likely to be found in cultures oriented toward science and technology.

Another of Piaget's views on formal operations which subsequent researchers have partly refuted is his notion that formal operations cannot be taught to younger children. Researchers have succeeded in teaching formal operations to youngsters in later middle childhood as well as to adolescents who previously showed no formal operational reasoning. Although these findings contradict Piaget's original thesis, their importance remains unclear. For one thing, rather than teaching pre-adolescent youngsters qualitatively different new skills, perhaps the training just brings out latent competencies in the children.

While Piaget's theories on the "how and why" of adolescent cognitive development have been thrown into doubt, the outlines of what those skills are remain largely intact. In truth, however, we remain less knowledgeable about how the thinking of adolescents varies from that of children than we are about describing how the two age groups differ in their approaches to solving various problems.

Focusing Questions

1. How might lack of specific knowledge about a particular task of higher-level reasoning impede an adolescent's ability to use formal operational thinking?

2. In a test designed to study adolescent formal operational reasoning, who would you expect to score higher, a 15-year-old Japanese boy or a 15-year-old Nepalese boy? Why?

Other Cognitive Changes of Adolescence

In a popular novel of the 1960s, *Up the Down Staircase*, a female high school student who does not feel that she fits in very well with her peers develops a crush on a male English teacher and writes him a love letter. The teacher responds by correcting the grammatical errors in the letter and giving it back to the girl. Emotionally crushed, the girl kills herself.

The novel's story illustrates one aspect of adolescent cognitive change which is usually less tragic. As adolescents experience both dramatic physical change and expanded abilities to think about their own thought processes, they increasingly imagine that others are watching them and commenting critically on them. In this form of egocentrism, the adolescent feels observed by an *imaginary audience*. Since I'm obsessed by my pudgy thighs, thinks the adolescent, or hideous pimples, or croaking voice, so is everyone else. And as adolescents begin to feel new emotions and formulate new concepts, they develop the idea that they are unique and are experiencing these feelings and thoughts for the first time, ever. This is known as having your own *personal fable*. In the case of the embarrassed girl in the novel, her inexperience about her own emotions and her inability to judge the reactions of others accurately led her into tragedy.

Adolescence is also the time of thinking about values and of questioning what is right and wrong – as any exasperated parent of teenagers is likely to know. For the first time, the changing cognitive abilities of adolescents allow them to consider the wider implications of abstract notions which until now they have just accepted as "true" because it's what their parents or teachers have told them. Closely related to questions of values are issues of moral reasoning. Adolescence is when children begin thinking seriously about the right course of action in a given situation. Whereas younger children tend to think of morality as absolute and unalterable, with adolescence teenagers become aware of the ambiguities involved in moral decisions and to recognize that there may be differing opinions about what is right or wrong in a given instance.

In Piaget's view, moral development was a result of cognitive development and social experience. Piaget thought that adolescents develop the powers of moral reasoning through a process beginning with an amoral stage in early childhood. From about age 7, children progress to the stage of moral realism, in which morality is absolute. With late middle childhood or early adolescence, children then emerge into the stage of *autonomous morality*, in which moral rules are seen not as absolute but rather as the result of social agreement. Another model of moral development has been created by Lawrence Kohlberg, who organizes the growth of moral reasoning from early childhood to young adulthood in six stages. Both Piaget's and Kohlberg's theories have been criticized for focusing on moral intentions as opposed to the actual behavior which individuals practice.

Key Terms

>   Imaginary audience
>   Personal fable
>   Autonomous morality

Focusing Questions

1. How does adolescent egocentrism differ from the egocentrism of infants and preschoolers?

2. Why is it almost a developmental necessity that adolescents question the values which they've inherited from their parents and other adults?

Questions for Understanding

As you read these questions, often raised by parents, educators, and other childcare providers, first try to answer the questions yourself. Then read the answer following each question and compare your response to it.

1. *If it is the level of sex hormones in the blood that sets off puberty, what is it that causes the brain to signal the gonads to increase the production of sex hormones?*

While the mechanism that causes the brain to send the message to the gonads that actually sets off puberty is unknown, there are a few theories. According to the critical weight hypothesis, the beginning of puberty may be related to weight. Among the evidence in this direction is data suggesting that menarche occurs at a relatively constant weight in girls although there are studies of dancers and swimmers which might contradict this. The theory suggests that when the body reaches some critical overall weight, this causes a change in metabolic rate, which in turn brings about a change in blood chemistry that then brings on the events that result in a greater output of sex hormones. Currently, however, some researchers believe that instead of being the main biological signal that sets off adolescent sex changes, weight is just one related factor.

2. *I've heard that the brains of teenagers change during adolescence. Could this account for the unpredictable behavior of my 14-year-old?*

It doesn't seem likely. Behavior that to adults seems "unpredictable" may well be just the reaction of your son to the numerous psychological and physiological changes that his body is going through now. As for the neurological changes which you refer to, researchers differ as to their existence, though the evidence for change in the brain during this period is mounting.

For one thing, it has been noted that the brains of young children heal more quickly from injuries than do the brains of adults, an ability which seems to change around the time of puberty. Other research has reported that the synapses in certain areas of an adult's brain are less dense than corresponding areas of a child's brain. Furthermore, medical studies have shown that between the ages of 10 or 11 and 13 or 14, the amount of energy used in certain parts of the brain decreases by about 50 percent. Both of these findings seem to indicate that the adult's brain is more "efficient." In other words, a child's brain has extra synapses, which are eliminated at puberty. Other research indicates that the hormonal changes of puberty end the development of specialization in brain hemisphere functions.

But while these and other examples of changes in brain structure as a result of – or at least coincident with – puberty are intriguing, there is little consensus among scientists as to their meaning. And certainly, you can't try to explain your son's behavior by any specific neurological changes which occur during puberty.

3. *My 12-year-old son isn't showing any signs of entering puberty yet – his voice hasn't deepened, he's still quite short, his face doesn't even have peach fuzz. His 15-year-old sister, on the other hand, began menstruation when she was 11. Should I worry about my son's development?*

Not at all. For one thing, it is normal for girls to enter puberty on an average of about two years earlier than boys. At his age, your son is still within the normal range for boys to begin producing sperm, which can be as young as 10 years and as old as 19 years. For girls, on the other hand, the range for the onset of menstruation is as young as 10 years and as old as 16 years.

Keep in mind, also, that during puberty an individual's secondary sex characteristics may develop at varying rates. For instance, it is possible for a male to be fairly well along in the development of his genitals and yet have only sparsely developed pubic hair. The growth spurts that occur during puberty will also proceed at different rates in different parts of the body, with, for example, arms and legs growing faster than the torso for a time. It is important for both you and your son to remember that these apparent inconsistencies in his growth are normal, though they may be a source of self-consciousness to him.

4. *Do most adults consistently use the type of reasoning abilities that Piaget referred to as formal operations when solving problems?*

According to studies by a number of researchers, it is fairly uncommon for adolescents and even adults to use formal operations to solve problems. For example, one study found that in a group of 15 year olds, only 32 percent used formal reasoning, while in a group of 18 year olds, just 34 percent used formal reasoning. Furthermore, of these two groups, only 13 percent of the 15 year olds and 19 percent of the 18 year olds used formal operations in mature ways.

While these findings may be surprising and seem to cast doubt on the soundness of Piaget's conclusions, keep in mind that formal operations seem to be best suited for solving the kinds of academic problems which students face in school. Also, individuals may fail to apply formal reasoning to a problem because they lack some specific knowledge necessary to apply a higher form of reasoning. Most of us, for example, may have faced the task of resetting the clock on a video cassette recorder after the machine has been unplugged. If, in exasperation at your lack of understanding of the clock's programming sequence, you just begin punching buttons at random, then you'll have some idea of why people may often have trouble applying formal operational thinking to problems.

5. *Recently, it's a daily struggle to get my 14-year-old daughter to go to school. Even getting her to leave her room is an effort. She's especially difficult when her skin breaks out, even if only slightly. "People stare at me and laugh behind my back," she says. Is this kind of behavior normal for teenagers?*

Yes. To varying degrees, self-consciousness is a normal reaction to the many physical changes which accompany puberty and will affect most adolescents. Because they are so engrossed by the changes which are reshaping their bodies, including the maturing of their genitals and the growth of secondary sex characteristics such as breasts and pubic hair, they often believe that other people are too. Another reason for your daughter's concern about the thoughts of others is that now she is better able to understand them; during adolescence, children further develop their ability to understand how other people think. Ironically, since teenagers are also inexperienced, these new insights into other people's thought processes lead them to believe their attention is focused on the teenager.

This self-absorption, known as adolescent egocentrism, is probably the underlying reason for your daughter's sensitivity; she's appalled by her skin problems and thinks that other people pay as much attention to them as she does. One result of this over-sensitivity is a desire for privacy.

6. *I thought I'd done a pretty good job of instilling decent values in my son. Now that he's 15, however, he seems determined to question everything he's ever learned about right and wrong. Not only that, but if I so much as speed up to get through a yellow traffic light before it turns red, he accuses me of being a hypocrite. Why is my son rejecting my values?*

While it may seem as though your son is rejecting all the values you've taught him, in truth he is actually examining them in depth for the first time. He is doing this now because, due to the advances in understanding which adolescents experience, he is able to consider the underlying abstract principles that govern our judgments about what actions are right or wrong. When children are young, they are unable to understand abstract concepts and so just accept what they are told about proper behavior by parents and teachers.

Now, however, your son is becoming able to think systematically about his values. As a result, he is reassessing what you and others have taught him is the correct way to behave. And because your son is also going through the stage of adolescent egocentrism, he may think that only his ideas are right and that you should intuitively grasp the logical necessity of his views. With time and experience, your son will learn that values are often subjective matters and that circumstances often have a strong effect on what people consider to be acceptable or unacceptable behavior. Because adolescents' improved thinking skills allow them to see the possible, they often become idealistic and intolerant of anything less than perfection in both their own behavior and in the behavior of others.

SELF-TEST

The following multiple choice and short answer test questions should help you assess your understanding of the points covered in the text and the video. After answering all the questions, check your answers against the key and use the accuracy of your answers to gauge how well you have met the lesson objectives.

Multiple Choice Questions

1. On the average, occurrences of acne and body odors during adolescence are

   a. more a problem for girls than boys.
   b. more a problem for boys than girls.
   c. an equal problem for boys and girls.
   d. not a real problem for either sex.

2. Among a group of high school students, the one group most likely to be dissatisfied with their bodies are 14-year-old

   a. boys who are maturing late.
   b. boys who matured early.
   c. girls who matured early.
   d. girls who are maturing late.

3. Among a group of pre-adolescent girls, the one most likely to experience a delayed puberty is the girl who is

   a. a serious student of ballet.
   b. slightly overweight.
   c. a championship chess player.
   d. tall for her age.

4. Between the ages of about 10 or 11 and 13 or 14, the amount of energy used within certain areas of the brain of the average person

   a. decreases by 25 percent.
   b. decreases by 50 percent.
   c. remains the same.
   d. more than doubles.

5. John, a 15-year-old computer whiz, is trying to figure out why his father erased a file accidentally on a microcomputer: "Let's see, you said you have the full menu selection clicked on . . . How about folders, did you have your file nested in a folder? Maybe that's what you did wrong." The type of problem-solving skill which John is using is known as

   a. having an imaginary audience.
   b. hypothetical-deductive reasoning.
   c. a study of all-possible-combinations.
   d. flexibility.

6. In part, Piaget used the term formal operations to refer to the new thinking skills which adolescents use to

   a. manipulate information about abstract concepts.
   b. understand how other people think.
   c. think about the changes in their bodies.
   d. think about formal ways of behaving.

7. You would probably be most likely to find formal operational thinking being used to solve problems by the

   a. 16-year-old son of Chinese peasants.
   b. 12-year-old daughter of New Zealand sheep ranchers.
   c. 17-year-old son of French computer programmers.
   d. 14-year-old daughter of Peruvian gold miners.

8. When 15-year-old Amelia stormed out of a shoe store because, as she told her mother later, "that smart-aleck sales woman thought it was so funny that I have such big feet," she was demonstrating

    a. adolescent moral reasoning.
    b. formal operational thinking.
    c. adolescent egocentrism.
    d. bad manners.

9. The term *personal fable* is used to refer to the idea adolescents have that

    a. people are talking about them.
    b. their bodies are out of proportion.
    c. privacy is the most important thing in their lives.
    d. no one has ever before felt as they are feeling.

10. The number of people who reach Kohlberg's sixth stage of post-conventional morality probably

    a. includes everyone.
    b. is a majority of the population, but not everyone.
    c. is about half the population.
    d. is a minority of the population.

Short Answer Questions

The following questions should be answered in a paragraph or two. You should identify several key points for each answer and use these to form the framework for your response.

1. What are some of the major physical changes that boys and girls undergo during puberty?

2. What are the four main cognitive advances adolescents experience?

3. What are the six stages that make up Kohlberg's model of moral development?

23

Social and Emotional Development in Adolescence

LESSON ASSIGNMENT

Completing the following steps will help you master the lesson objectives and achieve the goal for this lesson:

STEP 1: Read the INTRODUCING THE LESSON section to provide a context for what you will learn in this lesson.

STEP 2: Read the lesson's GOAL and LESSON OBJECTIVES so that you will know what you are expected to learn.

STEP 3: Read the text assignment, Chapter 14, pages 514-541. Pay particular attention to the key terms and concepts in the Chapter Summary on page 547; they will help you when you watch the video.

STEP 4: Review the VIEWING GUIDE in the telecourse guide. It lists several points to consider as you watch the video.

STEP 5: Watch the video.

STEP 6: Read the UNDERSTANDING THE LESSON section in the telecourse guide. Make sure you understand the key terms and can answer the focusing questions included there.

STEP 7: Complete the SELF-TEST.

STEP 8: Go back to the LESSON OBJECTIVES and make sure you can respond to each of them.

INTRODUCING THE LESSON

Do you remember saying "I'm having an identity crisis"? Chances are you might, since the words and the concept they describe relate to one of the major developmental turning points of adolescence. During adolescence, rapid cognitive and physical development make the questions, "Who am I? What do I believe? What do I want from life?" issues of everyday concern. Furthermore – though the knowledge may be small comfort years after you've lived through the emotional turmoil of an identity crisis – such inner struggles are signs of healthy adjustment to the demands of adolescence.

"If all your friends jumped off a building, would you jump, too?"

Does that classic response of exasperated parents to the urge that young teenagers have to conform to group norms sound familiar? During adolescence, peer groups evolve into refuges of mutual support and understanding for teens as they struggle to achieve a unique identity and to de-identify themselves from their parents. As a natural result of their exploration of self, adolescents increasingly influence one another – though perhaps not in the areas and to the degree that parents may fear.

"I know math isn't an easy subject, but knowing it is important for your future. You'll probably need it in your career, no matter what you might decide on."

Perhaps this familiar parental litany evokes memories, as well. After all, adolescence is the time when parents and teachers increase their directives to teenagers to consider the future and encourage them to begin thinking about careers, or higher education, or the responsibilities of having a family. Adolescence is a time of transition when the clear-cut limitations and privileges of childhood are crumbling away but have yet to be replaced by the responsibilities and freedoms of adulthood.

The emotional and social challenges of adolescence take many forms. As their bodies grow in sudden spurts and begin maturing sexually, adolescents go through a variety of emotional fluctuations, sometimes bewildering, sometimes exhilarating. They seek to establish a unique and autonomous sense of the self, and are increasingly able – and likely – to examine the values which they previously accepted from parents and teachers without much thought. Friendships deepen, peer groups re-form into cliques and then into groups, and families mold and bend into new shapes under the winds of adolescent change.

In this lesson you will examine in detail the ways in which adolescents cope with their changing self-concepts, parental authority, and the possible effects of divorce in their families. You will take a look at the need adolescents feel to establish a sense of personal identity and how they work toward that in peer groups. As part of this process, you will find, adolescents seek intimacy in deeper friendships and treasure the personal insights which they gain through partaking of self-disclosure with peers. In the process you may encounter some bittersweet memories of your own teenage friendships and identity crises – lingering echoes of your own passage through adolescence, the doorway to adulthood.

GOAL

The purpose of this lesson is to provide an overview of the numerous emotional and social changes adolescents face as they develop a new sense of self, form new and deeper friendships, and adjust to the challenges of their unfolding sexuality.

LESSON OBJECTIVES

After reading the text assignment, completing the exercises in this telecourse guide, and viewing the lesson's video portion, you will be able to:

1. Relate the stress that can be encountered during adolescence to patterns of growth, the age of the teenager, and cultural perspectives.

2. Identify the key tasks of social development in adolescence.

3. Discuss the concept of personal identity and recognize individual differences in identity formation.

4. Describe the changes in self-concept that occur across the teen years.

5. Characterize the nature of friendship and peer group membership and the relative influence of peers during adolescence.

6. Describe the relationship between parenting patterns and adolescent behavior and the influence of adolescent behavior on parental behavior.

7. Describe the impact of divorce on adolescents.

VIEWING GUIDE

In this lesson, the budding young men and women of the adolescent stage of development speak to you of their search for an identity. Through their cliques and heart-felt friendships, you will examine how adolescents struggle to understand the changes affecting their bodies and minds as they grow toward adulthood. After reading the text material and learning the important terms included there, you are ready to view the lesson's video portion. First, review the questions in the Self-Test at the end of this telecourse guide lesson to give you an idea of important points to watch for in the video. Then read the following Points to Consider to give you an idea of what the video will cover. Keep these points in mind while watching.

Points to Consider

☐ *Leaping into the world*: Contrary to the views of Anna Freud and the 1950s movie, *Rebel Without a Cause*, adolescence is not necessarily a period of great conflict. Look for examples of how other cultures provide adolescents with rites of passage to adulthood. Be aware of the numerous tasks which adolescents face in regard to forming a new concept of the self.

☐ *Finding a true I.D.*: In many ways, adolescence is a voyage of discovery into the mysteries of the self. Notice how developing a sense of identity is by no means a foregone conclusion for adolescents. Keep an eye out for Erik Erikson's recipe for establishing a personal identity.

☐ *Seeing the self through peer eyes*: During adolescence, peer groups offer teenagers emotional refuge, mirrors for self discovery, and forums for exploring values. Be alert for the ways in which friendships change for adolescents. Pay attention to the new forms that peer groups assume as teenagers join cliques and crowds.

☐ *Shaking up the family*: Adolescents are the ones whose bodies grow and whose self-concepts change at this stage, but their families change along with them. Be on the lookout for examples of how parents alter their behavior in response to the new cognitive skills of their adolescent offspring. Pay attention to the impact divorce may have on teenagers.

UNDERSTANDING THE LESSON

In a national park campground, a group of young teenagers emerges from a cluster of tents. "Did you hear what happened last night?" one boy asks another. "Mr. Spetzer was mad 'cause some guys were making a lot of noise, but I was sound asleep. And now I think everybody's going to get in trouble."

"It was just Bill, Andre and I that were waking people up," another boy says. "If anybody gets in trouble, it should just be us."

Across the lane from this group another gathering of teenagers is also waking up. Two 19-year-old girls sip tea by the campfire and laugh with a boy of the same age; another older teen walks over to his late-model Jeep and turns on the radio to a rock station. "So what do you think?" one boy asks the girls, "Should we take the hike to the lake or the one to the meadows today?"

One set of youngsters gathers in same-sex peer groups to compare behaviors and wrestle with authority; another set mixes males and females in a forum of self-responsibility free of adult supervision. It is between these two natural poles of development that the social and emotional changes of adolescence take place.

The Social World of Adolescence

Not long ago, it was popularly believed that lemmings, hamster-like rodents common to Scandinavia, would periodically make mass migrations to the coast and cast themselves into the sea. Now, however, science has discredited this popular idea; lemmings are not intentionally suicidal, but rather sometimes the victims of over-population.

In similar fashion, current developmental theories debunk the long-popular notion that adolescence is inevitably a tumultuous time of conflict and emotional upheaval. While adolescence is a time when teenagers struggle to establish a sense of their own identity that is both autonomous and unique, this does not necessarily result in a break with parents or in other forms of conflict. The degree of conflict which adolescents experience depends on a variety of factors, with the age of the teenager and his or her socio-economic status being of major importance. Studies indicate that the kind of struggles with parents which are one form of adolescent turmoil, for example, are most typical of younger teens. And even in these cases, young teens and parents tend to fight over relatively minor items, such as household chores, hair styles, and clothing rather than over basic values or beliefs.

The culture in which a person grows up also partly determines the developmental outlines of their adolescence. In advanced industrial societies such as America, with their demands for well-educated, skillful adults, adolescence is prolonged, lasting for many individuals into their twenties. This period, when individuals are no longer children but are not yet accepted by their culture as adults, can be frustrating for adolescents. In other societies, however, such as ones focused on agriculture, children are given responsibility for taking care of siblings or helping in the fields from a very young age. In these societies, the transition from childhood to adulthood may be clearly marked by ceremonies known as *puberty rites*.

But no matter how an adolescent's society is structured, the tasks they face remain largely similar. An adolescent must forge a sense of personal identity, which includes having a sense of whom one is and a sense that the self is continuous over time, as well as a feeling of uniqueness. Related to this task is an understanding that one's self contains many parts and that one may sometimes need to act differently with different people. Adolescents must establish new levels of trust with peers, usually beginning with those of their own gender, and gain more adult status within the family. And, finally, adolescents must establish greater autonomy in regard to the world at large, which means making career choices and choosing their own values, among other things. Overall, one main chore of teenagers can be summed up as creating themselves as separate, unique individuals, while at the same time maintaining their already established ties to family, friends, and other groups.

Key Terms

Puberty rites

Focusing Questions

1. Holden Caulfield, the adolescent hero of J.D. Salinger's book, *The Catcher in the Rye*, has long been a favorite of teenagers because of his rebellion against adult hypocrisy. Does this mean that most teenagers wish to reject the values of their parents and other elders?

2. Why did such psychologists as Anna Freud characterize adolescence as "stormy," and emphasize its stressfulness for both teenagers and parents?

Development of the Self

As you saw in the video segment of this lesson, musing about the self, assessing their own motives and desires, as well as thinking about how others view them and their behavior occupy a great deal of the average adolescent's time and energy. The cognitive developments of adolescents, as detailed in Lesson 22, enable them now to think about themselves in ways that were impossible to them as children. These new concerns crystallize around the adolescent's need to find a *personal identity*, which developmentalists describe as composing a coherent whole of the individual's past experiences, ongoing personal changes, and the demands of society. In the views of Erik Erikson, this process of self discovery leads to individual *identity crises*, as adolescents cope with their changing self-concepts and adjust to the new expectations they now face from parents and other adults.

According to James Marcia, the paths individual adolescents take to a personal identity vary greatly. The responses of teenagers include *foreclosure*, in which adolescents more or less decline to choose their own role and instead adopt those assigned by parents and other adults. Teenagers who are overwhelmed by life's choices and tend to have few commitments and no long-range goals are experiencing *identity diffusion*. Adolescents who follow the path of *moratorium* do explore alternative roles but take a long time about settling on a final identity. And in *identity achievement*, the adolescent confidently explores alternative roles and makes conscious choices, eventually arriving at an individual ideology and sense of purpose.

In Erikson's view, those adolescents who are most successful at achieving a sense of personal identity have, from middle childhood, confidence in their own competence and abilities, as well as a basic sense of trust and autonomy. The other essential ingredient is a supportive environment, in which the individual feels safe to try out new roles in both fantasy and practice.

As adolescents begin forming their first tentative self-concepts, they are unsure of them and tend to feel that others can easily see through them. This latter feeling is related to the sense of an imaginary audience, as described in Lesson 22. This feeling of the fragility of the self underlies both the adolescent's claims of invulnerability as well as their tendency to fantasize; both are defenses against sensations of fragility. Adolescents will overcome these feelings as they pass through this period.

During this time, an adolescent's self-concepts become more differentiated and individuated, and they become more concerned about the character traits which define their place in the social structure. Teenagers also become more aware of their powers of self-reflection and begin to see the self as a coherent system made up of numerous parts. As their cognitive abilities – reflected in their growing powers of formal operational skills – advance, so do their self-concepts.

Key Terms

Personal identity
Identity crisis

Focusing Questions

1. Which adolescent is more likely to have experienced an identity crisis, one who has established an identity as the result of foreclosure, or one who has established one as the result of identity achievement?

2. If a teenager at 17 has a different view of himself as a son from the one he had at 13, is that a sign of emotional instablity? Why or why not?

Peer Relations in Adolescence

As you saw in Lesson 18, peer groups first become important to children during middle childhood, and it is worth noting that the peer group is becoming important at an increasingly early age. With adolescence, peer groups take on a new depth of meaning for individuals, becoming forums for self-discovery and identity achievement. Now, as adolescents understand themselves better, they improve in their understanding of the feelings and behavior of others. These cognitive changes lead to changes in adolescent friendships. With new powers of mutual understanding, teenagers feel a need for self-disclosure, by which they both deepen their friendships and their self-understanding. Teenage friendships are characterized by *intimacy*, loyalty, and fidelity. A very important ingredient of the recipe for teenage friendship is an ability to keep secrets among friends. These changes are especially significant during early- to mid-adolescence. During later adolescence, teenagers are better able to coordinate a broader range of friends. The friendships of older teens also tend to be more stable than those of younger adolescents.

It also becomes more important during adolescence for individuals to belong to a group; younger adolescents especially consider it important that the group be popular. Adolescents form *cliques*, small clusters of close friends who associate with one another more or less exclusively. A *crowd* is a larger, looser group which may be made up of several cliques. Across the years of adolescence, the progression is from the precrowd stage to unisex cliques interacting within loosely formed groups to a transitional stage where certain high-status cliques begin forming heterosexual cliques. In the next-to-last stage, several heterosexual cliques form a crowd, which in the final stage dissolves into loosely linked groups of couples. These transitions form the context within which most adolescents begin dating, experimenting with their sexuality, and, in later adolescence, establishing intimacy with an opposite-sex friend.

The influence that peer groups have on adolescents varies with the stage of development. Generally speaking, the younger the adolescent, the more likely he or she is influenced by peers, especially in such superficial matters as dress and mannerisms. Probably, this greater dependence upon their peers helps adolescents to achieve autonomy from their parents. The degree to which adolescents tend to conform to their peers varies also, with middle teens being the most likely to follow the lead of their peers. And, not surprisingly, adolescents tend to be more influenced by their long-term friends than by acquaintances.

Key Terms

Self-disclosure
Intimacy
Clique
Crowd

Focusing Questions

1. What are some of the ways peer groups facilitate the adolescent task of de-identifying with parents?

2. Why do the friendships of older adolescents tend to be less exclusive than they were earlier in development?

Family Relations in Adolescence

Sixteen-year-old Marc is arguing with his father: "But Dad, why can't I get my ear pierced?" he demands.

"Why not? I can't believe I'm hearing this," replies his father. "For one thing, only women pierce their ears."

"Dad, if that's the case, then there are several women in the NBA."

"I don't care who else is piercing their ears, you're not because I said you're not."

The changes of adolescence affect not only the teenagers in whose bodies hormones are percolating, but also their families. As a result of the formal operational skills now at their command, teenagers are able to counter their parent's arguments with increasing logic and reason. Also, teenagers no longer automatically defer to their parents' authority and, at least by late adolescence, tend to see mutual tolerance and respect as the basis of the relationship with their parents.

At the same time, parents are most likely going through their own developmental changes, with many experiencing a midlife crisis during the adolescence of their children. The conflict which arises from these converging changes tends to peak during mid-adolescence and diminish in late adolescence. Research has shown a gradual evolution of the power structure in families toward a more symmetrical arrangement during these years. As part of this evolution, parents must turn over increasing responsibility to growing adolescents as they steer them toward adulthood. Now, as in earlier periods of development, the parental patterns of warmth, support, and authoritativeness tend to be the most successful approaches.

The continuity of development is echoed in how different children evoke different parenting responses, and vice versa. For instance, research has shown that a girl who experiences early menarche is more likely to have conflict with her father. Not only that but, in reciprocal fashion, girls who experience greater parental conflict appear to achieve puberty faster than girls who do not. Likewise, girls tend to seek recognition for their emerging uniqueness within the family, whereas boys often struggle to escape the home.

Not surprisingly, adolescents from homes where there has been a divorce are at greater risk for behavioral problems than those from families where the parents remain together. It also appears that divorce can cause problems among children during adolescence, even if it has been years since the family breakup. The effects of divorce during adolescence continue to differ for males and females, with at least one study suggesting that the remarriage of mothers may be a more difficult transition for girls than for boys in adolescence.

Focusing Questions

1. What are some of the developmental factors that increasingly make it difficult for teenagers to accept their parents' dictates as they once did?

2. Why might some parents resent the kinds of idealistic conclusions toward which their teenagers' new cognitive skills are leading them?

Questions for Understanding

As you read these questions, often raised by parents, educators, and other childcare providers, first try to answer the question yourself. Then read the answer following each question and compare your response to it.

1. *My daughter and I fought like cats and dogs when she was a teenager; it seemed like all she was interested in was flouting my authority. On the other hand, her brother is now 16, and I've hardly had to question his behavior in the last two years. What accounts for the difference in how my two children and I relate?*

The differences in how various adolescents relate to their parents will depend on a variety of factors, which include individual temperament, developmental history, and possible effects of birth order. One factor that has been found to affect the quality of an adolescent's adjustment, however, is the timing of puberty. Girls who have early puberty tend to have long periods of conflict with parents. These girls tend to be dissatisfied with their bodies, are more likely to be assessed negatively by their peers, and have a greater chance of depression. These considerations, however, apply mainly to the early stage of their adolescence; by their middle and late teens, they tend to have worked through some of their turmoil.

With boys, on the other hand, it is late maturing boys who tend to have the most problems with parents. They are often considered by others to be bossy, tense, and restless; when they reach early adulthood, they may be thought of as impulsive and nonconforming. But even adolescents who frequently clash with their parents are more likely to do so on such matters as hair and clothing styles rather than fundamental values and beliefs.

2. *Why are adolescents so self-absorbed? All my teenage son can talk about is me, me, me. Am I raising an especially selfish son?*

Probably not. The self absorption and concern with personal matters that seems to be an obsessive trait of many adolescents, especially during the early teens, is actually a sign of healthy development. Although children have a concept of the self prior to adolescence, it is not a "wide angle" view. That is, children are not able to look at themselves from the point of view of others. This becomes possible with the cognitive advances of adolescence, which include the capacity to reflect upon oneself. Thus, adolescents are aware that other people notice them and are aware of their own awareness.

At the same time, the adolescent is learning to think of himself as unique and knows that the person he is today, when he is "blue" and disgusted with himself, is also the same boy who last week was elated at having won the regional division of a chess championship. Out of this welter of conflicting emotions and insights, he must forge a personal identity. Add to this the fact that his body is changing from a boy's into a man's, with sexual potential, and it's hardly surprising that your adolescent finds himself so interesting.

3. *When my daughter was in puberty, she was very hard to be around. She was extra quarrelsome and took exception to every effort we made to guide her, saying we were always trying to stifle her. But now when she's in the twelfth grade, she's become a joy to be around. We can actually have discussions that don't automatically become arguments, and she's always eager to be of help around the house. What's going on?*

Just the natural course of events. Rather than viewing adolescence as a single phase of development, most experts now consider it to consist of two subphases, early and late adolescence. During early adolescence, as children first experience the changes in both their bodies and thought processes that come with puberty, they tend to experience more turmoil. Furthermore, adolescents who value conformity to adult norms are not usually popular among their peers – you can imagine the reaction of the healthy young teenager to this perception.

In the second, later subphase of adolescence, however, teenagers have made great advances in their self-understanding. They have a greater awareness of the complexity of their mental processes and a correspondingly greater ability to adjust to their vagaries. As a partial consequence of this improved self-awareness, older teens are less self-conscious than they were previously. Your "new, improved," easier-to-get-along-with daughter is just the late adolescent model of the same girl who, as a young teen, was so hard to live with.

4. *I recently saw a television show about the rites of passage which other cultures enact for their adolescents. In one African tribe, girls at menarche were isolated from the group for a few days, then brought back in later with great celebration. Why don't Western societies have similar customs?*

One main reason is probably because the demands of the two societies are very different. Countries such as the United States are highly industrialized technological societies which require a high level of knowledge and skill on the part of their citizens. Gaining these skills requires many years of schooling, often reaching into a young person's middle and late twenties, during which young people are discouraged or prevented from taking on the full responsibilities of adulthood. American society, at least superficially, discourages adolescents from assuming fully sexual roles, even though, after puberty, they are physically ready for them. All these special conditions often contribute to a sense of frustration and ambiguity among adolescents about their status, and result in Western societies' placing less emphasis on "rites of passage."

5. *Is the AIDS epidemic having any effect on the sexual practices of young people?*

A study of adolescents at age 18 from the class of 1988 cited in the text showed that over 60 percent of the girls had had intercourse, as had almost as high a percentage of the boys. In early 1992, the national Centers for Disease Control reported the findings of a 1990 survey of teen health habits. The section of the survey asking if teens had had sexual intercourse, if they had used contraceptives, and if they had had a sexually transmitted disease showed that 54 percent of all 9th through 12th graders were sexually active, and by the 12th grade, 72 percent of the teens surveyed had had sex. Overall, boys were more likely to have had sex than girls, and one in 25 students had contracted a sexually transmitted disease.

Of the students who reported themselves to be sexually active, 78 percent had used some form of contraception during their most recent intercourse. But fewer than half of the students (49 percent of the boys and 40 percent of the girls) reported that condoms – one of the major methods recommended for preventing the spread of the HIV virus that leads to AIDS – had been used at that time.

6. *Our son has always had a number of good friends, most of whom were well-behaved and thoughtful children. Since entering high school, however, both he and his buddies seem to have become clones of each other. They all wear the same clothing, mimic one another's talk, and appear to share the same opinions. Are these kids exceptionally conformist?*

On the contrary, the image you convey is of perfectly healthy male friends in early adolescence. At this age peers adopt similar clothing and styles of behavior as a way of both affirming and concealing their uniqueness, while at the same time de-identifying with their parents. These new behaviors may be a little unsettling for you, but they are part of the adolescent's need to establish greater autonomy from their parents. In turn, these peer group interactions may actually help your son develop a more mature relationship with you.

As for the apparently conformist behavior of your son and his friends, this too is a natural part of development, especially for young adolescents. Young teenagers demonstrate a high level of conformity to peer group standards because they have well-developed abilities to compare their actions and beliefs with those of others, but are also very self-conscious about how others view them. By the time they are 17 or 18, however, they will have largely outgrown their sense of having an imaginary audience and will begin thinking and acting more for themselves.

In the meantime, though, it might console you to know that the influence which teenagers have on one another is largely superficial, involving what kind of clothes are "cool," and what is proper slang. In areas of values and ethics, however, even young teenagers tend to reflect the beliefs of their parents rather than their friends.

SELF-TEST

The following multiple choice and short answer test questions should help you assess your understanding of the points covered in the text and video. After answering all the questions, check your answers against the key and use the accuracy of your answers to gauge how well you have met the lesson objectives.

Multiple Choice Questions

1. Although Monica was raised in a conservative religious faith, when she turned 13 she began arguing with her parents about religion. She acquired a "punk" hairdo, began listening to "heavy metal" music, and had her nose pierced. The kind of extreme rejection of parental values which Monica is practicing is expressed by

   a. all girls her age.
   b. a quarter of all girls her age.
   c. a small number of all girls her age.
   d. very few, if any, girls her age.

2. Among the adolescents who are most likely to have conflict with their parents are

   a. early maturing girls.
   b. early maturing boys.
   c. older teenage boys.
   d. older teenage girls.

3. Elaine's mother criticizes her for being sulky one afternoon. Elaine points out to her mom that she's the same girl her mother used to call "Effervescent Elaine"; but now that she's older, she has a more complicated life and more complicated feelings. Elaine's comment refers to the task an adolescent has of achieving a

   a. new status in the family.
   b. new level of trust with peers.
   c. more autonomous stance toward the world.
   d. sense of the unity and continuity of the self over time.

4. Fifteen-year-old Patty is an honor student and member of her high school debating team and considers herself an "intellectual." Patty has always thought that kids who admire pop idols are "silly." But recently Patty saw a movie and developed a crush on the star. Now she is confused and can't understand how someone with her "deeper" values could be impressed by a shallow pop star. According to the theories of Erik Erikson, Patty is experiencing

   a. a puberty rite.
   b. identity diffusion.
   c. foreclosure.
   d. an identity crisis.

5. A teenager who seeks to form a sense of personal identity by adopting the values and roles imposed on them by their parents is following the course of

   a. moratorium.
   b. foreclosure.
   c. identity achievement.
   d. identity diffusion.

6. Around the time that Abigail turned 13, she began describing herself as being ". . . really good with my hands; I like to string beads and carve wood and stuff. Maybe I'll be an artist." This attempt to define her self-concept is an example of

   a. differentiation.
   b. concern for stable personality traits that define her in the social network.
   c. individuation.
   d. the idea that her self is a coherent, integrated system.

7. Teenagers feel they need self-disclosure with friends because of their

   a. feelings of guilt during puberty.
   b. growing capacity for mutual understanding.
   c. belief in their own invulnerability.
   d. sense of having an imaginary audience.

8. Cleo has just met her fiance's parents and asks them if their son, her fiance Leon, has always been eccentric. "Oh no," says his mother. "At one point he was a regular clone of all the other kids; all he wanted was to win his friends' approval. Let's see, that would have been when he was about

   a. 7 or 8."
   b. 12 or 13."
   c. 16 or 17."
   d. 18 or 19."

9. Parents interested in promoting their child's quest for identity achievement would do well to practice

   a. authoritarian parenting.
   b. "hands-off" parenting.
   c. democratic parenting.
   d. confrontational parenting.

10. A male psychologist conducted a series of interviews with adolescent girls. Some of the girls consistently sat close to the psychologist and tended to lean toward him. These girls made regular eye contact and even flirted with him. The researcher found that the one thing almost all those girls had in common was that they lived with

   a. divorced mothers.
   b. both natural parents.
   c. widowed mothers.
   d. divorced fathers.

Short Answer Questions

The following questions should be answered in a paragraph or two. You should identify several key points for each answer and use these to form the framework for your response.

1. What are some of the special characteristics of an adolescent's new sense of personal identity as that concept is defined by Erik Erikson?

2. What are some of the signs of how an adolescent's view of friendship is changing at this time?

3. How do the tasks of parenting change during adolescence, and what are the best ways for parents to adapt to these changes?

24

Challenges of Adolescence

LESSON ASSIGNMENT

Completing the following steps will help you master the lesson objectives and achieve the goal for this lesson:

STEP 1: Read the INTRODUCING THE LESSON section to provide a context for what you will learn in this lesson.

STEP 2: Read the lesson's GOAL and LESSON OBJECTIVES so that you will know what you are expected to learn.

STEP 3: Read the text assignment, Chapter 13, pages 494-496 and Chapter 14, pages 514-521, 530-534, and 540-546. Also review Chapter 15, pages 579-582. Pay particular attention to the key terms and concepts in the Chapter Summaries for each chapter; they will help you when you watch the video.

STEP 4: Review the VIEWING GUIDE section in the telecourse guide. It lists several points to consider as you watch the video.

STEP 5: Watch the video.

STEP 6: Read the telecourse guide chapter's UNDERSTANDING THE LESSON section in the telecourse guide. Make sure you understand the key terms and can answer the focusing questions included there.

STEP 7: Complete the SELF-TEST.

STEP 8: Go back to the LESSON OBJECTIVES and make sure you can respond to each of them.

INTRODUCING THE LESSON

Anyone who reads the newspapers or watches the evening news knows that it can be tough being a teenager these days. Drug-sniffing dogs prowl the corridors of urban high schools, checking lockers for drugs. In other high schools, teenage mothers-to-be attend special pre-natal classes and courses on caring for babies while they continue their education.

Across the land, where previously the only visible signs in front of schools read SLOW DOWN WHEN CHILDREN ARE PRESENT, telephone poles now sprout declarations of DRUG-FREE ZONES. In "drive by" incidents, cars filled with gang members cruise past schoolyards and spray the area with bullets.

Violence, in fact, seems endemic. A 1990 survey among some 11,500 U.S. high school students in all 50 states, the District of Columbia, Puerto Rico, and the Virgin Islands discovered that one in five high school students sometimes carries a weapon for self defense. The same survey of high schoolers' behavior, which was conducted by the Centers for Disease Control (CDC), also disclosed that "one in two kids drinks, one in three smokes, and one in four has seriously considered suicide." Clearly, getting through adolescence is more difficult now than it has ever been.

Or is it? While the focus of television cameras on such dramatic instances of teenage turmoil as teenage alcoholism or gang warfare certainly makes modern adolescence seem exceptionally difficult, the fact is that this transition period has always been accompanied by challenges. The cognitive, social, physical, and emotional changes that accompany puberty, as detailed in Lessons 22 and 23, bring new difficulties of adjustment and self-control to all teenagers. And though the risks confronting contemporary teens can certainly be formidable, they are hardly unique.

Take, for example, the troubles that afflicted that classic pair of teenage lovers, Romeo and Juliet. If ever a pair of adolescents had a hard time reconciling their awakening sexual urges with the restrictions imposed upon them by their society, those two did. By falling in love against the wishes of their families, Romeo and Juliet faced conflict with their parents that eventually led to tragedy. Like many youngsters of today who feel misunderstood by their parents, the unhappy lovers ran away from home. Even the violence that mars so many modern high school hallways is but an echo of the street fights between the warring factions of the Capulets and Montagues – a parallel that was echoed in a modern retelling of the tale as a clash between teenage gangs, *West Side Story*. And, like the one out of four teenagers mentioned in the CDC's survey who have at least considered suicide, Romeo and Juliet saw no other way out of their problems than to kill themselves.

Clearly, the challenges of adolescence may vary from country to country, from decade to decade, and from individual to individual, but all teenagers face them to varying degrees. With this lesson, you examine in detail what some of these specific challenges look like to adolescents today. You explore the special difficulties that teenagers face when confronted with decisions about whether or not to drink alcohol, use illegal drugs, or begin smoking. You learn some of the reasons that individual teenagers might develop behavior problems and look at some of the problems facing adolescents who become pregnant. And you get a glimpse of some of the ways in which emotional development can go awry at this time, in instances such as adolescent depression and suicide, as well as disorders like anorexia nervosa and bulimia.

Not all teenagers are star-crossed lovers who solve their problems by committing suicide, nor will all teenagers be struck by violence on the school grounds. But, in one form or another, each adolescent will be faced with and have to somehow conquer one or another of the challenges of development which arise at this time.

GOAL

The purpose of this lesson is to survey the variety of serious problems that teenagers may be exposed to, including suicide, unwed pregnancy, and drug use.

LESSON OBJECTIVES

After reading the text assignment, completing the exercises in this telecourse guide, and viewing the lesson's video portion, you will be able to:

1. Identify the most common problems of teenagers in Western culture and the frequency with which they occur.

2. Given the dangers associated with drugs, suggest reasons for the high incidence of drug use by teenagers.

3. Cite reasons for the frequency of teenage pregnancies and the consequences that often result when children have children.

4. Develop a profile of a typical victim of bulimia or anorexia nervosa; indicate why someone would engage in self-starvation and what therapeutic approaches tend to help those who are afflicted.

5. Describe individual tendencies and contexts associated with teenage suicide.

VIEWING GUIDE

With this lesson, you take a look at the circumstances under which an adolescent's development can take a turn down a problematic or even tragic path. For some adolescents, the hurdles of development are higher than for others – and in a few cases, may be insurmountable. After reading the text material and learning the important terms included there, you are ready to view the lesson's video portion. First, review the questions in the Self-Test at the end of this telecourse guide lesson to give you an idea of important points to watch for in the video. Then, read the following Points to Consider to give you an idea of what the video will cover. Keep these points in mind while watching.

Points to Consider

☐ *Possible wrong turnings*: For some adolescents, the new demands and states of mind that come with puberty bring great difficulties. Pay attention to the ways in which normal tensions with parents may become prolonged cases of devastating conflict for some teenagers. Notice the range of problems, including drug and alcohol use, unwed pregnancy, suicide, and depression, which may affect some adolescents.

☐ *What to do about drinking and drugs*: It is a rare adolescent who is not faced with decisions about using alcohol, marijuana, and other drugs during high school. Keep track of the general incidence of alcohol and drug use among adolescents. Be aware of the various pressures and underlying problems that might lead an adolescent to become involved with alcohol and drug use.

☐ *Teenage motherhood*: Pay attention to some of the factors that may be involved in a particular girl's becoming pregnant. Be aware of some of the long-term consequences that may accompany teenage pregnancy.

☐ *Disasters of adolescence*: For a few teenagers, the challenges of adolescence lead to tragic consequences and may include death. Be aware of the types of emotional and social problems that may accompany an adolescent's suicide. Notice ways in which the changes involved with puberty may be a part of anorexia nervosa.

UNDERSTANDING THE LESSON

In a doctor's office, a 15-year-old girl receives the word that she is pregnant. "I'll keep the baby," the girl tells the doctor. "At least a baby would love me, not like my mom and dad."

Outside a high school dance, a teenager passes his friend a joint. "Go ahead," he tells the other boy, "take a toke; it makes it a lot easier to talk to girls."

In a high school counselor's office, a 14-year-old-girl slumps in a chair, her head bent forward, her voice low. "Nobody at home cares if I flunk out," the girl says. "They don't notice anything I do; I might as well be dead."

Pregnancy, illicit drug use, depression and thoughts of suicide – for some teenagers, the challenges of adolescence are severe and overwhelming. In combination with prior developmental history, family context, genetics, and socioeconomic conditions, the pressures that come to some teenagers with puberty and their changing self-concepts lead to great difficulties – and sometimes tragedy.

Problems of Adolescence

As you learned in Lesson 23, not all developmentalists now consider adolescence a time of inevitable conflict for all teenagers. For one thing, as a transitional period between childhood and adulthood, adolescence seems to be more troublesome during its early years, when young teens are usually undergoing puberty and its attendant changes. Most teenagers manage to get through these years with no parental difficulties greater than arguing over clothing styles, dating habits, and doing homework.

But for some youngsters, adolescence is a troubled time. A number of teens develop problems with alcohol or drugs, become pregnant, or develop the eating disorders of anorexia nervosa or bulimia. And for some teenagers, the normal emotional doubts and quandaries of these years may take the form of debilitating depression and even suicide.

The reason that some teenagers fall into such serious problems depends upon a variety of developmental factors, including the individual's prior history of development, socioeconomic contexts, and family history. About one-half of all adolescents in one study reported feelings of unhappiness. Among boys, about one-quarter experience what is called tumultuous growth, filled with conflict and crisis. Recall also that early-maturing girls often have a long period of conflict with their parents, while for boys, it is those who mature late who tend to have more problems with parents and peers.

Early-maturing girls tend to have a poor body image, tending to be dissatisfied with their weight and height when in their early teens. Some studies have found a connection between early menarche and such problems as truancy, poor grades, drug and alcohol use, running away, and shoplifting.

The school setting, with its high degree of regimentation and demand for conformity, can cause teenagers to feel frustration as they strive to achieve a sense of themselves as unique and differentiated. To some extent, the success with which adolescents cope with scholastic challenges will depend upon whether they have an internal or an external locus of control, as described in Lesson 18. And for an increasing number of adolescents, working may cause them extra stress at this time. By their senior year, about 75 percent of all high schoolers have a part-time job. And while a job may contribute to an adolescent's sense of self-esteem, having a job may also cause them to neglect schoolwork and spend less time with friends.

One cause of frustration for teenagers is their status as "marginal persons," as they were labeled by the psychologist Kurt Lewin. While they have matured physically, adolescents are not yet accorded the rights and responsibilities of adults and still have much to learn about handling their new emotional and mental capabilities. And, lacking clear-cut rites of passage to adulthood, some adolescents may become confused about their position in their families and the world. All of these factors contribute to the possibility that a teenager may develop serious problems during this time.

Focusing Questions

1. What are the differences in the ages at which boys and girls are most likely to experience problems with parents during adolescence?

2. What are some of the reasons an adolescent might feel frustration about the expectations and rules which are imposed upon him or her by parents, teachers, and possibly employers?

Decisions about Drinking and Drugs

It's Saturday night, and a man in his early twenties pulls up to a convenience store. As he gets out of his car, a teenage boy approaches him.

"Hi. I wonder if you could do me a favor?" says the boy. "While you're in there, could you pick up a half case for me?"

"Uh, sure, I suppose," says the man. "I used to do the same thing myself. What's your brand?"

It is an unusual teenager who will not be faced with the question of whether to drink alcohol during high school and possibly before. The scene depicted above is probably acted out, in one form or another, many times every weekend. Among adolescents at least, getting drunk is viewed as a rite of passage, as indicated by the finding of one study in the 1980s that over 90 percent of high school students had some contact with drinking. And while the majority of adolescents are able to experiment with alcohol without suffering apparent harm, some five percent of seniors are daily drinkers, while 37.5 percent have had more than five drinks in a short time at least once.

As a legal drug, alcohol at least has some degree of social acceptability. Marijuana, on the other hand, is illegal for everyone, not just minors. Yet, while its overall use by teenagers may have declined in recent years, just over 50 percent of American high school students have tried marijuana. And, of course, "crack" cocaine remains a serious problem among some segments of the adolescent population.

Whatever form an adolescent chooses, teenagers who try drugs all probably try them for similar reasons. For one thing, adolescence is a natural time for trying new experiences and for seeking out activities that are forbidden or criticized by one's elders. Drinking and drug taking are seen by some teenagers as ways of moving away from their parents and identifying with peers. And, just as adults do, teenagers gravitate toward alcohol and drugs to lower tension in social situations, to have a good time, and to reduce feelings of self-consciousness.

One important factor involved in a teenager's choice to use or not use alcohol and drugs is the influence of peers. While an individual is mainly influenced by his or her peers on such matters as style and dress, teenagers do tend to want to be accepted by their peers. And when all of an individual's friends may be cracking a few cans of beer or toking a few joints, it may be hard to resist. And as you'll recall from your text material, teenagers tend to follow the lead of good friends when it comes to smoking marijuana. At the same time, according to the findings of one study of young adolescents, by the age of 14 teenagers were more likely to listen to friends about smoking cigarettes or marijuana, but to the advice of their parents about other drugs.

Focusing Questions

1. What are some of the possible ways in which an adolescent's involvement with a particular clique might influence his or her use of alcohol or drugs?

2. Should parents be worried about the influence that their children's friends might have upon their behavior, particularly as regards drinking alcohol or using illicit drugs?

Problems with Sex and Pregnancy

Rhonda and Stephen Melvern are ecstatic as they show their new baby to friends. "Isn't she beautiful?" Rhonda exclaims, holding up her 2-week-old adopted daughter. "She's a little small, of course, but she's very healthy. She's small because her mother was just a child of 15 herself. It's so sad, you know, that somebody so young has to give up her baby, but she was smart enough to know that she wasn't ready to raise her."

Becoming pregnant during adolescence is a problem that teenagers handle in different ways. Some pregnant teenagers choose to have abortions; others choose to have the child and keep it; and others have the baby and give it up for adoption. And, tragically, an occasional teenage mother will abandon her baby soon after birth. For the majority of adolescent females, though their bodies are fully mature and ready for childbearing, their emotional abilities and social skills are not sufficiently developed for the challenges of being a parent. Having a child while still a teenager is complicated even further by the likelihood that the pregnant girl will have to face her situation alone, without the support of the father.

Over the past two decades, the number of married teenagers giving birth has actually dropped. On the other hand, the proportion of unwed teenage girls giving birth has risen. For teenage girls who become pregnant, the consequences include a higher chance of dropping out of school, getting low-paying jobs, going on welfare, and having an unstable marriage. As for teenage fathers, there is little information about them other than that they provide little support for these families.

While it may not seem surprising that girls become pregnant during adolescence, it isn't simply a result of the sexual desires and possibilities which are brought on by puberty. Teenage mothers tend to have a variety of problems that other girls do not have, including frequent school suspensions, truancy, running away from home, marijuana use, and fighting. At the same time, pregnancy is a natural consequence, at least in part, of the inexperience of adolescents. For one thing, few teenagers report using contraceptives during their first act of intercourse. The reasons for this range from lack of information, the perception among teens that using condoms will mark them as "loose," and the common adolescent belief in individual invulnerability. Recently, however, there is evidence that educational programs about contraceptives may be reducing the number of early pregnancies, especially among African Americans.

As you'll recall from Lesson 23, most adolescents don't begin sexual experimentation until mid-adolescence. Even then, masturbation is the primary sexual release, especially for boys. Toward the end of adolescence, girls begin to accept their full sexual capacity, while boys accept that sexuality is a part of mutual understanding. Also, divorce may have an effect on the sexual behavior of adolescents, particularly girls. As recounted by the study of girls described in Chapter 14, girls from homes where the father was absent due to divorce were more likely to behave toward men in a forward, even provocative manner.

Focusing Questions

1. What are some of the reasons, specific to her development as an adolescent, that a teenage mother might choose to have and keep her baby, even though she is unable to fully provide for its care?

2. Why do you think teenage girls who get pregnant tend to have other problems, as related above?

Serious Emotional Problems of Teenagers

The black comedy, *Heathers*, is a movie that satirizes the importance of popularity and of belonging to the "right" clique in high school. In the movie, an unpopular student murders a girl who belongs to the clique of the prettiest girls in school, disguising it as a suicide. After another staged suicide of a popular student makes it seem like the "in" thing to do, less-popular students begin attempting suicide.

While the movie makes its points about adolescent behavior by carrying its idea into absurdity, the problem of teenage suicide is a real one. As you know from your text material, six percent of seventh grade boys and nine percent of seventh grade girls have attempted suicide, and by the twelfth grade, these figures have risen to eight and 18 percent, respectively. And while the figures for successful suicide are much smaller, two percent of boys and girls who had previously attempted suicide say they would kill themselves if they had the chance.

Thoughts of suicide are not surprising when a person is depressed, and depression is a common enough emotion during adolescence. After all, adolescents are now capable of self-reflection and analysis, and their sense of being the subject of other people's attention may serve to exaggerate a low sense of self-esteem. Serious levels of depression, however, tend to be related to drug problems, conflict in the family, and to emotional rejection and lack of closeness with the parents.

Furthermore, as you'll recall from Lesson 20, some youngsters suffer from clinical depression, which is much deeper and more prolonged than the sense of blues and self-pity that any normal teenager is subject to. Teenagers who suffer from depression have feelings of hopelessness, help-lessness, and low self-worth, and tend to be lethargic and unmotivated. Among depressed adolescents, those who have lost a parent before the age of 16 tend to have more suicidal thoughts than peers from intact families.

Depression is also closely related to two other emotional problems most common among adolescents, anorexia nervosa and bulimia, both of which were covered in Lesson 20. As you'll recall, victims of anorexia nervosa, who are almost always adolescent girls or young women, deprive themselves of food because they believe that they are overweight. A re-lated disorder involving food is bulimia, in which individuals eat large quan-tities of food, but then force themselves to regurgitate it. Among the theories of why a teenager would voluntarily starve herself is that anorexics come from families that demand perfection of their children. According to this theory, adolescent girls gain some control over their parents by refusing to eat. Remember, also, that girls who experience early menarche have negative self-perceptions, particularly as regards being overweight.

Focusing Questions

1. What are some of the cognitive changes, including changes in their self-concepts, that adolescents undergo that might contribute to thoughts of suicide or feelings of depression?

2. How might the feelings that she has about her body image affect an adolescent girl, particularly in terms of how it might interact with eating disorders such as anorexia nervosa or bulimia?

Questions for Understanding

As you read these questions, often raised by parents, educators, and other childcare providers, first try to answer the questions yourself. Then read the answer following each question and compare your response to it.

1. *My son is 13 years old right now and is just beginning to show signs of puberty. When can I expect him to begin challenging my authority?*

   For one thing, it's not an automatic part of adolescence that your son will begin "challenging your authority," as you put it. While it is normal for adolescents to differ with their parents on such matters as what the youngsters are allowed to do or wear or how they behave, this doesn't mean that your son and you are fated to have serious disagreements during his teen years. In fact, only five to nine percent of male teenagers reject their parents outright.

   Overall, about one-quarter of boys have tumultuous growth, which is filled with conflict and crisis. Another third have surgent growth, characterized by reasonable adjustment interspersed with flare-ups of difficult expressions such as anger, defiance, and general immaturity. And about one-quarter experience what is called continuous growth and demonstrate self-assurance, a sense of purpose, and mutual respect between parents and child. The remaining percentage can't be easily classified. So you can see that the degree of difficulty of your son's own adolescence includes a variety of factors, including his rate of puberty, previous developmental history, personal temperament, and genetics, as well as, of course, his relationship with his parents.

2. *I recently found out that my 16-year-old son has been smoking marijuana. When I confronted him with this, he said that it helps him relax around his friends and that since I was always pushing him to be more outgoing, I shouldn't criticize his use of marijuana. He likened his use of marijuana to relax to my social drinking. What can I tell him?*

   One obvious difference between alcohol and marijuana, both of which are mind-altering drugs, is that one is legal for adults and the other is not. And while this may not be a strong argument to teenagers, who tend to make their moral judgments on a grander, more ideal scale than adults do, it is one that has great possible consequences for smokers of marijuana.

As for your son's assertion that smoking marijuana will help him become more social, you might point out that the reduction of anxiety and increase in self-esteem that he may feel with marijuana use are temporary – as they are with alcohol, also. Furthermore, adolescents who use drugs such as marijuana to enhance social interaction may find it interfering with the mutual exploration and self-disclosure that are a necessary part of their social and emotional development now. The apparent solutions of emotional problems that smoking marijuana brings also may tend to hinder adolescents from developing their own effective coping skills.

3. *I realize that condoms are becoming more available as a result of public health campaigns to encourage people to practice safer sex. Has this had any effect on the sexual practices of teenagers?*

There is some evidence that educational programs about contraceptives may be reducing the number of teenage pregnancies, especially among African-Americans. On the other hand, teenagers still tend not to use contraceptives during their first sexual experience, possibly because they believe that having a contraceptive available would cause them to be labeled as immoral. More simply, adolescents may not rely on contraceptives simply because they don't believe that it can happen to them, that they can become pregnant or acquire a sexually transmitted disease.

4. *Are all teenage mothers probably going to have problems making a good home for their children?*

While it is true that having a child while a teenager tends to predispose a girl toward problems such as having low-paying jobs and unstable marriages, it doesn't guarantee these results. Obviously, the effects of an early pregnancy on any female are going to be influenced by the support she has from her family and community.

There is great diversity in how, and how well, teenagers eventually cope with early childbearing. On average, early childbearers are more likely than those who delay childbearing to be economically disadvantaged. If, however, the teen mother is able to finish school, establish a stable marriage, and have only a small number of children, her chances of having a good life improve. Of such mothers, about half report doing well by the time their child is 17.

5. *Is there any connection between the drinking problems that some teenage girls develop and the time at which they enter puberty?*

In some cases, yes. A Swedish research project discovered that girls who matured early in comparison with other girls of the same age experienced a number of behavior problems, including truancy, shoplifting, running away, and drug and alcohol use. In another study, this one of Finnish girls, researchers found similar problems concerning drinking among girls who had matured early. These researchers found that since girls who had experienced early menarche had matured earlier than others of their age group, they had taken part longer in the kind of social activities likely to involve drinking than their late-developing peers. At the same time, other studies, which followed their subjects beyond mid-adolescence, have found that these problems tend to be temporary.

6. *I'm concerned about my 14-year-old daughter, who is a very skilled gymnast. She enjoys her sport, works very hard at it, and regularly competes at tournaments. But she has yet to have her first period, and I'm worried about her. Because of her sports involvement, she is very concerned about her weight and eats like a bird. She looks at least two or three years younger than her classmates. My worry is that she might develop anorexia nervosa. Could her training as an athlete lead her into this eating problem?*

From the way you describe her situation, probably not. Because the physiological onset of menarche appears to be related to the percentage of fat to lean tissue, girls who do not have the necessary amount of fat in the body will not begin menarche. Since young female athletes engaged in intense physical training, such as your daughter, are likely to have a low proportion of fat in their bodies, they sometimes experience delayed menarche. This sounds like the case with your daughter.

As to whether this might lead her to develop anorexia nervosa, that is hard to say. While it is true anorexic girls deliberately stop eating as a result of an obsessive concern over their weight, research indicates that they do this for certain psychological reasons. One theory holds that anorexics are the children of very demanding, controlling parents, and that the child becomes anorexic as a way of gaining control over the parents. In other words, anorexia is a problem that is strongly entangled within the victim's family. In that respect, you probably need to consider both your relationship with your daughter, and her concern about keeping within certain weight limits as a gymnast, as she develops through adolescence and eventually enters puberty.

SELF-TEST

The following multiple choice and short answer test questions should help you assess your understanding of the points covered in the text and the video. After answering all the questions, check your answers against the key and use the accuracy of your answers to gauge how well you have met the lesson objectives.

Multiple Choice Questions

1. One example of a serious developmental problem during adolescence would be

   a. self-disclosure.
   b. anorexia nervosa.
   c. egocentrism.
   d. an identity crisis.

2. At the age of 16, Christine is painfully shy. She lacks self-confidence and dreads having to speak up in class or talk with people she doesn't know well. When her good friend Karla tells her that she has tried

marijuana, Christine is most attracted by Karla's comment that smoking marijuana

a. "made colors seem so much brighter."
b. "gave me less of a hangover than I usually get drinking beer."
c. "made me feel extremely nervous."
d. "really relaxed me; I didn't feel self-conscious at all."

3. According to studies, the percentage of high school students who have had some contact with alcohol is

a. less than 25 percent.
b. between 50 and 75 percent.
c. between 76 and 90 percent.
d. over 90 percent.

4. Parents Anita and Brian are talking about their son Ken; they're worried that the 17 year old may have begun smoking cigarettes. The parents should be most concerned about the influence of

a. his best friend Clarence who smokes.
b. his favorite heavy metal band who include smoking in their music videos.
c. the smoking in the "classic" movies he rents from the video store.
d. the advertising in magazines.

5. Four girls in the junior class at Central High School became pregnant last year. Of these four, one had an abortion; the other three carried their babies to term. The one who had the abortion most likely is

a. white, middle class, and an honors student.
b. white, lower class, and a poor student who has two friends who are mothers.
c. African-American, middle class, and a poor student.
d. white, middle class, and married to an 18-year-old high school graduate.

6. When 16-year-old Wendy told her parents that she was pregnant, they asked her why she and her boyfriend hadn't used a contraceptive. Among her answers, she is LEAST likely to say,

a. "I didn't want him to think I was loose."
b. "I didn't think it could happen to me."
c. "I don't know what a contraceptive is."
d. "I did it to have someone to love me."

7. Among a group of teenagers, the one most likely to develop anorexia nervosa is probably

a. Glenn, who is from a low-income family, a poor student, and not interested in sports.
b. Rosemarie, who is an honors student, noted for her good manners, and something of a perfectionist.
c. Anne, who is a poor student and something of a rebel and who is noted for her easy-going, relaxed personality.
d. Jeannie, who is a good student but has frequent arguments with her parents and is slightly overweight.

8. According to one psychological theory, anorexia may be a way that an adolescent

    a. speeds up her sexual development.
    b. gains some control over her parents.
    c. can become closer to her parents.
    d. prepares for sports.

9. As they enter adolescence, boys and girls become much more likely to commit suicide than before. While all of the following statements may be true, which is the most likely reason that teenagers are more likely than younger children to commit suicide?

    a. Teenagers are now capable of self-reflection and analysis.
    b. They are now stronger and more capable of hurting themselves.
    c. They begin using alcohol and drugs at this time.
    d. They are depressed by the changes their bodies are undergoing.

10. Among teenagers, the group with the highest reported percentage of attempted suicide is

    a. urban females.
    b. urban males.
    c. rural females.
    d. rural males.

Short Answer Questions

The following questions should be answered in a paragraph or two. You should identify several key points for each answer and use these to form the framework for your response.

1. In relation to the developmental tasks of adolescence, what are some of the possible reasons that teenagers become involved with drugs and alcohol?

2. Other than as a result of normal sexual experimentation at this time, what are some of the reasons that teenage girls become pregnant?

3. What are some of the circumstances under which teenagers commit suicide?

25

A Look at the Whole Child: The Teen Years

LESSON ASSIGNMENT

Completing the following steps will help you master the lesson objectives and achieve the goal for this lesson:

STEP 1: Read the INTRODUCING THE LESSON section to provide a context for what you will learn in this lesson.

STEP 2: Read the lesson's GOAL and LESSON OBJECTIVES so that you will know what you are expected to learn.

STEP 3: Read the text assignment, Chapter 13, pages 486-511, and Chapter 14, pages 514-551. Pay particular attention to the key terms and concepts in the Chapter Summaries; they will help you when you watch the video.

STEP 4: Review the VIEWING GUIDE section in the telecourse guide. It lists several points to consider as you watch the video.

STEP 5: Watch the video.

STEP 6: Read the UNDERSTANDING THE LESSON section in the telecourse guide. Make sure you understand the key terms and can answer the focusing questions included there.

STEP 7: Complete the SELF-TEST.

STEP 8: Go back to the LESSON OBJECTIVES and make sure you can respond to each of them.

INTRODUCING THE LESSON

After dinner, Shannon and Dean talk about their 16-year-old daughter Noreen with their friend Bob who has known the girl since she was a baby.

"She'd like to go to the state university," says Shannon, "but we just can't afford it. What we'd like her to do is go to City Central College for two years, then transfer."

"What does she think?" asks Bob.

"Oh, she wants to go. City's still away from home; she's talking with her friend Jill about sharing an apartment."

"Jill will last about one month in a place of her own," says Dean. "She's used to having her mother do everything for her; Noreen knows how to take care of herself, and she likes her room neat; she'll get tired of Jill's flakiness."

"She knows that, but she says she'd like to give Jill a chance," says Shannon. "She says Jill just hasn't had a chance to be responsible. Can you believe she'd ever say something like that? Three years ago, it was 'Woe is me, who sold me to these awful people when I was a baby? They can't be my *real* parents!'"

"Did she show you her car?" Dean asks.

"Yes; she said you two picked it out, you bought it, and she's buying it from you," Bob answers. "She's really proud of it."

"Uh huh, she's paying it off with the money she makes at the pizza parlor. It's only got 65 thousand miles on it; for $1500, it's a great deal. Jill's dad bought her a new Honda, but Noreen says she's happier with hers, since she's paying for it. She values her independence."

"She always has," says her mother. "When she was about 13, that was *all* she valued. But lately she's amazing, she's so level-headed, so mature; I love being with her, talking about ideas and her plans for the future. It's hard to realize she's the same person who I used to go around and around with, always hassling about something. And now that she's turned into this really interesting, neat person, she's going to leave us."

As their daughter Noreen approaches the end of adolescence and prepares to begin life on her own, her parents feel a mix of emotions. Their understandable pride in her new-found maturity and clear goals is tempered by frustration at her lack of experience. They know she has to leave the nest soon and begin making her own mistakes, but they lie awake nights worrying about how she'll cope. And through it all, as they assess this young woman they're preparing to launch, they remember the little girl she was just a few short years ago – and sometimes still seems to be.

For both parents and youngsters, adolescence is an eventful, exhilarating period. In some ways, a child at the threshold of adolescence is like a Polaroid photograph in the first moments of its exposure. The outline of the individual is there, both physically and emotionally, but the fine details haven't yet filled in. During adolescence, many details of individual personality, emotional outlook, and intellectual ability take on a finer focus.

In this lesson you look back over the whole of adolescence to get a coherent view of the amazing changes that occur during this process. During adolescence, puberty literally reshapes each of us. Boys and girls enter it loathing one another, and leave it chasing the opposite sex. And as their bodies grow and develop into those of young men and women, so do their inner worlds expand and mature, setting the stage for the self-reliance and full independence of adulthood. As you have learned in the preceding three lessons, adolescence is a time when each individual again works through several of the earlier stages of development, becoming a more complex, individuated person in the process.

GOAL

The purpose of this lesson is to provide a comprehensive picture of the biological, cognitive, social, and emotional changes which adolescents are undergoing during this period.

LESSON OBJECTIVES

After reading the text assignment, completing the exercises in this tele-course guide, and viewing the lesson's video portion, you will be able to:

1. Explain why adolescence is referred to as the second revolution in development.

2. Describe the biological changes children experience in adolescence.

3. Summarize, in general, the cognitive changes that children experience in adolescence.

4. Indicate the extent to which self-awareness and individuation play a role in the teen years.

5. Contrast peer relationships among adolescents with peer relationships among 6 to 12 year olds.

6. Recognize the ways in which relationships with parents change and mature during adolescence.

VIEWING GUIDE

With this lesson and the many upheavals of adolescence, we reach the end of childhood development. Appropriately, during the two subphases of adolescence, individuals re-enact certain significant portions of earlier development. But with the final teenage years, the children of our study are moving into young adulthood. After reading the text material and learning the important terms included there, you are ready to view the lesson's video portion. First, review the questions in the Self-Test at the end of this telecourse guide lesson to give you an idea of important points to watch for in the video. Then read the following Points to Consider to give you an idea of what the video will cover. Keep these points in mind while watching.

Points to Consider

☐ *Let's get physical*: For most youngsters, the many challenges of adolescence begin with the onset of puberty. Be aware of the impact that the physical changes of sexual maturity have on adolescents. Notice the variety of ways in which the timing of puberty affects individual development.

☐ *Whose mind is it?* During adolescence, youngsters build a new wealth and strength of mental abilities on the foundation of previous development. Notice how teenagers become more self-analytical and better able to handle abstract subjects. Be aware of how their new mental abilities can affect their relations with others, especially parents.

☐ *Self-exploration*: The new physical and mental attributes of adolescence require new self-concepts. Keep an eye on the different ways in which teenagers adjust to the challenge of establishing a sense of personal identity. Recognize how an adolescent's new sense of self grows out of previous stages of development.

☐ *Shifting alliances*: Under the influence of their maturing bodies and minds, adolescents move toward new peer relationships. Pay attention to how same-sex friendships deepen during adolescence. Be aware of the stages that adolescents move through as they progress from same-sex friendships to mixed cliques, dating in crowds, and eventually paired couples.

UNDERSTANDING THE LESSON

Since it was first published in 1947, *The Diary of Anne Frank* has been a favorite book among teenagers. The record of an adolescent Jewish girl's emotional growth while in hiding from the Nazis in World War II Holland, Anne Frank's words echo the emotions of all teenagers as they cope with changing bodies and minds. In spite of her life in hiding, Anne Frank struck a note of high idealism that any teenager can recognize: "In spite of everything I still believe that people are really good at heart."

Anne Frank's words and short life touch deep chords of sympathy and compassion in most teens. Like her, they are involved in a personal drama of self-discovery, approaching adulthood and the future with rapidly growing bodies and expanding intellects. Anne Frank's diary, for many reflective teens, captures the essence of their own emotions and insights during an especially eventful phase of development.

Changing Bodies

For many youngsters, adolescence might be called the time of mirror gazing. Up to this point, growing for most children has been a gradual, predictable process that is too slow to notice. When they look in the mirror from day to day, they see the same boy or girl as the last time they looked. During middle childhood, their bodies grow steadily and predictably, like young evergreens straining upward.

But somewhere near the beginning of the teen years, children find that they have suddenly become more like bamboo, a fast-growing grass, than a slow-growing pine. For perhaps the first time, looking into a mirror becomes a fascinating, sometimes harrowing process. What's that bump on the side of my nose? When did I start sprouting hair *there*? Will the skin stretch out if I *don't* wear a supporter? Every day brings the possibility of new changes in the shape and content of their bodies; mirrors become fascinating, dreaded messengers of the physical advance of adolescence.

As you know from Lesson 22, adolescence brings with it a number of significant and – to the teenager – startling physical changes. With the onset of puberty, hormones are released in teenagers' bodies to begin making them sexually mature. A number of glands, including the pituitary and the hypothalamus, produce the triggering hormones that start puberty. For girls, puberty begins with menarche, a girl's first menstruation, and is followed a few months later by ovulation. As the girl's ovaries develop, they will secrete the hormones estrogen and progesterone and some androgen, that stimulate further changes in the body. As you'll recall, the timing of a girl's puberty will depend upon a combination of heredity, nutrition, stress level, and amount of exercise.

For boys, puberty begins with the production of live sperm from the testes and the development of secondary sexual characteristics. During puberty, a boy will notice a variety of changes. Among the most notable changes, his voice will become deeper, his shoulders will begin growing broader, and he will begin to grow facial hair. These changes are a result of increased levels in the body of the hormones known as androgens.

As a result of these puberty-triggered developments, the bodies of both boys and girls change dramatically during the teenage years. Before adolescence, a group of young children will usually be distinguishable as boys and girls, of course, but the physical differences between them will not be great. If, for example, you watch a mixed group of 9 or 10 year olds playing baseball, all dressed in jeans and t-shirts, with their hair covered by caps, you'll have trouble telling the boys from the girls. In middle childhood, both sexes have slender hips, narrow shoulders, and high-pitched voices.

But if you leap forward six or seven years for the same group of ball players and observe their co-educational athletics during their junior and senior years of high school, you'll have no trouble separating the boys from the girls. For starters, the boys will now be an average of two or three inches taller than the girls, heavier, and broader through the shoulders. The boy's voices will now be easily discernible from those of the girls. And the girls will have developed figures, with the fuller breasts and widened hips of sexually mature females. And an even closer inspection would reveal that the smooth skin of childhood has, for some adolescents, become splotched with the blemishes of acne. A high school baseball team will even smell stronger than a younger one, since adolescence stimulates growth in the skin and sweat glands of both boys and girls.

And as you know from the preceding three lessons, all these physical changes alter the way in which adolescents view themselves, as well as how their families, friends, and others relate to them – as well as making repeated trips to the mirror a normal part of adolescent development.

Focusing Questions

1. What are some of the ways that environmental factors, such as nutrition and athletic activities, might affect the start of puberty for an individual adolescent?

2. As an adolescent's body changes during puberty, what are some of the ways in which other people may begin to respond differently to him or her?

Changing Minds

When Jesse was 8 years old, he heard a story in Sunday School that made a big impression on him. In II Kings, the prophet Elisha was going past the city of Bethel when some children came out and made fun of him. As the Bible tells it, the kids made fun of the holy man's baldness: "Go away, baldhead! Go away, baldhead!" Elisha was obviously sensitive about his looks, because, according to the story, he "cursed them in the name of the Lord. Then two she-bears came out of the woods and mauled forty-two of the boys."

This made a big impression on the elementary schoolboy, who took it as evidence that making fun of holy men was not a good idea. But several years later, when Jesse came across the same Bible passage again, the story had an entirely different effect on him.

"Now how can this be right?" the 14 year old asked his pastor. "Surely you can't believe that it was an act of God for these bears to come out of the woods and eat up 42 kids, just because they made fun of this guy's baldness? No way, that can't be right. That's not fair. It wouldn't be fair to punish little kids just for being rude; I don't care if Elisha was the messenger of God. If that's the way God treats people, then I'm not sure I want to have anything to do with him."

As a teenager, Jesse is no longer content just to accept what his elders tell him about moral issues. The trusting, credulous 8 year old has become an inquisitive, thoughtful teenager who is beginning to think for himself and to realize that moral issues often aren't as simple as they appear on the surface.

As you learned in Lesson 22, during adolescence youngsters go through a number of cognitive changes that enable them to think more maturely and in new ways about the issues of their existence. For example, adolescents become capable of thinking about possibilities rather than being limited to what physically exists. They become capable of hypothetico-deductive reasoning, the ability to think up and systematically test hypothetical solutions to problems. In other words, teenagers develop the ability to imagine possible future problems and formulate their solutions.

Adolescents are also able to form abstract concepts and to mentally organize them in relationships. For example, Jesse now is able to apply the concept of justice to the story of the Old Testament prophet and the teasing children, and to think about the story's implications in relation to his own developing ideas about fairness and mercy.

Adolescents now develop an ability to accept a degree of uncertainty in regard to some questions. Whereas younger children need to have a definite answer to a problem – "Of course there are such things as UFOs," says the 10 year old – adolescents can now accept that some problems may have a variety of answers, or may even be unsolvable – "I don't really know what I think about UFO's; they seem possible, but the evidence isn't very good," says the 16 year old.

As one result of their expanding metacognitive skills and powers of abstract thought, teenagers now enter a new stage of egocentrism. This time, though, instead of believing that other people and objects exist only in the presence of the child, as infants seem to, adolescents become very self-conscious and imagine that everyone is talking about them or noticing them. This reaction is related in part to the physical changes of their bodies that are so prominent in the thoughts of teenagers. A related change is the teenager's belief that his or her ideas are unique and that no one else can possibly understand them. You have seen numerous examples of how these cognitive changes account for much of the touchiness and need for privacy that are so common among teenagers, especially during early adolescence.

Another motivation for Jesse's comments to his pastor is the urge that teenagers feel to apply their new powers of cognition to the questions of morals and values. Whereas Jesse just accepted what he was told about right or wrong when he was younger because he lacked the cognitive skills to examine the abstract issues involved, now he is scrutinizing the beliefs of his parents and culture with his emerging cognitive abilities. Teenagers are now able to consider the consequences and implications of their own behavior with a new level of understanding.

Focusing Questions

1. Once a teenager has developed the power of hypothetico-deductive thinking, will he or she always apply it to solving appropriate problems? What are some of the limitations of hypothetico-deductive thinking?

2. What are some of the ways in which the changes brought about by puberty might affect an adolescent's efforts to establish his or her own moral standards?

Discovering the Self Anew

A high school English class is having a discussion about Shakespeare's play *Hamlet*. "Well, what do you think, Joel?" asks the teacher. "Are we supposed to take what Polonius says to Laertes seriously?"

"Um, some of it, yeah, I think so," answers Joel. "Sure, Shakespeare's made Polonius look pretty goofy up to now, but the stuff he's saying to his son all makes pretty good sense. I mean, when he tells him to be 'neither a borrower nor a lender,' that's good advice. And that line about being true to yourself – that's really good."

"You mean," says Mr. Anderson, leafing through the textbook, "this: 'This above all: to thine own self be true, and it must follow, as the night the day, thou canst not then be false to any man.' What does that mean to you?"

"Well, just that if you know who you are and do what you believe in, then other people will respect you, and they'll treat you right. And that you gotta know who you are before other people can really know you or trust you," says the teenager.

At a time when they are concerned with developing a clear sense of self amid the many physical and emotional changes of adolescence, Polonius's counsel for personal integrity rings true to many teens. The problem for many of them is figuring out just who that self is. If Joel's teacher had asked him how he thought of himself, Joel might have had a hard time answering. As an average 16 year old, Joel is sexually mature – but his parents and other adults don't consider him ready yet for sexual relations. He may have a license to drive a car – but he has to ask his father for permission to drive the family car. He may feel pride at his country's ability to mount a swift military campaign against Iraq's military – but he is troubled by the many homeless people he sees begging on the streets of his hometown.

One of the larger tasks facing an adolescent is the need to establish a personal identity. In view of the sometimes contradictory demands that teenagers feel at this time and of the emotional turmoil which they experience as a result of the biological changes that puberty brings, it isn't surprising that most teenagers suffer through one or more identity crises as they mature. As you saw in Lesson 23, James Marcia laid out four main statuses which adolescents may be in with regard to personal identity: foreclosure, identity diffusion, moratorium, and identity achievement.

As part of this process of finding a personal identity, and as a result of their developing bodies and increased powers of cognition, adolescents go through a number of changes in self-concept. An adolescent's sense of self becomes more differentiated and more individuated, and she becomes increasingly concerned about the stability of her social personality traits. Also, adolescents see themselves as more self-reflective and as a coherent whole composed of many different elements. As you have seen in the preceding lessons, the degree of success with which individual teenagers negotiate these tasks will vary greatly. In some cases, such as teenage suicides or anorexics or severely depressed teens, they are unable to successfully form a sense of "thine own self" to be true to.

Focusing Questions

1. What are some of the cognitive changes teenagers experience that affect their self-concepts?

2. Who would you expect to have higher levels of self-esteem, teenagers who have chosen the path of foreclosure to the challenge of finding a personal identity, or those who tend toward identity achievement?

Changing Relationships

Children first begin forming peer relationships during middle childhood. As you'll recall from earlier lessons, one characteristic of same-sex peer groups is that they are formed at least in part to keep the opposite sex out. To 9-year-old boys, girls are "creepy," and the girls return the sentiment with interest. You may remember the comic strip character Dennis the Menace interacts with his neighbor Margaret only to tease her.

With adolescence, however, the purposes and forms of peer groups begin to change. With their advancing cognitive abilities, teenagers become more aware of both themselves and others. Their deeper understanding of their own motives and inner selves allows them to better understand others. This development of mutual understanding leads to deeper friendships and a strong sense of loyalty and commitment to those friends.

In early adolescence, teenagers still form unisex groups, known as cliques. Gradually, though, same-sex cliques begin interacting with cliques of the opposite sex in loosely formed crowds, often at events like school dances or other social events. This enables the clique members to safely begin exploring contacts with the opposite sex. Gradually, this kind of interaction leads to the formation of heterosexual groups and, finally, the stage in late adolescence when individuals pair off in couples. As you are aware by now, these stages emerge from the need adolescents feel for self disclosure and greater intimacy with friends as they progress through the changes of puberty and the parallel quest for personal identity.

As an important part of their quest for identity, adolescents will also be seeking different relationships in their families, often resulting in conflict with parents. For one thing, teenagers may seek to individuate themselves by resisting the influence of their parents and more actively questioning the limits put upon them. For their parts, parents may feel threatened by their child's new assertiveness, or resent the need that sensitive teens now feel for privacy. The time that teens wish to spend with peers is often a bone of contention with their parents, too. For many teens, these years can be a tug of war for commitment between themselves and their peer groups on one side and their parents on the other. Keep in mind, though, that the amount of conflict or difficulty any one adolescent will experience with his or her parents will vary greatly from individual to individual.

Focusing Questions

1. What are some of the developmental factors that change boy-hating girls of 10 into boy-crazy teens of 14?

2. What are some of the cognitive changes which teenagers experience that have a direct effect on their relationships with peers and parents?

Questions for Understanding

As you read these questions, often raised by parents, educators, and other childcare providers, first try to answer the questions yourself. Then read the answer following each question and compare your response to it.

1. Are the emotional changes that adolescents undergo unique to this stage of development?

Not at all. As a matter of fact, several of the major tasks of adolescence involve the reworking of issues that the teenager already went through as a young child. Take, for example, the teenager's need to establish greater autonomy with parents. Toddlers must also establish a level of autonomy with parents as they begin to walk and stand on their own two feet. For adolescents, however, "standing on their own two feet" involves taking more responsibility for their own decisions and asserting themselves as newly capable, self-aware individuals.

Likewise, the need that adolescents have to spend time with peer groups echoes their development during middle childhood. In middle childhood, children sought out same-sex groups as places to cement their senses of gender, learn how to interact socially, achieve status and popularity, and master the fundamentals of friendship. Adolescents, however, need peer group interaction as a means of deepening their understanding of themselves and others, learning how to be intimate with others, and preparing themselves for dating and relationships with members of the opposite sex.

2. *I realize that boys and girls enter puberty at different ages. Does this make any difference in how they experience adolescence?*

It can. The range of ages at which children enter puberty is very broad, spanning from the preteen years to late adolescence. Because of this range, the age at which a child enters puberty can have major effects on his or her development. For one thing, the timing of a teenager's puberty can have an effect on his or her body image. For example, girls who enter puberty early tend to have a poorer body image than do girls who begin a little later.

While you might think that girls would be pleased to begin maturing early, the effect actually seems to be that they are displeased at the gain in weight which they experience. The same thing seems to be true of their height for these girls. Later-maturing girls, on the other hand, tend to grow tall before putting on the fat deposits that come with puberty and so have better self-images. For boys, the effect of maturing early has just the opposite effect on self-image, since they tend to view themselves as more attractive than later-developing boys.

An additional burden on earlier-maturing adolescents is in the area of parental expectations. Recent studies have shown that parents of early-maturing teens, especially girls, have difficulty dealing with their children. The parents are unsure of how much they can expect – and may tend to expect too much – from adolescents who look older than they really are.

3. *As the mother of two children, an 8-year-old boy and a 14-year-old girl, I am continually amazed at the contrast in their mental abilities. For one thing, my son seems to be limited in what he can imagine. For example, I recently told him we were going to a Mexican dinner at our church. When we arrived and he saw that the people serving the food were the usual group of people he knows, he asked, "Where are the Mexicans?" My daughter, on the other hand, doesn't have any trouble understanding abstract or figurative speech. Are their differences in understanding because of their ages, their abilities, or their gender?*

Almost certainly their ages. Among the numerous cognitive changes that adolescents experience is an advance in their logical thinking abilities. That is, adolescents become capable of thinking about what might exist instead of what does exist. Younger children, on the other hand, are much more constrained by what is in the here and now; they seem to need to have physical evidence of problems before they can answer them. In your son's case, he interpreted the word Mexican literally, to include both the type of food served at the dinner and the people putting on the dinner. Children of your son's age are still restricted by the concept of contingent truth: they have to be able to see the elements of a problem before they can assemble them for a solution. By your daughter's age, though, he will undoubtedly have broken free of this restraint.

4. *My 17-year-old daughter has a friend her own age who worries me. Barbara is a very nice girl, but she seems almost a clone of her mother and father, who are very wealthy. Barbara parrots their opinions, dresses as her mother suggests, and never has a word of criticism about either one of her parents – in marked contrast to my daughter, I might add. Cindy, my daughter, has a mind of her own and isn't afraid to let me know when she disagrees with me. My worry about Barbara is that she isn't really her own person and may some day resent the smothering influence of her parents. Is this a ridiculous notion?*

Not necessarily. One of the tasks which adolescents face is to establish a sense of their own identity. To do this, they need to develop a sense of their own autonomy, which for most teenagers means asserting themselves to their parents to some degree. Establishing a sense of identity also requires forming a sense of the self as unique and differentiated from others, including one's parents. In the course of this search for self, it is normal for adolescents to experience an identity crisis, as well as a certain amount of conflict with parents.

Some youngsters faced with these challenges, however, evade them by just adopting wholesale the values and roles that their parents choose for them. This move, known to developmentalists as foreclosure, means that all their choices for a career, individual roles, and beliefs are just a reflection of what they think their parents would choose for them. In other words, foreclosure is a way of sidestepping the hard choices and uncertainty that come with finding one's own identity. It sounds like Barbara has taken the route of foreclosure (at least for now). As for your concerns, they could be warranted. The type of "pseudo-identity" that foreclosure brings is often too rigid and shallow to support the inevitable crises that Barbara will encounter as an adult.

5. *When my son turned 13, I expected him to become interested in girls. However, he's now 14, and he and his male friends still seem more interested in hanging out together and seeing movies than they do in dating girls. Is this normal?*

Certainly. While you are right to assume that your son and his friends will soon begin demonstrating an interest in the opposite sex, they'll get around to it at their own speed. At present, it sounds as if they are still in the stage of practicing their new depths of self and mutual understanding with their peers. This is the stage of deep and intimate friendships among same-sex peers. As they consolidate the emotional and cognitive changes that accompany puberty, your son and his friends will undoubtedly turn their attentions outside of their clique to their peers of the opposite sex.

6. *What are some of the reasons that relationships between parents and children change during adolescence?*

With puberty, children become capable of sexual activities, which is bound to alter the way their parents consider them. Adolescents, and especially girls, may find their parents becoming more concerned about their behavior toward the opposite sex at this age. The understanding and logical skills of adolescents are also becoming more sophisticated, making them more likely to see inconsistencies in their parents' arguments. Teenagers also have a better understanding of parent-child relationships and can imagine ways of changing their family relations. Even the simple fact that they are now physically larger, more nearly the size of their parents, inclines children to assert themselves more and seek a more equal relationship with their parents.

SELF-TEST

The following multiple choice and short answer test questions should help you assess your understanding of the points covered in the text and the video. After answering all the questions, check your answers against the key and use the accuracy of your answers to gauge how well you have met the lesson objectives.

Multiple Choice Questions

1. When Richard was 2 years old, he began forming a sense of himself as distinct from other people. Now that he is 14, Richard is again developing a renewed sense of himself, especially in terms of how he is a unique individual. Unlike his earlier period of self-development, however, Richard now

    a. looks mainly to his parents for guidance.
    b. will not rely on any cognitive changes to shape his insights.
    c. has fully matured physically and is at ease with his body.
    d. must discover himself partly through interactions with his peers.

2. If you are walking past an elementary school when it lets out and a flock of 10 year olds scurries past you, the boys and girls will be of a similar height. If you could fast-forward their growth by two years, however, at 12 years old

    a. all the children will still be about the same average height.
    b. those girls who have begun puberty will be taller than the boys; the rest will be much shorter than the boys.
    c. the boys will on average be an inch or two taller than the girls.
    d. the girls will on average be an inch or two taller than the boys.

3. Fourteen-year-old Kelly and her 10-year-old brother Mike were watching a TV program about mysterious circles that were appearing in corn and wheat fields all across England. "I think they're UFOs," said Mike, "just like that guy said." Kelly wasn't so sure. "I suppose they could be," she said, "but how come nobody's ever seen any lights in the sky or things like that?"

    A few months later, Kelly sees an article in the paper that reports the cornfield circles were a hoax, the product of two mischievous Australians. "Look at this," Kelly says to her brother. "This proves it was these guys." But Mike refuses to change his mind. "I bet the aliens planted those guys," he says; "brainwashed 'em." Kelly's acceptance of the new evidence is a result of cognitive changes that

a. force her to rely on contingent truth.
b. enable her to use hypothetico-deductive reasoning.
c. enable her to think about relationships among abstract concepts.
d. give her a willingness to accept a lack of closure about a subject.

4. In the above example, the kind of cognitive powers that Kelly uses in comparison with Mike's thinking fall under Piaget's category of

a. formal operations.
b. egocentrism.
c. an imaginary audience.
d. a personal fable.

5. In terms of development, one thing that teenagers have in common with toddlers is that both

a. must establish a certain level of autonomy from their parents.
b. are experiencing immense neurological changes.
c. must form new peer relationships.
d. must establish new levels of intimacy with friends.

6. When Jessica's mother teases her for wanting to be like a rock singer because the girl's new hairstyle copies that of a popular singer, the 15-year-old gets angry. "Just because I like her hair doesn't mean I want to be like her, Mom. You don't understand anything. I'm not like anybody else, and I wouldn't want to be. Nobody else could even imagine the thoughts in my head, so don't even try." Jessica's sentiments are an example of the adolescent's need for

a. identity diffusion.
b. foreclosure.
c. individuation.
d. intimacy.

7. With regard to interaction with their friends, teenagers spend a greater percentage of their time than other age groups

a. playing imaginative board games.
b. engaging in active sports.
c. discussing life experiences on the telephone.
d. taking part in activities with same-sex groups.

8. According to studies, children are more likely to go along with the opinions of their friends, even if they are wrong, during the ages of

a. 7 to 8.
b. 12 to 13.
c. 16 to 17.
d. 18 to 19.

9. The parents of 15-year-old Pamela feel as though they're always fighting with their daughter. Either they're at her to pick up her room, or offended by the music she listens to, or upset by the amount of eyeshadow she wears. When they talk with a friend who is a psychologist, she tells them

   a. "You should try to get along at all costs; avoid conflict if possible."
   b. "Don't worry about it. It's normal for young teens and parents to have conflict."
   c. "You and Pamela need therapy; your family sounds dysfunctional."
   d. "Pamela needs professional help; she's obviously very troubled."

10. To help their children achieve the new levels of responsibility which they are striving for during adolescence, parents are best advised to

   a. stay involved and offer guidance with limits.
   b. be very watchful and strict.
   c. adopt a distant, hands off attitude to their children.
   d. resign themselves to several years of tumultuous conflict.

Short Answer Questions

The following questions should be answered in a paragraph or two. You should identify several key points for each answer and use these to form the framework for your response.

1. In his experiment called the law of floating bodies study, Piaget examined how an adolescent's mind becomes able to reason systematically about abstract concepts. How do the minds of adolescents differ from those of younger children as demonstrated by this experiment?

2. What are some of the developmental stages that adolescents are working through for the second time in their lives?

3. What are some of the biological and cognitive changes that impel adolescents to form a new sense of personal identity?

MODULE VII:

EPILOGUE

26

Does Childhood Matter?
Issues in Child Development

LESSON ASSIGNMENT

Completing the following steps will help you master the lesson objectives and achieve the goal for this lesson:

STEP 1: Read the INTRODUCING THE LESSON section below to provide a context for what you will learn in this lesson.

STEP 2: Read the lesson's GOAL and LESSON OBJECTIVES so that you will know what you are expected to learn.

STEP 3: Review the text assignments for the course, with a focus on the "A Look at the Whole Child" telecourse guide and video segments, Lessons 8, 12, 16, 21, and 25. Pay particular attention to the key terms and concepts in the Chapter Summary for each text chapter; they will help you when you watch the video.

STEP 4: Review the VIEWING GUIDE section in the telecourse guide. It lists several points to consider as you watch the video.

STEP 5: Watch the video.

STEP 6: Read the UNDERSTANDING THE LESSON section in the telecourse guide. Make sure you understand the key terms and can answer the focusing questions included there.

STEP 7: Complete the SELF-TEST.

STEP 8: Go back to the LESSON OBJECTIVES and make sure you can respond to each of them.

INTRODUCING THE LESSON

O ne of the earliest theories known on the relationship of childhood development to adulthood may be found in the Bible, in I Corinthians 13:11. In modern vocabulary, that says "When I was a child, I spoke like a child, I thought like a child, I reasoned like a child; when I became an adult, I put an end to childish ways" (New Revised Standard Version).

In its originally intended meaning, concerning of the necessity of taking on new responsibilities with adulthood – supporting one's self, finding an emotional partner, fulfilling the obligations of citizenship – this bit of ancient wisdom still rings true. As adults, we no longer make the conceptual mistakes typical of preschoolers – imagining, for instance, that the setting sun makes clouds when it sinks into the ocean. We are no longer likely to tease and mock people with whom we have differences – not to their faces, anyway. Nor do we undergo the kind of confusion and doubt that accompanies a teenager's quest for self-identity. To be mature means to be "complete and finished in natural growth or development," according to the dictionary.

And yet who among us does not retain some trace of the child we once were – within our actions, thoughts, and emotions? The adult appeal of movies such as *E.T.* depends to a great deal upon the power of its message of childhood's passion and sense of loyalty to hold true for grown-ups. If, as this course has repeatedly emphasized, the process of childhood development is orderly, sequential, and cumulative, then it seems reasonable to assume that traces of our developmental paths remain with us, like the bubbles of old air that freeze within a glacier's ice.

With Lesson 26 you reach the conclusion of your exploration of childhood development and take time to look back over the process of development as a whole. From the pre-natal period to adolescence, you will go over again the major phases and challenges of development, looking for examples of change and growth that are echoed in the patterns of maturity. In the video portion of the lesson, you will hear the debate among experts in the field of child development of the effect upon adults of such milestones of growth as attachment, the development of autonomy in toddlers, teenage cliques, and adolescent idealism. And once again, you will see and hear evidence of the dynamic, interactive process of human growth and development.

GOAL

To gain a comprehensive overview of the course of child development, and to assess the degree to which an individual's childhood is reflected in his or her maturity.

LESSON OBJECTIVES

After reading the text assignment, completing the exercises in this telecourse guide, and viewing the lesson's video portion, you will be able to:

1. Summarize the arguments about the contribution of childhood experiences to adult development.

2. Recognize the extent and variety of developmental issues that exist.

3. Discuss some major developmental issues that remain for the field of child development.

4. Describe the interaction between a culture's beliefs and values and its social policies related to child development.

VIEWING GUIDE

All of us reach adulthood through a similar sequence of maturation. And yet every individual is unique, with wide differences in character and outlook, even among people of similar background. In Lesson 26 you examine for one last time some of the major forces of childhood responsible for shaping our adult personalities. After reading the text material and learning the important terms included there, you are ready to view the lesson's video portion. First, try answering the questions in the Self-Test at the end of this telecourse guide lesson to give you an idea of important points to watch for in the video. Then read the following Points to Consider to give you an idea of what the video will cover. Keep these points in mind while watching.

Points to Consider

☐ *Back to year one*: The first year of life sets each child on the course of development. Notice how infants are preadapted to meet certain demands of their environments. Look for examples of how infancy might influence later stages of development.

☐ *Toddling toward the future*: With toddlerhood, the child's sense of self begins to emerge. Be aware of how toddlers struggle to achieve autonomy. Look for ways a toddler's growth is shaped by his or her parents.

☐ *Growing playfully*: Early childhood marks a time of expanding conceptual and cognitive abilities. Pay attention to the role temperament plays in development now. Consider ways that developmental concepts such as scripts are carried forward into later stages.

☐ *A middle ground*: Middle childhood is a time of consolidation. Recall how children now deepen their foundations of memory and cognition. Pay attention to the ways that the social advances of this period will develop during adolescence.

☐ *Concluding with adolescence*: Teenagers are the culmination of a sequential chain of events. Keep track of the evidence that shows how a milestone of adolescence carries over into adulthood.

UNDERSTANDING THE LESSON

In a sense, childhood development doesn't end with the passing of our teenage years. As part of life's journey, the developmental changes of childhood really reach their end only with death. Life is a process of continual change. By necessity, the effects of events and choices made during previous ages remain with us throughout our lives. In one sense, perhaps that is what is meant by a "second childhood" for many people in old age, when memories of the past become more real than day-to-day ones.

At the same time, since childhood development is capped by the end of adolescence, it is appropriate to pause at the frontier of adulthood for a look backward at the significant events of childhood. Because the milestones of childhood make up the foundation of individual growth, it is fitting to look among them for clues and hints of what that person's mature growth will hold.

The First Year of Development

An individual's journey to adulthood begins with birth. As you will recall from the early lessons in this course, each child begins his or her life's journey with certain genetic preadaptations, the most basic of which are reflexes. Building upon reflexes such as those of rooting and sucking, each child begins gaining mastery over his or her body. As you now know, a child's successive stages of growth will evolve from earlier ones, with the mastery of early motor skills and other challenges of infancy setting the stage for successive phases of growth.

As infants gain control over their bodies, they are also gaining learning skills that will remain with them throughout their lifetimes. Habituation, for example, which allows infants to gradually become used to and thus undistracted by repeated stimulation, is a familiar concept to any adult who has gotten used to sleeping in a noisy apartment. Likewise, the skills of associative and imitative learning that children acquire within their first year form the basis of much of an adult's ability to master new habits of thought and behavior.

Some of an individual's social skills and emotional outlook are also grounded in the first year of development. A particularly important phase of first-year development is the child's attachment to care givers. In both the text material and video segments you saw many examples of how the child's type of attachment, secure or otherwise, will play a part in the stages of emotional and cognitive development that come later. While the results are not conclusive, studies have shown that infants raised in sterile institutions, or subjected to either insensitive or abusive care, for example, often tend to have problems at later stages. Among infants who were institutionalized, for instance, some were found to have trouble establishing friendships during adolescence and later developed problems as parents.

But while a child's first year of development establishes the foundation for later development, it doesn't necessarily represent a blueprint that will shape all later growth. By the end of year one, a child remains a highly resilient organism that still faces many opportunities – as well as challenges – on the road to maturity.

Focusing Questions

1. Are all children who form secure attachments in infancy guaranteed a smooth course of development in the stages of development that follow? For example, is being securely attached a sure sign that the child will easily learn to walk and talk, and successfully face the other challenges of the next few years such as establishing autonomy?

2. Infants are born preadapted to form social ties. As an adult, can you think of any ways you respond to infants that may be related to the ways infant's behave reflexively? (Hint: What is the first reaction of most adults to a smiling baby?)

The Toddler Years

Both biologically and philosophically, the thread of any individual's life can be said to stretch backwards from now to the moment of their conception. But consciously, for most people, existence trails behind them in a string of memories that begin with vague glimmers of awareness arising out of toddlerhood. As toddlers begin walking and talking, forming the rudiments of sociability, they are continuing to follow their individual paths to maturity. Recall that Piaget thought that the ability to think symbolically first emerged in toddlerhood.

As an adult, however, one of each person's most important legacies from the developmental stage of toddlerhood is likely to be a sense of selfhood. In a very real sense, the search for a sense of self begins in the toddler years, with the first emergence of a sense of "me" and the recognition of the option to say "no." As toddlers develop a growing sense of self and strive to establish their autonomy, they also become increasingly social. Out of these early stages will grow later abilities to form relationships and get along with others. Remember, too, that socialization – that mechanism by which we all learn the rules and expectations of our particular social group – begins working on each of us during the toddler years.

Toddlerhood is the period when children encounter new limits put upon them by their parents. Here again, the form of attachment children have established will partly determine the success with which they accomplish the tasks of becoming more self-reliant and separating from their parents. As with other stages of development, the actual course of any given phase continues to be framed by the outcome of earlier ones.

Focusing Questions

1. What are two ways in which the parent-child relationship changes during toddlerhood?

2. What are some of the dramatic qualitative changes that a toddler undergoes?

Early Childhood

In the course of any average week, you make use of a number of conceptual tools. For instance, you might quickly estimate the number of cup hangers you need to buy based on a remembered glimpse of a kitchen cupboard. Maybe you estimate how long it will take a bathtub to fill with water or perhaps you organize a collection of books on a shelf according to their size. Whenever you apply any of these skills with full adult awareness, you're simply taking advantage of a process of self-development that you entered during your preschool years. Your adult ability to concentrate and your gifts of communication have their roots in your early childhood development.

During early childhood, we make great strides in mastering the conceptual skills that will guide us toward maturity. In addition to the influence of previous stages of development, preschoolers also continue to develop according to individual differences in temperament. The degree of self-reliance which children develop during this time will shape their future growth. And if you recall the concept of scripts – symbolic mental outlines of actions needed to reach a goal – that preschoolers begin to acquire, you'll recognize the basic pattern of dozens of actions you repeat every day as an adult.

This course has repeatedly stressed that each stage of individual development proceeds from the previous one, following paths much like a river course traces its bed. During early childhood, a child's success or failure mastering self-control and developing a degree of ego resiliency will affect later stages of his or her development. The lessons covering early childhood point out that a child's behavior, whether prosocial or aggressive, tends to be coherent over time.

Focusing Questions

1. Preschoolers learn – among other things – to tolerate frustration, delay gratification, and inhibit actions. Why are these important milestones along the individual path of social and emotional development?

Middle Childhood

In the video segments covering the years of middle childhood, you saw several examples of how children consolidate and expand upon the skills and abilities that they acquired during earlier stages of development. Elementary school children gain in height, put on weight, and improve their coordination. Cognitively, children of this period deepen and broaden their grasp of such concepts as conservation of liquid and volume and of classification. Also during middle childhood, children gain an increasing awareness of their own memory weaknesses and strengths – known as metamemory – laying the foundation for more mature memory control in later years.

Middle childhood youngsters spend a great deal of time in same-sex peer groups, establishing the basis for the social skills they'll need in later life. Likewise, children now gain a more sophisticated sense both of themselves and of others, as shown by a growing sense of empathy. Youngsters of this age are combining various concepts of the self into a coherent self-image, a process that is molded by past contexts of biology and environment.

Children face a number of challenges during middle childhood, including that of consolidating a sense of self, gaining confidence in their own abilities, forming peer friendships, joining peer groups, and successfully adjusting to school. To a great degree, those who successfully meet these challenges will be the ones with a solid basis of development from previous stages. In other words, if children have developed in ways that built up their self-confidence and self-esteem, they tend to present themselves to others in positive ways that elicit favorable reactions, further enhancing their self-confidence.

Focusing Questions

1. During middle childhood, teasing and taunting begins to replace physical violence in disputes between children. What developmental changes account for this?

2. What are some of the ways a child's sense of self-esteem affects his or her cognitive and social development during middle childhood?

Adolescence

With adolescence, the phases of childhood development reach a plateau. By the time they are in their late teens, most children will have matured sexually, developed newly sophisticated social and cognitive skills, and established a sense of personal identity. As a result of a myriad of influences that have been molding them physically, socially, emotionally, and cognitively since before birth, the children of our studies are now about to embark on the continuing path of adult development.

At least over the short term, adolescence would appear to have a strong influence over an individual's course through life. After all, it is during adolescence that children must evolve a coherent sense of self, motivated in part by their new sexual capacities. They must also set new levels of intimacy with peers and navigate the unknown passages of relationships based upon sexual attraction. Adolescents must reach fresh forms of understanding with parents and prepare themselves for greater involvement with the world at large. Adolescence is the time when children choose the shape of the values and morality that will guide them as they enter adulthood.

Keep in mind, however, the importance of continuity throughout each individual's development. Since each new stage of development emerges from the previous one, the "new" adolescent individual can trace his or her emotions, thoughts, values, and even physical form back through a line of growth and the influences that shaped it. Just as the child's development was a dynamic interchange of influences among cultural, social, economic, environmental, and biological contexts, so will it be for the adult. And though, as you saw in the video, developmentalists may disagree over the importance of the influence that specific aspects or events of childhood development exert on an adult, they all will agree that the course of childhood pointed the way to the emerging adult. As the poet Wordsworth once phrased it, "The child is father of the man."

Focusing Questions

1. Some of the developmental challenges that teenagers face are, to some degree, repetitions of earlier phases of development. Discuss some of these challenges.

2. What are some of the cognitive changes which children will undergo during adolescence?

Questions for Understanding

As you read these questions, often raised by parents, educators, and other childcare providers, first try to answer the questions yourself. Then read the answer following each question and compare your response to it.

1. *If a child receives poor care as an infant, how will that affect him or her in later life?*

The long-term effects of inadequate care on infants are hard to pin down. Certainly, the effects of extreme mistreatment on infants, such as raising them in near-total isolation, tend to show up as marked abnormalities in social development. For instance, children raised in large institutions were shown in one study to have trouble establishing friendships during adolescence and later to have had problems as parents.

At the same time, some studies have shown that children are remarkably resilient. For instance, children who were first raised in very deprived settings were then placed in favorable surroundings and showed improved intellectual functioning. Social and emotional development, however, may not be as resilient. Generally speaking, psychologists tend to believe that the earlier an intervention program for a deprived child begins, the better are his or her chances of showing an improved developmental path.

2. *Are children who are abused in danger of becoming abusers themselves if they become parents?*

In many cases, yes. Although not all abusing parents were victims of abuse themselves, many were. Psychologists theorize that abused children learn maladaptive responses to the pressures of child rearing, which they as parents then apply to their own children. These tendencies will be strengthened in families that encounter problems such as low income, isolation, poor education, and stress.

Keep in mind, however, the importance of context for any phase of development. Even victims of child abuse may overcome their past when they become parents if they can receive high degrees of social support. One study found that mothers who themselves were mistreated as children were unlikely to abuse their own children if they had adequate social support. A history of abuse does not doom a child to later abnormal development, but is a significant and possibly influential factor in one's developmental history.

3. *When do children begin exhibiting behavior traits that parents can consider useful indicators of what their child's personality will be like at later stages of development?*

Temperament, which becomes individually discernible during the child's first year, tends to be a stable indicator of the direction of development of a child's characteristics over time. Kagan, in studying inhibited vs. outgoing behavior, found that a small number of children classified as either very timid or very bold at 2 years of age were still classified the same way two years later. It appears that classifications of temperament tend to become stable and the characteristics they are based on influence the behavior of parents and others.

The response that young children have to the challenges of developing self-control also can predict later behavior. Individual differences in level of self-control tend to become apparent by about age 3 and have been found to be quite stable even into middle childhood and adolescence. In other words, the impulsive 4 year old is likely to also be impulsive as a 7 year old and a 16 year old.

4. *What are some of the effects that the different types of attachment will have on a child's later development?*

During preschool, children who were securely attached tend to be more competent with peers, have higher self-esteem, greater self-reliance, and more flexibility in their self-management. They express more positive emotions toward peers, as well as more empathy and less aggression toward others. During elementary school, the high self-esteem of these children tends to translate into success in school, even in the area of reading ability. These traits tend to be stable over time and predict probable feelings of high self-esteem during the teen years and into adulthood.

Among preschoolers with a history of anxious attachment, on the other hand, self-esteem is lower, as are peer competence and capacity for flexible self-management. Children with histories of avoidant attachment are often hostile and aggressive toward other children, or they may be emotionally isolated. Such children may have strong dependency needs. But even these children have been shown to respond to the persistent efforts of caring teachers.

5. *Will elementary school children who are skilled at getting along with their peers probably be socially competent in adolescence and even later?*

While developmentalists do not look upon successful peer interactions of middle childhooders as determining later healthy development, it is clear that effective peer relationships are important to healthy development. In one long-term study of the interrelationships of a group of third-graders' intelligence test scores, attendance records, and measures of peer acceptance, for instance, rejection by peers at ages 8 and 9 turned out to be the best school predictor of mental health problems in early adulthood. Keep in mind, however, that signs such as poor peer relations do not destine a person to later problems. Rather, such childhood difficulties are seen as indicators of later developmental problems. A number of developmental factors, including changing environment, adjustments in child care, and changes in the family, will continue to have an effect on individual growth.

SELF-TEST

The following multiple choice and short answer test questions should help you assess your understanding of the points covered in the text and the video. After answering all the questions, check your answers against the key and use the accuracy of your answers to gauge how well you have met the lesson objectives.

Multiple Choice Questions

1. One developmental challenge that individuals must go through as both toddlers and teenagers is to develop

   a. peer friendships.
   b. a sense of empathy.
   c. a new sense of the self.
   d. symbolic thought.

2. During early childhood, one developmental trait that tends to be a predictor of the individual's behavior during later childhood and even the teen years is the

   a. age a child begins talking.
   b. degree to which a child masters conservation.
   c. age when a child overcomes egocentrism.
   d. degree to which a child learns to tolerate frustration.

3. A basic tenet of childhood development is that at any given moment, a child's development is

   a. solely determined by the previous stage of development.
   b. largely unaffected by previous stages of development.
   c. orderly, sequential, and cumulative.
   d. completely out of the child's control.

4. As a 3-month-old infant, Randy would kick his legs and wave his arms around whenever he heard his mother's approaching footsteps. As a first grader, his enthusiasm made him a natural leader in games. As a teenager, his sense of humor and positive self-image made him popular with girls. One developmental principle that characterizes Randy's development as described is the

   a. limitations constraining each stage of development.
   b. extent to which individuals actively take part in their own development.
   c. importance of secure attachment during infancy.
   d. central importance of family in individual development.

5. During all ages, each child's course of development will be affected by his or her

   a. reflexes.
   b. relationships with others.
   c. peer relationships.
   d. order of birth in the family.

6. Researchers have been able to predict the likelihood of teenage drug abuse from earlier measures of self-control versus impulsiveness. The developmental theme that underlies this finding is the

   a. need of teenagers to rebel.
   b. importance of environmental factors.
   c. central role played by attachment.
   d. continuity of development.

7. In developmental terms, the word autonomy refers to a child's

   a. tendency to work out conflicts during fantasy play.
   b. desire to get a driver's license during the teen years.
   c. need at various stages to establish a level of self-reliance.
   d. dependency on care givers for guidance.

8. Research shows that teenage mothers have a better chance of raising a child relatively free of developmental problems if they

   a. have the baby after they are 16.
   b. finish high school.
   c. have adequate support from their families.
   d. attend Lamaze child-birthing classes before giving birth.

9. In several studies of grade-school children, researchers found that teachers tended to interact more with boys and to give boys more positive feedback, while criticizing girls more. This is one example of the power that school exerts over a child's

   a. search for autonomy.
   b. gender-role learning.
   c. prosocial behavior.
   d. understanding of conceptual tools.

10. Some cultures have established specific ceremonies or rituals that mark the transition of a teenager from a child into a man or a woman. In North America, some observers see this same turning point being heralded by a teen's first license, or voting, or a first job. The type of socially sanctioned rite that's described here is known as

    a. puberty.
    b. an identity crisis.
    c. tumultuous growth.
    d. a rite of passage.

Short Answer Questions

The following questions should be answered in a paragraph or two. You should identify several key points for each answer and use these to form the framework for your response.

1. What is an example, for each of the five main periods of childhood development, of the sequential nature of development?

2. What are some specific examples of patterns of developmental change that persist from various stages into adulthood?

3. Throughout this course in childhood development, you have seen that the early phases of development clearly have an effect on later individual development. What are some of those phases?

ANSWER KEY

FOR THE

SELF-TEST

LESSON 1
The Nature and Theories of Development

Multiple Choice Questions

1. a (Text page 14) Lesson Objective #5
2. b (Text pages 5-6) Lesson Objective #2
3. a (Text pages 7-8) Lesson Objective #3
4. a (Text page 8) Lesson Objective #4
5. c (Text page 12) Lesson Objective #1
6. b (Text page 20) Lesson Objective #6
7. b (Text page 17) Lesson Objective #6
8. a (Text pages 26-27) Lesson Objective #8
9. a (Text pages 26-27) Lesson Objective #8
10. c (Text page 23) Lesson Objective #7

Short Answer Questions

The following are examples of key points or ideas you might have used in your answers to these questions.

Question 1:

- Infant development involves both qualitative and quantitative changes.

- As children progress through the stages of development, their ability to organize their behavior in new and more complex ways increases.

- The changes that children experience are orderly, cumulative, and directional.

- An individual's particular stage of development depends upon his or her genetic developmental plan, plus his or her previous developmental history.

- Development is also affected by the environment.

Question 2:

- The psychoanalytic theory of Sigmund Freud states that children first possess only a primitive instinctual drive, known as the id. Next the growing child develops the ego, followed finally by the superego. Individuals are capable of being "stuck" at any one of several important developmental milestones during their youth.

- Jean Piaget's cognitive theory of development focuses on the child's increasing cognitive development. Children of different ages have greatly different abilities to understand and learn about the world.

- The adaptational theory of John Bowlby is a blend of Freud's views on individual development, Darwin's theory of evolution, and

Piaget's cognitive theories. Infants are predisposed to form attachments with their care givers. Depending upon their early experiences with care givers, infants form expectations called internal working models that guide their later development.

– Information-processing theory holds that developmental change is the result of gradual cognitive change. As children improve in their powers of memory, attention, and thought, they are increasingly able to interpret events and devise solutions to problems.

– Social learning theory focuses on gradual change that arises out of individual experience. The theory focuses on differences among children of the same age and emphasizes the important role that the current environment plays in shaping behavior. In addition, reinforcement history plays a critical role in this theory.

Question 3:

– Laboratory experiments are controlled situations in special settings that are designed to gather information under very specific circumstances.

– An advantage of laboratory experiments is that they can be very systematically controlled, using sophisticated equipment; a disadvantage is that people sometimes behave differently in laboratory settings than they would in uncontrolled circumstances.

– Trained researchers can take observations of children in real-life settings, using the techniques of naturalistic observation.

– Naturalistic observation has the advantage of describing human behavior in actual situations; a disadvantage is that the conclusions that can be drawn from what observers report is limited.

LESSON 2
Children in Context

Multiple Choice Questions

1. a (Telecourse Guide) Lesson Objective #4
2. b (Text page 48) Lesson Objective #1
3. b (Video) Lesson Objective #2
4. a (Text page 49) Lesson Objective #1
5. c (Text page 50) Lesson Objective #3
6. d (Telecourse Guide) Lesson Objective #3
7. c (Text page 74) Lesson Objective #7
8. b (Text pages 68-70) Lesson Objective #6
9. c (Text page 67) Lesson Objective #5
10. c (Text page 75) Lesson Objective #8

Short Answer Questions

The following are examples of key points or ideas you might have used in your answers to these questions:

Question 1:

- If the father is supportive of the mother in her role as a mother, she will feel more positive about her role and will function more effectively.

- When both mother and father interact with their children, they tend to reinforce each other and deal more positively with the child than if only one parent participated in the child's care.

- The father's influence in a home usually produces male children who are more competitive and independent than those from a home with no male influence.

- The father's role is especially important in dealing with the toddler, because the father's way of relating to the child at this stage is different from the mother's.

Question 2:

- In a traditional classroom, material is presented by a teacher, individual students practice using the material, and the teacher then asks questions to which students respond individually.

- Some subcultures emphasize cooperation and assisted performance. Native Hawaiians, for example, use this pattern which prepares children for group problem solving – not a pattern generally encouraged in the traditional classroom.

- Native American communities teach tasks and skills holistically. A child learns an entire process, rather than learning steps in the process.

- The African-American tradition encourages children to challenge and outwit adults, which is viewed as disruptive in the traditional classroom.

Question 3:

- Children growing up in poverty experience more health problems than the general population of children. As a result, such children tend to miss school more often.

- Accidents are more common than in middle-class homes because the environments are not as safe.

- As they grow older, they receive poor health care and do not eat well. Both of these factors lead to loss of time in school.

- Stress is more common in the low income home than in the middle-class home. Children from stressful environments do not adjust as well to school and exhibit more behavior problems. They also have more emotional problems and are more likely to be learning disabled.

– Children of poverty experience more real violence than middle-class children. Child abuse is more common, and the low income child is more likely to be a victim of crime than a child from a more affluent home.

LESSON 3
Conception and Prenatal Development

Multiple Choice Questions

1. b   (Text page 84) Lesson Objective #3
2. c   (Text page 97) Lesson Objective #1
3. a   (Text page 85) Lesson Objective #2
4. d   (Text page 85) Lesson Objective #4
5. b   (Text page 91) Lesson Objective #5
6. b   (Text page 94) Lesson Objective #5
7. a   (Text page 100) Lesson Objective #6
8. d   (Text page 104) Lesson Objective #8
9. a   (Text page 87) Lesson Objective #8
10. d   (Text page 106) Lesson Objective #7

Short Answer Questions

The following are examples of key points or ideas you might have used in your answers to these questions:

Question 1:

– Male infertility is caused by reduced numbers of sperm in each ejaculation or by sperm with low activity and a low survival rate. A doctor might suggest pooling the sperm from several ejaculations and inserting them into the uterus – a process called artificial insemination. In a case where the man is completely sterile, the woman may be artificially inseminated with sperm from another man.

– A woman may be unable to conceive because of blockage of the fallopian tubes or cervical mucus that is hostile to sperm. Surgical procedures and drug and hormone therapies are solutions to some problems of female infertility.

– If a woman is completely sterile, sperm from the man can be used to artificially inseminate another woman who will give birth to the fetus.

– In vitro fertilization is a technique that can be used to help couples who are fertile, but cannot conceive. A fertile egg from the woman is fertilized in the laboratory with sperm from the man. If cell division occurs, the developing cell mass is placed in the woman's uterus to develop to full term.

Question 2:

- Rubella or German measles can have devastating effects on the developing embryo or fetus if the mother contracts the disease between the third or fourth week of pregnancy through the third month. If the mother is infected, the probability of birth defects runs from about 50 percent in the early weeks of pregnancy to 7 percent in the third month. Blindness, deafness, mental retardation, heart defects, and deformed or missing limbs are some of the defects that appear in children whose mothers contracted rubella in the early months of pregnancy. A vaccine for rubella was introduced to the public in 1969; unfortunately not all women of child-bearing age have been immunized.

- The HIV virus can penetrate the placenta. It is possible to carry the HIV virus for as long as eleven years without exhibiting symptoms, and a woman may not know that she is carrying the disease when she becomes pregnant. Newborns infected with the virus may have abnormally small heads or facial deformities; other newborns may appear normal, but later fail to grow, contract numerous infections, and exhibit cognitive deficits.

- Various types of sexually transmitted disease as well as the viruses that cause diseases such as mumps or influenza can also damage a developing embryo or fetus. Adequate prenatal care can assist a pregnant woman in avoiding some of these dangers.

Question 3:

- Babies born prematurely are obvious candidates for low birth weight. Low birth weight may also be due to retarded growth and development in the uterus.

- Low birth weight is common in conditions of poverty where prenatal care is poor or absent.

- Very young mothers and women who are toward the end of the childbearing years are at risk for low birth weight babies.

- Smoking, alcohol abuse, and drug use are also behaviors that contribute to low birth weight infants.

- Babies who are too small show a greater than normal incidence of neurological handicaps, physical abnormalities, and lung problems.

LESSON 4
Birth and the Neonate

Multiple Choice Questions

1. b (Text pages 95-96 and 107) Lesson Objective #2
2. d (Text page 108) Lesson Objective #2
3. a (Text page 108, Table 3.3) Lesson Objective #2
4. b (Text page 111) Lesson Objective #2

5. c (Text page 111) Lesson Objective #5

6. b (Text page 128) Lesson Objective #4

7. d (Text page 128) Lesson Objective #3

8. b (Text pages 136-137) Lesson Objective #3

9. d (Text page 106) Lesson Objective #5

10. a (Text page 109) Lesson Objective #1

Short Answer Questions

The following are examples of key points or ideas you might have used in your answers to these questions:

Question 1:

- If the doctor recommends inducing labor, then Sheila will be given oxytocin.

- In a breech birth, using drugs may dangerously cut off the supply of oxygen to the baby.

- The doctor may recommend performing a Caesarean section.

- This birth is an example of a complicated one; the parents must make some hard decisions about how to deliver their child safely.

Question 2:

- There has been a shift toward natural methods of childbirth, which usually include having the mother and her partner take part in pre-natal classes.

- These methods usually train the mother in breathing and stretching exercises designed to lower her anxiety and pain during the birth.

- Hospitals have increasingly remodeled their delivery rooms with the thought of the newborn's comfort in mind.

- Mothers can now sometimes choose to deliver in rooms with muted lighting, and their partners are often allowed to be present.

- Midwives and other paraprofessionals are also often involved in the birth process, often for long periods before and after the birth.

Question 3:

- A newborn's behavior is divided into six states: quiet sleep; active sleep; awake and quiet; awake and active; fussing; and crying.

- A newborn will tend to sleep about 16 hours a day, with its wake-and-sleep cycle fairly evenly divided throughout the day and night.

- All of its physical behaviors, such as sucking, moving, and crying, are the result of reflex action.

- It will cry in the three distinct patterns of being hungry, upset, or in pain.

LESSON 5
First Adaptations

Multiple Choice Questions

1. c (Text page 130; Telecourse Guide) Lesson Objective #2
2. a (Text page 125; Telecourse Guide) Lesson Objective #6
3. a (Text page 129) Lesson Objective #2
4. d (Text page 136) Lesson Objective #3
5. b (Text page 137, Telecourse Guide, Video) Lesson Objective #4
6. a (Text page 142, Video) Lesson Objective #4
7. c (Text page 145) Lesson Objective #3
8. a (Text page 132, Video) Lesson Objective #5
9. d (Text page 148) Lesson Objective #1
10. b (Text page 150, Video) Lesson Objective #6

Short Answer Questions

The following are examples of key points or ideas you might have used in your answers to these questions.

Question 1:

- Infant learning includes strong interaction of genetic control and experience.

- Prepared responses are precursor to many infant learning tasks.

- Infant learning involves the decline of reflexive behaviors and the re-establishment of the behaviors under voluntary control.

- Infants learn a lot of their new behavior through imitation.

Question 2:

- Depth perception develops through development of binocular and monocular depth cues.

- Shape and size constancy develop in infants.

- Ability of infants to perceive faces changes.

Question 3:

- There are many examples that can be given here. The important point is that your example for classical conditioning must include a behavior that the child already knows how to do – such as crying, sucking, grasping. Learning that involves establishing new behaviors is best explained using operant conditioning.

- In your example for classical conditioning, identify the conditioned and unconditioned stimuli and responses.

– Note that often the conditioned and unconditioned responses are very similar and, in fact, may appear the same.

– In operant conditioning, make sure that the consequence – positive reinforcement, negative reinforcement, punishment – is specified.

– Remember that negative reinforcement is *not* the same as punishment.

LESSON 6
Infant Cognitive Development

Multiple Choice Questions

1. b   (Text pages 159-160) Lesson Objective #1
2. d   (Text pages 162-163) Lesson Objective #1
3. c   (Text pages 164-165) Lesson Objective #2
4. c   (Text page 167) Lesson Objective #2
5. a   (Text page 172) Lesson Objective #3
6. d   (Text page 174) Lesson Objective #3
7. a   (Text page 178) Lesson Objective #4
8. c   (Text page 181) Lesson Objective #4
9. c   (Text page 161) Lesson Objective #5
10. a   (Text page 177) Lesson Objective #6

Short Answer Questions

The following are examples of key points or ideas you might have used in your answers to these questions.

Question 1:

– This is an example of a secondary circular reaction as described by Piaget where an infant actively experiences the effects of its behavior on an external object.

– The first occurrence of this activity is an accident. Then the baby will purposely repeat the action to observe the consequence again.

– After discovering such a reaction, a baby will repeat the triggering actions, eventually modifying his movements so that only the ones relevant to the desired consequence remain and extraneous movements are deleted.

– The baby ultimately acquires a rudimentary understanding of the connection between a movement and a resulting consequence.

– According to Piaget, the baby does not understand the connection between the movement and the result; he simply learns a connection between a motor behavior and a sensory consequence.

Question 2:

- Babies at this age show strong ties to their parents, proving that they have developed a set of memories about these important individuals.

- Most babies in the second half-year of life begin to speak. The mastery of language requires a long-term memory.

- At this age, babies demonstrate an ability to remember a category that has been introduced to them. Further, they are able to react when they perceive an object that does not fit into a memorized category.

- Experiments show that infants in the second 6 months of life can begin to categorize examples shown to them by a given combination of features – such as animals with a certain type of body, feet, and tail.

- Infants at this stage of life display an ability to perceive numerosity, or the concept of "how many." Studies have shown that babies in the second half-year are aware of a connection between the number of objects they see in a group and the number of drumbeats they hear.

Question 3:

- To accomplish some of the more complex tasks that babies begin to master in the second 6 months of life, they must be able to combine two or more learned behaviors – for example, the ability to remember objects and to control behaviors. If the working memory is overloaded with too large a string of learned behaviors before the goal is achieved, the baby will not be able to make any more progress. The task will remain unfinished.

- As the size of the working memory increases, the capacity to accomplish more complicated tasks increases also.

- The baby's experiences in working with certain processes may turn a skill into one block of behavior instead of a series of steps, freeing up working memory space. This new ability can become a stepping stone to even more complex skills.

- The progression of mental processes seems to be from one action to two related actions to a series of related actions and finally to single representations of more complicated actions.

LESSON 7
Infant Social and Emotional Development

Multiple Choice Questions

1. b (Text pages 219-220) Lesson Objective #7
2. b (Text pages 191-192) Lesson Objective #1

3. d   (Text page 196) Lesson Objective #2
4. d   (Text page 194) Lesson Objective #2
5. c   (Text page 201) Lesson Objective #3
6. a   (Text page 202) Lesson Objective #3
7. d   (Text page 205) Lesson Objective #4
8. b   (Text page 216) Lesson Objective #5
9. d   (Text page 210) Lesson Objective #6
10. a   (Text page 220) Lesson Objective #8

Short Answer Questions

The following are examples of key points or ideas you might have used in your answers to these questions.

Question 1:

- For children 12 months old and above, most research has lead to the conclusion that day care is not harmful.

- Day care may be beneficial to the child, at least in terms of promoting cognitive and social development.

- Children placed in day care seem still to attach securely to their primary care givers.

- Studies show that some infants under 12 months old who are placed in day care, however, appear to be at risk for forming anxious attachment.

Question 2:

- Adults tend to act in a number of sensitive ways when relating to children.

- Adults tend to lean down close to a baby's face and move their head from side to side as they talk.

- The high-pitched "baby talk" that adults babble to babies seems to especially attract children.

- Adults seem to be predisposed to smile at infants.

Question 3:

- Reciprocity refers to a mutual give and take in communication.

- Babies do not initiate any communication other than by their reflexive reactions to internal and external stimuli.

- The baby is staying alert for longer periods of time, and gaining greater control over his or her motor activities.

- A sensitive care giver is able to engage the infant's attention and frame or guide their reactions in specific directions – the child reciprocates the communication.

LESSON 8
A Look at the Whole Child: The First Year

Multiple Choice Questions

1. c (Text pages 134-136) Lesson Objective #1
2. a (Text page 136) Lesson Objective #1
3. b (Text page 150) Lesson Objective #2
4. d (Text page 163) Lesson Objective #5
5. d (Text page 174) Lesson Objective # 4
6. a (Text pages 191-192) Lesson Objective #3
7. c (Text page 163) Lesson Objective #2
8. a (Text pages 150-151) Lesson Objective #4
9. a (Text page 208) Lesson Objective #3
10. b (Text pages 194-196) Lesson Objective #5

Short Answer Questions

The following are examples of key points or ideas you might have used in your answers to these questions.

Question 1:

- In the area of motor skills, the child's overall coordination and balance are immensely advanced over those of a newborn's. The 1 year old is able to combine a series of movements to perform such planned actions as reaching and grasping, as well as standing upright with assistance.

- The 1 year old is able to learn by imitation, which indicates impressive memory abilities. To imitate, the infant must also be able to form a connection between something seen and actions of his or her own body.

- The 1 year old is aware that objects exist outside of its own presence.

- The 1 year old is initiating responses from others with an idea of the effect she or he will achieve. The ability to anticipate the results of his or her actions is also a skill that 1 year olds possess.

Question 2:

- The child must have enough memory ability to be able to remember a word from one moment to another.

- To be able to properly identify things in order to name them, the child must have developed a certain ability to form concepts.

- The child must be able to imitate the way other people move their lips and use their voices to make words.

- The child must also have developed social and emotional ties that are strong enough to encourage it to want to communicate.

Question 3:

- Clifton is able to make a decision based on contingencies, which in this case is that his appearance will make his mother share her treat with him. He has also learned to associate the opening of the refrigerator door with ice cream.

- His motor skills have advanced to the point where he is able to move to the source of the food, where earlier he had to rely on his mother to bring food to him.

- He is able to form plans and to act purposefully to accomplish them.

- He is capable of reciprocating actively with others, and may even be able to form a few simple words – such as "eye keem," for example.

LESSON 9
Toddler Language and Thinking

Multiple Choice Questions

1. c   (Text pages 245-246) Lesson Objective #1
2. b   (Text page 253) Lesson Objective #1
3. a   (Text page 241) Lesson Objective #2
4. b   (Text page 242) Lesson Objective #3
5. c   (Text page 244) Lesson Objective #3
6. d   (Text page 249) Lesson Objective #5
7. a   (Text page 252) Lesson Objective #5
8. a   (Text page 255) Lesson Objective #5
9. b   (Text pages 257-258) Lesson Objective #6
10. c   (Text pages 261-264) Lesson Objective #4

Short Answer Questions

The following are examples of key points or ideas you might have used in your answers to these questions.

Question 1:

- If Elizabeth is saying two words with a pause between them, she is probably just expressing two separate and unrelated thoughts. She probably is using sentences, though, since most children begin forming sentences between 18 and 24 months.

- Most of her words will be nouns, verbs, and adjectives; she probably won't use any articles, conjunctions, or prepositions.

- Her speech will be telegraphic, meaning that her words do form sentences, but sentences stripped of all nonessential words.

- She will only talk about a limited number of subjects, with the meanings of sentences confined to things such as identification, lo-

cation, and recurrence. She may express possession – "Ball mine" –
or ask questions – "Where Daddy?"

Question 2:

- Phonology is the study of the sounds of a language. The smallest
  unit of sound that can change the meaning of a word is a phoneme.
  English has 41 phonemes.

- Morphology is the study of words in their smallest meaningful size.
  Words are broken down in single units of meaning, called morphemes, and single units which only have meaning when added to
  other words, which are called grammatical morphemes.

- Syntax refers to the rules that govern how words are organized into
  sentences and what kind of information they convey through that
  order. In English, for example, the standard word order of a sentence is subject, verb, object.

- Semantics covers the meaning of words as they are used within
  sentences. Words may be placed correctly in sentences according
  to syntax and still be meaningless if they contradict semantic rules –
  as in a grammatically correct but ridiculous sentence such as "The
  cow milked the farmer."

Question 3:

- Children first learn to make yes/no, or "closed" questions; these
  questions are always answered yes or no. This behavior appears at
  about age 3.

- Also at about the age of 3, children learn to make yes/no questions
  by moving the auxiliary verb in a declarative sentence to in front of
  the verb. The sentence "Johnny can run" becomes "Can Johnny
  run?"

- Children begin making yes/no questions first, at about 3 years of
  age. They are beginning to use auxiliary verbs in sentences by this
  time.

- Children next learn how to make "wh" questions, which are those
  beginning with what, where, when, why, who, how. These are also
  called "open" questions.

- To make open questions, children must choose the correct interrog-
  ative word and place it, along with an auxiliary verb, at the front of a
  sentence. "Where did Johnny go?"

- Children begin making open questions around 4½, toward the end
  of the toddler period.

LESSON 10
Toddler Social and Emotional Development

Multiple Choice Questions

1. a   (Text pages 273-274) Lesson Objective #4
2. b   (Text page 280) Lesson Objective #1
3. c   (Text page 281) Lesson Objective #1
4. b   (Text page 278) Lesson Objective #2
5. d   (Text page 278) Lesson Objective #3
6. b   (Text page 272) Lesson Objective #2
7. c   (Text pages 283-284) Lesson Objective #3
8. a   (Text page 287) Lesson Objective #5
9. b   (Text pages 286-292) Lesson Objective #5
10. b   (Text page 285) Lesson Objective #2

Short Answer Questions

The following are examples of key points or ideas you might have used in your answers to these questions.

Question 1:

- Socialization from the outside was based mainly on Freud's early theories, but it is also characteristic of earlier attitudes, for example Puritan child-rearing. Freud thought that babies were seething masses of biological desires that had to be channeled and controlled.

- In Freud's thinking, parents socialized children by imposing rules upon them from without. This blocking of goals is called sublimation.

- Social learning theorists also thought socialization had to be imposed from outside; they thought children would obey the imposed rules in order to maintain closeness with their parents.

- Those who believe socialization springs from within children base their opinions on humanity's evolution as a group-living species. Children naturally wish to please their parents in order to gain their approval and affection.

- When children have a harmonious relationship with care givers, they naturally enjoy pleasing them; resistance to the clear limits which care givers impose on toddlers isn't an inescapable reaction.

Question 2:

- Children do not inevitably begin opposing their parents' wishes when they become toddlers, but they do feel urges toward independence and active exploration.

- A certain amount of negativism from children is natural because the child is moving toward greater self-reliance. But the child generally expresses resistance mainly when the child's goals are in conflict with the parent's.

- Children whose care givers have been consistently responsive to them tend to form secure attachments and to be relatively compliant with parental wishes.

- When a child consistently opposes its parents' wishes, modern developmentalists tend to regard this as a sign of a problem in the parent-child relationship, not something inherently wrong in the child's nature or personality.

Question 3:

- As they become more mobile, toddlers separate themselves from their care givers and begin communicating over distances. This prepares them for seeking out and playing with other children.

- Toddlers are inclined to share their discoveries with others. This habit of sharing objects which they are interested in indicates that they are aware of the need of a receptive partner for communication.

- Affective sharing is another way toddlers indicate their growing sociability.

- Through social referencing, toddlers show that they are noticing other people and being influenced by them.

LESSON 11
Abuse and Neglect of Children

Multiple Choice Questions

1. c (Text page 291) Lesson Objective #1
2. a (Text pages 288-289) Lesson Objective #1
3. d (Text page 293) Lesson Objective #2
4. d (Video) Lesson Objective #3
5. b (Text page 293) Lesson Objective #4
6. a (Text page 293) Lesson Objective #5
7. d (Text page 294) Lesson Objective #5
8. d (Text page 296) Lesson Objective #6
9. c (Text page 296) Lesson Objective #6
10. a (Text page 296) Lesson Objective #6

Short Answer Questions

The following are examples of key points or ideas you might have used in your answers to these questions.

Question 1:

- Individuals aren't doomed by prior developmental history because individual growth continues to be affected by present circumstances.

- The long-term effects of abuse on a child can be lessened if the child is able to form at least one positive relationship with an adult during his or her childhood.

- Abused children who undergo extensive psychotherapy as adults are less likely to abuse their own children. Individual working models can be changed; self esteem can be improved.

- Perhaps most important is that parents who were themselves abused have a supportive partner for child rearing.

Question 2:

- Because Amanda is a single, young woman with no experience of child rearing, all the stress of raising a baby will fall on her alone. Isolation of the care giver is one indicator of risk for child abuse.

- Amanda is already expressing ambivalent feelings about being pregnant. If she is unable to find some way of coping with her feelings, she may be greatly confused and frightened by them after the baby arrives.

- Amanda appears to have unrealistic expectations about her baby. If the baby doesn't live up to her expectations for it, Amanda may resent the child.

- If Amanda doesn't become better prepared for the realities of parenting before giving birth, she runs the risk of becoming hostile and perhaps abusive toward a baby which she didn't ask for and isn't emotionally or financially ready to raise.

Question 3:

- The child's stage of development may be a difficult one for the parent to deal with. For example, crying, the infant's way of communicating, may merely irritate some parents when a toddler does it.

- The larger context of the parent's world greatly affects parent-child relations. The stress of losing a job or perhaps being homeless brings added stress to the task of raising children.

- If a mother is involved in a destructive relationship, it can affect her relations with her child for the worse.

- The developmental histories of parents have a bearing on how they relate to their own children. Women who have had chaotic early lives themselves tend to be more likely to have children with developmental problems.

LESSON 12
A Look at the Whole Child: Age 1 to 2½

Multiple Choice Questions

1. b   (Text page 279) Lesson Objective #4
2. b   (Text pages 278-279) Lesson Objective #1
3. c   (Text pages 266-267) Lesson Objective #2
4. c   (Text page 253) Lesson Objective #2
5. a   (Text page 281) Lesson Objective #3
6. d   (Text page 282) Lesson Objective #3
7. b   (Text page 284) Lesson Objective #4
8. c   (Text pages 240-241) Lesson Objective #5
9. c   (Text pages 273-274) Lesson Objective #5
10. a   (Text pages 242-243) Lesson Objective #5

Short Answer Questions

The following are examples of key points or ideas you might have used in your answers to these questions.

Question 1:

- Even before children begin speaking, adults treat their babbling as though it had meaning. Parents will engage their infants in reciprocal "conversations" that prepare the child for actual conversation.

- Adults talk to toddlers in the modified speech known as "child directed speech;" they tend to speak in a high-pitched voice, exaggerate their intonations, and use simple words and grammar. Men and women tend to use different types of CDS.

- Toddlers practice "affective sharing," which means that they are compelled to share their excitement and discoveries with care givers. This increases opportunities for communicating and learning words.

- Toddlers pick up cues about other people and situations through "social referencing," which is the ability to make judgments about a situation by "reading" a care giver's face. This gives the child greater confidence about what to say or do in social situations.

Question 2:

- Mothers continue to play the main nurturing role with the child. During the toddler period, however, this role will change as the mother must begin setting firm limits on the child's behavior.

- Mothers must strike a balance between intimacy with the child and a certain distance as the child strives to establish autonomy.

- Fathers attend more to their children as they become toddlers; fathers commonly play more with their children at this time.

- Fathers tend to be more involved with the child as it establishes distance from the mother, which can ease the transition for both mother and child.

- Fathers talk to their children differently than do mothers, using longer words and asking for more repetitions and clarifications.

Question 3:

- Securely attached children feel confident of their parents' support; they are able to separate from the mother and strive to establish autonomy without excessive anxiety.

- Anxiously resistant attached children feel ambivalent about their care givers and are not confident of the responses their actions will receive; their struggle for autonomy may be marked by timidity, preoccupation with the parent, and power struggles.

- Anxiously avoidant attached children show distinct aversion for their care givers and try to avoid interaction with them; they may refuse to obey their parents, try to get away from them, and show little pleasure or enthusiasm for activities that involve them with care givers.

- Disorganized/disoriented attached children react in a dazed or confused manner to stimulus; this form of attachment was created to describe children who have been abused. Physically abused children tend to react to pressures and stimuli in maladaptive ways, including apathy, trouble dealing with peers, and an inability to experience pleasure.

LESSON 13
Early Childhood Cognitive Development

Multiple Choice Questions

1. b (Text page 310) Lesson Objective #1
2. a (Text page 313) Lesson Objective #4
3. d (Text page 315) Lesson Objective #2
4. c (Text page 325) Lesson Objective #3
5. b (Text page 332) Lesson Objective #6
6. a (Text page 335) Lesson Objective #7
7. b (Text page 338) Lesson Objective #7
8. a (Text page 341) Lesson Objective #5
10. c (Text page 323) Lesson Objective #8

Short Answer Questions

The following are examples of key points or ideas you might have used in your answers to these questions.

Question 1:

- Preschoolers are unable to focus on more than one part of a problem at a time, a limitation known as centration.

- Preschoolers often have trouble distinguishing between appearance and reality.

- Preschoolers have difficulty thinking of memory strategies that they can use to solve problems.

- Preschoolers tend to be egocentric, which means that they are unable to see or imagine another person's point of view.

Question 2:

- A script is a mental list of actions needed to accomplish a task. For example, picking up a phone when it rings, saying "hello," and carrying on a conversation would be one example of a script.

- Having a script to follow would allow a child to perform a sequence of actions without having to think about them, thus overcoming the limitations imposed by cognition.

- Scripts are probably more helpful to children when communicating with each other than when they are talking to adults, since adults are capable of carrying much more of the conversation than the child.

Question 3:

- In stage 1, children do not grasp the concept of conservation. Stage 1 children do not understand that a quantity of liquid will remain the same, no matter what size container it is poured into. This stage is generally from age 3 to 4.

- In stage 2, children become unsure of questions about liquid volume and often change their minds about such questions. This is a transitional period, when children are beginning to suspect that their understanding is faulty and to seek a consistent basis for understanding. This stage lasts from about age 5 to 6.

- In stage 3, children are able to understand conservation and comprehend its underlying principles. By now, children consider the issue very easy to grasp. This stage generally starts at about age 7 for most children.

LESSON 14
Social and Emotional Development
in Early Childhood

Multiple Choice Questions

1. c (Text page 348) Lesson Objective #1
2. a (Text page 351) Lesson Objective #2
3. c (Text page 351) Lesson Objective #2
4. b (Text pages 357-358) Lesson Objective #3
5. b (Text pages 358-359) Lesson Objective #4
6. a (Text page 369) Lesson Objective #5
7. c (Text page 369) Lesson Objective #5
8. a (Text page 365) Lesson Objective #6
9. d (Text pages 363-364) Lesson Objective #7
10. d (Text page 364) Lesson Objective #8

Short Answer Questions

The following are examples of key points or ideas you might have used in your answers to these questions.

Question 1:

- Emotional dependency describes preschoolers who are unable to make the move from infantile dependence to greater independence. Such children show less autonomy than other children of the same age and cling to care givers.

- Emotionally dependent children seek constant reassurance and attention from care givers; they frequently require physical contact, such as being held. They need attention not only when upset, but virtually all the time.

- These children typically have not had a secure attachment with a parent. They act doubtful that adults will respond to their needs.

- Instrumental dependency means that when a child is unable to solve a problem, he or she seeks help from an adult. This is appropriate behavior for preschoolers and not indicative of a problem.

Question 2:

- The ability to inhibit one's own actions. Toddlers find it very hard to resist taking an action once an impulse has struck them. By about age 3 or 4, though, children are much more capable of inhibiting their own actions.

- The ability to delay gratification. Preschoolers are becoming able to deliberately delay doing something now, in anticipation of having a better time doing the same thing later.

– The ability to tolerate frustration. At about age 2, children begin developing the ability to control their emotions when they do not obtain their wishes. Instead of throwing tantrums when they are thwarted, children are increasingly able to keep from getting extremely upset.

– The ability to adjust their self-control to the situation. Children now develop ego resiliency, which indicates that they can evaluate when a situation calls for self-control and when it does not. They are developing the ability to exercise self-restraint voluntarily.

Question 3:

– When children understand that a person's gender is permanent no matter what that person is wearing, or if they age or change their hair style or behavior, they have a sense of gender constancy. Three year olds usually understand that they are boys or girls, but may be vague on gender constancy.

– Earlier researchers used simple drawings in their tests for gender constancy; the tested children may have thought questions about gender just referred to the pictures. More recently, however, researchers have used anatomically accurate photographs of people to study gender constancy. These recent studies indicate that children acquire gender constancy earlier than previously thought.

– Preschool children do seem to have some confusion about gender in children other than themselves. Gender constancy becomes firm by middle childhood.

LESSON 15
Play and Imagination

Multiple Choice Questions

1. c (Text pages 357-358) Lesson Objective #1
2. d (Text page 350) Lesson Objective #1
3. a (Text page 352) Lesson Objective #1
4. c (Text page 353) Lesson Objective #2
5. d (Text pages 368-369) Lesson Objective #2
6. b (Text pages 359-360) Lesson Objective #3
7. a (Text page 369) Lesson Objective #3
8. c (Text page 371) Lesson Objective #3
9. d (Text pages 372-373) Lesson Objective #4
10. a (Text page 353) Lesson Objective #5

Short Answer Questions

The following are examples of key points or ideas you might have used in your answers to these questions.

Question 1:

- Children must first develop an ability to inhibit their physical actions. Toddlers are unable to inhibit their impulses, making it difficult for them to participate in group games.

- Children must develop a certain degree of ego resiliency, which enables them to gain control over when to be quiet and when to play.

- Children must begin forming new understandings of the self, specifically the ability to "uncouple" various aspects of experience. To be able to engage in true fantasy play, for instance, children need to be able simultaneously to pretend and to watch themselves pretending.

- Children must begin developing an understanding that they have dispositions, or ways of being, that are consistent through time.

Question 2:

- Socially competent children show high levels of curiosity and often have a tendency to get into things. You would expect them to be eager to try new games or explore new situations.

- Socially competent children are able to collaborate on making up elaborate rules for fantasy play.

- Socially competent children would be more likely to show high levels of cooperation with peers during group play.

- Socially competent children tend to get lots of attention from other children during play. They also tend to be the ones other children enjoy playing with.

- Socially competent children display high levels of enthusiasm and energy when playing and generally express positive emotions toward peers.

Question 3:

- Sex-typed behavior: Preschool children act out their grasp of what they are learning as correct or expected behavior of males and females in their society. Boys tend to roughhouse, while girls show a greater interest in babies.

- Gender preferences: Preschool children have begun forming gender-related preferences in toys, with boys playing largely with trucks and cars and girls leaning toward dolls and soft, cuddly toys.

- Gender constancy: By about age 4, children should have formed an awareness that they remain boys or girls in spite of superficial changes in their appearance such as different clothing or a haircut.

LESSON 16
A Look at the Whole Child: Ages 2½ through 5

Multiple Choices

1. b   (Text page 355) Lesson Objective #1
2. a   (Text page 324) Lesson Objective #2
3. d   (Text page 314) Lesson Objective #2
4. c   (Text pages 367-368) Lesson Objective #3
5. b   (Text page 336) Lesson Objective #3
6. d   (Text pages 334-335) Lesson Objective 3
7. c   (Text page 348) Lesson Objective #4
8. d   (Text page 349) Lesson Objective #4
9. b   (Text pages 378-379) Lesson Objective #4
10. b   (Text page 379) Lesson Objective #5

Short Answer Questions

The following are examples of key points or ideas you might have used in your answers to these questions.

Question 1:

– Children must first begin to overcome some of the limitations of egocentrism. This includes a knowledge of existence – the awareness that other people have feelings and motivations different from one's own.

– Children must begin to develop the skill of social inference, or the ability to "read" other people's emotions.

– Children must begin to develop the capacity to take the role of others.

– Children must begin to develop the awareness that they are independent agents responsible for their own actions.

Question 2:

– The preschooler's growing powers of self-resilience enable him or her to adapt flexibly to a variety of situations. Increasingly, the child is able to choose when to be reserved and disciplined and when to "let go" in play.

– With the development of gender constancy, children can act out the roles of either their mothers or fathers without fearing any alteration in their own sex.

– The preschooler's enhanced sense of self includes an ability to "uncouple" from what he or she is doing at any moment and, in a sense, take a step backward and observe him- or herself playing.

    – The child has learned that his or her disposition is consistent through time.

Question 3:

    – Preschoolers don't fully understand the concept of conservation until they're about 7 years old; gaining that understanding, in fact, is one mark of the transition to middle childhood.

    – Preschoolers still have only a shaky control of their powers of attention. They have not yet developed the information-scanning abilities that they will have later.

    – Preschoolers still have relatively poor memories. In particular, they have not yet formed an awareness of the need to have strategies for remembering things.

LESSON 17
Cognitive Development in Middle Childhood

Multiple Choice Questions

1. b (Text page 397) Lesson Objective #1
2. d (Text page 399) Lesson Objective #2
3. a (Text page 405) Lesson Objective #3
4. a (Text page 408) Lesson Objective #3
5. c (Text page 430) Lesson Objective #7
6. d (Text page 413) Lesson Objective #4
7. b (Text page 415) Lesson Objective #4
8. c (Text page 420) Lesson Objective #5
9. d (Text page 424) Lesson Objective #6
10. c (Text page 425) Lesson Objective #6

Short Answer Questions

The following are examples of key points or ideas you might have used in your answers to these questions.

Question 1:

    – Children become able to appreciate jokes, puns, and riddles. Piaget thought this was the result of overall cognitive changes at this age; social learning theorists believe children develop these skills through observing others; and information-processing theorists believe that children have now acquired the skills needed to understand and tell jokes.

    – Children can consider more than one piece of a problem at a time and are no longer so constrained by the limits of centration.

- They are able to perceive deeper truths below surface appearances and develop a much greater understanding of the conservation of liquids, number, weight, and length.

- Children show great improvements in memory, and gain the ability to think about how to remember, a process called metamemory.

Question 2:

- Children begin using constructive memory, which is the ability to remember new information better because it can be connected with previously acquired knowledge. Children make inferences about new information based on old.

- Children begin using mnemonic strategies to remember things. These include rehearsing information, organizing new information according to classification schemes, and adopting little "tricks" to jog their memory.

- Children begin using metamemory strategies; they begin paying attention to the process of remembering. They become aware of the need to consciously make an effort to recall important items of information and of their own memory strengths and weaknesses.

Question 3:

- Developmentalists agree that a number of genes contribute to an individual's intelligence. Studies of identical twins have shown definite correlation between their intelligence levels.

- Studies done on adoptive children have shown that a child raised in an advantaged environment can develop a significantly higher IQ than that of his or her natural mother. This indicates that environment has an influence on the development of an individual's intelligence.

- Genes establish the minimum and maximum levels possible for an individual's intelligence; this is called the reaction range. The level of the actual intelligence a person achieves appears to be greatly influenced by their environment.

- While it appears that the IQ scores of disadvantaged children can be raised by an improvement in their environments, these changes will remain stable over time only if the children remain in the improved environment.

LESSON 18
Social and Emotional Development in Middle Childhood: Self and Peers

Multiple Choice Questions

1. b   (Text page 5) Lesson Objective #1
2. c   (Text page 11) Lesson Objective #1

3. d (Text page 16) Lesson Objective #2

4. a (Text page 37) Lesson Objective #3

5. a (Text page 40) Lesson Objective #3

6. c (Text page 27) Lesson Objective #4

7. b (Text page 32) Lesson Objective #4

8. a (Text page 39) Lesson Objective #5

9. c (Text page 25) Lesson Objective #1

10. c (Text page 35) Lesson Objective #3

Short Answer Questions

The following are examples of key points or ideas you might have used in your answers to these questions.

Question 1:

- Preschoolers tend to think of the self in physical terms; they often think that the self is a physical part of the body.

- A preschooler tends to describe him- or herself in physical terms, often listing items such as hair color or clothing as distinguishing characteristics.

- Preschoolers have a very broad sense of what constitutes selfhood and may say that dogs, cats, even objects such as trees or cars can have a "self."

- By middle childhood, children are beginning to think of themselves in psychological terms. They tend to describe themselves according to psychological traits.

- Elementary school children make a distinction between the mind and the body.

- Elementary school children have a better understanding of the uniqueness of each individual than preschoolers have. They also grasp more firmly the concept that each person has an inner, private self.

Question 2:

- The 4 year olds may resort to instrumental aggression – hitting as a means of getting what they want – to decide who will play with the robot. In that case, the stronger or more assertive child will get the toy.

- To settle their dispute, the preschoolers are more likely to call upon an adult to resolve the issue – or at least the one who doesn't get the toy may.

- The 9 year olds are more likely to resort to negotiations to decide who plays first. One child may offer to trade the other one another toy or a favor for first turn at the game.

- The older children may invoke issues of fairness to settle the question ("You got to choose the video last night.") or appeal to the norm of sharing.

- If the older children cannot resolve the problem, they may vent their frustration in hostile aggression. But their hostility is more likely to take the form of verbal insults than physical violence.

Question 3:

- Children tend to be well-liked by peers as a consequence of their personal characteristics which others see as favorable. For example, popular children are described as being kind, or fair, or capable of organizing games.

- Popular children tend to have high self-esteem; in other words, they think of themselves as basically competent and likable. They are also outgoing and are able to give and receive positive reinforcement.

- Popular children have a good grasp of the techniques for making friends.

- Unpopular children are perceived by their peers as having undesirable traits; for example, other children see them as "mean," "whiny," or "wimpy."

- Once other children have categorized them as unlikable, unpopular children tend to think of themselves in unflattering terms. Such self-perpetuating negative images may stem from a sense of low self-esteem established during earlier stages of development.

LESSON 19
Social and Emotional Development
in Middle Childhood: Family Influence

Multiple Choice Questions

1. a (Text page 462) Lesson Objective #1
2. b (Text page 465) Lesson Objective #2
3. d (Text page 466) Lesson Objective #2
4. b (Text page 467) Lesson Objective #3
5. a (Text page 466) Lesson Objective #3
6. c (Text page 467) Lesson Objective #4
7. d (Text page 459) Lesson Objective #5
8. b (Text page 460) Lesson Objective #5
9. a (Text pages 460-461) Lesson Objective #6
10. c (Text page 463) Lesson Objective #7

Short Answer Questions

The following are examples of key points or ideas you might have used in your answers to these questions.

Question 1:

- Authoritative parents are nurturing and responsive toward their children. When they discipline their children, they try to give the child a reason for the punishment.

- Authoritative parents set firm limits for their children and expect them to behave responsibly. At the same time, they show respect for the child's point of view.

- The children of authoritative parents are likely to be energetic, friendly, and self-reliant. They are more likely to take the initiative and to rise to challenges.

- Authoritarian parents tend to enforce rules harshly and without making any effort to explain why the child is being punished.

- Authoritarian parents usually don't bother to find out their child's point of view.

- The children of authoritarian parents are often irritable and conflict-ridden.

Question 2:

- Boys often react to divorce by showing increased aggression and impulse control problems; girls may react by showing inhibition and anxiety.

- After a divorce, children usually stay with the mother; thus, boys often are no longer influenced by the example and control of their fathers.

- Boys may respond more negatively than girls to living with the opposite-sex parent.

- Researchers now believe that gender is not an important factor in how much divorce affects a child; boys and girls both are affected by the breakup of a family, but simply express it differently.

Question 3:

- The age difference between siblings affects their attitudes toward one another. Children who are close to each other in age, for example, tend to express a great deal of ambivalence in their mutual feelings about each other.

- Siblings are affected by how well the parents prepare a child for the birth of a new child. An older brother or sister who is told about a new sibling by thoughtful parents will have a better relationship with that child than one whose parents just leave things to chance.

- Parents who show favoritism to one child over another run the risk of breeding rivalry and ill-will between the siblings.

– The children's developing personalities or temperaments will have an effect on how well the two children get along.

LESSON 20
Prosocial and Aggressive Behavior

Multiple Choice Questions

1. d (Text pages 359-360) Lesson Objective #1
2. b (Text page 358) Lesson Objective #2
3. a (Text page 359) Lesson Objective #3
4. a (Text page 377) Lesson Objective #3
5. d (Text pages 458-460) Lesson Objective #4
6. d (Text pages 360-362) Lesson Objective #5
7. b (Text pages 559-560) Lesson Objective #6
8. b (Text pages 565-566) Lesson Objective #6
9. a (Text page 581) Lesson Objective #7
10. a (Text page 557) Lesson Objective #7

Short Answer Questions

The following are examples of key points or ideas you might have used in your answers to these questions.

Question 1:

– Children must first understand that they are independent agents responsible for their own actions.

– Children must grasp that they are capable of actions that cause feelings in other people which are different from those they themselves are feeling.

– Parents can best encourage empathy in their children by modeling it in their own actions.

– When reprimanding their child for hurting someone else, the parent should try to explain how the other child feels and explain the principles of kindness. The parent should also underline their seriousness by using a sincere tone.

Question 2:

– Even though infants may sometimes act roughly and seem to be aggressive, they aren't capable of true aggression until they are more cognitively advanced. Aggression involves an intent to cause someone harm, an ability that the child will develop along with conceptual thought.

– Toddlers have angry outbursts toward parents as a result of the increasing restraints that parents impose on the child. Toddlers also engage in negative interactions with peers, usually concerning objects. But the toddler still isn't expressing personal negative intent toward the other child.

- True aggressive behavior appears in the preschool period, as children develop concepts of the self as an agent and of the idea of fairness.

- During late preschool and early elementary school years, children show less instrumental aggression and begin exhibiting hostile aggression. "Getting even" becomes a common reason for aggression at this age.

Question 3:

- A psychologist who follows a traditional medical model might assume that the boy suffers from a form of mental illness and look for underlying physiological causes of the boy's aggressiveness. Treatment might include some form of drug therapy.

- A psychologist who follows a genetic model might assume that the boy has inherited a tendency toward aggression and antisocial behavior. The psychologist might study the boy's parental background in search of similar behavioral problems. Probably the psychologist would assume that any genetic influence would be the result of a combination of genes, rather than any single gene.

- A psychologist who follows a psychodynamic model would assume that the boy's actions are a result of underlying thoughts and feelings. The psychologist might recommend that the boy enter therapy to uncover what past experiences or assumptions may now be causing the antisocial behavior.

- A psychologist who follows a family model would assume that the boy's behavior is just a manifestation of a larger disturbance within the boy's family. The psychologist would look to the boy's overall family structure in search of problems. The search for problem causes might go back to "the family of origin" – the families in which the boy's parents grew up. Treatment might include group counseling for the entire family.

LESSON 21
A Look at the Whole Child: Ages 6 through 12

Multiple Choice Questions

1. b (Text page 397) Lesson Objective #2
2. d (Text page 398) Lesson Objective #2
3. b (Text pages 407-408) Lesson Objective #2
4. a (Text page 442) Lesson Objective #3
5. c (Text page 442) Lesson Objective #3
6. c (Text page 449) Lesson Objective #3
7. b (Text pages 442-443) Lesson Objective #4

8. b (Text page 438) Lesson Objective #1

9. c (Text page 431) Lesson Objective #5

10. a (Text page 470) Lesson Objective #5

Short Answer Questions

The following are examples of key points or ideas you might have used in your answers to these questions.

Question 1:

- Children learn from one another; a child with a better understanding of a problem can help a less informed child understand the problem.

- When children cooperate to gain an understanding of a problem, their new knowledge often is transferable to related problems. For example, children who gained an understanding of number conservation through cooperation were able to apply their new understanding to problems of the conservation of liquid volume.

- In a cooperative learning situation, at least one child needs to have certain prerequisite skills. Furthermore, the learning situation requires that the two children trade information in a give-and-take manner; learning isn't just a matter of child A giving the answer to child B.

- Children are able to use scaffolding to teach one another, particularly in didactic learning situations.

Question 2:

- At home, children are given problems to solve within an embedded context; that is, parents ask children questions about real-life situations, such as how much money it takes to buy a certain candy bar or if the cat has been fed. In school, however, children are asked to solve problems that are disembodied or decontextualized; that is, school problems are abstract, self-contained, and often removed from "real life."

- At home, children are used to talking about problems; at school, they must begin to receive information in written form.

- At school, children will be exposed to many forces for socialization. For example, schools encourage children to be competitive, to work hard, to strive for achievement, and to obey authority.

- Children may be exposed to more clearly defined distinctions between gender roles at school than at home. For instance, elementary school teachers often form girls' and boys' lines for activities and organize group activities along gender lines – as in spelling contests pitting boys against girls.

Question 3:

- Research indicates that children with high self-esteem approach the world with positive expectations, which in turn increases their success.

- Children with high self-esteem approach tasks with the expectation that they will succeed. Likewise, they approach individuals and groups with the expectation that they will be accepted.

- Positive self-esteem is one of the factors which enables children to be popular within their peer groups.

- Children who achieve high status among their peers tend to have their positive views of themselves reinforced, further encouraging their sense of self-esteem. Likewise, this tends to encourage their peer acceptance and popularity.

LESSON 22
Physical and Cognitive Development in Adolescence

Multiple Choice Questions

1. b   (Text page 491) Lesson Objective #1
2. c   (Text page 494) Lesson Objective #1
3. a   (Text page 488) Lesson Objective #1
4. b   (Text page 493) Lesson Objective #2
5. b   (Text page 497) Lesson Objective #3
6. a   (Text page 498) Lesson Objective #3
7. c   (Text page 503) Lesson Objective #4
8. c   (Text page 505) Lesson Objective #5
9. d   (Text page 505) Lesson Objective #5
10. d   (Text page 509) Lesson Objective #6

Short Answer Questions

The following are examples of key points or ideas you might have used in your answers to these questions.

Question 1:

- For both boys and girls, the secretion of sex hormones into their blood streams stimulates secondary sex characteristics. Their skeletons grow, their body fat becomes redistributed, and hair grows on certain parts of the body.

- The sweat glands of both boys and girls will become more active, and their skin becomes more oily. Both also go through a growth spurt.

- Girls will begin to develop breasts; proportionally, their growth leads to narrower shoulders, broader hips, and shorter legs relative to torso. Girls also develop fat deposits on the thighs, hips, buttocks, and upper arms.

- Boys' voices will deepen; proportionally, their growth leads to broader shoulders, narrower hips, and longer legs relative to torso.

Question 2:

- Adolescents become able to apply logical thinking skills to abstract concepts; whereas earlier they could only think in this fashion about specific, concrete objects, now they can consider ideas that are only possibilities.

- Adolescents develop hypothetico-deductive reasoning, which allows them to imagine hypothetical solutions to a real problem and then to apply a systematic, logical plan to using the hypotheses to solve the problem.

- Adolescents are able to form abstract concepts from concrete ones and then to think systematically about the relationships between the abstract concepts.

- Adolescents are able to keep their minds more open about the final solution to a problem and to accept that maybe their particular solution to a problem isn't the best or final answer.

Question 3:

- Kohlberg considers his first two steps to be in the preconventional period. During stage 1, the child's definition of good is shaped by a desire not to be punished by some external authority. In stage 2, good becomes whatever satisfies the child's own needs.

- The next phase of Kohlberg's model is known as the period of conventional morality. During stage 3, which is known as the good-boy, good-girl orientation, the child strives to act in ways that others will approve of. In stage 4, which Kohlberg called the law and order orientation, the child begins making moral judgments based on what are perceived as one's duties according to society's laws.

- The final phase of Kohlberg's model of moral development is called postconventional or principled morality. In stage 5, the individual tries to meet the goal of keeping society running smoothly; Kohlberg referred to this as the social contract orientation. In stage 6, individuals try to make decisions based on the highest relevant moral principle; Kohlberg referred to this as the hierarchy of principle orientation.

LESSON 23
Social and Emotional Development in Adolescence

Multiple Choice Questions

1. d (Text page 515) Lesson Objective #1
2. a (Text page 516) Lesson Objective #1
3. d (Text page 518) Lesson Objective #2
4. d (Text page 519) Lesson Objective #3
5. b (Text page 520) Lesson Objective #3
6. c (Text page 523) Lesson Objective #4

7. b   (Text page 528) Lesson Objective #5
8. b   (Text page 532) Lesson Objective #5
9. c   (Text page 538) Lesson Objective #6
10. a   (Text page 541) Lesson Objective #7

Short Answer Questions

The following are examples of key points or ideas you might have used in your answers to these questions.

Question 1:

- The adolescent is pursuing personal discovery by asking questions such as "Who am I?" and "What is the meaning of my life?"

- The adolescent is beginning to form a coherent self image by integrating past experiences, current personal changes, and the expectations that society at large has for their future.

- The adolescent is constructing a structure of beliefs, abilities, and past experiences regarding the self that helps them understand their own strengths and weaknesses.

- As part of the struggle to establish a personal identity, adolescents will often experience an identity crisis that challenges them to adjust to the biological and cognitive changes that they are undergoing.

Question 2:

- As a result of their increased awareness of their own uniqueness, adolescents are capable of much greater mutual understanding with others.

- Their increased understanding of how others feel leads them to desire mutual disclosure, by which they share important inner feelings.

- These and other cognitive developments enable adolescents to achieve new levels of intimacy with friends. This sense of intimacy is reflected in deep levels of emotional commitment with friends, which is expressed in strong bonds of loyalty and fidelity among them.

- Adolescents are better able now to share and keep confidences with one another. Being able to trust a friend is an important aspect of adolescent friendships.

Question 3:

- Because their children are now striving for autonomy, self-expression, and influence, parents need to find ways of handing over responsibility to their children.

- As a result of their developing formal operational skills, adolescents are better able to counter their parents' arguments, putting pressure on parents to give their children more chance to offer their own reasons and points of view.

- Parents need to be aware that their children may have new cognitive abilities which enable them to share responsibly in making decisions about their behavior. Parents also need to be aware of possible changes in their own lives, such as midlife crises.

- Research indicates that a democratic style of parenting, where the parents share power with teenagers while still setting limits, is one which greatly helps teenagers achieve identity.

LESSON 24
Challenges of Adolescence

Multiple Choice Questions

1. b   (Text page 579) Lesson Objective #1
2. d   (Text page 545) Lesson Objective #2
3. d   (Text page 544) Lesson Objective #2
4. a   (Text page 534) Lesson Objective #2
5. a   (Text page 546) Lesson Objective #3
6. c   (Text pages 545-546) Lesson Objective #3
7. b   (Text page 580) Lesson Objective #4
8. b   (Text page 580) Lesson Objective #4
9. a   (Text page 546) Lesson Objective #5
10. a   (Text page 546) Lesson Objective #5

Short Answer Questions

The following are examples of key points or ideas you might have used in your answers to these questions.

Question 1:

- Adolescents are influenced by their friends to drink and smoke marijuana at a time when the support and approval of peer groups is very important.

- At a time when they are feeling the focus of attention from other people, some teenagers turn to alcohol and illicit drugs as a means of reducing their levels of self-consciousness.

- To some degree, teenagers may feel that drinking or taking drugs signifies that they are now mature; in fact, drinking and drug-taking may represent a form of rite of passage to maturity in the view of some adolescents in our society.

- Adolescents are interested in having new experiences and exploring their feelings, and may think they'll be able to do this through the use of alcohol and drugs.

Question 2:

- Some teenagers become pregnant as a way of getting out of an unhappy home situation.

- Some teenagers become pregnant in hopes of gaining someone to love them, either in the form of the baby's father or the baby.

- Parents may contribute to a teenager's pregnancy by failing to monitor their daughter's dating behavior. Conflict with parents also is involved with pregnancy during adolescence.

- In view of the fact that many pregnant teenagers also have problems of truancy, poor academic performance, marijuana use, and fighting, it is possible that for some girls, pregnancy may represent another form of rebellion against their parents or the school system.

Question 3:

- Teenagers may commit suicide as the result of worry about their school performance.

- Teenagers may commit suicide as the result of the use of drugs or alcohol, which are themselves often associated with adolescent depression.

- Young adults who have lost a parent before the age of 16 have a higher incidence of suicidal thoughts than peers from intact families.

- Teenagers may commit suicide as a result of conflict in the family and of emotional rejection and a lack of closeness with parents.

LESSON 25
A Look at the Whole Child: The Teen Years

Multiple Choice Questions

1. d   (Text page 514) Lesson Objective #1
2. d   (Text pages 491-492) Lesson Objective #2
3. b   (Text pages 497-498) Lesson Objective #3
4. a   (Text page 498) Lesson Objective #3
5. a   (Text page 514) Lesson Objective #4
6. c   (Text page 523) Lesson Objective #4
7. c   (Text page 528) Lesson Objective #5
8. b   (Text page 532) Lesson Objective #5
9. b   (Text page 536) Lesson Objective #6
10. a   (Text page 538) Lesson Objective #6

Short Answer Questions

The following are examples of key points or ideas you might have used in your answers to these questions.

Question 1:

- The reasoning of younger children is often unsystematic and illogical; teenagers are more likely to catch their own inconsistencies.

- Elementary school children understand volume and weight and so can solve conservation problems. But they do not yet grasp the idea of density because they don't understand the concept of proportion.

- Adolescents begin to understand the idea of proportions. This is because they are able to relate two abstract concepts – number and weight – with a third – volume – for the first time.

- The cognitive abilities that adolescents use to reason about problems of density and proportion emerge from the abilities that they developed in middle childhood.

Question 2:

- Egocentrism: Babies are egocentric because they seem to believe that objects exist only when they perceive them; toddlers are egocentric because they confuse other people's desires for their own; and teenagers are egocentric because they think that other people think about them as much as they think about themselves.

- Autonomy: Toddlers must achieve a balance between self-reliance and dependence on parents as they begin forming a sense of individual selfhood and walking; adolescents must establish new levels of independence and responsibility from their parents as they grope toward a sense of personal identity.

- Relationships with peers: Toddlers and preschoolers must begin mastering the rules of social behavior and learn how to play with peers; middle childhooders develop the ability and need for same-sex friendships; and adolescents move toward mutual understanding and intimacy with friends, first of the same sex, and later of the opposite sex.

Question 3:

- The physical changes that puberty brings cause adolescents to change their self-concepts. Not only are they now bigger and stronger, but they are sexual beings also. These physical changes affect the way others relate to them.

- Adolescents have a greater capacity for self analysis and are more aware of their own thinking processes. With their new capacity to comprehend abstract thought, they are challenged to think about values in new, more sophisticated ways.

- In early adolescence, teenagers have a fragile sense of the self as they come to grips with these many changes. They feel that others are scrutinizing them and may become guarded and in need of privacy. As they mature, their sense of self becomes more assured and less fragile.

LESSON 26
Does Childhood Matter?
Issues in Child Development

Multiple Choice Questions

1. c (Telecourse Guide Lesson 12 and Lesson 25) Lesson Objective #1
2. d (Text page 357) Lesson Objective #1
3. c (Telecourse Guide Lesson 8) Lesson Objective #2
4. b (Text page 187) Lesson Objective #2
5. b (Throughout the text) Lesson Objective #2
6. d (Text page 382) Lesson Objective #3
7. c (Text pages 298-299) Lesson Objective #3
8. c (Text page 237) Lesson Objective #4
9. b (Text pages 468-469) Lesson Objective #4
10. d (Text pages 516-517) Lesson Objective #4

Short Answer Questions

The following are examples of key points or ideas you might have used in your answers to these questions.

Question 1:

- Before development can proceed for an infant, he or she must be born. Then, initial motor skills such as reaching and grasping or voluntary looking are based upon such reflexes as sucking, grasping, and blinking.

- In the toddler period, language learning is built upon the child's improving motor skills, as well as the relationships which have been formed with care givers—particularly in terms of attachment.

- In early childhood, children struggle for a new level of self-sufficiency based upon an existing relationship of trust with the care giver. Cognitive development, including grasping the basics of conservation, seriation, and ordering, relies upon the child's understanding of language.

- With middle childhood, children begin mastering the self-aware concepts of metacognition, based upon their previous mastery of basic memory processes.

- During adolescence, the success with which children establish intimate friendships and a new sense of self-identity will be shaped by an earlier sense of self-esteem. The degree to which teens successfully negotiate a new relationship with parents will in large part depend upon the course of previous adjustments in parent-child relationships.

Question 2:

- Among the innate forms of learning with which we are born, habituation is one that remains with us throughout life.

- Scripts, the abstract representations of sequences of actions that a child learns to perform to meet goals, form the basis of many actions throughout life. For example, the script that a 6 year old learns to get through show-and-tell is not that far removed from the script that an office worker follows to get through a weekly staff meeting.

- The role-playing that children use as a means of acting out conflicts is reflected in the skill with which mature adults shift from one social role to another in their daily interactions.

Question 3:

- The nature of individual attachment has been shown repeatedly to affect later development. In early childhood, for example, children who have formed anxious or avoidant attachments will often have difficulty interacting prosocially with other children. And in middle childhood, the children who have had secure attachment are more likely to achieve peer acceptance than those who have had anxious or avoidant attachment.

- Parenting styles form a major context for individual development at all ages. During preschool, for example, the children of authoritative parents tend to be energetic, friendly, and self-reliant. Children of authoritarian parents, on the other hand, tend to be irritable and conflict-ridden. During middle childhood, children of authoritative parents have a greater tendency than other children to take initiative and to try to influence events.